Python Machine Learning

Unlock deeper insights into machine learning with this vital guide to cutting-edge predictive analytics

Sebastian Raschka

BIRMINGHAM - MUMBAI

Python Machine Learning

First published: September 2015

Production reference: 3150416

Published by Packt Publishing Ltd.
Livery Place
35 Livery Street
Birmingham B3 2PB, UK.

ISBN 978-1-78355-513-0

www.packtpub.com

Credits

Author
Sebastian Raschka

Reviewers
Richard Dutton
Dave Julian
Vahid Mirjalili
Hamidreza Sattari
Dmytro Taranovsky

Commissioning Editor
Akram Hussain

Acquisition Editors
Rebecca Youe
Meeta Rajani

Content Development Editor
Riddhi Tuljapurkar

Technical Editors
Madhunikita Sunil Chindarkar
Taabish Khan

Copy Editors
Roshni Banerjee
Stephan Copestake

Project Coordinator
Kinjal Bari

Proofreader
Safis Editing

Indexer
Hemangini Bari

Graphics
Sheetal Aute
Abhinash Sahu

Production Coordinator
Shantanu N. Zagade

Cover Work
Shantanu N. Zagade

Foreword

We live in the midst of a data deluge. According to recent estimates, 2.5 quintillion (10^{18}) bytes of data are generated on a daily basis. This is so much data that over 90 percent of the information that we store nowadays was generated in the past decade alone. Unfortunately, most of this information cannot be used by humans. Either the data is beyond the means of standard analytical methods, or it is simply too vast for our limited minds to even comprehend.

Through Machine Learning, we enable computers to process, learn from, and draw actionable insights out of the otherwise impenetrable walls of big data. From the massive supercomputers that support Google's search engines to the smartphones that we carry in our pockets, we rely on Machine Learning to power most of the world around us — often, without even knowing it.

As modern pioneers in the brave new world of big data, it then behooves us to learn more about Machine Learning. What is Machine Learning and how does it work? How can I use Machine Learning to take a glimpse into the unknown, power my business, or just find out what the Internet at large thinks about my favorite movie? All of this and more will be covered in the following chapters authored by my good friend and colleague, Sebastian Raschka.

When away from taming my otherwise irascible pet dog, Sebastian has tirelessly devoted his free time to the open source Machine Learning community. Over the past several years, Sebastian has developed dozens of popular tutorials that cover topics in Machine Learning and data visualization in Python. He has also developed and contributed to several open source Python packages, several of which are now part of the core Python Machine Learning workflow.

Owing to his vast expertise in this field, I am confident that Sebastian's insights into the world of Machine Learning in Python will be invaluable to users of all experience levels. I wholeheartedly recommend this book to anyone looking to gain a broader and more practical understanding of Machine Learning.

Dr. Randal S. Olson
Artificial Intelligence and Machine Learning Researcher, University of Pennsylvania

About the Author

Sebastian Raschka is a PhD student at Michigan State University, who develops new computational methods in the field of computational biology. He has been ranked as the number one most influential data scientist on GitHub by Analytics Vidhya. He has many years of experience with coding in Python and he has conducted several seminars on the practical applications of data science and machine learning. Talking and writing about data science, machine learning, and Python really motivated Sebastian to write this book in order to help people develop data-driven solutions without necessarily needing to have a machine learning background.

He has also actively contributed to open source projects and methods that he implemented, which are now successfully used in machine learning competitions, such as Kaggle. In his free time, he works on models for sports predictions, and if he is not in front of the computer, he enjoys playing sports.

I would like to thank my professors, Arun Ross and Pang-Ning Tan, and many others who inspired me and kindled my great interest in pattern classification, machine learning, and data mining.

I would like to take this opportunity to thank the great Python community and developers of open source packages who helped me create the perfect environment for scientific research and data science.

A special thanks goes to the core developers of scikit-learn. As a contributor to this project, I had the pleasure to work with great people, who are not only very knowledgeable when it comes to machine learning, but are also excellent programmers.

Lastly, I want to thank you all for showing an interest in this book, and I sincerely hope that I can pass on my enthusiasm to join the great Python and machine learning communities.

About the Reviewers

Richard Dutton started programming the ZX Spectrum when he was 8 years old and his obsession carried him through a confusing array of technologies and roles in the fields of technology and finance.

He has worked with Microsoft, and as a Director at Barclays, his current obsession is a mashup of Python, machine learning, and block chain.

If he's not in front of a computer, he can be found in the gym or at home with a glass of wine while he looks at his iPhone. He calls this balance.

Dave Julian is an IT consultant and teacher with over 15 years of experience. He has worked as a technician, project manager, programmer, and web developer. His current projects include developing a crop analysis tool as part of integrated pest management strategies in greenhouses. He has a strong interest in the intersection of biology and technology with a belief that smart machines can help solve the world's most important problems.

Vahid Mirjalili received his PhD in mechanical engineering from Michigan State University, where he developed novel techniques for protein structure refinement using molecular dynamics simulations. Combining his knowledge from the fields of statistics, data mining, and physics he developed powerful data-driven approaches that helped him and his research group to win two recent worldwide competitions for protein structure prediction and refinement, CASP, in 2012 and 2014.

While working on his doctorate degree, he decided to join the Computer Science and Engineering Department at Michigan State University to specialize in the field of machine learning. His current research projects involve the development of unsupervised machine learning algorithms for the mining of massive datasets. He is also a passionate Python programmer and shares his implementations of clustering algorithms on his personal website at http://vahidmirjalili.com.

Hamidreza Sattari is an IT professional and has been involved in several areas of software engineering, from programming to architecture, as well as management. He holds a master's degree in software engineering from Herriot-Watt University, UK, and a bachelor's degree in electrical engineering (electronics) from Tehran Azad University, Iran. In recent years, his areas of interest have been big data and Machine Learning. He coauthored the book *Spring Web Services 2 Cookbook* and he maintains his blog at `http://justdeveloped-blog.blogspot.com/`.

Dmytro Taranovsky is a software engineer with an interest and background in Python, Linux, and machine learning. Originally from Kiev, Ukraine, he moved to the United States in 1996. From an early age, he displayed a passion for science and knowledge, winning mathematics and physics competitions. In 1999, he was chosen to be a member of the U.S. Physics Team. In 2005, he graduated from the Massachusetts Institute of Technology, majoring in mathematics. Later, he worked as a software engineer on a text transformation system for computer-assisted medical transcriptions (eScription). Although he originally worked on Perl, he appreciated the power and clarity of Python, and he was able to scale the system to very large data sizes. Afterwards, he worked as a software engineer and analyst for an algorithmic trading firm. He also made significant contributions to the foundation of mathematics, including creating and developing an extension to the language of set theory and its connection to large cardinal axioms, developing a notion of constructive truth, and creating a system of ordinal notations and implementing them in Python. He also enjoys reading, likes to go outdoors, and tries to make the world a better place.

www.PacktPub.com

Support files, eBooks, discount offers, and more

For support files and downloads related to your book, please visit www.PacktPub.com.

Did you know that Packt offers eBook versions of every book published, with PDF and ePub files available? You can upgrade to the eBook version at www.PacktPub.com and as a print book customer, you are entitled to a discount on the eBook copy. Get in touch with us at service@packtpub.com for more details.

At www.PacktPub.com, you can also read a collection of free technical articles, sign up for a range of free newsletters and receive exclusive discounts and offers on Packt books and eBooks.

https://www2.packtpub.com/books/subscription/packtlib

Do you need instant solutions to your IT questions? PacktLib is Packt's online digital book library. Here, you can search, access, and read Packt's entire library of books.

Why subscribe?

- Fully searchable across every book published by Packt
- Copy and paste, print, and bookmark content
- On demand and accessible via a web browser

Free access for Packt account holders

If you have an account with Packt at www.PacktPub.com, you can use this to access PacktLib today and view 9 entirely free books. Simply use your login credentials for immediate access.

Table of Contents

Preface

I probably don't need to tell you that machine learning has become one of the most exciting technologies of our time and age. Big companies, such as Google, Facebook, Apple, Amazon, IBM, and many more, heavily invest in machine learning research and applications for good reasons. Although it may seem that machine learning has become the buzzword of our time and age, it is certainly not a hype. This exciting field opens the way to new possibilities and has become indispensable to our daily lives. Talking to the voice assistant on our smart phones, recommending the right product for our customers, stopping credit card fraud, filtering out spam from our e-mail inboxes, detecting and diagnosing medical diseases, the list goes on and on.

If you want to become a machine learning practitioner, a better problem solver, or maybe even consider a career in machine learning research, then this book is for you! However, for a novice, the theoretical concepts behind machine learning can be quite overwhelming. Yet, many practical books that have been published in recent years will help you get started in machine learning by implementing powerful learning algorithms. In my opinion, the use of practical code examples serve an important purpose. They illustrate the concepts by putting the learned material directly into action. However, remember that with great power comes great responsibility! The concepts behind machine learning are too beautiful and important to be hidden in a black box. Thus, my personal mission is to provide you with a different book; a book that discusses the necessary details regarding machine learning concepts, offers intuitive yet informative explanations on how machine learning algorithms work, how to use them, and most importantly, how to avoid the most common pitfalls.

If you type "machine learning" as a search term in Google Scholar, it returns an overwhelmingly large number-1,800,000 publications. Of course, we cannot discuss all the nitty-gritty details about all the different algorithms and applications that have emerged in the last 60 years. However, in this book, we will embark on an exciting journey that covers all the essential topics and concepts to give you a head start in this field. If you find that your thirst for knowledge is not satisfied, there are many useful resources that can be used to follow up on the essential breakthroughs in this field.

If you have already studied machine learning theory in detail, this book will show you how to put your knowledge into practice. If you have used machine learning techniques before and want to gain more insight into how machine learning really works, this book is for you! Don't worry if you are completely new to the machine learning field; you have even more reason to be excited. I promise you that machine learning will change the way you think about the problems you want to solve and will show you how to tackle them by unlocking the power of data.

Before we dive deeper into the machine learning field, let me answer your most important question, "why Python?" The answer is simple: it is powerful yet very accessible. Python has become the most popular programming language for data science because it allows us to forget about the tedious parts of programming and offers us an environment where we can quickly jot down our ideas and put concepts directly into action.

Reflecting on my personal journey, I can truly say that the study of machine learning made me a better scientist, thinker, and problem solver. In this book, I want to share this knowledge with you. Knowledge is gained by learning, the key is our enthusiasm, and the true mastery of skills can only be achieved by practice. The road ahead may be bumpy on occasions, and some topics may be more challenging than others, but I hope that you will embrace this opportunity and focus on the reward. Remember that we are on this journey together, and throughout this book, we will add many powerful techniques to your arsenal that will help us solve even the toughest problems the data-driven way.

What this book covers

Chapter 1, Giving Computers the Ability to Learn from Data, introduces you to the main subareas of machine learning to tackle various problem tasks. In addition, it discusses the essential steps for creating a typical machine learning model building pipeline that will guide us through the following chapters.

Chapter 2, Training Machine Learning Algorithms for Classification, goes back to the origin of machine learning and introduces binary perceptron classifiers and adaptive linear neurons. This chapter is a gentle introduction to the fundamentals of pattern classification and focuses on the interplay of optimization algorithms and machine learning.

Chapter 3, A Tour of Machine Learning Classifiers Using Scikit-learn, describes the essential machine learning algorithms for classification and provides practical examples using one of the most popular and comprehensive open source machine learning libraries, scikit-learn.

Chapter 4, Building Good Training Sets – Data Preprocessing, discusses how to deal with the most common problems in unprocessed datasets, such as missing data. It also discusses several approaches to identify the most informative features in datasets and teaches you how to prepare variables of different types as proper inputs for machine learning algorithms.

Chapter 5, Compressing Data via Dimensionality Reduction, describes the essential techniques to reduce the number of features in a dataset to smaller sets while retaining most of their useful and discriminatory information. It discusses the standard approach to dimensionality reduction via principal component analysis and compares it to supervised and nonlinear transformation techniques.

Chapter 6, Learning Best Practices for Model Evaluation and Hyperparameter Tuning, discusses the do's and don'ts for estimating the performances of predictive models. Moreover, it discusses different metrics for measuring the performance of our models and techniques to fine-tune machine learning algorithms.

Chapter 7, Combining Different Models for Ensemble Learning, introduces you to the different concepts of combining multiple learning algorithms effectively. It teaches you how to build ensembles of experts to overcome the weaknesses of individual learners, resulting in more accurate and reliable predictions.

Chapter 8, Applying Machine Learning to Sentiment Analysis, discusses the essential steps to transform textual data into meaningful representations for machine learning algorithms to predict the opinions of people based on their writing.

Chapter 9, Embedding a Machine Learning Model into a Web Application, continues with the predictive model from the previous chapter and walks you through the essential steps of developing web applications with embedded machine learning models.

Chapter 10, Predicting Continuous Target Variables with Regression Analysis, discusses the essential techniques for modeling linear relationships between target and response variables to make predictions on a continuous scale. After introducing different linear models, it also talks about polynomial regression and tree-based approaches.

Chapter 11, Working with Unlabeled Data – Clustering Analysis, shifts the focus to a different subarea of machine learning, unsupervised learning. We apply algorithms from three fundamental families of clustering algorithms to find groups of objects that share a certain degree of similarity.

Chapter 12, Training Artificial Neural Networks for Image Recognition, extends the concept of gradient-based optimization, which we first introduced in *Chapter 2, Training Machine Learning Algorithms for Classification*, to build powerful, multilayer neural networks based on the popular backpropagation algorithm.

Chapter 13, Parallelizing Neural Network Training with Theano, builds upon the knowledge from the previous chapter to provide you with a practical guide for training neural networks more efficiently. The focus of this chapter is on Theano, an open source Python library that allows us to utilize multiple cores of modern GPUs.

What you need for this book

The execution of the code examples provided in this book requires an installation of Python 3.4.3 or newer on Mac OS X, Linux, or Microsoft Windows. We will make frequent use of Python's essential libraries for scientific computing throughout this book, including SciPy, NumPy, scikit-learn, matplotlib, and pandas.

The first chapter will provide you with instructions and useful tips to set up your Python environment and these core libraries. We will add additional libraries to our repertoire and installation instructions are provided in the respective chapters: the NLTK library for natural language processing (*Chapter 8, Applying Machine Learning to Sentiment Analysis*), the Flask web framework (*Chapter 9, Embedding a Machine Learning Algorithm into a Web Application*), the seaborn library for statistical data visualization (*Chapter 10, Predicting Continuous Target Variables with Regression Analysis*), and Theano for efficient neural network training on graphical processing units (*Chapter 13, Parallelizing Neural Network Training with Theano*).

Who this book is for

If you want to find out how to use Python to start answering critical questions of your data, pick up *Python Machine Learning* — whether you want to start from scratch or want to extend your data science knowledge, this is an essential and unmissable resource.

Conventions

In this book, you will find a number of text styles that distinguish between different kinds of information. Here are some examples of these styles and an explanation of their meaning.

Code words in text, database table names, folder names, filenames, file extensions, pathnames, dummy URLs, user input, and Twitter handles are shown as follows: "And already installed packages can be updated via the `--upgrade` flag."

A block of code is set as follows:

```
>>> import matplotlib.pyplot as plt
>>> import numpy as np

>>> y = df.iloc[0:100, 4].values
>>> y = np.where(y == 'Iris-setosa', -1, 1)
>>> X = df.iloc[0:100, [0, 2]].values
>>> plt.scatter(X[:50, 0], X[:50, 1],
...             color='red', marker='x', label='setosa')
>>> plt.scatter(X[50:100, 0], X[50:100, 1],
...             color='blue', marker='o', label='versicolor')
>>> plt.xlabel('sepal length')
>>> plt.ylabel('petal    length')
>>> plt.legend(loc='upper left')
>>> plt.show()
```

Any command-line input or output is written as follows:

```
> dot -Tpng tree.dot -o tree.png
```

New terms and **important words** are shown in bold. Words that you see on the screen, for example, in menus or dialog boxes, appear in the text like this: "After we click on the **Dashboard** button in the top-right corner, we have access to the control panel shown at the top of the page."

 Warnings or important notes appear in a box like this.

 Tips and tricks appear like this.

Reader feedback

Feedback from our readers is always welcome. Let us know what you think about this book—what you liked or disliked. Reader feedback is important for us as it helps us develop titles that you will really get the most out of.

To send us general feedback, simply e-mail feedback@packtpub.com, and mention the book's title in the subject of your message.

If there is a topic that you have expertise in and you are interested in either writing or contributing to a book, see our author guide at www.packtpub.com/authors.

Customer support

Now that you are the proud owner of a Packt book, we have a number of things to help you to get the most from your purchase.

Downloading the example code

You can download the example code files from your account at http://www.packtpub.com for all the Packt Publishing books you have purchased. If you purchased this book elsewhere, you can visit http://www.packtpub.com/support and register to have the files e-mailed directly to you.

Errata

Although we have taken every care to ensure the accuracy of our content, mistakes do happen. If you find a mistake in one of our books—maybe a mistake in the text or the code—we would be grateful if you could report this to us. By doing so, you can save other readers from frustration and help us improve subsequent versions of this book. If you find any errata, please report them by visiting http://www.packtpub.com/submit-errata, selecting your book, clicking on the **Errata Submission Form** link, and entering the details of your errata. Once your errata are verified, your submission will be accepted and the errata will be uploaded to our website or added to any list of existing errata under the Errata section of that title.

To view the previously submitted errata, go to https://www.packtpub.com/books/content/support and enter the name of the book in the search field. The required information will appear under the **Errata** section.

Piracy

Piracy of copyrighted material on the Internet is an ongoing problem across all media. At Packt, we take the protection of our copyright and licenses very seriously. If you come across any illegal copies of our works in any form on the Internet, please provide us with the location address or website name immediately so that we can pursue a remedy.

Please contact us at copyright@packtpub.com with a link to the suspected pirated material.

We appreciate your help in protecting our authors and our ability to bring you valuable content.

Questions

If you have a problem with any aspect of this book, you can contact us at questions@packtpub.com, and we will do our best to address the problem.

1

Giving Computers the Ability to Learn from Data

In my opinion, *machine learning*, the application and science of algorithms that makes sense of data, is the most exciting field of all the computer sciences! We are living in an age where data comes in abundance; using the self-learning algorithms from the field of machine learning, we can turn this data into knowledge. Thanks to the many powerful open source libraries that have been developed in recent years, there has probably never been a better time to break into the machine learning field and learn how to utilize powerful algorithms to spot patterns in data and make predictions about future events.

In this chapter, we will learn about the main concepts and different types of machine learning. Together with a basic introduction to the relevant terminology, we will lay the groundwork for successfully using machine learning techniques for practical problem solving.

In this chapter, we will cover the following topics:

- The general concepts of machine learning
- The three types of learning and basic terminology
- The building blocks for successfully designing machine learning systems
- Installing and setting up Python for data analysis and machine learning

Building intelligent machines to transform data into knowledge

In this age of modern technology, there is one resource that we have in abundance: a large amount of structured and unstructured data. In the second half of the twentieth century, machine learning evolved as a subfield of *artificial intelligence* that involved the development of self-learning algorithms to gain knowledge from that data in order to make predictions. Instead of requiring humans to manually derive rules and build models from analyzing large amounts of data, machine learning offers a more efficient alternative for capturing the knowledge in data to gradually improve the performance of predictive models, and make data-driven decisions. Not only is machine learning becoming increasingly important in computer science research but it also plays an ever greater role in our everyday life. Thanks to machine learning, we enjoy robust e-mail spam filters, convenient text and voice recognition software, reliable Web search engines, challenging chess players, and, hopefully soon, safe and efficient self-driving cars.

The three different types of machine learning

In this section, we will take a look at the three types of machine learning: *supervised learning*, *unsupervised learning*, and *reinforcement learning*. We will learn about the fundamental differences between the three different learning types and, using conceptual examples, we will develop an intuition for the practical problem domains where these can be applied:

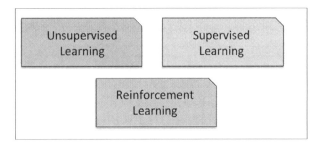

Making predictions about the future with supervised learning

The main goal in supervised learning is to learn a model from labeled *training* data that allows us to make predictions about unseen or future data. Here, the term *supervised* refers to a set of samples where the desired output signals (labels) are already known.

Considering the example of e-mail spam filtering, we can train a model using a supervised machine learning algorithm on a corpus of labeled e-mail, e-mail that are correctly marked as spam or not-spam, to predict whether a new e-mail belongs to either of the two categories. A supervised learning task with discrete *class labels*, such as in the previous e-mail spam-filtering example, is also called a *classification* task. Another subcategory of supervised learning is *regression*, where the outcome signal is a continuous value:

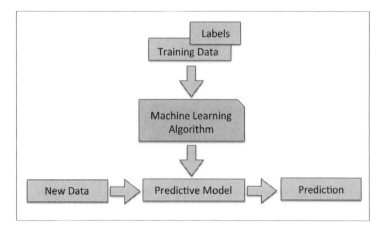

Classification for predicting class labels

Classification is a subcategory of supervised learning where the goal is to predict the categorical class labels of new instances based on past observations. Those class labels are discrete, unordered values that can be understood as the *group memberships* of the instances. The previously mentioned example of e-mail-spam detection represents a typical example of a *binary classification* task, where the machine learning algorithm learns a set of rules in order to distinguish between two possible classes: spam and non-spam e-mail.

However, the set of class labels does not have to be of a binary nature. The predictive model learned by a supervised learning algorithm can assign any class label that was presented in the training dataset to a new, unlabeled instance. A typical example of a *multi-class classification* task is handwritten character recognition. Here, we could collect a training dataset that consists of multiple handwritten examples of each letter in the alphabet. Now, if a user provides a new handwritten character via an input device, our predictive model will be able to predict the correct letter in the alphabet with certain accuracy. However, our machine learning system would be unable to correctly recognize any of the digits zero to nine, for example, if they were not part of our training dataset.

The following figure illustrates the concept of a binary classification task given 30 training samples: 15 training samples are labeled as *negative class* (circles) and 15 training samples are labeled as *positive class* (plus signs). In this scenario, our dataset is two-dimensional, which means that each sample has two values associated with it: x_1 and x_2. Now, we can use a supervised machine learning algorithm to learn a rule — the decision boundary represented as a black dashed line — that can separate those two classes and classify new data into each of those two categories given its x_1 and x_2 values:

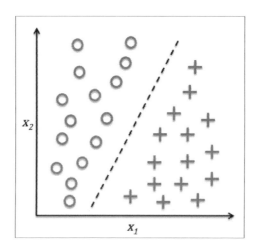

Regression for predicting continuous outcomes

We learned in the previous section that the task of classification is to assign categorical, unordered labels to instances. A second type of supervised learning is the prediction of continuous outcomes, which is also called regression analysis. In *regression analysis*, we are given a number of *predictor* (explanatory) variables and a continuous response variable (outcome), and we try to find a relationship between those variables that allows us to predict an outcome.

For example, let's assume that we are interested in predicting the Math SAT scores of our students. If there is a relationship between the time spent studying for the test and the final scores, we could use it as training data to learn a model that uses the study time to predict the test scores of future students who are planning to take this test.

> The term *regression* was devised by Francis Galton in his article *Regression Towards Mediocrity in Hereditary Stature* in 1886. Galton described the biological phenomenon that the variance of *height* in a population does not increase over time. He observed that the height of parents is not passed on to their children but the children's height is regressing towards the population mean.

The following figure illustrates the concept of *linear regression*. Given a predictor variable *x* and a response variable *y*, we fit a straight line to this data that minimizes the distance — most commonly the average squared distance — between the sample points and the fitted line. We can now use the intercept and slope learned from this data to predict the outcome variable of new data:

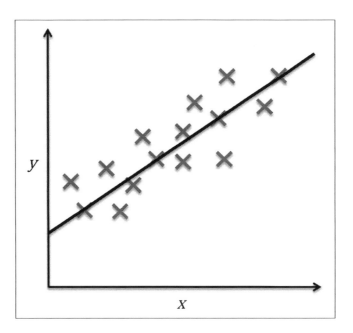

Solving interactive problems with reinforcement learning

Another type of machine learning is reinforcement learning. In reinforcement learning, the goal is to develop a system (*agent*) that improves its performance based on interactions with the *environment*. Since the information about the current state of the environment typically also includes a so-called *reward* signal, we can think of reinforcement learning as a field related to *supervised* learning. However, in reinforcement learning this feedback is not the correct ground truth label or value, but a measure of how well the action was measured by a *reward* function. Through the interaction with the environment, an agent can then use reinforcement learning to learn a series of actions that maximizes this reward via an exploratory trial-and-error approach or deliberative planning.

A popular example of reinforcement learning is a chess engine. Here, the agent decides upon a series of moves depending on the state of the board (the environment), and the reward can be defined as *win* or *lose* at the end of the game:

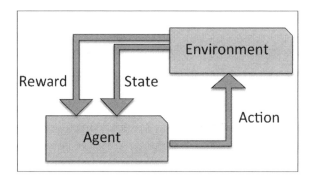

Discovering hidden structures with unsupervised learning

In supervised learning, we know the *right answer* beforehand when we train our model, and in reinforcement learning, we define a measure of *reward* for particular actions by the agent. In unsupervised learning, however, we are dealing with unlabeled data or data of *unknown structure*. Using unsupervised learning techniques, we are able to explore the structure of our data to extract meaningful information without the guidance of a known outcome variable or reward function.

Finding subgroups with clustering

Clustering is an exploratory data analysis technique that allows us to organize a pile of information into meaningful subgroups (*clusters*) without having any prior knowledge of their group memberships. Each cluster that may arise during the analysis defines a group of objects that share a certain degree of similarity but are more dissimilar to objects in other clusters, which is why clustering is also sometimes called "unsupervised classification." Clustering is a great technique for structuring information and deriving meaningful relationships among data, For example, it allows marketers to discover customer groups based on their interests in order to develop distinct marketing programs.

The figure below illustrates how clustering can be applied to organizing unlabeled data into three distinct groups based on the similarity of their features x_1 and x_2:

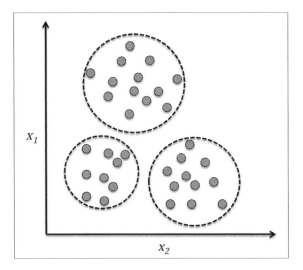

Dimensionality reduction for data compression

Another subfield of unsupervised learning is *dimensionality reduction*. Often we are working with data of high dimensionality—each observation comes with a high number of measurements—that can present a challenge for limited storage space and the computational performance of machine learning algorithms. Unsupervised dimensionality reduction is a commonly used approach in feature preprocessing to remove noise from data, which can also degrade the predictive performance of certain algorithms, and compress the data onto a smaller dimensional subspace while retaining most of the relevant information.

Sometimes, dimensionality reduction can also be useful for visualizing data—for example, a high-dimensional feature set can be projected onto one-, two-, or three-dimensional feature spaces in order to visualize it via 3D- or 2D-scatterplots or histograms. The figure below shows an example where non-linear dimensionality reduction was applied to compress a 3D *Swiss Roll* onto a new 2D feature subspace:

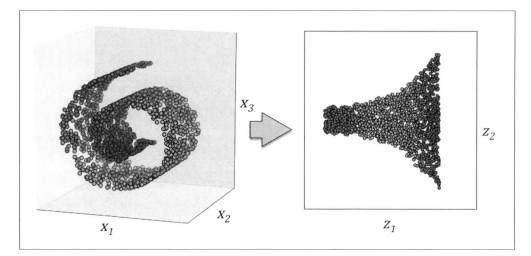

An introduction to the basic terminology and notations

Now that we have discussed the three broad categories of machine learning—supervised, unsupervised, and reinforcement learning—let us have a look at the basic terminology that we will be using in the next chapters. The following table depicts an excerpt of the *Iris* dataset, which is a classic example in the field of machine learning. The Iris dataset contains the measurements of 150 iris flowers from three different species: *Setosa*, *Versicolor*, and *Virginica*. Here, each flower sample represents one row in our data set, and the flower measurements in centimeters are stored as columns, which we also call the features of the dataset:

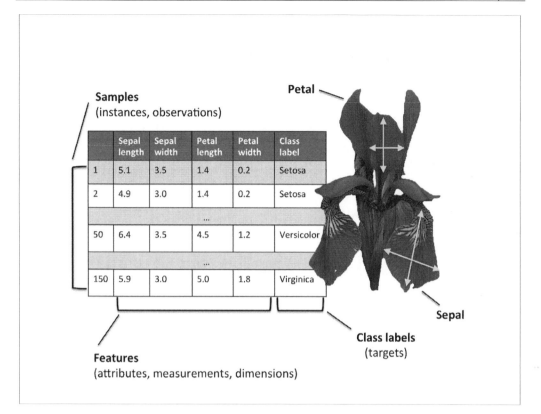

To keep the notation and implementation simple yet efficient, we will make use of some of the basics of *linear algebra*. In the following chapters, we will use a *matrix* and *vector* notation to refer to our data. We will follow the common convention to represent each sample as separate row in a feature matrix X, where each feature is stored as a separate column.

The Iris dataset, consisting of 150 samples and 4 features, can then be written as a 150×4 matrix $X \in \mathbb{R}^{150 \times 4}$:

$$\begin{bmatrix} x_1^{(1)} & x_2^{(1)} & x_3^{(1)} & x_4^{(1)} \\ x_1^{(2)} & x_2^{(2)} & x_3^{(2)} & x_4^{(2)} \\ \vdots & \vdots & \vdots & \vdots \\ x_1^{(150)} & x_2^{(150)} & x_3^{(150)} & x_4^{(150)} \end{bmatrix}$$

For the rest of this book, we will use the superscript *(i)* to refer to the *i*th training sample, and the subscript *j* to refer to the *j*th dimension of the training dataset.

We use lower-case, bold-face letters to refer to vectors $\left(x \in \mathbb{R}^{n \times 1}\right)$ and upper-case, bold-face letters to refer to matrices, respectively ($X \in \mathbb{R}^{n \times m}$). To refer to single elements in a vector or matrix, we write the letters in italics ($x^{(n)}$ or $x_{(m)}^{(n)}$, respectively).

For example, x_1^{150} refers to the first dimension of flower sample 150, the *sepal length*. Thus, each row in this feature matrix represents one flower instance and can be written as four-dimensional row vector $x^{(i)} \in \mathbb{R}^{1 \times 4}$,

$$x^{(i)} = \begin{bmatrix} x_1^{(i)} & x_2^{(i)} & x_3^{(i)} & x_4^{(i)} \end{bmatrix}.$$

Each feature dimension is a 150-dimensional column vector $x_j \in \mathbb{R}^{150 \times 1}$, for example:

$$x_j = \begin{bmatrix} x_j^{(1)} \\ x_j^{(2)} \\ \vdots \\ x_j^{(150)} \end{bmatrix}.$$

Similarly, we store the target variables (here: class labels) as a 150-dimensional column vector $y = \begin{bmatrix} y^{(1)} \\ \dots \\ y^{(150)} \end{bmatrix} \left(y \in \{\text{Setosa, Versicolor, Virginica}\}\right).$

A roadmap for building machine learning systems

In the previous sections, we discussed the basic concepts of machine learning and the three different types of learning. In this section, we will discuss other important parts of a machine learning system accompanying the learning algorithm. The diagram below shows a typical workflow diagram for using machine learning in *predictive modeling*, which we will discuss in the following subsections:

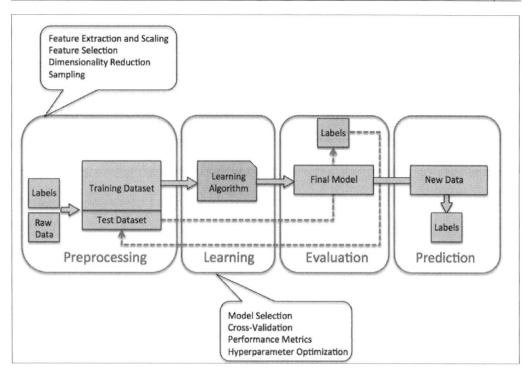

Preprocessing – getting data into shape

Raw data rarely comes in the form and shape that is necessary for the optimal performance of a learning algorithm. Thus, the *preprocessing* of the data is one of the most crucial steps in any machine learning application. If we take the Iris flower dataset from the previous section as an example, we could think of the raw data as a series of flower images from which we want to extract meaningful features. Useful features could be the color, the hue, the intensity of the flowers, the height, and the flower lengths and widths. Many machine learning algorithms also require that the selected features are on the same scale for optimal performance, which is often achieved by transforming the features in the range [0, 1] or a standard normal distribution with zero mean and unit variance, as we will see in the later chapters.

Some of the selected features may be highly correlated and therefore redundant to a certain degree. In those cases, dimensionality reduction techniques are useful for compressing the features onto a lower dimensional subspace. Reducing the dimensionality of our feature space has the advantage that less storage space is required, and the learning algorithm can run much faster.

To determine whether our machine learning algorithm not only performs well on the training set but also generalizes well to new data, we also want to randomly divide the dataset into a separate training and test set. We use the training set to train and optimize our machine learning model, while we keep the test set until the very end to evaluate the final model.

Training and selecting a predictive model

As we will see in later chapters, many different machine learning algorithms have been developed to solve different problem tasks. An important point that can be summarized from David Wolpert's famous *No Free Lunch Theorems* is that we can't get learning "for free" (*The Lack of A Priori Distinctions Between Learning Algorithms*, D.H. Wolpert 1996; *No Free Lunch Theorems for Optimization*, D.H. Wolpert and W.G. Macready, 1997). Intuitively, we can relate this concept to the popular saying, "*I suppose it is tempting, if the only tool you have is a hammer, to treat everything as if it were a nail*" (Abraham Maslow, 1966). For example, each classification algorithm has its inherent biases, and no single classification model enjoys superiority if we don't make any assumptions about the task. In practice, it is therefore essential to compare at least a handful of different algorithms in order to train and select the best performing model. But before we can compare different models, we first have to decide upon a metric to measure performance. One commonly used metric is classification accuracy, which is defined as the proportion of correctly classified instances.

One legitimate question to ask is: *how do we know which model performs well on the final test dataset and real-world data if we don't use this test set for the model selection but keep it for the final model evaluation?* In order to address the issue embedded in this question, different cross-validation techniques can be used where the training dataset is further divided into training and *validation subsets* in order to estimate the *generalization performance* of the model. Finally, we also cannot expect that the default parameters of the different learning algorithms provided by software libraries are optimal for our specific problem task. Therefore, we will make frequent use of hyperparameter *optimization techniques* that help us to fine-tune the performance of our model in later chapters. Intuitively, we can think of those hyperparameters as parameters that are not learned from the data but represent the knobs of a model that we can turn to improve its performance, which will become much clearer in later chapters when we see actual examples.

Evaluating models and predicting unseen data instances

After we have selected a model that has been fitted on the training dataset, we can use the test dataset to estimate how well it performs on this unseen data to estimate the generalization error. If we are satisfied with its performance, we can now use this model to predict new, future data. It is important to note that the parameters for the previously mentioned procedures—such as feature scaling and dimensionality reduction—are solely obtained from the training dataset, and the same parameters are later re-applied to transform the test dataset, as well as any new data samples—the performance measured on the test data may be overoptimistic otherwise.

Using Python for machine learning

Python is one of the most popular programming languages for data science and therefore enjoys a large number of useful add-on libraries developed by its great community.

Although the performance of interpreted languages, such as Python, for computation-intensive tasks is inferior to lower-level programming languages, extension libraries such as *NumPy* and *SciPy* have been developed that build upon lower layer Fortran and C implementations for fast and vectorized operations on multidimensional arrays.

For machine learning programming tasks, we will mostly refer to the *scikit-learn* library, which is one of the most popular and accessible open source machine learning libraries as of today.

Installing Python packages

Python is available for all three major operating systems—Microsoft Windows, Mac OS X, and Linux—and the installer, as well as the documentation, can be downloaded from the official Python website: `https://www.python.org`.

This book is written for Python version >= 3.4.3, and it is recommended you use the most recent version of Python 3 that is currently available, although most of the code examples may also be compatible with Python >= 2.7.10. If you decide to use Python 2.7 to execute the code examples, please make sure that you know about the major differences between the two Python versions. A good summary about the differences between Python 3.4 and 2.7 can be found at `https://wiki.python.org/moin/Python2orPython3`.

The additional packages that we will be using throughout this book can be installed via the *pip* installer program, which has been part of the Python standard library since Python 3.3. More information about pip can be found at `https://docs.python.org/3/installing/index.html`.

After we have successfully installed Python, we can execute pip from the command line terminal to install additional Python packages:

```
pip install SomePackage
```

Already installed packages can be updated via the `--upgrade` flag:

```
pip install SomePackage --upgrade
```

A highly recommended alternative Python distribution for scientific computing is Anaconda by Continuum Analytics. Anaconda is a free—including commercial use—enterprise-ready Python distribution that bundles all the essential Python packages for data science, math, and engineering in one user-friendly cross-platform distribution. The Anaconda installer can be downloaded at `http://continuum.io/downloads#py34`, and an Anaconda quick start-guide is available at `https://store.continuum.io/static/img/Anaconda-Quickstart.pdf`.

After successfully installing Anaconda, we can install new Python packages using the following command:

```
conda install SomePackage
```

Existing packages can be updated using the following command:

```
conda update SomePackage
```

Throughout this book, we will mainly use *NumPy*'s multi-dimensional arrays to store and manipulate data. Occasionally, we will make use of *pandas*, which is a library built on top of NumPy that provides additional higher level data manipulation tools that make working with tabular data even more convenient. To augment our learning experience and visualize quantitative data, which is often extremely useful to intuitively make sense of it, we will use the very customizable *matplotlib* library.

The version numbers of the major Python packages that were used for writing this book are listed below. Please make sure that the version numbers of your installed packages are equal to, or greater than, those version numbers to ensure the code examples run correctly:

- NumPy 1.9.1
- SciPy 0.14.0
- scikit-learn 0.15.2
- matplotlib 1.4.0
- pandas 0.15.2

Summary

In this chapter, we explored machine learning on a very high level and familiarized ourselves with the big picture and major concepts that we are going to explore in the next chapters in more detail.

We learned that supervised learning is composed of two important subfields: classification and regression. While classification models allow us to categorize objects into known classes, we can use regression analysis to predict the continuous outcomes of target variables. Unsupervised learning not only offers useful techniques for discovering structures in unlabeled data, but it can also be useful for data compression in feature preprocessing steps.

We briefly went over the typical roadmap for applying machine learning to problem tasks, which we will use as a foundation for deeper discussions and hands-on examples in the following chapters. Eventually, we set up our Python environment and installed and updated the required packages to get ready to see machine-learning in action.

In the following chapter, we will implement one of the earliest machine learning algorithms for classification that will prepare us for *Chapter 3, A Tour of Machine Learning Classifiers Using Scikit-learn*, where we cover more advanced machine learning algorithms using the scikit-learn open source machine learning library. Since machine learning algorithms learn from data, it is critical that we feed them useful information, and in *Chapter 4, Building Good Training Sets – Data Preprocessing* we will take a look at important data preprocessing techniques. In *Chapter 5, Compressing Data via Dimensionality Reduction*, we will learn about dimensionality reduction techniques that can help us to compress our dataset onto a lower-dimensional feature subspace, which can be beneficial for computational efficiency. An important aspect of building machine learning models is to evaluate their performance and to estimate how well they can make predictions on new, unseen data. In *Chapter 6, Learning Best Practices for Model Evaluation and Hyperparameter Tuning* we will learn all about the best practices for model tuning and evaluation. In certain scenarios, we still may not be satisfied with the performance of our predictive model although we may have spent hours or days extensively tuning and testing. In *Chapter 7, Combining Different Models for Ensemble Learning* we will learn how to combine different machine learning models to build even more powerful predictive systems.

After we covered all of the important concepts of a typical machine learning pipeline, we will implement a model for predicting emotions in text in *Chapter 8, Applying Machine Learning to Sentiment Analysis*, and in *Chapter 9, Embedding a Machine Learning Model into a Web Application*, we will embed it into a Web application to share it with the world. In *Chapter 10, Predicting Continuous Target Variables with Regression Analysis* we will then use machine learning algorithms for regression analysis that allow us to predict continuous output variables, and in *Chapter 11, Working with Unlabelled Data – Clustering Analysis* we will apply clustering algorithms that will allow us to find hidden structures in data. The last two chapters in this book will cover artificial neural networks that will allow us to tackle complex problems, such as image and speech recognition, which is currently one of the hottest topics in machine-learning research.

2

Training Machine Learning Algorithms for Classification

In this chapter, we will make use of one of the first algorithmically described machine learning algorithms for classification, the *perceptron* and *adaptive linear neurons*. We will start by implementing a perceptron step by step in Python and training it to classify different flower species in the Iris dataset. This will help us to understand the concept of machine learning algorithms for classification and how they can be efficiently implemented in Python. Discussing the basics of optimization using adaptive linear neurons will then lay the groundwork for using more powerful classifiers via the scikit-learn machine-learning library in *Chapter 3, A Tour of Machine Learning Classifiers Using Scikit-learn*.

The topics that we will cover in this chapter are as follows:

- Building an intuition for machine learning algorithms
- Using pandas, NumPy, and matplotlib to read in, process, and visualize data
- Implementing linear classification algorithms in Python

Artificial neurons – a brief glimpse into the early history of machine learning

Before we discuss the perceptron and related algorithms in more detail, let us take a brief tour through the early beginnings of machine learning. Trying to understand how the biological brain works to design artificial intelligence, Warren McCullock and Walter Pitts published the first concept of a simplified brain cell, the so-called *McCullock-Pitts (MCP) neuron*, in 1943 (W. S. McCulloch and W. Pitts. *A Logical Calculus of the Ideas Immanent in Nervous Activity*. The bulletin of mathematical biophysics, 5(4):115–133, 1943). Neurons are interconnected nerve cells in the brain that are involved in the processing and transmitting of chemical and electrical signals, which is illustrated in the following figure:

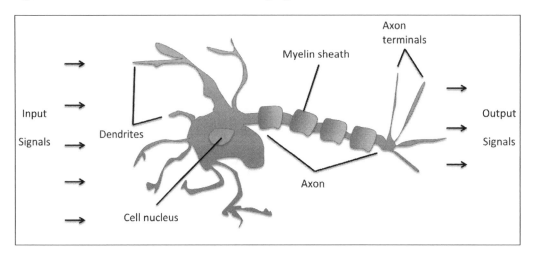

McCullock and Pitts described such a nerve cell as a simple logic gate with binary outputs; multiple signals arrive at the dendrites, are then integrated into the cell body, and, if the accumulated signal exceeds a certain threshold, an output signal is generated that will be passed on by the axon.

Only a few years later, Frank Rosenblatt published the first concept of the perceptron learning rule based on the MCP neuron model (F. Rosenblatt, *The Perceptron, a Perceiving and Recognizing Automaton*. Cornell Aeronautical Laboratory, 1957). With his perceptron rule, Rosenblatt proposed an algorithm that would automatically learn the optimal weight coefficients that are then multiplied with the input features in order to make the decision of whether a neuron fires or not. In the context of supervised learning and classification, such an algorithm could then be used to predict if a sample belonged to one class or the other.

More formally, we can pose this problem as a binary classification task where we refer to our two classes as 1 (positive class) and -1 (negative class) for simplicity. We can then define an *activation function* $\phi(z)$ that takes a linear combination of certain input values x and a corresponding weight vector w, where z is the so-called net input ($z = w_1 x_1 + \ldots + w_m x_m$):

$$w = \begin{bmatrix} w_1 \\ \vdots \\ w_m \end{bmatrix}, \quad x = \begin{bmatrix} x_1 \\ \vdots \\ x_m \end{bmatrix}$$

Now, if the activation of a particular sample $x^{(i)}$, that is, the output of $\phi(z)$, is greater than a defined threshold θ, we predict class 1 and class -1, otherwise. In the perceptron algorithm, the activation function $\phi(\cdot)$ is a simple *unit step function*, which is sometimes also called the *Heaviside step function*:

$$\phi(z) = \begin{cases} 1 & \text{if } z \geq \theta \\ -1 & \text{otherwise} \end{cases}$$

For simplicity, we can bring the threshold θ to the left side of the equation and define a weight-zero as $w_0 = -\theta$ and $x_0 = 1$, so that we write z in a more compact form $z = w_0 x_0 + w_1 x_1 + \ldots + w_m x_m = \boldsymbol{w}^T \boldsymbol{x}$ and $\phi(z) = \begin{cases} 1 & \text{if } z \geq 0 \\ -1 & \text{otherwise} \end{cases}$.

In the following sections, we will often make use of basic notations from linear algebra. For example, we will abbreviate the sum of the products of the values in $\boldsymbol{x}$ and $\boldsymbol{w}$ using a *vector dot product*, whereas superscript T stands for *transpose*, which is an operation that transforms a column vector into a row vector and vice versa:

$$z = w_0 x_0 + w_1 x_1 + \cdots + w_m x_m = \sum_{j=0}^{m} x_j w_j = \boldsymbol{w}^T \boldsymbol{x}$$

For example: $\begin{bmatrix} 1 & 2 & 3 \end{bmatrix} \times \begin{bmatrix} 4 \\ 5 \\ 6 \end{bmatrix} = 1 \times 4 + 2 \times 5 + 3 \times 6 = 32$.

Furthermore, the transpose operation can also be applied to a matrix to reflect it over its diagonal, for example:

$$\begin{bmatrix} 1 & 2 \\ 3 & 4 \\ 5 & 6 \end{bmatrix}^T = \begin{bmatrix} 1 & 3 & 5 \\ 2 & 4 & 6 \end{bmatrix}$$

In this book, we will only use the very basic concepts from linear algebra. However, if you need a quick refresher, please take a look at Zico Kolter's excellent Linear Algebra Review and Reference, which is freely available at http://www.cs.cmu.edu/~zkolter/course/linalg/linalg_notes.pdf.

The following figure illustrates how the net input $z = \boldsymbol{w}^T \boldsymbol{x}$ is squashed into a binary output (-1 or 1) by the activation function of the perceptron (left subfigure) and how it can be used to discriminate between two linearly separable classes (right subfigure):

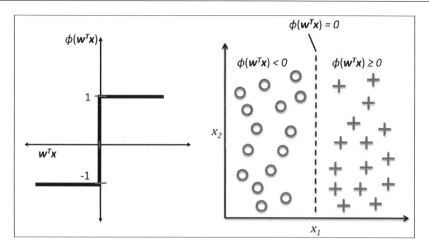

The whole idea behind the MCP neuron and Rosenblatt's *thresholded* perceptron model is to use a reductionist approach to mimic how a single neuron in the brain works: it either *fires* or it doesn't. Thus, Rosenblatt's initial perceptron rule is fairly simple and can be summarized by the following steps:

1. Initialize the weights to 0 or small random numbers.

2. For each training sample $x^{(i)}$ perform the following steps:

    1. Compute the output value $\hat{y}$.
    2. Update the weights.

Here, the output value is the class label predicted by the unit step function that we defined earlier, and the simultaneous update of each weight w_j in the weight vector w can be more formally written as:

$$w_j := w_j + \Delta w_j$$

The value of Δw_j, which is used to update the weight w_j, is calculated by the perceptron learning rule:

$$\Delta w_j = \eta \left(y^{(i)} - \hat{y}^{(i)} \right) x_j^{(i)}$$

Where η is the learning rate (a constant between 0.0 and 1.0), $y^{(i)}$ is the true class label of the i th training sample, and $\hat{y}^{(i)}$ is the predicted class label. It is important to note that all weights in the weight vector are being updated simultaneously, which means that we don't recompute the $\hat{y}^{(i)}$ before all of the weights Δw_j were updated. Concretely, for a 2D dataset, we would write the update as follows:

$$\Delta w_0 = \eta\left(y^{(i)} - output^{(i)}\right)$$

$$\Delta w_1 = \eta\left(y^{(i)} - output^{(i)}\right)x_1^{(i)}$$

$$\Delta w_2 = \eta\left(y^{(i)} - output^{(i)}\right)x_2^{(i)}$$

Before we implement the perceptron rule in Python, let us make a simple thought experiment to illustrate how beautifully simple this learning rule really is. In the two scenarios where the perceptron predicts the class label correctly, the weights remain unchanged:

$$\Delta w_j = \eta\left(-1 - -1\right)x_j^{(i)} = 0$$

$$\Delta w_j = \eta\left(1 - 1\right)x_j^{(i)} = 0$$

However, in the case of a wrong prediction, the weights are being pushed towards the direction of the positive or negative target class, respectively:

$$\Delta w_j = \eta\left(1 - -1\right)x_j^{(i)} = \eta\left(2\right)x_j^{(i)}$$

$$\Delta w_j = \eta\left(-1 - 1\right)x_j^{(i)} = \eta\left(-2\right)x_j^{(i)}$$

To get a better intuition for the multiplicative factor $x_j^{(i)}$, let us go through another simple example, where:

$$y^{(i)} = +1, \ \hat{y}_j^{(i)} = -1, \ \eta = 1$$

Let's assume that $x_j^{(i)} = 0.5$, and we misclassify this sample as -1. In this case, we would increase the corresponding weight by 1 so that the activation $x_j^{(i)} \times w_j^{(i)}$ will be more positive the next time we encounter this sample and thus will be more likely to be above the threshold of the unit step function to classify the sample as +1:

$$\Delta w_j^{(i)} = \left(1--1\right)0.5 = \left(2\right)0.5 = 1$$

The weight update is proportional to the value of $x_j^{(i)}$. For example, if we have another sample $x_j^{(i)} = 2$ that is incorrectly classified as -1, we'd push the decision boundary by an even larger extent to classify this sample correctly the next time:

$$\Delta w_j = \left(1--1\right)2 = \left(2\right)2 = 4$$

It is important to note that the convergence of the perceptron is only guaranteed if the two classes are linearly separable and the learning rate is sufficiently small. If the two classes can't be separated by a linear decision boundary, we can set a maximum number of passes over the training dataset (*epochs*) and/or a threshold for the number of tolerated misclassifications—the perceptron would never stop updating the weights otherwise:

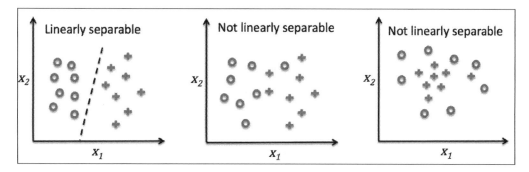

Now, before we jump into the implementation in the next section, let us summarize what we just learned in a simple figure that illustrates the general concept of the perceptron:

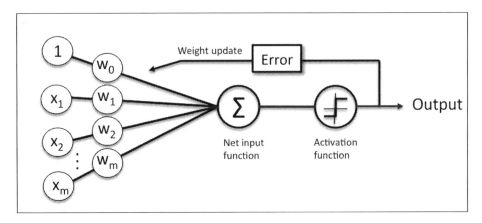

The preceding figure illustrates how the perceptron receives the inputs of a sample *x* and combines them with the weights *w* to compute the net input. The net input is then passed on to the activation function (here: the unit step function), which generates a binary output -1 or +1 — the predicted class label of the sample. During the learning phase, this output is used to calculate the error of the prediction and update the weights.

Implementing a perceptron learning algorithm in Python

In the previous section, we learned how Rosenblatt's perceptron rule works; let us now go ahead and implement it in Python and apply it to the Iris dataset that we introduced in *Chapter 1, Giving Computers the Ability to Learn from Data*. We will take an objected-oriented approach to define the perceptron interface as a Python `Class`, which allows us to initialize new perceptron objects that can learn from data via a `fit` method, and make predictions via a separate `predict` method. As a convention, we add an underscore to attributes that are not being created upon the initialization of the object but by calling the object's other methods — for example, `self.w_`.

If you are not yet familiar with Python's scientific libraries or need a refresher, please see the following resources:

NumPy: http://wiki.scipy.org/Tentative_NumPy_Tutorial

Pandas: http://pandas.pydata.org/pandas-docs/stable/tutorials.html

Matplotlib: http://matplotlib.org/users/beginner.html

Also, to better follow the code examples, I recommend you download the IPython notebooks from the Packt website. For a general introduction to IPython notebooks, please visit https://ipython.org/ipython-doc/3/notebook/index.html.

```
import numpy as np
class Perceptron(object):
    """Perceptron classifier.

    Parameters
    ------------
    eta : float
        Learning rate (between 0.0 and 1.0)
    n_iter : int
        Passes over the training dataset.

    Attributes
    -----------
    w_ : 1d-array
        Weights after fitting.
    errors_ : list
        Number of misclassifications in every epoch.

    """
    def __init__(self, eta=0.01, n_iter=10):
        self.eta = eta
        self.n_iter = n_iter

    def fit(self, X, y):
        """Fit training data.

        Parameters
        ----------
        X : {array-like}, shape = [n_samples, n_features]
            Training vectors, where n_samples
            is the number of samples and
```

```
            n_features is the number of features.
    y : array-like, shape = [n_samples]
            Target values.

    Returns
    -------
    self : object

    """
    self.w_ = np.zeros(1 + X.shape[1])
    self.errors_ = []

    for _ in range(self.n_iter):
        errors = 0
        for xi, target in zip(X, y):
            update = self.eta * (target - self.predict(xi))
            self.w_[1:] += update * xi
            self.w_[0] += update
            errors += int(update != 0.0)
        self.errors_.append(errors)
    return self

def net_input(self, X):
    """Calculate net input"""
    return np.dot(X, self.w_[1:]) + self.w_[0]

def predict(self, X):
    """Return class label after unit step"""
    return np.where(self.net_input(X) >= 0.0, 1, -1)
```

Using this perceptron implementation, we can now initialize new `Perceptron` objects with a given learning rate `eta` and `n_iter`, which is the number of epochs (passes over the training set). Via the `fit` method we initialize the weights in `self.w_` to a zero-vector $\mathbb{R}^{m+1}$ where m stands for the number of dimensions (features) in the dataset where we add 1 for the zero-weight (that is, the threshold).

NumPy indexing for one-dimensional arrays works similarly to Python lists using the square-bracket (`[]`) notation. For two-dimensional arrays, the first indexer refers to the row number, and the second indexer to the column number. For example, we would use `X[2, 3]` to select the third row and fourth column of a 2D array `X`.

After the weights have been initialized, the `fit` method loops over all individual samples in the training set and updates the weights according to the perceptron learning rule that we discussed in the previous section. The class labels are predicted by the `predict` method, which is also called in the `fit` method to predict the class label for the weight update, but `predict` can also be used to predict the class labels of new data after we have fitted our model. Furthermore, we also collect the number of misclassifications during each epoch in the list `self.errors_` so that we can later analyze how well our perceptron performed during the training. The `np.dot` function that is used in the `net_input` method simply calculates the vector dot product $w^T x$.

> Instead of using NumPy to calculate the vector dot product between two arrays a and b via `a.dot(b)` or `np.dot(a, b)`, we could also perform the calculation in pure Python via `sum([i*j for i,j in zip(a, b)])`. However, the advantage of using NumPy over classic Python for-loop structures is that its arithmetic operations are vectorized. **Vectorization** means that an elemental arithmetic operation is automatically applied to all elements in an array. By formulating our arithmetic operations as a sequence of instructions on an array rather than performing a set of operations for each element one at a time, we can make better use of our modern CPU architectures with **Single Instruction, Multiple Data (SIMD)** support. Furthermore, NumPy uses highly optimized linear algebra libraries, such as **Basic Linear Algebra Subprograms (BLAS)** and **Linear Algebra Package (LAPACK)** that have been written in C or Fortran. Lastly, NumPy also allows us to write our code in a more compact and intuitive way using the basics of linear algebra, such as vector and matrix dot products.

Training a perceptron model on the Iris dataset

To test our perceptron implementation, we will load the two flower classes *Setosa* and *Versicolor* from the Iris dataset. Although, the perceptron rule is not restricted to two dimensions, we will only consider the two features *sepal length* and *petal length* for visualization purposes. Also, we only chose the two flower classes *Setosa* and *Versicolor* for practical reasons. However, the perceptron algorithm can be extended to multi-class classification—for example, through the *One-vs.-All* technique.

> **One-vs.-All (OvA)**, or sometimes also called **One-vs.-Rest (OvR)**, is a technique used to extend a binary classifier to multi-class problems. Using OvA, we can train one classifier per class, where the particular class is treated as the positive class and the samples from all other classes are considered as the negative class. If we were to classify a new data sample, we would use our n classifiers, where n is the number of class labels, and assign the class label with the highest confidence to the particular sample. In the case of the perceptron, we would use OvA to choose the class label that is associated with the largest absolute net input value.

First, we will use the *pandas* library to load the Iris dataset directly from the *UCI Machine Learning Repository* into a `DataFrame` object and print the last five lines via the `tail` method to check that the data was loaded correctly:

```
>>> import pandas as pd
>>> df = pd.read_csv('https://archive.ics.uci.edu/ml/'
...     'machine-learning-databases/iris/iris.data', header=None)
>>> df.tail()
```

	0	1	2	3	4
145	6.7	3.0	5.2	2.3	Iris-virginica
146	6.3	2.5	5.0	1.9	Iris-virginica
147	6.5	3.0	5.2	2.0	Iris-virginica
148	6.2	3.4	5.4	2.3	Iris-virginica
149	5.9	3.0	5.1	1.8	Iris-virginica

Next, we extract the first 100 class labels that correspond to the 50 *Iris-Setosa* and 50 *Iris-Versicolor* flowers, respectively, and convert the class labels into the two integer class labels `1` (*Versicolor*) and `-1` (*Setosa*) that we assign to a vector `y` where the values method of a pandas `DataFrame` yields the corresponding NumPy representation. Similarly, we extract the first feature column (*sepal length*) and the third feature column (*petal length*) of those 100 training samples and assign them to a feature matrix `X`, which we can visualize via a two-dimensional scatter plot:

```
>>> import matplotlib.pyplot as plt
>>> import numpy as np

>>> y = df.iloc[0:100, 4].values
```

```
>>> y = np.where(y == 'Iris-setosa', -1, 1)
>>> X = df.iloc[0:100, [0, 2]].values
>>> plt.scatter(X[:50, 0], X[:50, 1],
...             color='red', marker='o', label='setosa')
>>> plt.scatter(X[50:100, 0], X[50:100, 1],
...             color='blue', marker='x', label='versicolor')
>>> plt.xlabel('sepal length')
>>> plt.ylabel('petal length')
>>> plt.legend(loc='upper left')
>>> plt.show()
```

After executing the preceding code example we should now see the following scatterplot:

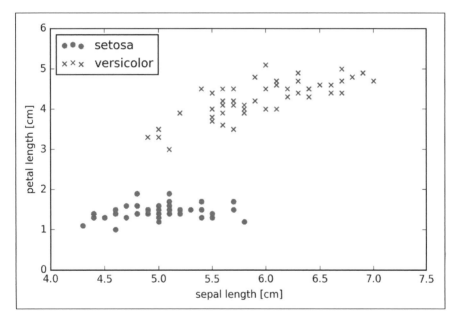

Now it's time to train our perceptron algorithm on the Iris data subset that we just extracted. Also, we will plot the `misclassification error` for each epoch to check if the algorithm converged and found a decision boundary that separates the two Iris flower classes:

```
>>> ppn = Perceptron(eta=0.1, n_iter=10)
>>> ppn.fit(X, y)
>>> plt.plot(range(1, len(ppn.errors_) + 1), ppn.errors_,
```

```
...             marker='o')
>>> plt.xlabel('Epochs')
>>> plt.ylabel('Number of misclassifications')
>>> plt.show()
```

After executing the preceding code, we should see the plot of the misclassification errors versus the number of epochs, as shown next:

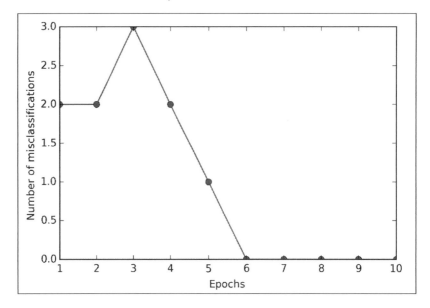

As we can see in the preceding plot, our perceptron already converged after the sixth epoch and should now be able to classify the training samples perfectly. Let us implement a small convenience function to visualize the decision boundaries for 2D datasets:

```
from matplotlib.colors import ListedColormap

def plot_decision_regions(X, y, classifier, resolution=0.02):

    # setup marker generator and color map
    markers = ('s', 'x', 'o', '^', 'v')
    colors = ('red', 'blue', 'lightgreen', 'gray', 'cyan')
```

```
cmap = ListedColormap(colors[:len(np.unique(y))])


# plot the decision surface
x1_min, x1_max = X[:, 0].min() - 1, X[:, 0].max() + 1
x2_min, x2_max = X[:, 1].min() - 1, X[:, 1].max() + 1
xx1, xx2 = np.meshgrid(np.arange(x1_min, x1_max, resolution),
                       np.arange(x2_min, x2_max, resolution))
Z = classifier.predict(np.array([xx1.ravel(), xx2.ravel()]).T)
Z = Z.reshape(xx1.shape)
plt.contourf(xx1, xx2, Z, alpha=0.4, cmap=cmap)
plt.xlim(xx1.min(), xx1.max())
plt.ylim(xx2.min(), xx2.max())


# plot class samples
for idx, cl in enumerate(np.unique(y)):
    plt.scatter(x=X[y == cl, 0], y=X[y == cl, 1],
                alpha=0.8, c=cmap(idx),
                marker=markers[idx], label=cl)
```

First, we define a number of `colors` and `markers` and create a color map from the list of colors via `ListedColormap`. Then, we determine the minimum and maximum values for the two features and use those feature vectors to create a pair of grid arrays `xx1` and `xx2` via the NumPy `meshgrid` function. Since we trained our perceptron classifier on two feature dimensions, we need to flatten the grid arrays and create a matrix that has the same number of columns as the Iris training subset so that we can use the `predict` method to predict the class labels `z` of the corresponding grid points. After reshaping the predicted class labels `z` into a grid with the same dimensions as `xx1` and `xx2`, we can now draw a contour plot via matplotlib's `contourf` function that maps the different decision regions to different colors for each predicted class in the grid array:

```
>>> plot_decision_regions(X, y, classifier=ppn)
>>> plt.xlabel('sepal length [cm]')
>>> plt.ylabel('petal length [cm]')
>>> plt.legend(loc='upper left')
>>> plt.show()
```

After executing the preceding code example, we should now see a plot of the decision regions, as shown in the following figure:

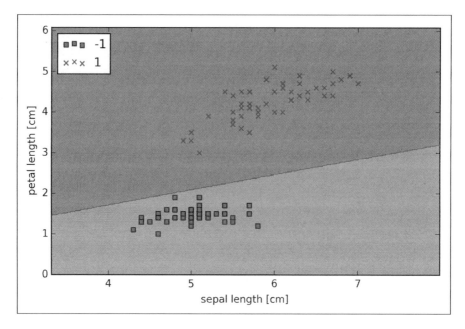

As we can see in the preceding plot, the perceptron learned a decision boundary that was able to classify all flower samples in the Iris training subset perfectly.

> Although the perceptron classified the two Iris flower classes perfectly, convergence is one of the biggest problems of the perceptron. Frank Rosenblatt proved mathematically that the perceptron learning rule converges if the two classes can be separated by a linear hyperplane. However, if classes cannot be separated perfectly by such a linear decision boundary, the weights will never stop updating unless we set a maximum number of epochs.

Adaptive linear neurons and the convergence of learning

In this section, we will take a look at another type of single-layer neural network: **ADAptive LInear NEuron (Adaline)**. Adaline was published, only a few years after Frank Rosenblatt's perceptron algorithm, by Bernard Widrow and his doctoral student Tedd Hoff, and can be considered as an improvement on the latter (B. Widrow et al. Adaptive *"Adaline" neuron using chemical "memistors"*. Number Technical Report 1553-2. Stanford Electron. Labs. Stanford, CA, October 1960). The Adaline algorithm is particularly interesting because it illustrates the key concept of defining and minimizing cost functions, which will lay the groundwork for understanding more advanced machine learning algorithms for classification, such as logistic regression and support vector machines, as well as regression models that we will discuss in future chapters.

The key difference between the Adaline rule (also known as the *Widrow-Hoff rule*) and Rosenblatt's perceptron is that the weights are updated based on a linear activation function rather than a unit step function like in the perceptron. In Adaline, this linear activation function $\phi(z)$ is simply the identity function of the net input so that $\phi(w^T x) = w^T x$.

While the linear activation function is used for learning the weights, a *quantizer*, which is similar to the unit step function that we have seen before, can then be used to predict the class labels, as illustrated in the following figure:

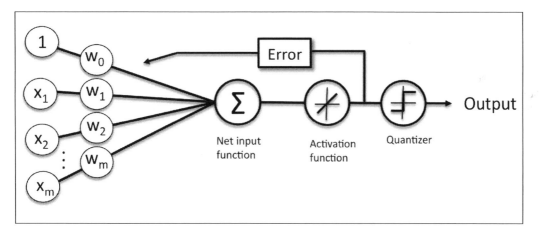

If we compare the preceding figure to the illustration of the perceptron algorithm that we saw earlier, the difference is that we know to use the continuous valued output from the linear activation function to compute the model error and update the weights, rather than the binary class labels.

Minimizing cost functions with gradient descent

One of the key ingredients of supervised machine learning algorithms is to define an *objective function* that is to be optimized during the learning process. This objective function is often a *cost function* that we want to minimize. In the case of Adaline, we can define the cost function J to learn the weights as the **Sum of Squared Errors (SSE)** between the calculated outcomes and the true class labels

$$J(w) = \frac{1}{2} \sum_i \left(y^{(i)} - \phi\left(z^{(i)}\right) \right)^2 .$$

The term $\frac{1}{2}$ is just added for our convenience; it will make it easier to derive the gradient, as we will see in the following paragraphs. The main advantage of this continuous linear activation function is — in contrast to the unit step function — that the cost function becomes differentiable. Another nice property of this cost function is that it is convex; thus, we can use a simple, yet powerful, optimization algorithm called *gradient descent* to find the weights that minimize our cost function to classify the samples in the Iris dataset.

As illustrated in the following figure, we can describe the principle behind gradient descent as *climbing down a hill* until a local or global cost minimum is reached. In each iteration, we take a step away from the gradient where the step size is determined by the value of the learning rate as well as the slope of the gradient:

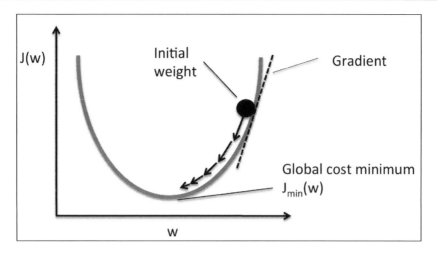

Using gradient descent, we can now update the weights by taking a step away from the gradient $\nabla J(w)$ of our cost function $J(w)$:

$$w := w + \Delta w$$

Here, the weight change Δw is defined as the negative gradient multiplied by the learning rate η:

$$\Delta w = -\eta \nabla J(w)$$

To compute the gradient of the cost function, we need to compute the partial derivative of the cost function with respect to each weight w_j, $\frac{\partial J}{\partial w_j} = -\sum_i \left(y^{(i)} - \phi(z^{(i)}) \right) x_j^{(i)}$, so that we can write the update of weight w_j as $\Delta w_j = -\eta \frac{\partial J}{\partial w_j} = \eta \sum_i \left(y^{(i)} - \phi(z^{(i)}) \right) x_j^{(i)}$.

Since we update all weights simultaneously, our Adaline learning rule becomes $w := w + \Delta w$.

For those who are familiar with calculus, the partial derivative of the SSE cost function with respect to the *j*th weight in can be obtained as follows:

$$\frac{\partial J}{\partial w_j} = \frac{\partial}{\partial w_j} \frac{1}{2} \sum_i \left(y^{(i)} - \phi\left(z^{(i)}\right) \right)^2$$

$$= \frac{1}{2} \frac{\partial}{\partial w_j} \sum_i \left(y^{(i)} - \phi\left(z^{(i)}\right) \right)^2$$

$$= \frac{1}{2} \sum_i 2\left(y^{(i)} - \phi\left(z^{(i)}\right) \right) \frac{\partial}{\partial w_j} \left(y^{(i)} - \phi\left(z^{(i)}\right) \right)$$

$$= \sum_i \left(y^{(i)} - \phi\left(z^{(i)}\right) \right) \frac{\partial}{\partial w_j} \left(y^{(i)} - \sum_i \left(w_j^{(i)} x_j^{(i)} \right) \right)$$

$$= \sum_i \left(y^{(i)} - \phi\left(z^{(i)}\right) \right) \left(-x_j^{(i)} \right)$$

$$= -\sum_i \left(y^{(i)} - \phi\left(z^{(i)}\right) \right) x_j^{(i)}$$

Although the Adaline learning rule looks identical to the perceptron rule, the $\phi\left(z^{(i)}\right)$ with $z^{(i)} = \boldsymbol{w}^T \boldsymbol{x}^{(i)}$ is a real number and not an integer class label. Furthermore, the weight update is calculated based on all samples in the training set (instead of updating the weights incrementally after each sample), which is why this approach is also referred to as "batch" gradient descent.

Implementing an Adaptive Linear Neuron in Python

Since the perceptron rule and Adaline are very similar, we will take the perceptron implementation that we defined earlier and change the `fit` method so that the weights are updated by minimizing the cost function via gradient descent:

```
class AdalineGD(object):
    """ADAptive LInear NEuron classifier.

    Parameters
    -----------
```

```
eta : float
    Learning rate (between 0.0 and 1.0)
n_iter : int
    Passes over the training dataset.

Attributes
-----------
w_ : 1d-array
    Weights after fitting.
errors_ : list
    Number of misclassifications in every epoch.

"""
def __init__(self, eta=0.01, n_iter=50):
    self.eta = eta
    self.n_iter = n_iter


def fit(self, X, y):
    """ Fit training data.

    Parameters
    ----------
    X : {array-like}, shape = [n_samples, n_features]
        Training vectors,
        where n_samples is the number of samples and
        n_features is the number of features.
    y : array-like, shape = [n_samples]
        Target values.

    Returns
    -------
    self : object

    """
    self.w_ = np.zeros(1 + X.shape[1])
    self.cost_ = []

    for i in range(self.n_iter):
        output = self.net_input(X)
        errors = (y - output)
        self.w_[1:] += self.eta * X.T.dot(errors)
        self.w_[0] += self.eta * errors.sum()
```

```
            cost = (errors**2).sum() / 2.0
            self.cost_.append(cost)
        return self

    def net_input(self, X):
        """Calculate net input"""
        return np.dot(X, self.w_[1:]) + self.w_[0]

    def activation(self, X):
        """Compute linear activation"""
        return self.net_input(X)

    def predict(self, X):
        """Return class label after unit step"""
        return np.where(self.activation(X) >= 0.0, 1, -1)
```

Instead of updating the weights after evaluating each individual training sample, as in the perceptron, we calculate the gradient based on the whole training dataset via `self.eta * errors.sum()` for the zero-weight and via `self.eta * X.T.dot(errors)` for the weights 1 to *m* where `X.T.dot(errors)` is a *matrix-vector multiplication* between our feature matrix and the error vector. Similar to the previous perceptron implementation, we collect the cost values in a list `self.cost_` to check if the algorithm converged after training.

Performing a matrix-vector multiplication is similar to calculating a vector dot product where each row in the matrix is treated as a single row vector. This vectorized approach represents a more compact notation and results in a more efficient computation using NumPy. For example:

$$\begin{bmatrix} 1 & 2 & 3 \\ 4 & 5 & 6 \end{bmatrix} \times \begin{bmatrix} 7 \\ 8 \\ 9 \end{bmatrix} = \begin{bmatrix} 1\times7+2\times8+3\times9 \\ 4\times7+5\times8+6\times9 \end{bmatrix} = \begin{bmatrix} 50 \\ 122 \end{bmatrix}$$

In practice, it often requires some experimentation to find a good learning rate η for optimal convergence. So, let's choose two different learning rates $\eta = 0.1$ and $\eta = 0.0001$ to start with and plot the cost functions versus the number of epochs to see how well the Adaline implementation learns from the training data.

The learning rate η, as well as the number of epochs n_iter, are the so-called *hyperparameters* of the perceptron and Adaline learning algorithms. In *Chapter 4, Building Good Training Sets – Data Preprocessing*, we will take a look at different techniques to automatically find the values of different hyperparameters that yield optimal performance of the classification model.

Let us now plot the cost against the number of epochs for the two different learning rates:

```
>>> fig, ax = plt.subplots(nrows=1, ncols=2, figsize=(8, 4))
>>> ada1 = AdalineGD(n_iter=10, eta=0.01).fit(X, y)
>>> ax[0].plot(range(1, len(ada1.cost_) + 1),
...            np.log10(ada1.cost_), marker='o')
>>> ax[0].set_xlabel('Epochs')
>>> ax[0].set_ylabel('log(Sum-squared-error)')
>>> ax[0].set_title('Adaline - Learning rate 0.01')
>>> ada2 = AdalineGD(n_iter=10, eta=0.0001).fit(X, y)
>>> ax[1].plot(range(1, len(ada2.cost_) + 1),
...            ada2.cost_, marker='o')
>>> ax[1].set_xlabel('Epochs')
>>> ax[1].set_ylabel('Sum-squared-error')
>>> ax[1].set_title('Adaline - Learning rate 0.0001')
>>> plt.show()
```

As we can see in the resulting cost function plots next, we encountered two different types of problems. The left chart shows what could happen if we choose a learning rate that is too large—instead of minimizing the cost function, the error becomes larger in every epoch because we *overshoot* the global minimum:

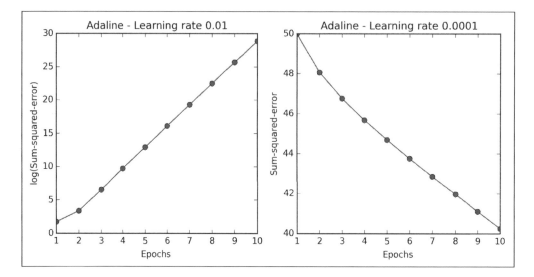

Although we can see that the cost decreases when we look at the right plot, the chosen learning rate $\eta = 0.0001$ is so small that the algorithm would require a very large number of epochs to converge. The following figure illustrates how we change the value of a particular weight parameter to minimize the cost function J (left subfigure). The subfigure on the right illustrates what happens if we choose a learning rate that is too large, we overshoot the global minimum:

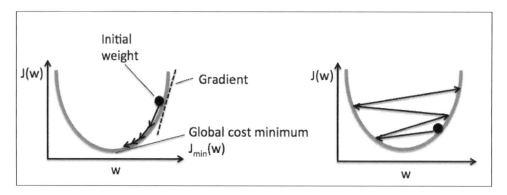

Many machine learning algorithms that we will encounter throughout this book require some sort of feature scaling for optimal performance, which we will discuss in more detail in *Chapter 3, A Tour of Machine Learning Classifiers Using Scikit-learn*. Gradient descent is one of the many algorithms that benefit from feature scaling. Here, we will use a feature scaling method called *standardization*, which gives our data the property of a standard normal distribution. The mean of each feature is centered at value 0 and the feature column has a standard deviation of 1. For example, to standardize the j th feature, we simply need to subtract the sample mean μ_j from every training sample and divide it by its standard deviation σ_j:

$$x'_j = \frac{x_j - \mu_j}{\sigma_j}$$

Here x_j is a vector consisting of the j th feature values of all training samples n.

Standardization can easily be achieved using the NumPy methods `mean` and `std`:

```
>>> X_std = np.copy(X)
>>> X_std[:,0] = (X[:,0] - X[:,0].mean()) / X[:,0].std()
>>> X_std[:,1] = (X[:,1] - X[:,1].mean()) / X[:,1].std()
```

After standardization, we will train the Adaline again and see that it now converges using a learning rate $\eta = 0.01$:

```
>>> ada = AdalineGD(n_iter=15, eta=0.01)
>>> ada.fit(X_std, y)
>>> plot_decision_regions(X_std, y, classifier=ada)
>>> plt.title('Adaline - Gradient Descent')
>>> plt.xlabel('sepal length [standardized]')
>>> plt.ylabel('petal length [standardized]')
>>> plt.legend(loc='upper left')
>>> plt.show()
>>> plt.plot(range(1, len(ada.cost_) + 1), ada.cost_, marker='o')
>>> plt.xlabel('Epochs')
>>> plt.ylabel('Sum-squared-error')
>>> plt.show()
```

After executing the preceding code, we should see a figure of the decision regions as well as a plot of the declining cost, as shown in the following figure:

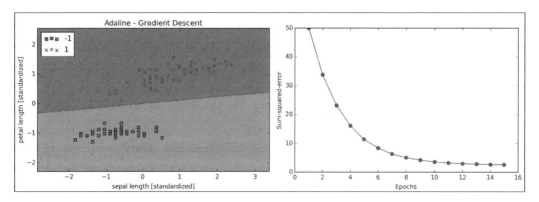

As we can see in the preceding plots, the Adaline now converges after training on the standardized features using a learning rate $\eta = 0.01$. However, note that the SSE remains non-zero even though all samples were classified correctly.

Large scale machine learning and stochastic gradient descent

In the previous section, we learned how to minimize a cost function by taking a step into the opposite direction of a gradient that is calculated from the whole training set; this is why this approach is sometimes also referred to as *batch* gradient descent. Now imagine we have a very large dataset with millions of data points, which is not uncommon in many machine learning applications. Running batch gradient descent can be computationally quite costly in such scenarios since we need to reevaluate the whole training dataset each time we take one step towards the global minimum.

A popular alternative to the batch gradient descent algorithm is *stochastic gradient descent*, sometimes also called *iterative* or *on-line* gradient descent. Instead of updating the weights based on the sum of the accumulated errors over all samples $x^{(i)}$:

$$\Delta w = \eta \sum_i \left(y^{(i)} - \phi\left(z^{(i)}\right)\right) x^{(i)},$$

We update the weights incrementally for each training sample:

$$\eta \left(y^{(i)} - \phi\left(z^{(i)}\right)\right) x^{(i)}$$

Although stochastic gradient descent can be considered as an approximation of gradient descent, it typically reaches convergence much faster because of the more frequent weight updates. Since each gradient is calculated based on a single training example, the error surface is noisier than in gradient descent, which can also have the advantage that stochastic gradient descent can escape shallow local minima more readily. To obtain accurate results via stochastic gradient descent, it is important to present it with data in a random order, which is why we want to shuffle the training set for every epoch to prevent cycles.

> In stochastic gradient descent implementations, the fixed learning rate η is often replaced by an adaptive learning rate that decreases over time, for example, $\frac{c_1}{[number\ of\ iterations] + c_2}$ where c_1 and c_2 are constants. Note that stochastic gradient descent does not reach the global minimum but an area very close to it. By using an adaptive learning rate, we can achieve further annealing to a better global minimum

Another advantage of stochastic gradient descent is that we can use it for *online learning*. In online learning, our model is trained on-the-fly as new training data arrives. This is especially useful if we are accumulating large amounts of data—for example, customer data in typical web applications. Using online learning, the system can immediately adapt to changes and the training data can be discarded after updating the model if storage space in an issue.

> A compromise between batch gradient descent and stochastic gradient descent is the so-called *mini-batch learning*. Mini-batch learning can be understood as applying batch gradient descent to smaller subsets of the training data—for example, 50 samples at a time. The advantage over batch gradient descent is that convergence is reached faster via mini-batches because of the more frequent weight updates. Furthermore, mini-batch learning allows us to replace the for-loop over the training samples in **Stochastic Gradient Descent (SGD)** by vectorized operations, which can further improve the computational efficiency of our learning algorithm.

Since we already implemented the Adaline learning rule using gradient descent, we only need to make a few adjustments to modify the learning algorithm to update the weights via stochastic gradient descent. Inside the `fit` method, we will now update the weights after each training sample. Furthermore, we will implement an additional `partial_fit` method, which does not reinitialize the weights, for on-line learning. In order to check if our algorithm converged after training, we will calculate the cost as the average cost of the training samples in each epoch. Furthermore, we will add an option to `shuffle` the training data before each epoch to avoid cycles when we are optimizing the cost function; via the `random_state` parameter, we allow the specification of a random seed for consistency:

```python
from numpy.random import seed

class AdalineSGD(object):
    """ADAptive LInear NEuron classifier.

    Parameters
    ------------
    eta : float
        Learning rate (between 0.0 and 1.0)
    n_iter : int
        Passes over the training dataset.

    Attributes
    -----------
    w_ : 1d-array
        Weights after fitting.
    errors_ : list
        Number of misclassifications in every epoch.
    shuffle : bool (default: True)
        Shuffles training data every epoch
        if True to prevent cycles.
    random_state : int (default: None)
        Set random state for shuffling
        and initializing the weights.

    """
    def __init__(self, eta=0.01, n_iter=10,
                 shuffle=True, random_state=None):
        self.eta = eta
        self.n_iter = n_iter
        self.w_initialized = False
        self.shuffle = shuffle
```

```python
        if random_state:
            seed(random_state)

    def fit(self, X, y):
        """ Fit training data.

        Parameters
        ----------
        X : {array-like}, shape = [n_samples, n_features]
            Training vectors, where n_samples
            is the number of samples and
            n_features is the number of features.
        y : array-like, shape = [n_samples]
            Target values.

        Returns
        -------
        self : object

        """
        self._initialize_weights(X.shape[1])
        self.cost_ = []
        for i in range(self.n_iter):
            if self.shuffle:
                X, y = self._shuffle(X, y)
            cost = []
            for xi, target in zip(X, y):
                cost.append(self._update_weights(xi, target))
            avg_cost = sum(cost)/len(y)
            self.cost_.append(avg_cost)
        return self

    def partial_fit(self, X, y):
        """"Fit training data without reinitializing the weights"""
        if not self.w_initialized:
            self._initialize_weights(X.shape[1])
        if y.ravel().shape[0] > 1:
            for xi, target in zip(X, y):
                self._update_weights(xi, target)
        else:
            self._update_weights(X, y)
        return self

    def _shuffle(self, X, y):
```

```
            """Shuffle training data"""
            r = np.random.permutation(len(y))
            return X[r], y[r]

        def _initialize_weights(self, m):
            """Initialize weights to zeros"""
            self.w_ = np.zeros(1 + m)
            self.w_initialized = True

        def _update_weights(self, xi, target):
            """Apply Adaline learning rule to update the weights"""
            output = self.net_input(xi)
            error = (target - output)
            self.w_[1:] += self.eta * xi.dot(error)
            self.w_[0] += self.eta * error
            cost = 0.5 * error**2
            return cost

    def net_input(self, X):
        """Calculate net input"""
        return np.dot(X, self.w_[1:]) + self.w_[0]

    def activation(self, X):
        """Compute linear activation"""
        return self.net_input(X)

    def predict(self, X):
        """Return class label after unit step"""
        return np.where(self.activation(X) >= 0.0, 1, -1)
```

The _shuffle method that we are now using in the AdalineSGD classifier works as follows: via the permutation function in numpy.random, we generate a random sequence of unique numbers in the range 0 to 100. Those numbers can then be used as indices to shuffle our feature matrix and class label vector.

We can then use the fit method to train the AdalineSGD classifier and use our plot_decision_regions to plot our training results:

```
>>> ada = AdalineSGD(n_iter=15, eta=0.01, random_state=1)
>>> ada.fit(X_std, y)
>>> plot_decision_regions(X_std, y, classifier=ada)
>>> plt.title('Adaline - Stochastic Gradient Descent')
>>> plt.xlabel('sepal length [standardized]')
>>> plt.ylabel('petal length [standardized]')
```

```
>>> plt.legend(loc='upper left')
>>> plt.show()
>>> plt.plot(range(1, len(ada.cost_) + 1), ada.cost_, marker='o')
>>> plt.xlabel('Epochs')
>>> plt.ylabel('Average Cost')
>>> plt.show()
```

The two plots that we obtain from executing the preceding code example are shown in the following figure:

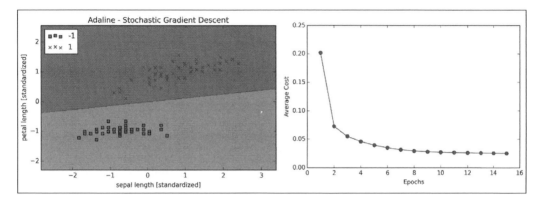

As we can see, the average cost goes down pretty quickly, and the final decision boundary after 15 epochs looks similar to the batch gradient descent with Adaline. If we want to update our model—for example, in an on-line learning scenario with streaming data—we could simply call the `partial_fit` method on individual samples—for instance, `ada.partial_fit(X_std[0, :], y[0])`.

Summary

In this chapter, we gained a good understanding of the basic concepts of linear classifiers for supervised learning. After we implemented a perceptron, we saw how we can train adaptive linear neurons efficiently via a vectorized implementation of gradient descent and on-line learning via stochastic gradient descent. Now that we have seen how to implement simple classifiers in Python, we are ready to move on to the next chapter where we will use the Python scikit-learn machine learning library to get access to more advanced and powerful off-the-shelf machine learning classifiers that are commonly used in academia as well as in industry.

3

A Tour of Machine Learning Classifiers Using Scikit-learn

In this chapter, we will take a tour through a selection of popular and powerful machine learning algorithms that are commonly used in academia as well as in the industry. While learning about the differences between several supervised learning algorithms for classification, we will also develop an intuitive appreciation of their individual strengths and weaknesses. Also, we will take our first steps with the scikit-learn library, which offers a user-friendly interface for using those algorithms efficiently and productively.

The topics that we will learn about throughout this chapter are as follows:

- Introduction to the concepts of popular classification algorithms
- Using the scikit-learn machine learning library
- Questions to ask when selecting a machine learning algorithm

Choosing a classification algorithm

Choosing an appropriate classification algorithm for a particular problem task requires practice: each algorithm has its own quirks and is based on certain assumptions. To restate the "No Free Lunch" theorem: no single classifier works best across all possible scenarios. In practice, it is always recommended that you compare the performance of at least a handful of different learning algorithms to select the best model for the particular problem; these may differ in the number of features or samples, the amount of noise in a dataset, and whether the classes are linearly separable or not.

Eventually, the performance of a classifier, computational power as well as predictive power, depends heavily on the underlying data that are available for learning. The five main steps that are involved in training a machine learning algorithm can be summarized as follows:

1. Selection of features.
2. Choosing a performance metric.
3. Choosing a classifier and optimization algorithm.
4. Evaluating the performance of the model.
5. Tuning the algorithm.

Since the approach of this book is to build machine learning knowledge step by step, we will mainly focus on the principal concepts of the different algorithms in this chapter and revisit topics such as feature selection and preprocessing, performance metrics, and hyperparameter tuning for more detailed discussions later in this book.

First steps with scikit-learn

In *Chapter 2*, *Training Machine Learning Algorithms for Classification*, you learned about two related learning algorithms for classification: the **perceptron** rule and **Adaline**, which we implemented in Python by ourselves. Now we will take a look at the scikit-learn API, which combines a user-friendly interface with a highly optimized implementation of several classification algorithms. However, the scikit-learn library offers not only a large variety of learning algorithms, but also many convenient functions to preprocess data and to fine-tune and evaluate our models. We will discuss this in more detail together with the underlying concepts in *Chapter 4*, *Building Good Training Sets – Data Preprocessing*, and *Chapter 5*, *Compressing Data via Dimensionality Reduction*.

Training a perceptron via scikit-learn

To get started with the scikit-learn library, we will train a perceptron model similar to the one that we implemented in *Chapter 2*, *Training Machine Learning Algorithms for Classification*. For simplicity, we will use the already familiar **Iris** dataset throughout the following sections. Conveniently, the Iris dataset is already available via scikit-learn, since it is a simple yet popular dataset that is frequently used for testing and experimenting with algorithms. Also, we will only use two features from the **Iris flower** dataset for visualization purposes.

We will assign the *petal length* and *petal width* of the 150 flower samples to the feature matrix X and the corresponding class labels of the flower species to the vector y:

```
>>> from sklearn import datasets
>>> import numpy as np
>>> iris = datasets.load_iris()
>>> X = iris.data[:, [2, 3]]
>>> y = iris.target
```

If we executed np.unique(y) to return the different class labels stored in iris. target, we would see that the Iris flower class names, *Iris-Setosa*, *Iris-Versicolor*, and *Iris-Virginica*, are already stored as integers (0, 1, 2), which is recommended for the optimal performance of many machine learning libraries.

To evaluate how well a trained model performs on unseen data, we will further split the dataset into separate training and test datasets. Later in *Chapter 5, Compressing Data via Dimensionality Reduction*, we will discuss the best practices around model evaluation in more detail:

```
>>> from sklearn.cross_validation import train_test_split
>>> X_train, X_test, y_train, y_test = train_test_split(
...             X, y, test_size=0.3, random_state=0)
```

Using the train_test_split function from scikit-learn's cross_validation module, we randomly split the X and y arrays into 30 percent test data (45 samples) and 70 percent training data (105 samples).

Many machine learning and optimization algorithms also require feature scaling for optimal performance, as we remember from the **gradient descent** example in *Chapter 2, Training Machine Learning Algorithms for Classification*. Here, we will standardize the features using the StandardScaler class from scikit-learn's preprocessing module:

```
>>> from sklearn.preprocessing import StandardScaler
>>> sc = StandardScaler()
>>> sc.fit(X_train)
>>> X_train_std = sc.transform(X_train)
>>> X_test_std = sc.transform(X_test)
```

Using the preceding code, we loaded the `StandardScaler` class from the preprocessing module and initialized a new `StandardScaler` object that we assigned to the variable `sc`. Using the `fit` method, `StandardScaler` estimated the parameters μ (sample mean) and σ (standard deviation) for each feature dimension from the training data. By calling the `transform` method, we then standardized the training data using those estimated parameters μ and σ. Note that we used the same scaling parameters to standardize the test set so that both the values in the training and test dataset are comparable to each other.

Having standardized the training data, we can now train a perceptron model. Most algorithms in scikit-learn already support multiclass classification by default via the **One-vs.-Rest (OvR)** method, which allows us to feed the three flower classes to the perceptron all at once. The code is as follows:

```
>>> from sklearn.linear_model import Perceptron
>>> ppn = Perceptron(n_iter=40, eta0=0.1, random_state=0)
>>> ppn.fit(X_train_std, y_train)
```

The scikit-learn interface reminds us of our perceptron implementation in *Chapter 2, Training Machine Learning Algorithms for Classification*: after loading the `Perceptron` class from the `linear_model` module, we initialized a new `Perceptron` object and trained the model via the `fit` method. Here, the model parameter `eta0` is equivalent to the learning rate `eta` that we used in our own perceptron implementation, and the parameter `n_iter` defines the number of epochs (passes over the training set). As we remember from *Chapter 2, Training Machine Learning Algorithms for Classification*, finding an appropriate learning rate requires some experimentation. If the learning rate is too large, the algorithm will overshoot the global cost minimum. If the learning rate is too small, the algorithm requires more epochs until convergence, which can make the learning slow—especially for large datasets. Also, we used the `random_state` parameter for reproducibility of the initial shuffling of the training dataset after each epoch.

Having trained a model in scikit-learn, we can make predictions via the `predict` method, just like in our own perceptron implementation in *Chapter 2, Training Machine Learning Algorithms for Classification*. The code is as follows:

```
>>> y_pred = ppn.predict(X_test_std)
>>> print('Misclassified samples: %d' % (y_test != y_pred).sum())
Misclassified samples: 4
```

On executing the preceding code, we see that the perceptron misclassifies 4 out of the 45 flower samples. Thus, the misclassification error on the test dataset is 0.089 or 8.9 percent $(4/45 \approx 0.089)$.

> Instead of the misclassification **error**, many machine learning practitioners report the classification **accuracy** of a model, which is simply calculated as follows:
>
> 1 - *misclassification error* = 0.911 or 91.1 percent.

Scikit-learn also implements a large variety of different performance metrics that are available via the `metrics` module. For example, we can calculate the classification accuracy of the perceptron on the test set as follows:

```
>>> from sklearn.metrics import accuracy_score
>>> print('Accuracy: %.2f' % accuracy_score(y_test, y_pred))
0.91
```

Here, `y_test` are the true class labels and `y_pred` are the class labels that we predicted previously.

> Note that we evaluate the performance of our models based on the test set in this chapter. In *Chapter 5, Compressing Data via Dimensionality Reduction*, you will learn about useful techniques, including graphical analysis such as learning curves, to detect and prevent **overfitting**. Overfitting means that the model captures the patterns in the training data well, but fails to generalize well to unseen data.

Finally, we can use our `plot_decision_regions` function from *Chapter 2, Training Machine Learning Algorithms for Classification*, to plot the **decision regions** of our newly trained perceptron model and visualize how well it separates the different flower samples. However, let's add a small modification to highlight the samples from the test dataset via small circles:

```
from matplotlib.colors import ListedColormap
import matplotlib.pyplot as plt

def plot_decision_regions(X, y, classifier,
                test_idx=None, resolution=0.02):

    # setup marker generator and color map
```

```
    markers = ('s', 'x', 'o', '^', 'v')
    colors = ('red', 'blue', 'lightgreen', 'gray', 'cyan')
    cmap = ListedColormap(colors[:len(np.unique(y))])

    # plot the decision surface
    x1_min, x1_max = X[:, 0].min() - 1, X[:, 0].max() + 1
    x2_min, x2_max = X[:, 1].min() - 1, X[:, 1].max() + 1
    xx1, xx2 = np.meshgrid(np.arange(x1_min, x1_max, resolution),
                           np.arange(x2_min, x2_max, resolution))
    Z = classifier.predict(np.array([xx1.ravel(), xx2.ravel()]).T)
    Z = Z.reshape(xx1.shape)
    plt.contourf(xx1, xx2, Z, alpha=0.4, cmap=cmap)
    plt.xlim(xx1.min(), xx1.max())
    plt.ylim(xx2.min(), xx2.max())

    # plot all samples
    for idx, cl in enumerate(np.unique(y)):
        plt.scatter(x=X[y == cl, 0], y=X[y == cl, 1],
                    alpha=0.8, c=cmap(idx),
                    marker=markers[idx], label=cl)

    # highlight test samples
    if test_idx:
        X_test, y_test = X[test_idx, :], y[test_idx]
        plt.scatter(X_test[:, 0], X_test[:, 1], c='',
                    alpha=1.0, linewidths=1, marker='o',
                    s=55, label='test set')
```

With the slight modification that we made to the plot_decision_regions function (highlighted in the preceding code), we can now specify the indices of the samples that we want to mark on the resulting plots. The code is as follows:

```
>>> X_combined_std = np.vstack((X_train_std, X_test_std))
>>> y_combined = np.hstack((y_train, y_test))
>>> plot_decision_regions(X=X_combined_std,
...                       y=y_combined,
...                       classifier=ppn,
...                       test_idx=range(105,150))
>>> plt.xlabel('petal length [standardized]')
>>> plt.ylabel('petal width [standardized]')
>>> plt.legend(loc='upper left')
>>> plt.show()
```

As we can see in the resulting plot, the three flower classes cannot be perfectly separated by a linear decision boundaries:

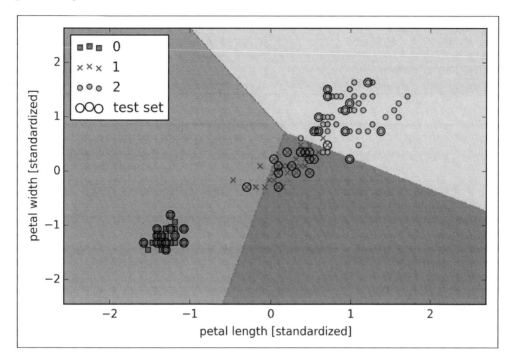

We remember from our discussion in *Chapter 2, Training Machine Learning Algorithms for Classification*, that the perceptron algorithm never converges on datasets that aren't perfectly linearly separable, which is why the use of the perceptron algorithm is typically not recommended in practice. In the following sections, we will look at more powerful linear classifiers that converge to a cost minimum even if the classes are not perfectly linearly separable.

> The Perceptron as well as other scikit-learn functions and classes have additional parameters that we omit for clarity. You can read more about those parameters using the help function in Python (for example, help(Perceptron)) or by going through the excellent scikit-learn online documentation at http://scikit-learn.org/stable/.

Modeling class probabilities via logistic regression

Although the perceptron rule offers a nice and easygoing introduction to machine learning algorithms for classification, its biggest disadvantage is that it never converges if the classes are not perfectly linearly separable. The classification task in the previous section would be an example of such a scenario. Intuitively, we can think of the reason as the weights are continuously being updated since there is always at least one misclassified sample present in each epoch. Of course, you can change the learning rate and increase the number of epochs, but be warned that the perceptron will never converge on this dataset. To make better use of our time, we will now take a look at another simple yet more powerful algorithm for linear and binary classification problems: **logistic regression**. Note that, in spite of its name, logistic regression is a model for classification, not regression.

Logistic regression intuition and conditional probabilities

Logistic regression is a classification model that is very easy to implement but performs very well on linearly separable classes. It is one of the most widely used algorithms for classification in industry. Similar to the perceptron and Adaline, the logistic regression model in this chapter is also a linear model for binary classification that can be extended to multiclass classification via the OvR technique.

To explain the idea behind logistic regression as a probabilistic model, let's first introduce the **odds ratio**, which is the odds in favor of a particular event. The odds ratio can be written as $\frac{p}{(1-p)}$, where p stands for the probability of the positive event. The term *positive event* does not necessarily mean *good*, but refers to the event that we want to predict, for example, the probability that a patient has a certain disease; we can think of the positive event as class label $y = 1$. We can then further define the **logit** function, which is simply the logarithm of the odds ratio (log-odds):

$$logit(p) = log \frac{p}{(1-p)}$$

The logit function takes input values in the range 0 to 1 and transforms them to values over the entire real number range, which we can use to express a linear relationship between feature values and the log-odds:

$$logit\left(p\left(y=1\mid x\right)\right)=w_0x_0+w_1x_1+\cdots+w_mx_m=\sum_{i=0}^{m}w_ix_i=\boldsymbol{w}^T\boldsymbol{x}$$

Here, $p(y=1\mid x)$ is the conditional probability that a particular sample belongs to class 1 given its features x.

Now what we are actually interested in is predicting the probability that a certain sample belongs to a particular class, which is the inverse form of the logit function. It is also called the *logistic* function, sometimes simply abbreviated as *sigmoid* function due to its characteristic S-shape.

$$\phi\left(z\right)=\frac{1}{1+e^{-z}}$$

Here, z is the net input, that is, the linear combination of weights and sample features and can be calculated as $z=\boldsymbol{w}^T\boldsymbol{x}=w_0+w_1x_1+\cdots+w_mx_m$.

Now let's simply plot the sigmoid function for some values in the range -7 to 7 to see what it looks like:

```
>>> import matplotlib.pyplot as plt
>>> import numpy as np
>>> def sigmoid(z):
...     return 1.0 / (1.0 + np.exp(-z))
>>> z = np.arange(-7, 7, 0.1)
>>> phi_z = sigmoid(z)
>>> plt.plot(z, phi_z)
>>> plt.axvline(0.0, color='k')
>>> plt.axhspan(0.0, 1.0, facecolor='1.0', alpha=1.0, ls='dotted')
>>> plt.axhline(y=0.5, ls='dotted', color='k')
>>> plt.yticks([0.0, 0.5, 1.0])
>>> plt.ylim(-0.1, 1.1)
>>> plt.xlabel('z')
>>> plt.ylabel('$\phi (z)$')
>>> plt.show()
```

As a result of executing the previous code example, we should now see the **S-shaped** (sigmoidal) curve:

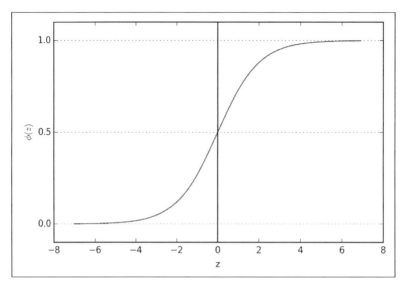

We can see that $\phi(z)$ approaches 1 if z goes towards infinity ($z \rightarrow \infty$), since e^{-z} becomes very small for large values of z. Similarly, $\phi(z)$ goes towards 0 for $z \rightarrow -\infty$ as the result of an increasingly large denominator. Thus, we conclude that this sigmoid function takes real number values as input and transforms them to values in the range [0, 1] with an intercept at $\phi(z) = 0.5$.

To build some intuition for the logistic regression model, we can relate it to our previous Adaline implementation in *Chapter 2, Training Machine Learning Algorithms for Classification*. In Adaline, we used the identity function $\phi(z) = z$ as the activation function. In logistic regression, this activation function simply becomes the sigmoid function that we defined earlier, which is illustrated in the following figure:

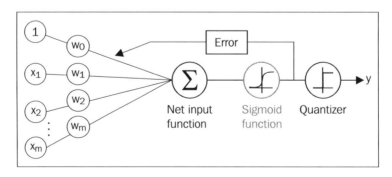

The output of the sigmoid function is then interpreted as the probability of particular sample belonging to class 1 $\phi(z) = P(y=1|x;w)$, given its features x parameterized by the weights w. For example, if we compute $\phi(z) = 0.8$ for a particular flower sample, it means that the chance that this sample is an Iris-Versicolor flower is 80 percent. Similarly, the probability that this flower is an Iris-Setosa flower can be calculated as $P(y=0|x;w) = 1 - P(y=1|x;w) = 0.2$ or 20 percent. The predicted probability can then simply be converted into a binary outcome via a quantizer (unit step function):

$$\hat{y} = \begin{cases} 1 & if\,\phi(z) \geq 0.5 \\ 0 & otherwise \end{cases}$$

If we look at the preceding sigmoid plot, this is equivalent to the following:

$$\hat{y} = \begin{cases} 1 & if\ z \geq 0.0 \\ 0 & otherwise \end{cases}$$

In fact, there are many applications where we are not only interested in the predicted class labels, but where estimating the class-membership probability is particularly useful. Logistic regression is used in weather forecasting, for example, to not only predict if it will rain on a particular day but also to report the chance of rain. Similarly, logistic regression can be used to predict the chance that a patient has a particular disease given certain symptoms, which is why logistic regression enjoys wide popularity in the field of medicine.

Learning the weights of the logistic cost function

You learned how we could use the logistic regression model to predict probabilities and class labels. Now let's briefly talk about the parameters of the model, for example, weights w. In the previous chapter, we defined the sum-squared-error cost function:

$$J(w) = \sum_i \frac{1}{2}\left(\phi\left(z^{(i)}\right) - y^{(i)}\right)^2$$

We minimized this in order to learn the weights w for our Adaline classification model. To explain how we can derive the cost function for logistic regression, let's first define the likelihood L that we want to maximize when we build a logistic regression model, assuming that the individual samples in our dataset are independent of one another. The formula is as follows:

$$L(w) = P(y \mid x; w) = \prod_{i=1}^{n} P\left(y^{(i)} \mid x^{(i)}; w\right) = \prod_{i=1}^{n} \left(\phi\left(z^{(i)}\right)\right)^{y^{(i)}} \left(1 - \phi\left(z^{(i)}\right)\right)^{1-y^{(i)}}$$

In practice, it is easier to maximize the (natural) log of this equation, which is called the log-likelihood function:

$$l(w) = \log L(w) = \sum_{i=1}^{n} \left[y^{(i)} \log\left(\phi\left(z^{(i)}\right)\right) + \left(1 - y^{(i)}\right) \log\left(1 - \phi\left(z^{(i)}\right)\right) \right]$$

Firstly, applying the log function reduces the potential for numerical underflow, which can occur if the likelihoods are very small. Secondly, we can convert the product of factors into a summation of factors, which makes it easier to obtain the derivative of this function via the addition trick, as you may remember from calculus.

Now we could use an optimization algorithm such as gradient ascent to maximize this log-likelihood function. Alternatively, let's rewrite the log-likelihood as a cost function J that can be minimized using gradient descent as in *Chapter 2, Training Machine Learning Algorithms for Classification*:

$$J(w) = \sum_{i=1}^{n} \left[-y^{(i)} \log\left(\phi\left(z^{(i)}\right)\right) - \left(1 - y^{(i)}\right) \log\left(1 - \phi\left(z^{(i)}\right)\right) \right]$$

To get a better grasp on this cost function, let's take a look at the cost that we calculate for one single-sample instance:

$$J(\phi(z), y; w) = -y \log(\phi(z)) - (1-y) \log(1 - \phi(z))$$

Looking at the preceding equation, we can see that the first term becomes zero if $y = 0$, and the second term becomes zero if $y = 1$, respectively:

$$J(\phi(z), y; w) = \begin{cases} -\log(\phi(z)) & \text{if } y = 1 \\ -\log(1 - \phi(z)) & \text{if } y = 0 \end{cases}$$

The following plot illustrates the cost for the classification of a single-sample instance for different values of $\phi(z)$:

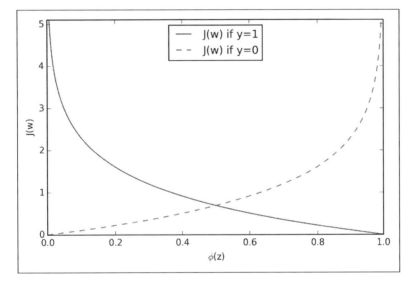

We can see that the cost approaches 0 (plain blue line) if we correctly predict that a sample belongs to class 1. Similarly, we can see on the y axis that the cost also approaches 0 if we correctly predict $y = 0$ (dashed line). However, if the prediction is wrong, the cost goes towards infinity. The moral is that we penalize wrong predictions with an increasingly larger cost.

Training a logistic regression model with scikit-learn

If we were to implement logistic regression ourselves, we could simply substitute the cost function J in our Adaline implementation from *Chapter 2, Training Machine Learning Algorithms for Classification,* by the new cost function:

$$J(w) = -\sum_i y^{(i)} \log\left(\phi\left(z^{(i)}\right)\right) + \left(1 - y^{(i)}\right) \log\left(1 - \phi\left(z^{(i)}\right)\right)$$

This would compute the cost of classifying all training samples per epoch and we would end up with a working logistic regression model. However, since scikit-learn implements a highly optimized version of logistic regression that also supports multiclass settings off-the-shelf, we will skip the implementation and use the `sklearn.linear_model.LogisticRegression` class as well as the familiar `fit` method to train the model on the standardized flower training dataset:

```
>>> from sklearn.linear_model import LogisticRegression
>>> lr = LogisticRegression(C=1000.0, random_state=0)
>>> lr.fit(X_train_std, y_train)
   >>> plot_decision_regions(X_combined_std,
...                          y_combined, classifier=lr,
...                          test_idx=range(105,150))
>>> plt.xlabel('petal length [standardized]')
>>> plt.ylabel('petal width [standardized]')
>>> plt.legend(loc='upper left')
>>> plt.show()
```

After fitting the model on the training data, we plotted the decision regions, training samples and test samples, as shown here:

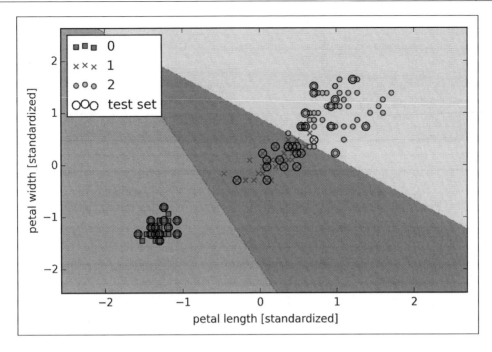

Looking at the preceding code that we used to train the `LogisticRegression` model, you might now be wondering, "What is this mysterious parameter C?" We will get to this in a second, but let's briefly go over the concept of overfitting and regularization in the next subsection first.

Furthermore, we can predict the class-membership probability of the samples via the `predict_proba` method. For example, we can predict the probabilities of the first Iris-Setosa sample:

```
>>> lr.predict_proba(X_test_std[0,:])
```

This returns the following array:

```
array([[  0.000,    0.063,    0.937]])
```

The preceding array tells us that the model predicts a chance of 93.7 percent that the sample belongs to the Iris-Virginica class, and a 6.3 percent chance that the sample is a Iris-Versicolor flower.

We can show that the weight update in logistic regression via gradient descent is indeed equal to the equation that we used in Adaline in *Chapter 2, Training Machine Learning Algorithms for Classification*. Let's start by calculating the partial derivative of the log-likelihood function with respect to the *j*th weight:

$$\frac{\partial}{\partial w_j} l(w) = \left(y \frac{1}{\phi(z)} - (1-y) \frac{1}{1-\phi(z)} \right) \frac{\partial}{\partial w_j} \phi(z)$$

Before we continue, let's calculate the partial derivative of the sigmoid function first:

$$\frac{\partial}{\partial z} \phi(z) = \frac{\partial}{\partial z} \frac{1}{1+e^{-z}} = \frac{1}{\left(1+e^{-z}\right)^2} e^{-z} = \frac{1}{1+e^{-z}} \left(1 - \frac{1}{1+e^{-z}} \right)$$

$$= \phi(z)(1-\phi(z))$$

Now we can resubstitute $\frac{\partial}{\partial z}\phi(z) = \phi(z)(1-\phi(z))$ in our first equation to obtain the following:

$$\left(y \frac{1}{\phi(z)} - (1-y) \frac{1}{1-\phi(z)} \right) \frac{\partial}{\partial w_j} \phi(z)$$

$$= \left(y \frac{1}{\phi(z)} - (1-y) \frac{1}{1-\phi(z)} \right) \phi(z)(1-\phi(z)) \frac{\partial}{\partial w_j} z$$

$$= \left(y(1-\phi(z)) - (1-y)\phi(z) \right) x_j$$

$$= (y - \phi(z)) x_j$$

Remember that the goal is to find the weights that maximize the log-likelihood so that we would perform the update for each weight as follows:

$$w_j := w_j + \eta \sum_{i=1}^{n} \left(y^{(i)} - \phi\left(z^{(i)}\right) \right) x_j^{(i)}$$

Since we update all weights simultaneously, we can write the general update rule as follows:

$$w := w + \Delta w$$

We define Δw as follows:

$$\Delta w = \eta \nabla l \left(w \right)$$

Since maximizing the log-likelihood is equal to minimizing the cost function J that we defined earlier, we can write the gradient descent update rule as follows:

$$\Delta w_j = -\eta \frac{\partial J}{\partial w_j} = \eta \sum_{i=1}^{n} \left(y^{(i)} - \phi\left(z^{(i)}\right) \right) x_j^{(i)}$$

$$w := w + \Delta w, \ \Delta w = -\eta \nabla J \left(w \right)$$

This is equal to the gradient descent rule in Adaline in *Chapter 2, Training Machine Learning Algorithms for Classification.*

Tackling overfitting via regularization

Overfitting is a common problem in machine learning, where a model performs well on training data but does not generalize well to unseen data (test data). If a model suffers from overfitting, we also say that the model has a high variance, which can be caused by having too many parameters that lead to a model that is too complex given the underlying data. Similarly, our model can also suffer from **underfitting** (high bias), which means that our model is not complex enough to capture the pattern in the training data well and therefore also suffers from low performance on unseen data.

Although we have only encountered linear models for classification so far, the problem of overfitting and underfitting can be best illustrated by using a more complex, nonlinear decision boundary as shown in the following figure:

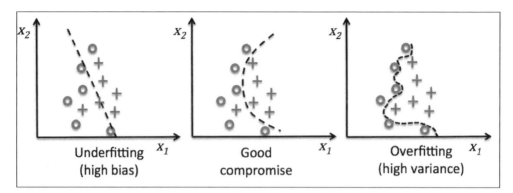

Variance measures the consistency (or variability) of the model prediction for a particular sample instance if we would retrain the model multiple times, for example, on different subsets of the training dataset. We can say that the model is sensitive to the randomness in the training data. In contrast, bias measures how far off the predictions are from the correct values in general if we rebuild the model multiple times on different training datasets; bias is the measure of the systematic error that is not due to randomness.

One way of finding a good bias-variance tradeoff is to tune the complexity of the model via regularization. Regularization is a very useful method to handle collinearity (high correlation among features), filter out noise from data, and eventually prevent overfitting. The concept behind regularization is to introduce additional information (bias) to penalize extreme parameter weights. The most common form of regularization is the so-called **L2 regularization** (sometimes also called L2 shrinkage or weight decay), which can be written as follows:

$$\frac{\lambda}{2}\|\boldsymbol{w}\|^2 = \frac{\lambda}{2}\sum_{j=1}^{m} w_j^2$$

Here, λ is the so-called regularization parameter.

> Regularization is another reason why feature scaling such as standardization is important. For regularization to work properly, we need to ensure that all our features are on comparable scales.

In order to apply regularization, we just need to add the regularization term to the cost function that we defined for logistic regression to shrink the weights:

$$J(w) = \sum_{i=1}^{n}\left[-y^{(i)}\log\left(\phi\left(z^{(i)}\right)\right)-\left(1-y^{(i)}\right)\log\left(1-\phi\left(z^{(i)}\right)\right)\right]+\frac{\lambda}{2}\|w\|^2$$

Via the regularization parameter λ, we can then control how well we fit the training data while keeping the weights small. By increasing the value of λ, we increase the regularization strength.

The parameter C that is implemented for the LogisticRegression class in scikit-learn comes from a convention in support vector machines, which will be the topic of the next section. C is directly related to the regularization parameter λ, which is its inverse:

$$C = \frac{1}{\lambda}$$

So we can rewrite the regularized cost function of logistic regression as follows:

$$J(w) = C\left[\sum_{i=1}^{n}\left(-y^{(i)}\log\left(\phi\left(z^{(i)}\right)\right)-\left(1-y^{(i)}\right)\right)\log\left(1-\phi\left(z^{(i)}\right)\right)\right]+\frac{1}{2}\|w\|^2$$

Consequently, decreasing the value of the inverse regularization parameter `C` means that we are increasing the regularization strength, which we can visualize by plotting the L2 regularization path for the two weight coefficients:

```
>>> weights, params = [], []
>>> for c in np.arange(-5, 5):
...     lr = LogisticRegression(C=10**c, random_state=0)
...     lr.fit(X_train_std, y_train)
...     weights.append(lr.coef_[1])
...     params.append(10**c)
>>> weights = np.array(weights)
>>> plt.plot(params, weights[:, 0],
...          label='petal length')
>>> plt.plot(params, weights[:, 1], linestyle='--',
...          label='petal width')
>>> plt.ylabel('weight coefficient')
>>> plt.xlabel('C')
>>> plt.legend(loc='upper left')
>>> plt.xscale('log')
>>> plt.show()
```

By executing the preceding code, we fitted ten logistic regression models with different values for the inverse-regularization parameter `C`. For the purposes of illustration, we only collected the weight coefficients of the class 2 vs. all classifier. Remember that we are using the OvR technique for multiclass classification.

As we can see in the resulting plot, the weight coefficients shrink if we decrease the parameter **C**, that is, if we increase the regularization strength:

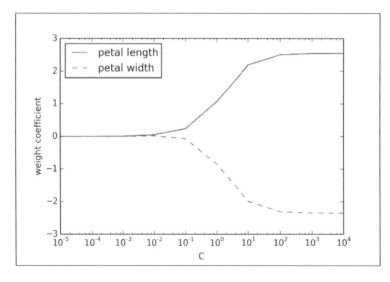

Since an in-depth coverage of the individual classification algorithms exceeds the scope of this book, I warmly recommend Dr. Scott Menard's *Logistic Regression: From Introductory to Advanced Concepts and Applications, Sage Publications*, to readers who want to learn more about logistic regression.

Maximum margin classification with support vector machines

Another powerful and widely used learning algorithm is the **support vector machine (SVM)**, which can be considered as an extension of the perceptron. Using the perceptron algorithm, we minimized misclassification errors. However, in SVMs, our optimization objective is to maximize the **margin**. The margin is defined as the distance between the separating hyperplane (decision boundary) and the training samples that are closest to this hyperplane, which are the so-called **support vectors**. This is illustrated in the following figure:

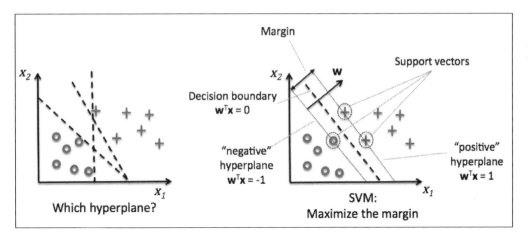

Maximum margin intuition

The rationale behind having decision boundaries with large margins is that they tend to have a lower generalization error whereas models with small margins are more prone to overfitting. To get an intuition for the margin maximization, let's take a closer look at those *positive* and *negative* hyperplanes that are parallel to the decision boundary, which can be expressed as follows:

$$w_0 + w^T x_{pos} = 1 \quad (1)$$

$$w_0 + w^T x_{neg} = -1 \quad (2)$$

If we subtract those two linear equations (1) and (2) from each other, we get:

$$\Rightarrow w^T \left(x_{pos} - x_{neg} \right) = 2$$

We can normalize this by the length of the vector w, which is defined as follows:

$$\|w\| = \sqrt{\sum_{j=1}^{m} w_j^2}$$

So we arrive at the following equation:

$$\frac{w^T \left(x_{pos} - x_{neg} \right)}{\|w\|} = \frac{2}{\|w\|}$$

The left side of the preceding equation can then be interpreted as the distance between the positive and negative hyperplane, which is the so-called margin that we want to maximize.

Now the objective function of the SVM becomes the maximization of this margin by maximizing $\frac{2}{\|w\|}$ under the constraint that the samples are classified correctly, which can be written as follows:

$$w_0 + \boldsymbol{w}^T \boldsymbol{x}^{(i)} \geq 1 \ if \ y^{(i)} = 1$$

$$w_0 + \boldsymbol{w}^T \boldsymbol{x}^{(i)} < -1 \ if \ y^{(i)} = -1$$

These two equations basically say that all negative samples should fall on one side of the negative hyperplane, whereas all the positive samples should fall behind the positive hyperplane. This can also be written more compactly as follows:

$$y^{(i)} \left(w_0 + \boldsymbol{w}^T \boldsymbol{x}^{(i)} \right) \geq 1 \ \forall_i$$

In practice, though, it is easier to minimize the reciprocal term $\frac{1}{2} \|w\|^2$, which can be solved by quadratic programming. However, a detailed discussion about quadratic programming is beyond the scope of this book, but if you are interested, you can learn more about **Support Vector Machines (SVM)** in Vladimir Vapnik's *The Nature of Statistical Learning Theory, Springer Science & Business Media*, or Chris J.C. Burges' excellent explanation in *A Tutorial on Support Vector Machines for Pattern Recognition* (Data mining and knowledge discovery, 2(2):121–167, 1998).

Dealing with the nonlinearly separable case using slack variables

Although we don't want to dive much deeper into the more involved mathematical concepts behind the margin classification, let's briefly mention the slack variable ξ. It was introduced by Vladimir Vapnik in 1995 and led to the so-called soft-margin classification. The motivation for introducing the slack variable ξ was that the linear constraints need to be relaxed for nonlinearly separable data to allow convergence of the optimization in the presence of misclassifications under the appropriate cost penalization.

The positive-values slack variable is simply added to the linear constraints:

$$w^T x^{(i)} \geq 1 - \xi^{(i)} \ \textit{if} \ y^{(i)} = 1$$

$$w^T x^{(i)} \leq -1 + \xi^{(i)} \ \textit{if} \ y^{(i)} = -1$$

So the new objective to be minimized (subject to the preceding constraints) becomes:

$$\frac{1}{2}\|w\|^2 + C\left(\sum_i \xi^{(i)}\right)$$

Using the variable c, we can then control the penalty for misclassification. Large values of c correspond to large error penalties whereas we are less strict about misclassification errors if we choose smaller values for c. We can then we use the parameter c to control the width of the margin and therefore tune the bias-variance trade-off as illustrated in the following figure:

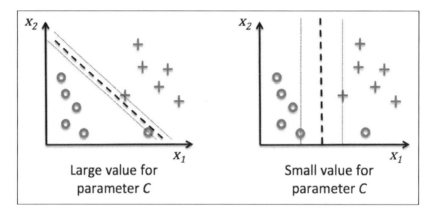

This concept is related to regularization, which we discussed previously in the context of regularized regression where increasing the value of c increases the bias and lowers the variance of the model.

Now that we learned the basic concepts behind the linear SVM, let's train a SVM model to classify the different flowers in our Iris dataset:

```
>>> from sklearn.svm import SVC
   >>> svm = SVC(kernel='linear', C=1.0, random_state=0)
>>> svm.fit(X_train_std, y_train)
>>> plot_decision_regions(X_combined_std,
...                         y_combined, classifier=svm,
...                         test_idx=range(105,150))
>>> plt.xlabel('petal length [standardized]')
>>> plt.ylabel('petal width [standardized]')
>>> plt.legend(loc='upper left')
>>> plt.show()
```

The decision regions of the SVM visualized after executing the preceding code example are shown in the following plot:

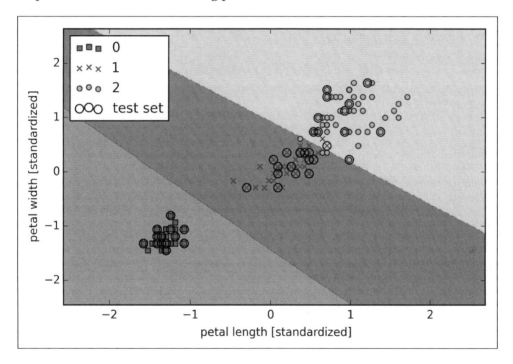

Logistic regression versus SVM

In practical classification tasks, linear logistic regression and linear SVMs often yield very similar results. Logistic regression tries to maximize the conditional likelihoods of the training data, which makes it more prone to outliers than SVMs. The SVMs mostly care about the points that are closest to the decision boundary (support vectors). On the other hand, logistic regression has the advantage that it is a simpler model that can be implemented more easily. Furthermore, logistic regression models can be easily updated, which is attractive when working with streaming data.

Alternative implementations in scikit-learn

The `Perceptron` and `LogisticRegression` classes that we used in the previous sections via scikit-learn make use of the LIBLINEAR library, which is a highly optimized C/C++ library developed at the National Taiwan University (http://www.csie.ntu.edu.tw/~cjlin/liblinear/). Similarly, the `SVC` class that we used to train an SVM makes use of LIBSVM, which is an equivalent C/C++ library specialized for SVMs (http://www.csie.ntu.edu.tw/~cjlin/libsvm/).

The advantage of using LIBLINEAR and LIBSVM over native Python implementations is that they allow an extremely quick training of large amounts of linear classifiers. However, sometimes our datasets are too large to fit into computer memory. Thus, scikit-learn also offers alternative implementations via the `SGDClassifier` class, which also supports online learning via the `partial_fit` method. The concept behind the `SGDClassifier` class is similar to the stochastic gradient algorithm that we implemented in *Chapter 2, Training Machine Learning Algorithms for Classification,* for Adaline. We could initialize the stochastic gradient descent version of the perceptron, logistic regression, and support vector machine with default parameters as follows:

```
>>> from sklearn.linear_model import SGDClassifier
>>> ppn = SGDClassifier(loss='perceptron')
>>> lr = SGDClassifier(loss='log')
>>> svm = SGDClassifier(loss='hinge')
```

Solving nonlinear problems using a kernel SVM

Another reason why SVMs enjoy high popularity among machine learning practitioners is that they can be easily *kernelized* to solve nonlinear classification problems. Before we discuss the main concept behind **kernel SVM**, let's first define and create a sample dataset to see how such a nonlinear classification problem may look.

Using the following code, we will create a simple dataset that has the form of an XOR gate using the `logical_xor` function from NumPy, where 100 samples will be assigned the class label 1 and 100 samples will be assigned the class label -1, respectively:

```
>>> np.random.seed(0)
>>> X_xor = np.random.randn(200, 2)
>>> y_xor = np.logical_xor(X_xor[:, 0] > 0, X_xor[:, 1] > 0)
>>> y_xor = np.where(y_xor, 1, -1)

>>> plt.scatter(X_xor[y_xor==1, 0], X_xor[y_xor==1, 1],
...             c='b', marker='x', label='1')
>>> plt.scatter(X_xor[y_xor==-1, 0], X_xor[y_xor==-1, 1],
...             c='r', marker='s', label='-1')
>>> plt.ylim(-3.0)
>>> plt.legend()
>>> plt.show()
```

After executing the code, we will have an XOR dataset with random noise, as shown in the following figure:

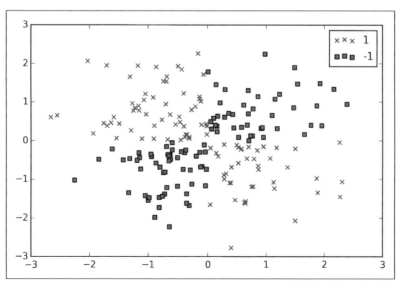

Obviously, we would not be able to separate samples from the positive and negative class very well using a linear hyperplane as the decision boundary via the linear logistic regression or linear SVM model that we discussed in earlier sections.

The basic idea behind kernel methods to deal with such linearly inseparable data is to create nonlinear combinations of the original features to project them onto a higher dimensional space via a mapping function $\phi(\cdot)$ where it becomes linearly separable. As shown in the next figure, we can transform a two-dimensional dataset onto a new three-dimensional feature space where the classes become separable via the following projection:

$$\phi(x_1, x_2) = (z_1, z_2, z_3) = \left(x_1, x_2, x_1^2 + x_2^2\right)$$

This allows us to separate the two classes shown in the plot via a linear hyperplane that becomes a nonlinear decision boundary if we project it back onto the original feature space:

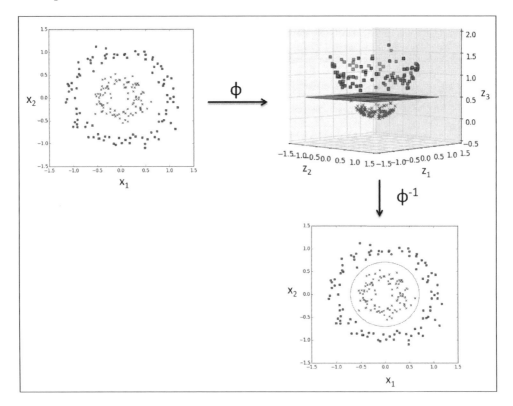

Using the kernel trick to find separating hyperplanes in higher dimensional space

To solve a nonlinear problem using an SVM, we transform the training data onto a higher dimensional feature space via a mapping function $\phi(\cdot)$ and train a linear SVM model to classify the data in this new feature space. Then we can use the same mapping function $\phi(\cdot)$ to transform new, unseen data to classify it using the linear SVM model.

However, one problem with this mapping approach is that the construction of the new features is computationally very expensive, especially if we are dealing with high-dimensional data. This is where the so-called kernel trick comes into play. Although we didn't go into much detail about how to solve the quadratic programming task to train an SVM, in practice all we need is to replace the dot product $x^{(i)T} x^{(j)}$ by $\phi\left(x^{(i)}\right)^T \phi\left(x^{(j)}\right)$. In order to save the expensive step of calculating this dot product between two points explicitly, we define a so-called kernel function:
$k\left(x^{(i)}, x^{(j)}\right) = \phi\left(x^{(i)}\right)^T \phi\left(x^{(j)}\right)$.

One of the most widely used kernels is the **Radial Basis Function kernel (RBF kernel)** or Gaussian kernel:

$$k\left(x^{(i)}, x^{(j)}\right) = \exp\left(-\frac{\left\|x^{(i)} - x^{(j)}\right\|^2}{2\sigma^2}\right)$$

This is often simplified to:

$$k\left(x^{(i)}, x^{(j)}\right) = \exp\left(-\gamma\left\|x^{(i)} - x^{(j)}\right\|^2\right)$$

Here, $\gamma = \frac{1}{2\sigma^2}$ is a free parameter that is to be optimized.

Roughly speaking, the term *kernel* can be interpreted as a *similarity function* between a pair of samples. The minus sign inverts the distance measure into a similarity score and, due to the exponential term, the resulting similarity score will fall into a range between 1 (for exactly similar samples) and 0 (for very dissimilar samples).

Now that we defined the big picture behind the kernel trick, let's see if we can train a kernel SVM that is able to draw a nonlinear decision boundary that separates the XOR data well. Here, we simply use the SVC class from scikit-learn that we imported earlier and replace the parameter kernel='linear' with kernel='rbf':

```
>>> svm = SVC(kernel='rbf', random_state=0, gamma=0.10, C=10.0)
>>> svm.fit(X_xor, y_xor)
>>> plot_decision_regions(X_xor, y_xor, classifier=svm)
>>> plt.legend(loc='upper left')
>>> plt.show()
```

As we can see in the resulting plot, the kernel SVM separates the XOR data relatively well:

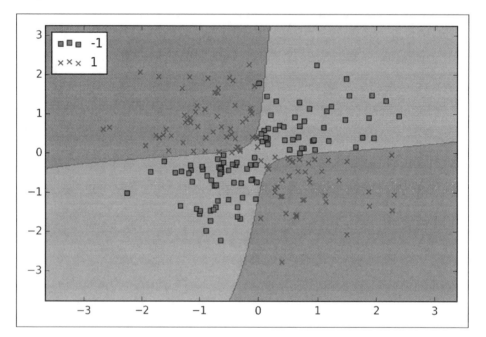

The γ parameter, which we set to gamma=0.1, can be understood as a *cut-off* parameter for the Gaussian sphere. If we increase the value for γ, we increase the influence or reach of the training samples, which leads to a softer decision boundary. To get a better intuition for γ, let's apply RBF kernel SVM to our Iris flower dataset:

```
>>> svm = SVC(kernel='rbf', random_state=0, gamma=0.2, C=1.0)
>>> svm.fit(X_train_std, y_train)
>>> plot_decision_regions(X_combined_std,
```

```
...                         y_combined, classifier=svm,
...                         test_idx=range(105,150))
>>> plt.xlabel('petal length [standardized]')
>>> plt.ylabel('petal width [standardized]')
>>> plt.legend(loc='upper left')
>>> plt.show()
```

Since we chose a relatively small value for γ, the resulting decision boundary of the RBF kernel SVM model will be relatively soft, as shown in the following figure:

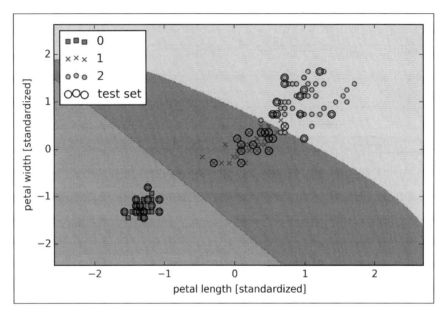

Now let's increase the value of γ and observe the effect on the decision boundary:

```
>>> svm = SVC(kernel='rbf', random_state=0, gamma=100.0, C=1.0)
>>> svm.fit(X_train_std, y_train)
>>> plot_decision_regions(X_combined_std,
...                         y_combined, classifier=svm,
...                         test_idx=range(105,150))
>>> plt.xlabel('petal length [standardized]')
>>> plt.ylabel('petal width [standardized]')
>>> plt.legend(loc='upper left')
>>> plt.show()
```

In the resulting plot, we can now see that the decision boundary around the classes 0 and 1 is much tighter using a relatively large value of γ:

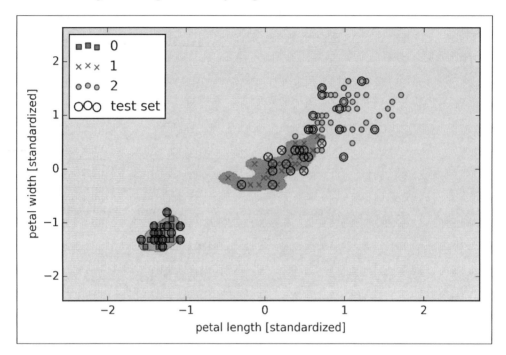

Although the model fits the training dataset very well, such a classifier will likely have a high generalization error on unseen data, which illustrates that the optimization of γ also plays an important role in controlling overfitting.

Decision tree learning

Decision tree classifiers are attractive models if we care about interpretability. Like the name *decision tree* suggests, we can think of this model as breaking down our data by making decisions based on asking a series of questions.

Let's consider the following example where we use a decision tree to decide upon an activity on a particular day:

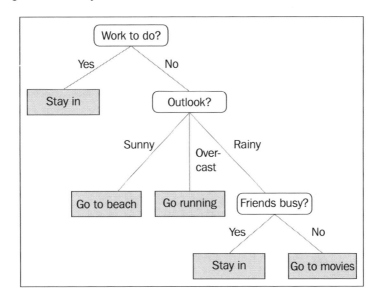

Based on the features in our training set, the decision tree model learns a series of questions to infer the class labels of the samples. Although the preceding figure illustrated the concept of a decision tree based on categorical variables, the same concept applies if our features are real numbers like in the Iris dataset. For example, we could simply define a cut-off value along the **sepal width** feature axis and ask a binary question "sepal width ≥ 2.8 cm?"

Using the decision algorithm, we start at the tree root and split the data on the feature that results in the largest **information gain** (**IG**), which will be explained in more detail in the following section. In an iterative process, we can then repeat this splitting procedure at each child node until the leaves are pure. This means that the samples at each node all belong to the same class. In practice, this can result in a very deep tree with many nodes, which can easily lead to overfitting. Thus, we typically want to *prune* the tree by setting a limit for the maximal depth of the tree.

Maximizing information gain – getting the most bang for the buck

In order to split the nodes at the most informative features, we need to define an objective function that we want to optimize via the tree learning algorithm. Here, our objective function is to maximize the information gain at each split, which we define as follows:

$$IG\left(D_p, f\right) = I\left(D_p\right) - \sum_{j=1}^{m} \frac{N_j}{N_p} I\left(D_j\right)$$

Here, f is the feature to perform the split, D_p and D_j are the dataset of the parent and jth child node, I is our impurity measure, N_p is the total number of samples at the parent node, and N_j is the number of samples in the jth child node. As we can see, the information gain is simply the difference between the impurity of the parent node and the sum of the child node impurities—the lower the impurity of the child nodes, the larger the information gain. However, for simplicity and to reduce the combinatorial search space, most libraries (including scikit-learn) implement binary decision trees. This means that each parent node is split into two child nodes, D_{left} and D_{right}:

$$IG\left(D_p, f\right) = I\left(D_p\right) - \frac{N_{left}}{N_p} I\left(D_{left}\right) - \frac{N_{right}}{N_p} I\left(D_{right}\right)$$

Now, the three impurity measures or splitting criteria that are commonly used in binary decision trees are **Gini impurity** (I_G), **entropy** (I_H), and the **classification error** (I_E). Let's start with the definition of entropy for all **non-empty** classes $p(i|t) \neq 0$:

$$I_H\left(t\right) = -\sum_{i=1}^{c} p\left(i|t\right) \log_2 p\left(i|t\right)$$

Here, $p(i|t)$ is the proportion of the samples that belongs to class i for a particular node t. The entropy is therefore 0 if all samples at a node belong to the same class, and the entropy is maximal if we have a uniform class distribution. For example, in a binary class setting, the entropy is 0 if $p(i=1|t)=1$ or $p(i=0|t)=0$. If the classes are distributed uniformly with $p(i=1|t)=0.5$ and $p(i=0|t)=0.5$, the entropy is 1. Therefore, we can say that the entropy criterion attempts to maximize the mutual information in the tree.

Intuitively, the Gini impurity can be understood as a criterion to minimize the probability of misclassification:

$$I_G(t) = \sum_{i=1}^{c} p(i|t)(1-p(i|t)) = 1 - \sum_{i=1}^{c} p(i|t)^2$$

Similar to entropy, the Gini impurity is maximal if the classes are perfectly mixed, for example, in a binary class setting ($c=2$):

$$1 - \sum_{i=1}^{c} 0.5^2 = 0.5$$

However, in practice both the Gini impurity and entropy typically yield very similar results and it is often not worth spending much time on evaluating trees using different impurity criteria rather than experimenting with different pruning cut-offs.

Another impurity measure is the classification error:

$$I_E = 1 - \max\{p(i|t)\}$$

This is a useful criterion for pruning but not recommended for growing a decision tree, since it is less sensitive to changes in the class probabilities of the nodes. We can illustrate this by looking at the two possible splitting scenarios shown in the following figure:

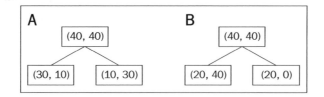

We start with a dataset D_p at the parent node D_p that consists of 40 samples from class 1 and 40 samples from class 2 that we split into two datasets D_{left} and D_{right}, respectively. The information gain using the classification error as a splitting criterion would be the same ($IG_E = 0.25$) in both scenario A and B:

$$I_E(D_p) = 1 - 0.5 = 0.5$$

$$A : I_E(D_{left}) = 1 - \frac{3}{4} = 0.25$$

$$A : I_E(D_{right}) = 1 - \frac{3}{4} = 0.25$$

$$A : IG_E = 0.5 - \frac{4}{8}0.25 - \frac{4}{8}0.25 = 0.25$$

$$B : I_E(D_{left}) = 1 - \frac{4}{6} = \frac{1}{3}$$

$$B : I_E(D_{right}) = 1 - 1 = 0$$

$$B : IG_E = 0.5 - \frac{6}{8} \times \frac{1}{3} - 0 = 0.25$$

However, the Gini impurity would favor the split in scenario $B(IG_G = 0.1\overline{6})$ over scenario $A(IG_G = 0.125)$, which is indeed more *pure*:

$$I_G(D_p) = 1 - (0.5^2 + 0.5^2) = 0.5$$

$$A: I_G(D_{left}) = 1 - \left(\left(\frac{3}{4}\right)^2 + \left(\frac{1}{4}\right)^2\right) = \frac{3}{8} = 0.375$$

$$A: I_G(D_{right}) = 1 - \left(\left(\frac{1}{4}\right)^2 + \left(\frac{3}{4}\right)^2\right) = \frac{3}{8} = 0.375$$

$$A: IG_G = 0.5 - \frac{4}{8}0.375 - \frac{4}{8}0.375 = 0.125$$

$$B: I_G(D_{left}) = 1 - \left(\left(\frac{2}{6}\right)^2 + \left(\frac{4}{6}\right)^2\right) = \frac{4}{9} = 0.\overline{4}$$

$$B: I_G(D_{right}) = 1 - (1^2 + 0^2) = 0$$

$$B: IG_G = 0.5 - \frac{6}{8}0.\overline{4} - 0 = 0.1\overline{6}$$

Similarly, the entropy criterion would favor scenario $B(IG_H = 0.31)$ over scenario $A(IG_H = 0.19)$:

$$I_H(D_p) = -(0.5 \log_2(0.5) + 0.5 \log_2(0.5)) = 1$$

$$A: I_H(D_{left}) = -\left(\frac{3}{4}\log_2\left(\frac{3}{4}\right) + \frac{1}{4}\log_2\left(\frac{1}{4}\right)\right) = 0.81$$

$$A : I_H \left(D_{right} \right) = - \left(\frac{1}{4} \log_2 \left(\frac{1}{4} \right) + \frac{3}{4} \log_2 \left(\frac{3}{4} \right) \right) = 0.81$$

$$A : IG_H = 1 - \frac{4}{8} 0.81 - \frac{4}{8} 0.81 = 0.19$$

$$B : I_H \left(D_{left} \right) = - \left(\frac{2}{6} \log_2 \left(\frac{2}{6} \right) + \frac{4}{6} \log_2 \left(\frac{4}{6} \right) \right) = 0.92$$

$$B : I_H \left(D_{right} \right) = 0$$

$$B : IG_H = 1 - \frac{6}{8} 0.92 - 0 = 0.31$$

For a more visual comparison of the three different impurity criteria that we discussed previously, let's plot the impurity indices for the probability range [0, 1] for class 1. Note that we will also add in a scaled version of the entropy (*entropy/2*) to observe that the Gini impurity is an intermediate measure between entropy and the classification error. The code is as follows:

```
>>> import matplotlib.pyplot as plt
>>> import numpy as np
>>> def gini(p):
...        return (p)*(1 - (p)) + (1 - p)*(1 - (1-p))
>>> def entropy(p):
...        return - p*np.log2(p) - (1 - p)*np.log2((1 - p))
>>> def error(p):
...        return 1 - np.max([p, 1 - p])
>>> x = np.arange(0.0, 1.0, 0.01)
>>> ent = [entropy(p) if p != 0 else None for p in x]
>>> sc_ent = [e*0.5 if e else None for e in ent]
>>> err = [error(i) for i in x]
>>> fig = plt.figure()
>>> ax = plt.subplot(111)
>>> for i, lab, ls, c, in zip([ent, sc_ent, gini(x), err],
...                     ['Entropy', 'Entropy (scaled)',
...                     'Gini Impurity',
```

```
...                        'Misclassification Error'],
...                        ['-', '-', '--', '-.'],
...                        ['black', 'lightgray',
...                         'red', 'green', 'cyan']):
...        line = ax.plot(x, i, label=lab,
...                       linestyle=ls, lw=2, color=c)
>>> ax.legend(loc='upper center', bbox_to_anchor=(0.5, 1.15),
...           ncol=3, fancybox=True, shadow=False)
>>> ax.axhline(y=0.5, linewidth=1, color='k', linestyle='--')
>>> ax.axhline(y=1.0, linewidth=1, color='k', linestyle='--')
>>> plt.ylim([0, 1.1])
>>> plt.xlabel('p(i=1)')
>>> plt.ylabel('Impurity Index')
>>> plt.show()
```

The plot produced by the preceding code example is as follows:

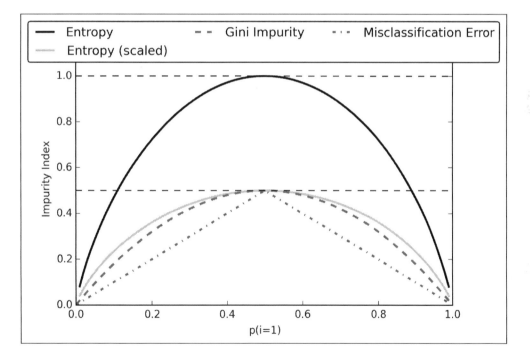

Building a decision tree

Decision trees can build complex decision boundaries by dividing the feature space into rectangles. However, we have to be careful since the deeper the decision tree, the more complex the decision boundary becomes, which can easily result in overfitting. Using scikit-learn, we will now train a decision tree with a maximum depth of 3 using entropy as a criterion for impurity. Although feature scaling may be desired for visualization purposes, note that feature scaling is not a requirement for decision tree algorithms. The code is as follows:

```
>>> from sklearn.tree import DecisionTreeClassifier
>>> tree = DecisionTreeClassifier(criterion='entropy',
...                               max_depth=3, random_state=0)
>>> tree.fit(X_train, y_train)
>>> X_combined = np.vstack((X_train, X_test))
>>> y_combined = np.hstack((y_train, y_test))
>>> plot_decision_regions(X_combined, y_combined,
...                       classifier=tree, test_idx=range(105,150))
>>>plt.xlabel('petal length [cm]')
>>>plt.ylabel('petal width [cm]')
>>> plt.legend(loc='upper left')
>>> plt.show()
```

After executing the preceding code example, we get the typical axis-parallel decision boundaries of the decision tree:

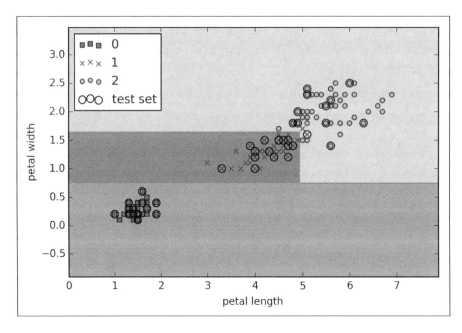

A nice feature in scikit-learn is that it allows us to export the decision tree as a
.dot file after training, which we can visualize using the GraphViz program. This
program is freely available at http://www.graphviz.org and supported by Linux,
Windows, and Mac OS X.

First, we create the .dot file via scikit-learn using the export_graphviz function
from the tree submodule, as follows:

```
>>> from sklearn.tree import export_graphviz
>>> export_graphviz(tree,
...                 out_file='tree.dot',
...                 feature_names=['petal length', 'petal width'])
```

After we have installed GraphViz on our computer, we can convert the tree.dot file
into a PNG file by executing the following command from the command line in the
location where we saved the tree.dot file:

```
> dot -Tpng tree.dot -o tree.png
```

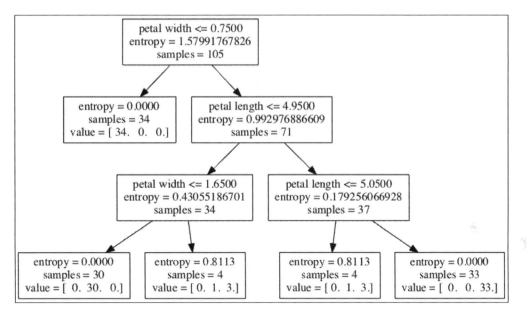

Looking at the decision tree figure that we created via GraphViz, we can now nicely
trace back the splits that the decision tree determined from our training dataset.
We started with 105 samples at the root and split it into two child nodes with 34
and 71 samples each using the **petal width** cut-off ≤ 0.75 cm. After the first split,
we can see that the left child node is already pure and only contains samples from
the Iris-Setosa class (entropy = 0). The further splits on the right are then used to
separate the samples from the Iris-Versicolor and Iris-Virginica classes.

Combining weak to strong learners via random forests

Random forests have gained huge popularity in applications of machine learning during the last decade due to their good classification performance, scalability, and ease of use. Intuitively, a random forest can be considered as an *ensemble* of decision trees. The idea behind ensemble learning is to combine **weak learners** to build a more robust model, a **strong learner**, that has a better generalization error and is less susceptible to overfitting. The random forest algorithm can be summarized in four simple steps:

1. Draw a random **bootstrap** sample of size n (randomly choose n samples from the training set with replacement).

2. Grow a decision tree from the bootstrap sample. At each node:

    1. Randomly select d features without replacement.

    2. Split the node using the feature that provides the best split according to the objective function, for instance, by maximizing the information gain.

3. Repeat the steps 1 to 2 k times.

4. Aggregate the prediction by each tree to assign the class label by **majority vote**. Majority voting will be discussed in more detail in *Chapter 7, Combining Different Models for Ensemble Learning*.

There is a slight modification in step 2 when we are training the individual decision trees: instead of evaluating all features to determine the best split at each node, we only consider a random subset of those.

Although random forests don't offer the same level of interpretability as decision trees, a big advantage of random forests is that we don't have to worry so much about choosing good hyperparameter values. We typically don't need to prune the random forest since the ensemble model is quite robust to noise from the individual decision trees. The only parameter that we really need to care about in practice is the number of trees k (step 3) that we choose for the random forest. Typically, the larger the number of trees, the better the performance of the random forest classifier at the expense of an increased computational cost.

Although it is less common in practice, other hyperparameters of the random forest classifier that can be optimized — using techniques we will discuss in *Chapter 5, Compressing Data via Dimensionality Reduction* — are the size n of the bootstrap sample (step 1) and the number of features d that is randomly chosen for each split (step 2.1), respectively. Via the sample size n of the bootstrap sample, we control the bias-variance tradeoff of the random forest. By choosing a larger value for n, we decrease the randomness and thus the forest is more likely to overfit. On the other hand, we can reduce the degree of overfitting by choosing smaller values for n at the expense of the model performance. In most implementations, including the RandomForestClassifier implementation in scikit-learn, the sample size of the bootstrap sample is chosen to be equal to the number of samples in the original training set, which usually provides a good bias-variance tradeoff. For the number of features d at each split, we want to choose a value that is smaller than the total number of features in the training set. A reasonable default that is used in scikit-learn and other implementations is $d = \sqrt{m}$, where m is the number of features in the training set.

Conveniently, we don't have to construct the random forest classifier from individual decision trees by ourselves; there is already an implementation in scikit-learn that we can use:

```
>>> from sklearn.ensemble import RandomForestClassifier
>>> forest = RandomForestClassifier(criterion='entropy',
...                                 n_estimators=10,
...                                 random_state=1,
...                                 n_jobs=2)
>>> forest.fit(X_train, y_train)
>>> plot_decision_regions(X_combined, y_combined,
...                 classifier=forest, test_idx=range(105,150))
>>> plt.xlabel('petal length')
>>> plt.ylabel('petal width')
>>> plt.legend(loc='upper left')
>>> plt.show()
```

After executing the preceding code, we should see the decision regions formed by the ensemble of trees in the random forest, as shown in the following figure:

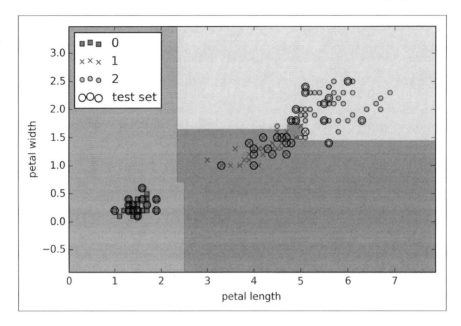

Using the preceding code, we trained a random forest from 10 decision trees via the `n_estimators` parameter and used the entropy criterion as an impurity measure to split the nodes. Although we are growing a very small random forest from a very small training dataset, we used the `n_jobs` parameter for demonstration purposes, which allows us to parallelize the model training using multiple cores of our computer (here, two).

K-nearest neighbors – a lazy learning algorithm

The last supervised learning algorithm that we want to discuss in this chapter is the **k-nearest neighbor classifier (KNN)**, which is particularly interesting because it is fundamentally different from the learning algorithms that we have discussed so far.

KNN is a typical example of a **lazy learner**. It is called *lazy* not because of its apparent simplicity, but because it doesn't learn a discriminative function from the training data but memorizes the training dataset instead.

Parametric versus nonparametric models

Machine learning algorithms can be grouped into **parametric** and **nonparametric** models. Using parametric models, we estimate parameters from the training dataset to learn a function that can classify new data points without requiring the original training dataset anymore. Typical examples of parametric models are the perceptron, logistic regression, and the linear SVM. In contrast, nonparametric models can't be characterized by a fixed set of parameters, and the number of parameters grows with the training data. Two examples of nonparametric models that we have seen so far are the decision tree classifier/random forest and the kernel SVM.

KNN belongs to a subcategory of nonparametric models that is described as **instance-based learning**. Models based on instance-based learning are characterized by memorizing the training dataset, and lazy learning is a special case of instance-based learning that is associated with no (zero) cost during the learning process.

The KNN algorithm itself is fairly straightforward and can be summarized by the following steps:

1. Choose the number of k and a distance metric.
2. Find the k nearest neighbors of the sample that we want to classify.
3. Assign the class label by majority vote.

The following figure illustrates how a new data point (**?**) is assigned the triangle class label based on majority voting among its five nearest neighbors.

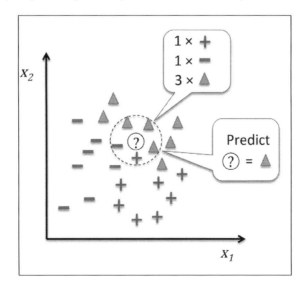

Based on the chosen distance metric, the KNN algorithm finds the k samples in the training dataset that are closest (most similar) to the point that we want to classify. The class label of the new data point is then determined by a majority vote among its k nearest neighbors.

The main advantage of such a memory-based approach is that the classifier immediately adapts as we collect new training data. However, the downside is that the computational complexity for classifying new samples grows linearly with the number of samples in the training dataset in the worst-case scenario — unless the dataset has very few dimensions (features) and the algorithm has been implemented using efficient data structures such as KD-trees. (J. H. Friedman, J. L. Bentley, and R. A. Finkel. An algorithm for finding best matches in logarithmic expected time. ACM Transactions on Mathematical Software (TOMS), 3(3):209–226, 1977.) Furthermore, we can't discard training samples since no *training* step is involved. Thus, storage space can become a challenge if we are working with large datasets.

By executing the following code, we will now implement a KNN model in scikit-learn using an Euclidean distance metric:

```
>>> from sklearn.neighbors import KNeighborsClassifier
>>> knn = KNeighborsClassifier(n_neighbors=5, p=2,
...                            metric='minkowski')
>>> knn.fit(X_train_std, y_train)
>>> plot_decision_regions(X_combined_std, y_combined,
...                       classifier=knn, test_idx=range(105,150))
>>> plt.xlabel('petal length [standardized]')
>>> plt.ylabel('petal width [standardized]')
>>> plt.show()
```

By specifying five neighbors in the KNN model for this dataset, we obtain a relatively smooth decision boundary, as shown in the following figure:

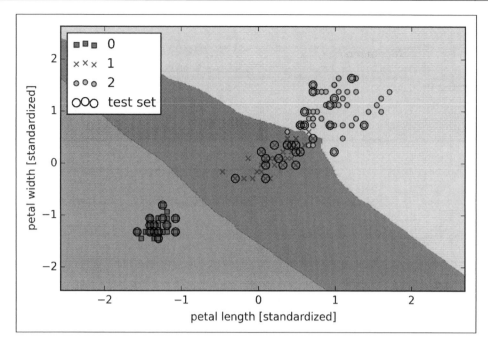

In the case of a tie, the scikit-learn implementation of the KNN algorithm will prefer the neighbors with a closer distance to the sample. If the neighbors have a similar distance, the algorithm will choose the class label that comes first in the training dataset.

The *right* choice of k is crucial to find a good balance between over- and underfitting. We also have to make sure that we choose a distance metric that is appropriate for the features in the dataset. Often, a simple Euclidean distance measure is used for real-valued samples, for example, the flowers in our Iris dataset, which have features measured in centimeters. However, if we are using a Euclidean distance measure, it is also important to standardize the data so that each feature contributes equally to the distance. The `'minkowski'` distance that we used in the previous code is just a generalization of the Euclidean and Manhattan distance that can be written as follows:

$$d\left(\boldsymbol{x}^{(i)}, \boldsymbol{x}^{(j)}\right) = \sqrt[p]{\sum_k \left|x_k^{(i)} - x_k^{(j)}\right|^p}$$

It becomes the Euclidean distance if we set the parameter p=2 or the Manhattan distance at p=1, respectively. Many other distance metrics are available in scikit-learn and can be provided to the metric parameter. They are listed at http://scikit-learn.org/stable/modules/generated/sklearn.neighbors.DistanceMetric.html.

The curse of dimensionality

It is important to mention that KNN is very susceptible to overfitting due to the **curse of dimensionality**. The curse of dimensionality describes the phenomenon where the feature space becomes increasingly sparse for an increasing number of dimensions of a fixed-size training dataset. Intuitively, we can think of even the closest neighbors being too far away in a high-dimensional space to give a good estimate.

We have discussed the concept of regularization in the section about logistic regression as one way to avoid overfitting. However, in models where regularization is not applicable such as decision trees and KNN, we can use feature selection and dimensionality reduction techniques to help us avoid the curse of dimensionality. This will be discussed in more detail in the next chapter.

Summary

In this chapter, you learned about many different machine algorithms that are used to tackle linear and nonlinear problems. We have seen that decision trees are particularly attractive if we care about interpretability. Logistic regression is not only a useful model for online learning via stochastic gradient descent, but also allows us to predict the probability of a particular event. Although support vector machines are powerful linear models that can be extended to nonlinear problems via the kernel trick, they have many parameters that have to be tuned in order to make good predictions. In contrast, ensemble methods such as random forests don't require much parameter tuning and don't overfit so easily as decision trees, which makes it an attractive model for many practical problem domains. The K-nearest neighbor classifier offers an alternative approach to classification via lazy learning that allows us to make predictions without any model training but with a more computationally expensive prediction step.

However, even more important than the choice of an appropriate learning algorithm is the available data in our training dataset. No algorithm will be able to make good predictions without informative and discriminatory features.

In the next chapter, we will discuss important topics regarding the preprocessing of data, feature selection, and dimensionality reduction, which we will need to build powerful machine learning models. Later in *Chapter 6, Learning Best Practices for Model Evaluation and Hyperparameter Tuning*, we will see how we can evaluate and compare the performance of our models and learn useful tricks to fine-tune the different algorithms.

4
Building Good Training Sets – Data Preprocessing

The quality of the data and the amount of useful information that it contains are key factors that determine how well a machine learning algorithm can learn. Therefore, it is absolutely critical that we make sure to examine and preprocess a dataset before we feed it to a learning algorithm. In this chapter, we will discuss the essential data preprocessing techniques that will help us to build good machine learning models.

The topics that we will cover in this chapter are as follows:

- Removing and imputing missing values from the dataset
- Getting categorical data into shape for machine learning algorithms
- Selecting relevant features for the model construction

Dealing with missing data

It is not uncommon in real-world applications that our samples are missing one or more values for various reasons. There could have been an error in the data collection process, certain measurements are not applicable, particular fields could have been simply left blank in a survey, for example. We typically see *missing values* as the blank spaces in our data table or as placeholder strings such as NaN (Not A Number).

Unfortunately, most computational tools are unable to handle such missing values or would produce unpredictable results if we simply ignored them. Therefore, it is crucial that we take care of those missing values before we proceed with further analyses. But before we discuss several techniques for dealing with missing values, let's create a simple example data frame from a **CSV (comma-separated values)** file to get a better grasp of the problem:

```
>>> import pandas as pd
>>> from io import StringIO
>>> csv_data = '''A,B,C,D
... 1.0,2.0,3.0,4.0
... 5.0,6.0,,8.0
... 10.0,11.0,12.0,'''
>>> # If you are using Python 2.7, you need
>>> # to convert the string to unicode:
>>> # csv_data = unicode(csv_data)
>>> df = pd.read_csv(StringIO(csv_data))
>>> df
    A   B   C    D
0   1   2   3    4
1   5   6 NaN    8
2  10  11  12  NaN
```

Using the preceding code, we read CSV-formatted data into a pandas `DataFrame` via the `read_csv` function and noticed that the two missing cells were replaced by `NaN`. The `StringIO` function in the preceding code example was simply used for the purposes of illustration. It allows us to read the string assigned to `csv_data` into a pandas `DataFrame` as if it was a regular CSV file on our hard drive.

For a larger `DataFrame`, it can be tedious to look for missing values manually; in this case, we can use the `isnull` method to return a `DataFrame` with Boolean values that indicate whether a cell contains a numeric value (`False`) or if data is missing (`True`). Using the `sum` method, we can then return the number of missing values per column as follows:

```
>>> df.isnull().sum()
A    0
B    0
C    1
D    1
dtype: int64
```

This way, we can count the number of missing values per column; in the following subsections, we will take a look at different strategies for how to deal with this missing data.

> Although scikit-learn was developed for working with NumPy arrays, it can sometimes be more convenient to preprocess data using pandas' DataFrame. We can always access the underlying NumPy array of the DataFrame via the values attribute before we feed it into a scikit-learn estimator:
>
> ```
> >>> df.values
> array([[  1.,   2.,   3.,   4.],
>        [  5.,   6.,  nan,   8.],
>        [ 10.,  11.,  12.,  nan]])
> ```

Eliminating samples or features with missing values

One of the easiest ways to deal with missing data is to simply remove the corresponding features (columns) or samples (rows) from the dataset entirely; rows with missing values can be easily dropped via the dropna method:

```
>>> df.dropna()
   A  B  C  D
0  1  2  3  4
```

Similarly, we can drop columns that have at least one NaN in any row by setting the axis argument to 1:

```
>>> df.dropna(axis=1)
    A   B
0   1   2
1   5   6
2  10  11
```

The dropna method supports several additional parameters that can come in handy:

```
# only drop rows where all columns are NaN
>>> df.dropna(how='all')

# drop rows that have not at least 4 non-NaN values
>>> df.dropna(thresh=4)

# only drop rows where NaN appear in specific columns (here: 'C')
>>> df.dropna(subset=['C'])
```

Although the removal of missing data seems to be a convenient approach, it also comes with certain disadvantages; for example, we may end up removing too many samples, which will make a reliable analysis impossible. Or, if we remove too many feature columns, we will run the risk of losing valuable information that our classifier needs to discriminate between classes. In the next section, we will thus look at one of the most commonly used alternatives for dealing with missing values: interpolation techniques.

Imputing missing values

Often, the removal of samples or dropping of entire feature columns is simply not feasible, because we might lose too much valuable data. In this case, we can use different interpolation techniques to estimate the missing values from the other training samples in our dataset. One of the most common interpolation techniques is **mean imputation**, where we simply replace the missing value by the mean value of the entire feature column. A convenient way to achieve this is by using the Imputer class from scikit-learn, as shown in the following code:

```
>>> from sklearn.preprocessing import Imputer
>>> imr = Imputer(missing_values='NaN', strategy='mean', axis=0)
>>> imr = imr.fit(df)
>>> imputed_data = imr.transform(df.values)
>>> imputed_data
array([[  1.,    2.,    3.,    4.],
       [  5.,    6.,    7.5,   8.],
       [ 10.,   11.,   12.,    6.]])
```

Here, we replaced each NaN value by the corresponding mean, which is separately calculated for each feature column. If we changed the setting axis=0 to axis=1, we'd calculate the row means. Other options for the strategy parameter are median or most_frequent, where the latter replaces the missing values by the most frequent values. This is useful for imputing categorical feature values.

Understanding the scikit-learn estimator API

In the previous section, we used the Imputer class from scikit-learn to impute missing values in our dataset. The Imputer class belongs to the so-called **transformer** classes in scikit-learn that are used for data transformation. The two essential methods of those estimators are fit and transform. The fit method is used to learn the parameters from the training data, and the transform method uses those parameters to transform the data. Any data array that is to be transformed needs to have the same number of features as the data array that was used to fit the model. The following figure illustrates how a transformer fitted on the training data is used to transform a training dataset as well as a new test dataset:

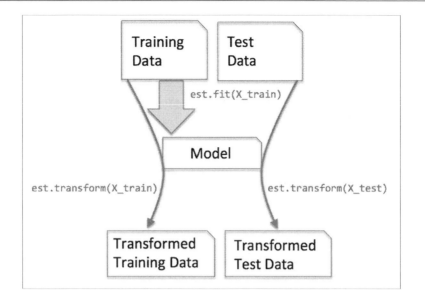

The classifiers that we used in *Chapter 3, A Tour of Machine Learning Classifiers Using Scikit-Learn*, belong to the so-called estimators in scikit-learn with an API that is conceptually very similar to the transformer class. Estimators have a `predict` method but can also have a `transform` method, as we will see later. As you may recall, we also used the `fit` method to learn the parameters of a model when we trained those estimators for classification. However, in supervised learning tasks, we additionally provide the class labels for fitting the model, which can then be used to make predictions about new data samples via the `predict` method, as illustrated in the following figure:

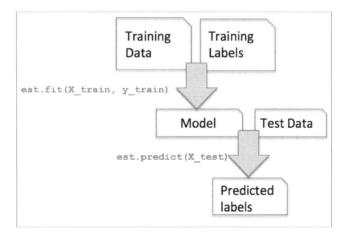

Handling categorical data

So far, we have only been working with numerical values. However, it is not uncommon that real-world datasets contain one or more categorical feature columns. When we are talking about categorical data, we have to further distinguish between **nominal** and **ordinal** features. Ordinal features can be understood as categorical values that can be sorted or ordered. For example, *T-shirt size* would be an ordinal feature, because we can define an order $XL > L > M$. In contrast, nominal features don't imply any order and, to continue with the previous example, we could think of *T-shirt color* as a nominal feature since it typically doesn't make sense to say that, for example, *red* is larger than *blue*.

Before we explore different techniques to handle such categorical data, let's create a new data frame to illustrate the problem:

```
>>> import pandas as pd
>>> df = pd.DataFrame([
...             ['green', 'M', 10.1, 'class1'],
...             ['red', 'L', 13.5, 'class2'],
...             ['blue', 'XL', 15.3, 'class1']])
>>> df.columns = ['color', 'size', 'price', 'classlabel']
>>> df
   color size  price classlabel
0  green    M   10.1     class1
1    red    L   13.5     class2
2   blue   XL   15.3     class1
```

As we can see in the preceding output, the newly created `DataFrame` contains a nominal feature (`color`), an ordinal feature (`size`), and a numerical feature (`price`) column. The class labels (assuming that we created a dataset for a supervised learning task) are stored in the last column. The learning algorithms for classification that we discuss in this book do not use ordinal information in class labels.

Mapping ordinal features

To make sure that the learning algorithm interprets the ordinal features correctly, we need to convert the categorical string values into integers. Unfortunately, there is no convenient function that can automatically derive the correct order of the labels of our `size` feature. Thus, we have to define the mapping manually. In the following simple example, let's assume that we know the difference between features, for example, $XL = L + 1 = M + 2$.

```
>>> size_mapping = {
...                 'XL': 3,
...                 'L': 2,
```

```
...                       'M': 1}
>>> df['size'] = df['size'].map(size_mapping)
>>> df
    color  size  price classlabel
0   green     1   10.1     class1
1     red     2   13.5     class2
2    blue     3   15.3     class1
```

If we want to transform the integer values back to the original string representation at a later stage, we can simply define a reverse-mapping dictionary inv_size_mapping = {v: k for k, v in size_mapping.items()} that can then be used via the pandas' map method on the transformed feature column similar to the size_mapping dictionary that we used previously.

Encoding class labels

Many machine learning libraries require that class labels are encoded as integer values. Although most estimators for classification in scikit-learn convert class labels to integers internally, it is considered good practice to provide class labels as integer arrays to avoid technical glitches. To encode the class labels, we can use an approach similar to the mapping of ordinal features discussed previously. We need to remember that class labels are *not* ordinal, and it doesn't matter which integer number we assign to a particular string-label. Thus, we can simply enumerate the class labels starting at 0:

```
>>> import numpy as np
>>> class_mapping = {label:idx for idx,label in
...                  enumerate(np.unique(df['classlabel']))}
>>> class_mapping
{'class1': 0, 'class2': 1}
```

Next we can use the mapping dictionary to transform the class labels into integers:

```
>>> df['classlabel'] = df['classlabel'].map(class_mapping)
>>> df
    color  size  price classlabel
0   green     1   10.1          0
1     red     2   13.5          1
2    blue     3   15.3          0
```

We can reverse the key-value pairs in the mapping dictionary as follows to map the converted class labels back to the original string representation:

```
>>> inv_class_mapping = {v: k for k, v in class_mapping.items()}
>>> df['classlabel'] = df['classlabel'].map(inv_class_mapping)
>>> df
    color  size  price  classlabel
0   green    1    10.1      class1
1     red    2    13.5      class2
2    blue    3    15.3      class1
```

Alternatively, there is a convenient LabelEncoder class directly implemented in scikit-learn to achieve the same:

```
>>> from sklearn.preprocessing import LabelEncoder
>>> class_le = LabelEncoder()
>>> y = class_le.fit_transform(df['classlabel'].values)
>>> y
array([0, 1, 0])
```

Note that the fit_transform method is just a shortcut for calling fit and transform separately, and we can use the inverse_transform method to transform the integer class labels back into their original string representation:

```
>>> class_le.inverse_transform(y)
array(['class1', 'class2', 'class1'], dtype=object)
```

Performing one-hot encoding on nominal features

In the previous section, we used a simple dictionary-mapping approach to convert the ordinal size feature into integers. Since scikit-learn's estimators treat class labels without any order, we used the convenient LabelEncoder class to encode the string labels into integers. It may appear that we could use a similar approach to transform the nominal color column of our dataset, as follows:

```
>>> X = df[['color', 'size', 'price']].values
>>> color_le = LabelEncoder()
>>> X[:, 0] = color_le.fit_transform(X[:, 0])
>>> X
array([[1, 1, 10.1],
       [2, 2, 13.5],
       [0, 3, 15.3]], dtype=object)
```

After executing the preceding code, the first column of the NumPy array X now holds the new `color` values, which are encoded as follows:

- blue → 0
- green → 1
- red → 2

If we stop at this point and feed the array to our classifier, we will make one of the most common mistakes in dealing with categorical data. Can you spot the problem? Although the color values don't come in any particular order, a learning algorithm will now assume that *green* is larger than *blue*, and *red* is larger than *green*. Although this assumption is incorrect, the algorithm could still produce useful results. However, those results would not be optimal.

A common workaround for this problem is to use a technique called **one-hot encoding**. The idea behind this approach is to create a new **dummy feature** for each unique value in the nominal feature column. Here, we would convert the `color` feature into three new features: `blue`, `green`, and `red`. Binary values can then be used to indicate the particular color of a sample; for example, a blue sample can be encoded as `blue=1`, `green=0`, `red=0`. To perform this transformation, we can use the `OneHotEncoder` that is implemented in the `scikit-learn.preprocessing` module:

```
>>> from sklearn.preprocessing import OneHotEncoder
>>> ohe = OneHotEncoder(categorical_features=[0])
>>> ohe.fit_transform(X).toarray()
array([[  0. ,   1. ,   0. ,   1. ,   10.1],
       [  0. ,   0. ,   1. ,   2. ,   13.5],
       [  1. ,   0. ,   0. ,   3. ,   15.3]])
```

When we initialized the `OneHotEncoder`, we defined the column position of the variable that we want to transform via the `categorical_features` parameter (note that `color` is the first column in the feature matrix X). By default, the `OneHotEncoder` returns a sparse matrix when we use the `transform` method, and we converted the sparse matrix representation into a regular (*dense*) NumPy array for the purposes of visualization via the `toarray` method. Sparse matrices are simply a more efficient way of storing large datasets, and one that is supported by many scikit-learn functions, which is especially useful if it contains a lot of zeros. To omit the `toarray` step, we could initialize the encoder as `OneHotEncoder(..., sparse=False)` to return a regular NumPy array.

An even more convenient way to create those dummy features via one-hot encoding is to use the `get_dummies` method implemented in pandas. Applied on a `DataFrame`, the `get_dummies` method will only convert string columns and leave all other columns unchanged:

```
>>> pd.get_dummies(df[['price', 'color', 'size']])
   price  size  color_blue  color_green  color_red
0  10.1   1          0            1           0
1  13.5   2          0            0           1
2  15.3   3          1            0           0
```

Partitioning a dataset in training and test sets

We briefly introduced the concept of partitioning a dataset into separate datasets for training and testing in *Chapter 1, Giving Computers the Ability to Learn from Data*, and *Chapter 3, A Tour of Machine Learning Classifiers Using Scikit-learn*. Remember that the test set can be understood as the *ultimate test* of our model before we let it loose on the real world. In this section, we will prepare a new dataset, the **Wine** dataset. After we have preprocessed the dataset, we will explore different techniques for feature selection to reduce the dimensionality of a dataset.

The Wine dataset is another open-source dataset that is available from the UCI machine learning repository (`https://archive.ics.uci.edu/ml/datasets/Wine`); it consists of 178 wine samples with 13 features describing their different chemical properties.

Using the pandas library, we will directly read in the open source Wine dataset from the UCI machine learning repository:

```
>>> df_wine = pd.read_csv('https://archive.ics.uci.edu/ml/machine-
learning-databases/wine/wine.data', header=None)
>>> df_wine.columns = ['Class label', 'Alcohol',
...                    'Malic acid', 'Ash',
...                    'Alcalinity of ash', 'Magnesium',
...                    'Total phenols', 'Flavanoids',
...                    'Nonflavanoid phenols',
...                    'Proanthocyanins',
...                    'Color intensity', 'Hue',
...                    'OD280/OD315 of diluted wines',
...                    'Proline']
>>>  print('Class labels', np.unique(df_wine['Class label']))
Class labels [1 2 3]
>>> df_wine.head()
```

The 13 different features in the **Wine** dataset, describing the chemical properties of the 178 wine samples, are listed in the following table:

	Class label	Alcohol	Malic acid	Ash	Alcalinity of ash	Magnesium	Total phenols	Flavanoids	Nonflavanoid phenols	Proanthocyanins	Color intensity	Hue	OD280/OD315 of diluted wines	Proline
0	1	14.23	1.71	2.43	15.6	127	2.80	3.06	0.28	2.29	5.64	1.04	3.92	1065
1	1	13.20	1.78	2.14	11.2	100	2.65	2.76	0.26	1.28	4.38	1.05	3.40	1050
2	1	13.16	2.36	2.67	18.6	101	2.80	3.24	0.30	2.81	5.68	1.03	3.17	1185
3	1	14.37	1.95	2.50	16.8	113	3.85	3.49	0.24	2.18	7.80	0.86	3.45	1480
4	1	13.24	2.59	2.87	21.0	118	2.80	2.69	0.39	1.82	4.32	1.04	2.93	735

The samples belong to one of three different classes, 1, 2, and 3, which refer to the three different types of grapes that have been grown in different regions in Italy.

A convenient way to randomly partition this dataset into a separate *test* and *training* dataset is to use the `train_test_split` function from scikit-learn's `cross_validation` submodule:

```
>>> from sklearn.cross_validation import train_test_split
>>> X, y = df_wine.iloc[:, 1:].values, df_wine.iloc[:, 0].values
>>> X_train, X_test, y_train, y_test = \
...         train_test_split(X, y, test_size=0.3, random_state=0)
```

First, we assigned the NumPy array representation of feature columns 1-13 to the variable X, and we assigned the class labels from the first column to the variable y. Then, we used the `train_test_split` function to randomly split X and y into separate training and test datasets. By setting `test_size=0.3` we assigned 30 percent of the wine samples to X_test and y_test, and the remaining 70 percent of the samples were assigned to X_train and y_train, respectively.

If we are dividing a dataset into training and test datasets, we have to keep in mind that we are withholding valuable information that the learning algorithm could benefit from. Thus, we don't want to allocate too much information to the test set. However, the smaller the test set, the more inaccurate the estimation of the generalization error. Dividing a dataset into training and test sets is all about balancing this trade-off. In practice, the most commonly used splits are 60:40, 70:30, or 80:20, depending on the size of the initial dataset. However, for large datasets, 90:10 or 99:1 splits into training and test subsets are also common and appropriate. Instead of discarding the allocated test data after model training and evaluation, it is a good idea to retrain a classifier on the entire dataset for optimal performance.

Bringing features onto the same scale

Feature scaling is a crucial step in our **preprocessing** pipeline that can easily be forgotten. Decision trees and random forests are one of the very few machine learning algorithms where we don't need to worry about feature scaling. However, the majority of machine learning and optimization algorithms behave much better if features are on the same scale, as we saw in *Chapter 2, Training Machine Learning Algorithms for Classification*, when we implemented the **gradient descent** optimization algorithm.

The importance of feature scaling can be illustrated by a simple example. Let's assume that we have two features where one feature is measured on a scale from 1 to 10 and the second feature is measured on a scale from 1 to 100,000. When we think of the squared error function in **Adaline** in *Chapter 2, Training Machine Learning Algorithms for Classification*, it is intuitive to say that the algorithm will mostly be busy optimizing the weights according to the larger errors in the second feature. Another example is the **k-nearest neighbors (KNN)** algorithm with a Euclidean distance measure; the computed distances between samples will be dominated by the second feature axis.

Now, there are two common approaches to bringing different features onto the same scale: **normalization** and **standardization**. Those terms are often used quite loosely in different fields, and the meaning has to be derived from the context. Most often, normalization refers to the rescaling of the features to a range of [0, 1], which is a special case of min-max scaling. To normalize our data, we can simply apply the min-max scaling to each feature column, where the new value $x_{norm}^{(i)}$ of a sample $x^{(i)}$ can be calculated as follows:

$$x_{norm}^{(i)} = \frac{x^{(i)} - x_{min}}{x_{max} - x_{min}}$$

Here, $x^{(i)}$ is a particular sample, x_{min} is the smallest value in a feature column, and x_{max} the largest value, respectively.

The min-max scaling procedure is implemented in scikit-learn and can be used as follows:

```
>>> from sklearn.preprocessing import MinMaxScaler
>>> mms = MinMaxScaler()
>>> X_train_norm = mms.fit_transform(X_train)
>>> X_test_norm = mms.transform(X_test)
```

Although normalization via min-max scaling is a commonly used technique that is useful when we need values in a bounded interval, standardization can be more practical for many machine learning algorithms. The reason is that many linear models, such as the logistic regression and SVM that we remember from *Chapter 3, A Tour of Machine Learning Classifiers Using Scikit-learn*, initialize the weights to 0 or small random values close to 0. Using standardization, we center the feature columns at mean 0 with standard deviation 1 so that the feature columns take the form of a normal distribution, which makes it easier to learn the weights. Furthermore, standardization maintains useful information about outliers and makes the algorithm less sensitive to them in contrast to min-max scaling, which scales the data to a limited range of values.

The procedure of standardization can be expressed by the following equation:

$$x_{std}^{(i)} = \frac{x^{(i)} - \mu_x}{\sigma_x}$$

Here, μ_x is the sample mean of a particular feature column and σ_x the corresponding standard deviation, respectively.

The following table illustrates the difference between the two commonly used feature scaling techniques, standardization and normalization on a simple sample dataset consisting of numbers 0 to 5:

input	standardized	normalized
0.0	-1.336306	0.0
1.0	-0.801784	0.2
2.0	-0.267261	0.4
3.0	0.267261	0.6
4.0	0.801784	0.8
5.0	1.336306	1.0

Similar to `MinMaxScaler`, scikit-learn also implements a class for standardization:

```
>>> from sklearn.preprocessing import StandardScaler
>>> stdsc = StandardScaler()
>>> X_train_std = stdsc.fit_transform(X_train)
>>> X_test_std = stdsc.transform(X_test)
```

Again, it is also important to highlight that we fit the StandardScaler only once on the training data and use those parameters to transform the test set or any new data point.

Selecting meaningful features

If we notice that a model performs much better on a training dataset than on the test dataset, this observation is a strong indicator for **overfitting**. Overfitting means that model fits the parameters too closely to the particular observations in the training dataset but does not generalize well to real data—we say that the model has a *high variance*. A reason for overfitting is that our model is too complex for the given training data and common solutions to reduce the generalization error are listed as follows:

- Collect more training data
- Introduce a penalty for complexity via regularization
- Choose a simpler model with fewer parameters
- Reduce the dimensionality of the data

Collecting more training data is often not applicable. In the next chapter, we will learn about a useful technique to check whether more training data is helpful at all. In the following sections and subsections, we will look at common ways to reduce overfitting by regularization and dimensionality reduction via feature selection.

Sparse solutions with L1 regularization

We recall from *Chapter 3, A Tour of Machine Learning Classifiers Using Scikit-learn*, that **L2 regularization** is one approach to reduce the complexity of a model by penalizing large individual weights, where we defined the L2 norm of our weight vector w as follows:

$$L2 : \|w\|_2^2 = \sum_{j=1}^{m} w_j^2$$

Another approach to reduce the model complexity is the related **L1 regularization**:

$$L1 : \|w\|_1 = \sum_{j=1}^{m} |w_j|$$

Here, we simply replaced the square of the weights by the sum of the absolute values of the weights. In contrast to L2 regularization, L1 regularization yields sparse feature vectors; most feature weights will be zero. Sparsity can be useful in practice if we have a high-dimensional dataset with many features that are irrelevant, especially cases where we have more irrelevant dimensions than samples. In this sense, L1 regularization can be understood as a technique for feature selection.

To better understand how L1 regularization encourages sparsity, let's take a step back and take a look at a geometrical interpretation of regularization. Let's plot the contours of a convex cost function for two weight coefficients w_1 and w_2. Here, we will consider the **sum of the squared errors (SSE)** cost function that we used for Adaline in *Chapter 2, Training Machine Learning Algorithms for Classification*, since it is symmetrical and easier to draw than the cost function of logistic regression; however, the same concepts apply to the latter. Remember that our goal is to find the combination of weight coefficients that minimize the cost function for the training data, as shown in the following figure (the point in the middle of the ellipses):

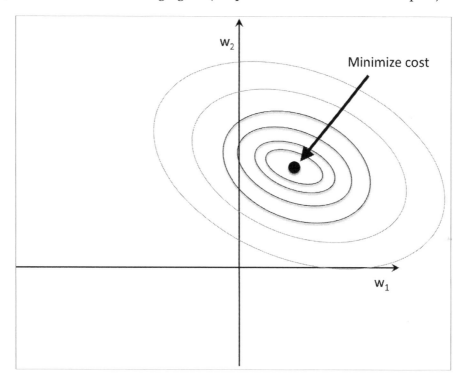

Now, we can think of regularization as adding a penalty term to the cost function to encourage smaller weights; or, in other words, we penalize large weights.

Thus, by increasing the regularization strength via the regularization parameter λ, we shrink the weights towards zero and decrease the dependence of our model on the training data. Let's illustrate this concept in the following figure for the L2 penalty term.

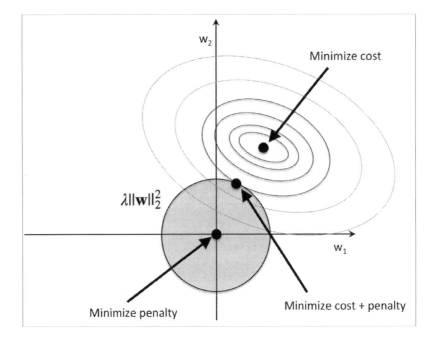

The quadratic L2 regularization term is represented by the shaded ball. Here, our weight coefficients cannot exceed our regularization *budget* — the combination of the weight coefficients cannot fall outside the shaded area. On the other hand, we still want to minimize the cost function. Under the penalty constraint, our best effort is to choose the point where the L2 ball intersects with the contours of the unpenalized cost function. The larger the value of the regularization parameter λ gets, the faster the penalized cost function grows, which leads to a narrower L2 ball. For example, if we increase the regularization parameter towards infinity, the weight coefficients will become effectively zero, denoted by the center of the L2 ball. To summarize the main message of the example: our goal is to minimize the sum of the unpenalized cost function plus the penalty term, which can be understood as adding bias and preferring a simpler model to reduce the variance in the absence of sufficient training data to fit the model.

Now let's discuss L1 regularization and sparsity. The main concept behind L1 regularization is similar to what we have discussed here. However, since the L1 penalty is the sum of the absolute weight coefficients (remember that the L2 term is quadratic), we can represent it as a diamond shape *budget*, as shown in the following figure:

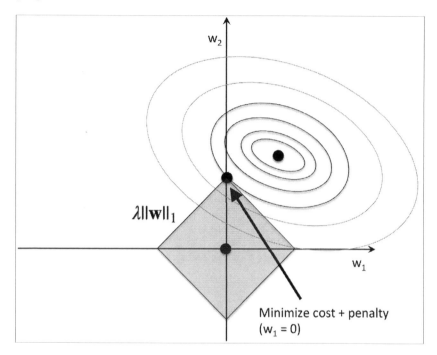

In the preceding figure, we can see that the contour of the cost function touches the L1 diamond at $w_1 = 0$. Since the contours of an L1 regularized system are sharp, it is more likely that the optimum—that is, the intersection between the ellipses of the cost function and the boundary of the L1 diamond—is located on the axes, which encourages sparsity. The mathematical details of why L1 regularization can lead to sparse solutions are beyond the scope of this book. If you are interested, an excellent section on L2 versus L1 regularization can be found in section 3.4 of *The Elements of Statistical Learning, Trevor Hastie, Robert Tibshirani, and Jerome Friedman, Springer*.

For regularized models in scikit-learn that support L1 regularization, we can simply set the penalty parameter to '11' to yield the sparse solution:

```
>>> from sklearn.linear_model import LogisticRegression
>>> LogisticRegression(penalty='l1')
```

Applied to the standardized Wine data, the L1 regularized logistic regression would yield the following sparse solution:

```
>>> lr = LogisticRegression(penalty='l1', C=0.1)
>>> lr.fit(X_train_std, y_train)
>>> print('Training accuracy:', lr.score(X_train_std, y_train))
Training accuracy: 0.983870967742
>>> print('Test accuracy:', lr.score(X_test_std, y_test))
Test accuracy: 0.981481481481
```

Both training and test accuracies (both 98 percent) do not indicate any overfitting of our model. When we access the intercept terms via the `lr.intercept_` attribute, we can see that the array returns three values:

```
>>> lr.intercept_
array([-0.38379237, -0.1580855 , -0.70047966])
```

Since we the fit the `LogisticRegression` object on a multiclass dataset, it uses the **One-vs-Rest (OvR)** approach by default where the first intercept belongs to the model that fits class 1 versus class 2 and 3; the second value is the intercept of the model that fits class 2 versus class 1 and 3; and the third value is the intercept of the model that fits class 3 versus class 1 and 2, respectively:

```
>>> lr.coef_
array([[ 0.280,  0.000,  0.000, -0.0282,  0.000,
         0.000,  0.710,  0.000,  0.000,  0.000,
         0.000,  0.000,  1.236],
       [-0.644, -0.0688 , -0.0572,  0.000,  0.000,
         0.000,  0.000,  0.000,  0.000, -0.927,
         0.060,  0.000, -0.371],
       [ 0.000,  0.061,  0.000,  0.000,  0.000,
         0.000, -0.637,  0.000,  0.000,  0.499,
        -0.358, -0.570,  0.000
       ]])
```

The weight array that we accessed via the `lr.coef_` attribute contains three rows of weight coefficients, one weight vector for each class. Each row consists of 13 weights where each weight is multiplied by the respective feature in the 13-dimensional Wine dataset to calculate the net input:

$$z = w_1 x_1 + \cdots + w_m x_m = \sum_{j=0}^{m} x_j w_j = \boldsymbol{w}^T \boldsymbol{x}$$

We notice that the weight vectors are sparse, which means that they only have a few non-zero entries. As a result of the L1 regularization, which serves as a method for feature selection, we just trained a model that is robust to the potentially irrelevant features in this dataset.

Lastly, let's plot the regularization path, which is the weight coefficients of the different features for different regularization strengths:

```
>>> import matplotlib.pyplot as plt
>>> fig = plt.figure()
>>> ax = plt.subplot(111)
>>> colors = ['blue', 'green', 'red', 'cyan',
...           'magenta', 'yellow', 'black',
...           'pink', 'lightgreen', 'lightblue',
...           'gray', 'indigo', 'orange']
>>> weights, params = [], []
>>> for c in np.arange(-4, 6):
...     lr = LogisticRegression(penalty='l1',
...                             C=10**c,
...                             random_state=0)
...     lr.fit(X_train_std, y_train)
...     weights.append(lr.coef_[1])
...     params.append(10**c)
>>> weights = np.array(weights)
>>> for column, color in zip(range(weights.shape[1]), colors):
...     plt.plot(params, weights[:, column],
...              label=df_wine.columns[column+1],
...              color=color)
>>> plt.axhline(0, color='black', linestyle='--', linewidth=3)
>>> plt.xlim([10**(-5), 10**5])
>>> plt.ylabel('weight coefficient')
>>> plt.xlabel('C')
>>> plt.xscale('log')
>>> plt.legend(loc='upper left')
>>> ax.legend(loc='upper center',
...           bbox_to_anchor=(1.38, 1.03),
...           ncol=1, fancybox=True)
>>> plt.show()
```

The resulting plot provides us with further insights about the behavior of L1 regularization. As we can see, all features weights will be zero if we penalize the model with a strong regularization parameter ($C < 0.1$); C is the inverse of the regularization parameter λ.

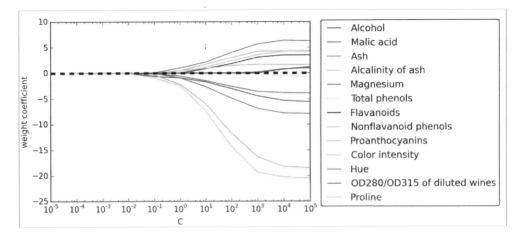

Sequential feature selection algorithms

An alternative way to reduce the complexity of the model and avoid overfitting is **dimensionality reduction** via feature selection, which is especially useful for unregularized models. There are two main categories of dimensionality reduction techniques: **feature selection** and **feature extraction**. Using feature selection, we select a subset of the original features. In feature extraction, we derive information from the feature set to construct a new feature subspace. In this section, we will take a look at a classic family of feature selection algorithms. In the next chapter, *Chapter 5, Compressing Data via Dimensionality Reduction*, we will learn about different feature extraction techniques to compress a dataset onto a lower dimensional feature subspace.

Sequential feature selection algorithms are a family of greedy search algorithms that are used to reduce an initial *d-dimensional* feature space to a *k-dimensional* feature subspace where *k < d*. The motivation behind feature selection algorithms is to automatically select a subset of features that are most relevant to the problem to improve computational efficiency or reduce the generalization error of the model by removing irrelevant features or noise, which can be useful for algorithms that don't support regularization. A classic sequential feature selection algorithm is **Sequential Backward Selection (SBS)**, which aims to reduce the dimensionality of the initial feature subspace with a minimum decay in performance of the classifier to improve upon computational efficiency. In certain cases, SBS can even improve the predictive power of the model if a model suffers from overfitting.

Greedy algorithms make locally optimal choices at each stage of a combinatorial search problem and generally yield a suboptimal solution to the problem in contrast to exhaustive search algorithms, which evaluate all possible combinations and are guaranteed to find the optimal solution. However, in practice, an exhaustive search is often computationally not feasible, whereas greedy algorithms allow for a less complex, computationally more efficient solution.

The idea behind the SBS algorithm is quite simple: SBS sequentially removes features from the full feature subset until the new feature subspace contains the desired number of features. In order to determine which feature is to be removed at each stage, we need to define criterion function J that we want to minimize. The criterion calculated by the criterion function can simply be the difference in performance of the classifier after and before the removal of a particular feature. Then the feature to be removed at each stage can simply be defined as the feature that maximizes this criterion; or, in more intuitive terms, at each stage we eliminate the feature that causes the least performance loss after removal. Based on the preceding definition of SBS, we can outline the algorithm in 4 simple steps:

1. Initialize the algorithm with $k = d$, where d is the dimensionality of the full feature space $\mathbf{X}_d$.

2. Determine the feature x^- that maximizes the criterion $x^- = \arg\max J\left(X_k - x\right)$ where $x \in X_k$.

3. Remove the feature x^- from the feature set: $X_{k-1} := X_k - x^-; k := k - 1$.

4. Terminate if k equals the number of desired features, if not, go to step 2.

You can find a detailed evaluation of several sequential feature algorithms in *Comparative Study of Techniques for Large Scale Feature Selection, F. Ferri, P. Pudil, M. Hatef, and J. Kittler. Comparative study of techniques for large-scale feature selection. Pattern Recognition in Practice IV, pages 403–413, 1994.*

Unfortunately, the SBS algorithm is not implemented in scikit-learn, yet. But since it is so simple, let's go ahead and implement it in Python from scratch:

```
from sklearn.base import clone
from itertools import combinations
import numpy as np
from sklearn.cross_validation import train_test_split
from sklearn.metrics import accuracy_score
```

```python
class SBS():
    def __init__(self, estimator, k_features,
        scoring=accuracy_score,
        test_size=0.25, random_state=1):
        self.scoring = scoring
        self.estimator = clone(estimator)
        self.k_features = k_features
        self.test_size = test_size
        self.random_state = random_state

    def fit(self, X, y):
        X_train, X_test, y_train, y_test = \
                train_test_split(X, y, test_size=self.test_size,
                                 random_state=self.random_state)

        dim = X_train.shape[1]
        self.indices_ = tuple(range(dim))
        self.subsets_ = [self.indices_]
        score = self._calc_score(X_train, y_train,
                                 X_test, y_test, self.indices_)
        self.scores_ = [score]

        while dim > self.k_features:
            scores = []
            subsets = []

            for p in combinations(self.indices_, r=dim-1):
                score = self._calc_score(X_train, y_train,
                                         X_test, y_test, p)
                scores.append(score)
                subsets.append(p)

            best = np.argmax(scores)
            self.indices_ = subsets[best]
            self.subsets_.append(self.indices_)
            dim -= 1

            self.scores_.append(scores[best])
        self.k_score_ = self.scores_[-1]

        return self

    def transform(self, X):
        return X[:, self.indices_]
```

```
def _calc_score(self, X_train, y_train,
                X_test, y_test, indices):
    self.estimator.fit(X_train[:, indices], y_train)
    y_pred = self.estimator.predict(X_test[:, indices])
    score = self.scoring(y_test, y_pred)
    return score
```

In the preceding implementation, we defined the `k_features` parameter to specify the desired number of features we want to return. By default, we use the `accuracy_score` from scikit-learn to evaluate the performance of a model and estimator for classification on the feature subsets. Inside the `while` loop of the `fit` method, the feature subsets created by the `itertools.combination` function are evaluated and reduced until the feature subset has the desired dimensionality. In each iteration, the accuracy score of the best subset is collected in a list `self.scores_` based on the internally created test dataset `X_test`. We will use those scores later to evaluate the results. The column indices of the final feature subset are assigned to `self.indices_`, which we can use via the `transform` method to return a new data array with the selected feature columns. Note that, instead of calculating the criterion explicitly inside the `fit` method, we simply removed the feature that is not contained in the best performing feature subset.

Now, let's see our SBS implementation in action using the KNN classifier from scikit-learn:

```
>>> from sklearn.neighbors import KNeighborsClassifier
>>> import matplotlib.pyplot as plt
>>> knn = KNeighborsClassifier(n_neighbors=2)
>>> sbs = SBS(knn, k_features=1)
>>> sbs.fit(X_train_std, y_train)
```

Although our SBS implementation already splits the dataset into a test and training dataset inside the `fit` function, we still fed the training dataset `X_train` to the algorithm. The SBS `fit` method will then create new training-subsets for testing (validation) and training, which is why this test set is also called **validation dataset**. *This approach is necessary to prevent our original test set becoming part of the training data.*

Remember that our SBS algorithm collects the scores of the best feature subset at each stage, so let's move on to the more exciting part of our implementation and plot the classification accuracy of the KNN classifier that was calculated on the validation dataset. The code is as follows:

```
>>> k_feat = [len(k) for k in sbs.subsets_]
>>> plt.plot(k_feat, sbs.scores_, marker='o')
>>> plt.ylim([0.7, 1.1])
```

```
>>> plt.ylabel('Accuracy')
>>> plt.xlabel('Number of features')
>>> plt.grid()
>>> plt.show()
```

As we can see in the following plot, the accuracy of the KNN classifier improved on the validation dataset as we reduced the number of features, which is likely due to a decrease of **the curse of dimensionality** that we discussed in the context of the KNN algorithm in *Chapter 3, A Tour of Machine Learning Classifiers Using Scikit-learn*. Also, we can see in the following plot that the classifier achieved 100 percent accuracy for *k={5, 6, 7, 8, 9, 10}*:

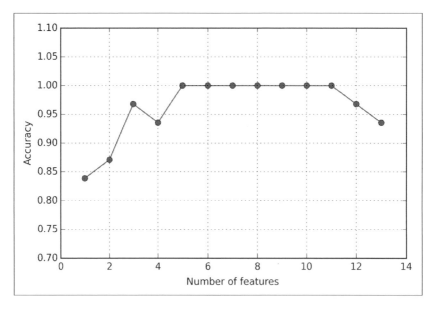

To satisfy our own curiosity, let's see what those five features are that yielded such a good performance on the validation dataset:

```
>>> k5 = list(sbs.subsets_[8])
>>> print(df_wine.columns[1:][k5])
Index(['Alcohol', 'Malic acid', 'Alcalinity of ash', 'Hue',
'Proline'], dtype='object')
```

Using the preceding code, we obtained the column indices of the 5-feature subset from the 9th position in the `sbs.subsets_` attribute and returned the corresponding feature names from the column-index of the pandas Wine `DataFrame`.

Next let's evaluate the performance of the KNN classifier on the original test set:

```
>>> knn.fit(X_train_std, y_train)
>>> print('Training accuracy:', knn.score(X_train_std, y_train))
Training accuracy: 0.983870967742
>>> print('Test accuracy:', knn.score(X_test_std, y_test))
Test accuracy: 0.944444444444
```

In the preceding code, we used the complete feature set and obtained ~98.4 percent accuracy on the training dataset. However, the accuracy on the test dataset was slightly lower (~94.4 percent), which is an indicator of a slight degree of overfitting. Now let's use the selected 5-feature subset and see how well KNN performs:

```
>>> knn.fit(X_train_std[:, k5], y_train)
>>> print('Training accuracy:',
...       knn.score(X_train_std[:, k5], y_train))
Training accuracy: 0.959677419355
>>> print('Test accuracy:',
...       knn.score(X_test_std[:, k5], y_test))
Test accuracy: 0.962962962963
```

Using fewer than half of the original features in the Wine dataset, the prediction accuracy on the test set improved by almost 2 percent. Also, we reduced overfitting, which we can tell from the small gap between test (~96.3 percent) and training (~96.0 percent) accuracy.

Feature selection algorithms in scikit-learn

There are many more feature selection algorithms available via scikit-learn. Those include recursive backward elimination based on feature weights, tree-based methods to select features by importance, and univariate statistical tests. A comprehensive discussion of the different feature selection methods is beyond the scope of this book, but a good summary with illustrative examples can be found at http://scikit-learn.org/stable/modules/feature_selection.html.

Assessing feature importance with random forests

In the previous sections, you learned how to use L1 regularization to zero out irrelevant features via logistic regression and use the SBS algorithm for feature selection. Another useful approach to select relevant features from a dataset is to use a random forest, an ensemble technique that we introduced in *Chapter 3, A Tour of Machine Learning Classifiers Using Scikit-learn*. Using a random forest, we can measure feature importance as the averaged impurity decrease computed from all decision trees in the forest without making any assumptions whether our data is linearly separable or not. Conveniently, the random forest implementation in scikit-learn already collects feature importances for us so that we can access them via the `feature_importances_` attribute after fitting a `RandomForestClassifier`. By executing the following code, we will now train a forest of 10,000 trees on the Wine dataset and rank the 13 features by their respective importance measures. Remember (from our discussion in *Chapter 3, A Tour of Machine Learning Classifiers Using Scikit-learn*) that we don't need to use standardized or normalized tree-based models. The code is as follows:

```
>>> from sklearn.ensemble import RandomForestClassifier
>>> feat_labels = df_wine.columns[1:]
>>> forest = RandomForestClassifier(n_estimators=10000,
...                                 random_state=0,
...                                 n_jobs=-1)
>>> forest.fit(X_train, y_train)
>>> importances = forest.feature_importances_
>>> indices = np.argsort(importances)[::-1]
>>> for f in range(X_train.shape[1]):
...     print("%2d) %-*s %f" % (f + 1, 30,
...                             feat_labels[indices[f]],
...                             importances[indices[f]]))
 1) Color intensity                0.182483
 2) Proline                        0.158610
 3) Flavanoids                     0.150948
 4) OD280/OD315 of diluted wines   0.131987
 5) Alcohol                        0.106589
 6) Hue                            0.078243
 7) Total phenols                  0.060718
 8) Alcalinity of ash              0.032033
 9) Malic acid                     0.025400
10) Proanthocyanins                0.022351
11) Magnesium                      0.022078
```

```
12) Nonflavanoid phenols             0.014645
13) Ash                              0.013916
>>> plt.title('Feature Importances')
>>> plt.bar(range(X_train.shape[1]),
...          importances[indices],
...          color='lightblue',
...          align='center')
>>> plt.xticks(range(X_train.shape[1]),
...            feat_labels[indices], rotation=90)
>>> plt.xlim([-1, X_train.shape[1]])
>>> plt.tight_layout()
>>> plt.show()
```

After executing the preceding code, we created a plot that ranks the different features in the Wine dataset by their relative importance; note that the feature importances are normalized so that they sum up to 1.0.

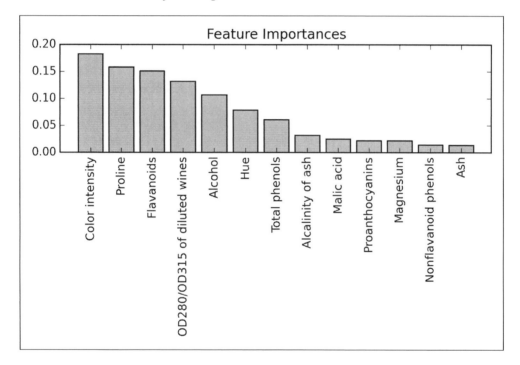

We can conclude that the color intensity of wine is the most discriminative feature in the dataset based on the average impurity decrease in the 10,000 decision trees. Interestingly, the three top-ranked features in the preceding plot are also among the top five features in the selection by the SBS algorithm that we implemented in the previous section. However, as far as interpretability is concerned, the random forest technique comes with an important *gotcha* that is worth mentioning. For instance, if two or more features are highly correlated, one feature may be ranked very highly while the information of the other feature(s) may not be fully captured. On the other hand, we don't need to be concerned about this problem if we are merely interested in the predictive performance of a model rather than the interpretation of feature importances. To conclude this section about feature importances and random forests, it is worth mentioning that scikit-learn also implements a `transform` method that selects features based on a user-specified threshold after model fitting, which is useful if we want to use the `RandomForestClassifier` as a feature selector and intermediate step in a scikit-learn pipeline, which allows us to connect different preprocessing steps with an estimator, as we will see in *Chapter 6, Learning Best Practices for Model Evaluation and Hyperparameter Tuning*. For example, we could set the threshold to 0.15 to reduce the dataset to the 3 most important features, **Color intensity**, **Proline**, and **Flavonoids** using the following code:

```
>>> X_selected = forest.transform(X_train, threshold=0.15)
>>> X_selected.shape
(124, 3)
```

Summary

We started this chapter by looking at useful techniques to make sure that we handle missing data correctly. Before we feed data to a machine learning algorithm, we also have to make sure that we encode categorical variables correctly, and we have seen how we can map ordinal and nominal features values to integer representations.

Moreover, we briefly discussed L1 regularization, which can help us to avoid overfitting by reducing the complexity of a model. As an alternative approach for removing irrelevant features, we used a sequential feature selection algorithm to select meaningful features from a dataset.

In the next chapter, you will learn about yet another useful approach to dimensionality reduction: feature extraction. It allows us to compress features onto a lower dimensional subspace rather than removing features entirely as in feature selection.

5
Compressing Data via Dimensionality Reduction

In *Chapter 4, Building Good Training Sets – Data Preprocessing,* you learned about the different approaches for reducing the dimensionality of a dataset using different feature selection techniques. An alternative approach to feature selection for dimensionality reduction is *feature extraction.* In this chapter, you will learn about three fundamental techniques that will help us to summarize the information content of a dataset by transforming it onto a new feature subspace of lower dimensionality than the original one. Data compression is an important topic in machine learning, and it helps us to store and analyze the increasing amounts of data that are produced and collected in the modern age of technology. In this chapter, we will cover the following topics:

- **Principal component analysis (PCA)** for unsupervised data compression
- **Linear Discriminant Analysis (LDA)** as a supervised dimensionality reduction technique for maximizing class separability
- Nonlinear dimensionality reduction via **kernel principal component analysis**

Unsupervised dimensionality reduction via principal component analysis

Similar to feature selection, we can use feature extraction to reduce the number of features in a dataset. However, while we maintained the original features when we used feature selection algorithms, such as *sequential backward selection*, we use feature extraction to transform or project the data onto a new feature space. In the context of dimensionality reduction, feature extraction can be understood as an approach to data compression with the goal of maintaining most of the relevant information. Feature extraction is typically used to improve computational efficiency but can also help to reduce the *curse of dimensionality*—especially if we are working with nonregularized models.

Principal component analysis (PCA) is an unsupervised linear transformation technique that is widely used across different fields, most prominently for dimensionality reduction. Other popular applications of PCA include exploratory data analyses and de-noising of signals in stock market trading, and the analysis of genome data and gene expression levels in the field of bioinformatics. PCA helps us to identify patterns in data based on the correlation between features. In a nutshell, PCA aims to find the directions of maximum variance in high-dimensional data and projects it onto a new subspace with equal or fewer dimensions that the original one. The orthogonal axes (principal components) of the new subspace can be interpreted as the directions of maximum variance given the constraint that the new feature axes are orthogonal to each other as illustrated in the following figure. Here, x_1 and x_2 are the original feature axes, and **PC1** and **PC2** are the principal components:

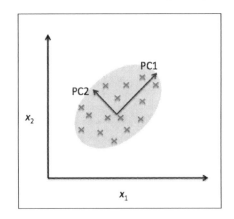

If we use PCA for dimensionality reduction, we construct a $d \times k$-dimensional transformation matrix W that allows us to map a sample vector x onto a new k-dimensional feature subspace that has fewer dimensions than the original d-dimensional feature space:

$$x = [x_1, x_2, \ldots, x_d], \quad x \in \mathbb{R}^d$$

$$\downarrow xW, \quad W \in \mathbb{R}^{d \times k}$$

$$z = [z_1, z_2, \ldots, z_k], \quad z \in \mathbb{R}^k$$

As a result of transforming the original d-dimensional data onto this new k-dimensional subspace (typically $k \ll d$), the first principal component will have the largest possible variance, and all consequent principal components will have the largest possible variance given that they are uncorrelated (orthogonal) to the other principal components. Note that the PCA directions are highly sensitive to data scaling, and we need to standardize the features *prior* to PCA if the features were measured on different scales and we want to assign equal importance to all features.

Before looking at the PCA algorithm for dimensionality reduction in more detail, let's summarize the approach in a few simple steps:

1. Standardize the d-dimensional dataset.
2. Construct the covariance matrix.
3. Decompose the covariance matrix into its eigenvectors and eigenvalues.
4. Select k eigenvectors that correspond to the k largest eigenvalues, where k is the dimensionality of the new feature subspace ($k \leq d$).
5. Construct a projection matrix W from the "top" k eigenvectors.
6. Transform the d-dimensional input dataset X using the projection matrix W to obtain the new k-dimensional feature subspace.

Total and explained variance

In this subsection, we will tackle the first four steps of a principal component analysis: standardizing the data, constructing the covariance matrix, obtaining the eigenvalues and eigenvectors of the covariance matrix, and sorting the eigenvalues by decreasing order to rank the eigenvectors.

First, we will start by loading the *Wine* dataset that we have been working with in *Chapter 4, Building Good Training Sets – Data Preprocessing*:

```
>>> import pandas as pd
>>> df_wine = pd.read_csv('https://archive.ics.uci.edu/ml/machine-
learning-databases/wine/wine.data', header=None)
```

Next, we will process the *Wine* data into separate training and test sets—using 70 percent and 30 percent of the data, respectively—and standardize it to unit variance.

```
>>> from sklearn.cross_validation import train_test_split
>>> from sklearn.preprocessing import StandardScaler
>>> X, y = df_wine.iloc[:, 1:].values, df_wine.iloc[:, 0].values
>>> X_train, X_test, y_train, y_test = \
...                 train_test_split(X, y,
...                 test_size=0.3, random_state=0)
>>> sc = StandardScaler()
>>> X_train_std = sc.fit_transform(X_train)
>>> X_test_std = sc.transform(X_test)
```

After completing the mandatory preprocessing steps by executing the preceding code, let's advance to the second step: constructing the covariance matrix. The symmetric $d \times d$-dimensional covariance matrix, where d is the number of dimensions in the dataset, stores the pairwise covariances between the different features. For example, the covariance between two features x_j and x_k on the population level can be calculated via the following equation:

$$\sigma_{jk} = \frac{1}{n}\sum_{i=1}^{n}\left(x_j^{(i)} - \mu_j\right)\left(x_k^{(i)} - \mu_k\right)$$

Here, μ_j and μ_k are the sample means of feature j and k, respectively. Note that the sample means are zero if we standardize the dataset. A positive covariance between two features indicates that the features increase or decrease together, whereas a negative covariance indicates that the features vary in opposite directions. For example, a covariance matrix of three features can then be written as (note that Σ stands for the Greek letter *sigma*, which is not to be confused with the *sum* symbol):

$$\Sigma = \begin{bmatrix} \sigma_1^2 & \sigma_{12} & \sigma_{13} \\ \sigma_{21} & \sigma_2^2 & \sigma_{23} \\ \sigma_{31} & \sigma_{32} & \sigma_3^2 \end{bmatrix}$$

The eigenvectors of the covariance matrix represent the principal components (the directions of maximum variance), whereas the corresponding eigenvalues will define their magnitude. In the case of the *Wine* dataset, we would obtain 13 eigenvectors and eigenvalues from the 13×13-dimensional covariance matrix.

Now, let's obtain the eigenpairs of the covariance matrix. As we surely remember from our introductory linear algebra or calculus classes, an eigen vector v satisfies the following condition:

$$\Sigma v = \lambda v$$

Here, λ is a scalar: the eigenvalue. Since the manual computation of eigenvectors and eigenvalues is a somewhat tedious and elaborate task, we will use the `linalg.eig` function from NumPy to obtain the eigenpairs of the *Wine* covariance matrix:

```
>>> import numpy as np
>>> cov_mat = np.cov(X_train_std.T)
>>> eigen_vals, eigen_vecs = np.linalg.eig(cov_mat)
>>> print('\nEigenvalues \n%s' % eigen_vals)
Eigenvalues
[ 4.8923083    2.46635032  1.42809973  1.01233462  0.84906459
0.60181514
0.52251546  0.08414846  0.33051429  0.29595018  0.16831254  0.21432212
0.2399553 ]
```

Using the `numpy.cov` function, we computed the covariance matrix of the standardized training dataset. Using the `linalg.eig` function, we performed the eigendecomposition that yielded a vector (`eigen_vals`) consisting of 13 eigenvalues and the corresponding eigenvectors stored as columns in a 13×13-dimensional matrix (`eigen_vecs`).

Although the numpy.linalg.eig function was designed to decompose nonsymmetric square matrices, you may find that it returns complex eigenvalues in certain cases.

A related function, numpy.linalg.eigh, has been implemented to decompose Hermetian matrices, which is a numerically more stable approach to work with symmetric matrices such as the covariance matrix; numpy.linalg.eigh always returns real eigenvalues.

Since we want to reduce the dimensionality of our dataset by compressing it onto a new feature subspace, we only select the subset of the eigenvectors (principal components) that contains most of the information (variance). Since the eigenvalues define the magnitude of the eigenvectors, we have to sort the eigenvalues by decreasing magnitude; we are interested in the top k eigenvectors based on the values of their corresponding eigenvalues. But before we collect those k most informative eigenvectors, let's plot the *variance explained ratios* of the eigenvalues.

The variance explained ratio of an eigenvalue λ_j is simply the fraction of an eigenvalue λ_j and the total sum of the eigenvalues:

$$\frac{\lambda_j}{\sum_{j=1}^{d} \lambda_j}$$

Using the NumPy cumsum function, we can then calculate the cumulative sum of explained variances, which we will plot via matplotlib's step function:

```
>>> tot = sum(eigen_vals)
>>> var_exp = [(i / tot) for i in
...                 sorted(eigen_vals, reverse=True)]
>>> cum_var_exp = np.cumsum(var_exp)

>>> import matplotlib.pyplot as plt
>>> plt.bar(range(1,14), var_exp, alpha=0.5, align='center',
...             label='individual explained variance')
>>> plt.step(range(1,14), cum_var_exp, where='mid',
...             label='cumulative explained variance')
>>> plt.ylabel('Explained variance ratio')
>>> plt.xlabel('Principal components')
>>> plt.legend(loc='best')
>>> plt.show()
```

The resulting plot indicates that the first principal component alone accounts for 40 percent of the variance. Also, we can see that the first two principal components combined explain almost 60 percent of the variance in the data:

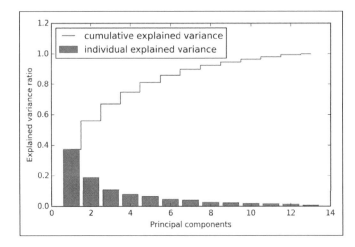

Although the explained variance plot reminds us of the feature importance that we computed in *Chapter 4, Building Good Training Sets – Data Preprocessing,* via random forests, we shall remind ourselves that PCA is an unsupervised method, which means that information about the class labels is ignored. Whereas a random forest uses the class membership information to compute the node impurities, variance measures the spread of values along a feature axis.

Feature transformation

After we have successfully decomposed the covariance matrix into eigenpairs, let's now proceed with the last three steps to transform the *Wine* dataset onto the new principal component axes. In this section, we will sort the eigenpairs by descending order of the eigenvalues, construct a projection matrix from the selected eigenvectors, and use the projection matrix to transform the data onto the lower-dimensional subspace.

We start by sorting the eigenpairs by decreasing order of the eigenvalues:

```
>>> eigen_pairs =[(np.abs(eigen_vals[i]),eigen_vecs[:,i])
...                 for i inrange(len(eigen_vals))]
>>> eigen_pairs.sort(reverse=True)
```

Next, we collect the two eigenvectors that correspond to the two largest values to capture about 60 percent of the variance in this dataset. Note that we only chose two eigenvectors for the purpose of illustration, since we are going to plot the data via a two-dimensional scatter plot later in this subsection. In practice, the number of principal components has to be determined from a trade-off between computational efficiency and the performance of the classifier:

```
>>> w= np.hstack((eigen_pairs[0][1][:, np.newaxis],
...                 eigen_pairs[1][1][:, np.newaxis]))
>>> print('Matrix W:\n',w)
Matrix W:
[[ 0.14669811  0.50417079]
 [-0.24224554  0.24216889]
 [-0.02993442  0.28698484]
 [-0.25519002 -0.06468718]
 [ 0.12079772  0.22995385]
 [ 0.38934455  0.09363991]
 [ 0.42326486  0.01088622]
 [-0.30634956  0.01870216]
 [ 0.30572219  0.03040352]
 [-0.09869191  0.54527081]
```

```
[ 0.30032535 -0.27924322]
[ 0.36821154 -0.174365   ]
[ 0.29259713  0.36315461]]
```

By executing the preceding code, we have created a 13×2-dimensional projection matrix W from the top two eigenvectors. Using the projection matrix, we can now transform a sample x (represented as 1×13-dimensional row vector) onto the PCA subspace obtaining x', a now two-dimensional sample vector consisting of two new features:

$$x' = xW$$

```
>>> X_train_std[0].dot(w)
array([ 2.59891628,  0.00484089])
```

Similarly, we can transform the entire 124×13-dimensional training dataset onto the two principal components by calculating the matrix dot product:

$$X' = XW$$

```
>>> X_train_pca = X_train_std.dot(w)
```

Lastly, let's visualize the transformed *Wine* training set, now stored as an 124×2-dimensional matrix, in a two-dimensional scatterplot:

```
>>> colors = ['r', 'b', 'g']
>>> markers = ['s', 'x', 'o']
>>> for l, c, m in zip(np.unique(y_train), colors, markers):
...     plt.scatter(X_train_pca[y_train==l, 0],
...                 X_train_pca[y_train==l, 1],
...                 c=c, label=l, marker=m)
>>> plt.xlabel('PC 1')
>>> plt.ylabel('PC 2')
>>> plt.legend(loc='lower left')
>>> plt.show()
```

As we can see in the resulting plot (shown in the next figure), the data is more spread along the *x*-axis—the first principal component—than the second principal component (*y*-axis), which is consistent with the explained variance ratio plot that we created in the previous subsection. However, we can intuitively see that a linear classifier will likely be able to separate the classes well:

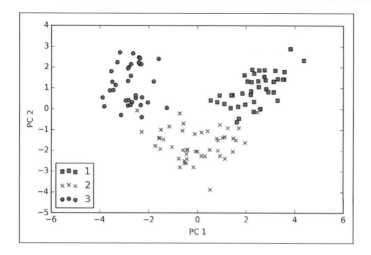

Although we encoded the class labels information for the purpose of illustration in the preceding scatter plot, we have to keep in mind that PCA is an unsupervised technique that doesn't use class label information.

Principal component analysis in scikit-learn

Although the verbose approach in the previous subsection helped us to follow the inner workings of PCA, we will now discuss how to use the PCA class implemented in scikit-learn. PCA is another one of scikit-learn's transformer classes, where we first fit the model using the training data before we transform both the training data and the test data using the same model parameters. Now, let's use the PCA from scikit-learn on the *Wine* training dataset, classify the transformed samples via logistic regression, and visualize the decision regions via the plot_decision_region function that we defined in *Chapter 2, Training Machine Learning Algorithms for Classification*:

```
from matplotlib.colors import ListedColormap

def plot_decision_regions(X, y, classifier, resolution=0.02):

    # setup marker generator and color map
    markers = ('s', 'x', 'o', '^', 'v')
    colors = ('red', 'blue', 'lightgreen', 'gray', 'cyan')
    cmap = ListedColormap(colors[:len(np.unique(y))])

    # plot the decision surface
```

```
      x1_min, x1_max = X[:, 0].min() - 1, X[:, 0].max() + 1
      x2_min, x2_max = X[:, 1].min() - 1, X[:, 1].max() + 1
      xx1, xx2 = np.meshgrid(np.arange(x1_min, x1_max, resolution),
                       np.arange(x2_min, x2_max, resolution))
      Z = classifier.predict(np.array([xx1.ravel(), xx2.ravel()]).T)
      Z = Z.reshape(xx1.shape)
      plt.contourf(xx1, xx2, Z, alpha=0.4, cmap=cmap)
      plt.xlim(xx1.min(), xx1.max())
      plt.ylim(xx2.min(), xx2.max())

      # plot class samples
      for idx, cl in enumerate(np.unique(y)):
          plt.scatter(x=X[y == cl, 0], y=X[y == cl, 1],
                    alpha=0.8, c=cmap(idx),
                    marker=markers[idx], label=cl)

>>> from sklearn.linear_model import LogisticRegression
>>> from sklearn.decomposition import PCA
>>> pca = PCA(n_components=2)
>>> lr = LogisticRegression()
>>> X_train_pca = pca.fit_transform(X_train_std)
>>> X_test_pca = pca.transform(X_test_std)
>>> lr.fit(X_train_pca, y_train)
>>> plot_decision_regions(X_train_pca, y_train, classifier=lr)
>>> plt.xlabel('PC1')
>>> plt.ylabel('PC2')
>>> plt.legend(loc='lower left')
>>> plt.show()
```

By executing the preceding code, we should now see the decision regions for the training model reduced to the two principal component axes.

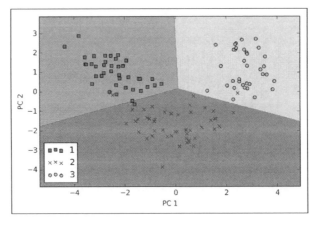

If we compare the PCA projection via scikit-learn with our own PCA implementation, we notice that the plot above is a mirror image of the previous PCA via our step-by-step approach. Note that this is not due to an error in any of those two implementations, but the reason for this difference is that, depending on the eigensolver, eigenvectors can have either negative or positive signs. Not that it matters, but we could simply revert the mirror image by multiplying the data with -1 if we wanted to; note that eigenvectors are typically scaled to unit length 1. For the sake of completeness, let's plot the decision regions of the logistic regression on the transformed test dataset to see if it can separate the classes well:

```
>>> plot_decision_regions(X_test_pca, y_test, classifier=lr)
>>> plt.xlabel('PC1')
>>> plt.ylabel('PC2')
>>> plt.legend(loc='lower left')
>>> plt.show()
```

After we plot the decision regions for the test set by executing the preceding code, we can see that logistic regression performs quite well on this small two-dimensional feature subspace and only misclassifies one sample in the test dataset.

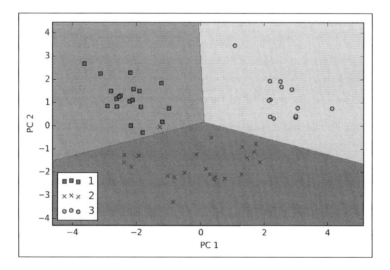

If we are interested in the explained variance ratios of the different principal components, we can simply initialize the PCA class with the n_components parameter set to None, so all principal components are kept and the explained variance ratio can then be accessed via the explained_variance_ratio_ attribute:

```
>>> pca = PCA(n_components=None)
>>> X_train_pca = pca.fit_transform(X_train_std)
>>> pca.explained_variance_ratio_
```

```
array([ 0.37329648,  0.18818926,  0.10896791,  0.07724389,
0.06478595,
0.04592014,  0.03986936,  0.02521914,  0.02258181,  0.01830924,
0.01635336,  0.01284271,  0.00642076])
```

Note that we set `n_components=None` when we initialized the PCA class so that it would return all principal components in sorted order instead of performing a dimensionality reduction.

Supervised data compression via linear discriminant analysis

Linear Discriminant Analysis (LDA) can be used as a technique for feature extraction to increase the computational efficiency and reduce the degree of over-fitting due to the curse of dimensionality in nonregularized models.

The general concept behind LDA is very similar to PCA, whereas PCA attempts to find the orthogonal component axes of maximum variance in a dataset; the goal in LDA is to find the feature subspace that optimizes class separability. Both LDA and PCA are linear transformation techniques that can be used to reduce the number of dimensions in a dataset; the former is an unsupervised algorithm, whereas the latter is supervised. Thus, we might intuitively think that LDA is a superior feature extraction technique for classification tasks compared to PCA. However, A.M. Martinez reported that preprocessing via PCA tends to result in better classification results in an image recognition task in certain cases, for instance, if each class consists of only a small number of samples (A. M. Martinez and A. C. Kak. *PCA Versus LDA*. Pattern Analysis and Machine Intelligence, IEEE Transactions on, 23(2):228–233, 2001).

Although LDA is sometimes also called Fisher's LDA, Ronald A. Fisher initially formulated *Fisher's Linear Discriminant* for two-class classification problems in 1936 (R. A. Fisher. *The Use of Multiple Measurements in Taxonomic Problems*. Annals of Eugenics, 7(2):179–188, 1936). Fisher's Linear Discriminant was later generalized for multi-class problems by C. Radhakrishna Rao under the assumption of equal class covariances and normally distributed classes in 1948, which we now call LDA (C. R. Rao. *The Utilization of Multiple Measurements in Problems of Biological Classification*. Journal of the Royal Statistical Society. Series B (Methodological), 10(2):159–203, 1948).

The following figure summarizes the concept of LDA for a two-class problem. Samples from class 1 are shown as crosses and samples from class 2 are shown as circles, respectively:

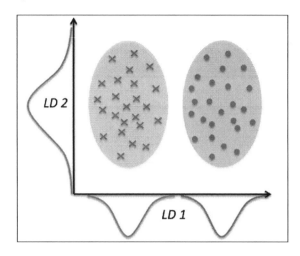

A linear discriminant, as shown on the x-axis (LD 1), would separate the two normally distributed classes well. Although the exemplary linear discriminant shown on the y-axis (LD 2) captures a lot of the variance in the dataset, it would fail as a good linear discriminant since it does not capture any of the class-discriminatory information.

One assumption in LDA is that the data is normally distributed. Also, we assume that the classes have identical covariance matrices and that the features are statistically independent of each other. However, even if one or more of those assumptions are slightly violated, LDA for dimensionality reduction can still work reasonably well (R. O. Duda, P. E. Hart, and D. G. Stork. *Pattern Classification*. 2nd. Edition. New York, 2001).

Before we take a look into the inner workings of LDA in the following subsections, let's summarize the key steps of the LDA approach:

1. Standardize the d-dimensional dataset (d is the number of features).
2. For each class, compute the d-dimensional mean vector.
3. Construct the between-class scatter matrix S_B and the within-class scatter matrix S_w.

4. Compute the eigenvectors and corresponding eigenvalues of the matrix $S_w^{-1}S_B$.

5. Choose the k eigenvectors that correspond to the k largest eigenvalues to construct a $d \times k$-dimensional transformation matrix W; the eigenvectors are the columns of this matrix.

6. Project the samples onto the new feature subspace using the transformation matrix W.

The assumptions that we make when we are using LDA are that the features are normally distributed and independent of each other. Also, the LDA algorithm assumes that the covariance matrices for the individual classes are identical. However, even if we violate those assumptions to a certain extent, LDA may still work reasonably well in dimensionality reduction and classification tasks (R. O. Duda, P. E. Hart, and D. G. Stork. *Pattern Classification*. 2nd. Edition. New York, 2001).

Computing the scatter matrices

Since we have already standardized the features of the *Wine* dataset in the PCA section at the beginning of this chapter, we can skip the first step and proceed with the calculation of the mean vectors, which we will use to construct the within-class scatter matrix and between-class scatter matrix, respectively. Each mean vector m_i stores the mean feature value μ_m with respect to the samples of class i:

$$m_i = \frac{1}{n_i}\sum_{x \in D_i}^{c} x_m$$

This results in three mean vectors:

$$m_i = \begin{bmatrix} \mu_{i,alcohol} \\ \mu_{i,malic\ acid} \\ \vdots \\ \mu_{i,proline} \end{bmatrix} \quad i \in \{1,2,3\}$$

```
>>> np.set_printoptions(precision=4)
>>> mean_vecs = []
>>> for label in range(1,4):
...      mean_vecs.append(np.mean(
...                X_train_std[y_train==label], axis=0))
...      print('MV %s: %s\n' % (label, mean_vecs[label-1]))
MV 1: [ 0.9259 -0.3091  0.2592 -0.7989  0.3039  0.9608  1.0515 -0.6306
0.5354
   0.2209  0.4855  0.798   1.2017]

MV 2: [-0.8727 -0.3854 -0.4437  0.2481 -0.2409 -0.1059  0.0187 -0.0164
0.1095
  -0.8796  0.4392  0.2776 -0.7016]

MV 3: [ 0.1637  0.8929  0.3249  0.5658 -0.01   -0.9499 -1.228   0.7436
-0.7652
   0.979  -1.1698 -1.3007 -0.3912]
```

Using the mean vectors, we can now compute the within-class scatter matrix S_W:

$$S_W = \sum_{i=1}^{c} S_i$$

This is calculated by summing up the individual scatter matrices S_i of each individual class i:

$$S_i = \sum_{x \in D_i} (x - m_i)(x - m_i)^T$$

```
>>> d = 13 # number of features
>>> S_W = np.zeros((d, d))
>>> for label,mv in zip(range(1,4), mean_vecs):
...      class_scatter = np.zeros((d, d))
...      for row in X_train[y_train == label]:
...           row, mv = row.reshape(d, 1), mv.reshape(d, 1)
...           class_scatter += (row-mv).dot((row-mv).T)
...      S_W += class_scatter
>>> print('Within-class scatter matrix: %sx%s'
...           % (S_W.shape[0], S_W.shape[1]))
Within-class scatter matrix: 13x13
```

The assumption that we are making when we are computing the scatter matrices is that the class labels in the training set are uniformly distributed. However, if we print the number of class labels, we see that this assumption is violated:

```
>>> print('Class label distribution: %s'
...        % np.bincount(y_train)[1:])
Class label distribution: [40 49 35]
```

Thus, we want to scale the individual scatter matrices S_i before we sum them up as scatter matrix S_w. When we divide the scatter matrices by the number of class samples N_i, we can see that computing the scatter matrix is in fact the same as computing the covariance matrix Σ_i. The covariance matrix is a normalized version of the scatter matrix:

$$\Sigma_i = \frac{1}{N_i} S_W = \frac{1}{N_i} \sum_{x \in D_i}^{c} (x - m_i)(x - m_i)^T$$

```
>>> d = 13 # number of features
>>> S_W = np.zeros((d, d))
>>> for label,mv in zip(range(1, 4), mean_vecs):
...        class_scatter = np.cov(X_train_std[y_train==label].T)
...        S_W += class_scatter
>>> print('Scaled within-class scatter matrix: %sx%s'
...        % (S_W.shape[0], S_W.shape[1]))
Scaled within-class scatter matrix: 13x13
```

After we have computed the scaled within-class scatter matrix (or covariance matrix), we can move on to the next step and compute the between-class scatter matrix S_B:

$$S_B = \sum_{i=1}^{c} N_i (m_i - m)(m_i - m)^T$$

Here, m is the overall mean that is computed, including samples from all classes.

```
>>> mean_overall = np.mean(X_train_std, axis=0)
>>> d = 13 # number of features
>>> S_B = np.zeros((d, d))
>>> for i,mean_vec in enumerate(mean_vecs):
...        n = X_train[y_train==i+1, :].shape[0]
...        mean_vec = mean_vec.reshape(d, 1)
...        mean_overall = mean_overall.reshape(d, 1)
    S_B += n * (mean_vec - mean_overall).dot(
```

```
...                (mean_vec - mean_overall).T)
print('Between-class scatter matrix: %sx%s'
...      % (S_B.shape[0], S_B.shape[1]))
Between-class scatter matrix: 13x13
```

Selecting linear discriminants for the new feature subspace

The remaining steps of the LDA are similar to the steps of the PCA. However, instead of performing the eigendecomposition on the covariance matrix, we solve the generalized eigenvalue problem of the matrix $S_w^{-1}S_B$:

```
>>>eigen_vals, eigen_vecs =\
...np.linalg.eig(np.linalg.inv(S_W).dot(S_B))
```

After we computed the eigenpairs, we can now sort the eigenvalues in descending order:

```
>>> eigen_pairs = [(np.abs(eigen_vals[i]), eigen_vecs[:,i])
...                 for i in range(len(eigen_vals))]
>>> eigen_pairs = sorted(eigen_pairs,
...                 key=lambda k: k[0], reverse=True)
>>> print('Eigenvalues in decreasing order:\n')
>>> for eigen_val in eigen_pairs:
...     print(eigen_val[0])


Eigenvalues in decreasing order:

452.721581245
156.43636122
8.11327596465e-14
2.78687384543e-14
2.78687384543e-14
2.27622032758e-14
2.27622032758e-14
1.97162599817e-14
1.32484714652e-14
1.32484714652e-14
1.03791501611e-14
5.94140664834e-15
2.12636975748e-16
```

In LDA, the number of linear discriminants is at most $c-1$ where c is the number of class labels, since the in-between class scatter matrix S_B is the sum of c matrices with rank 1 or less. We can indeed see that we only have two nonzero eigenvalues (the eigenvalues 3-13 are not exactly zero, but this is due to the floating point arithmetic in NumPy). Note that in the rare case of perfect collinearity (all aligned sample points fall on a straight line), the covariance matrix would have rank one, which would result in only one eigenvector with a nonzero eigenvalue.

To measure how much of the class-discriminatory information is captured by the linear discriminants (eigenvectors), let's plot the linear discriminants by decreasing eigenvalues similar to the explained variance plot that we created in the PCA section. For simplicity, we will call the content of the class-discriminatory information *discriminability*.

```
>>> tot = sum(eigen_vals.real)
>>> discr = [(i / tot) for i in sorted(eigen_vals.real, reverse=True)]
>>> cum_discr = np.cumsum(discr)
>>> plt.bar(range(1, 14), discr, alpha=0.5, align='center',
...         label='individual "discriminability"')
>>> plt.step(range(1, 14), cum_discr, where='mid',
...          label='cumulative "discriminability"')
>>> plt.ylabel('"discriminability" ratio')
>>> plt.xlabel('Linear Discriminants')
>>> plt.ylim([-0.1, 1.1])
>>> plt.legend(loc='best')
>>> plt.show()
```

As we can see in the resulting figure, the first two linear discriminants capture about 100 percent of the useful information in the *Wine* training dataset:

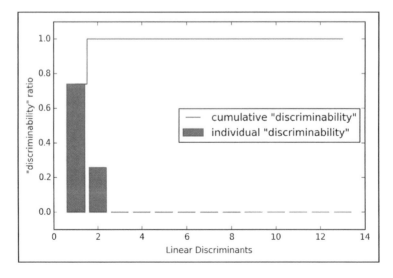

Let's now stack the two most discriminative eigenvector columns to create the transformation matrix W:

```
>>> w = np.hstack((eigen_pairs[0][1][:, np.newaxis].real,
...                eigen_pairs[1][1][:, np.newaxis].real))
>>> print('Matrix W:\n', w)
Matrix W:
[[ 0.0662 -0.3797]
 [-0.0386 -0.2206]
 [ 0.0217 -0.3816]
 [-0.184 0.3018]
 [ 0.0034 0.0141]
 [-0.2326 0.0234]
 [ 0.7747 0.1869]
 [ 0.0811 0.0696]
 [-0.0875 0.1796]
 [-0.185 -0.284 ]
 [ 0.066 0.2349]
 [ 0.3805 0.073 ]
 [ 0.3285 -0.5971]]
```

Projecting samples onto the new feature space

Using the transformation matrix W that we created in the previous subsection, we can now transform the training data set by multiplying the matrices:

$$X' = XW$$

```
>>> X_train_lda = X_train_std.dot(w)
>>> colors = ['r', 'b', 'g']
>>> markers = ['s', 'x', 'o']
>>> for l, c, m in zip(np.unique(y_train), colors, markers):
...     plt.scatter(X_train_lda[y_train==l, 0]*(-1)
...                 X_train_lda[y_train==l, 1]*(-1)
...                 c=c, label=l, marker=m)
>>> plt.xlabel('LD 1')
>>> plt.ylabel('LD 2')
>>> plt.legend(loc='lower right')
>>> plt.show()
```

As we can see in the resulting plot, the three wine classes are now linearly separable in the new feature subspace:

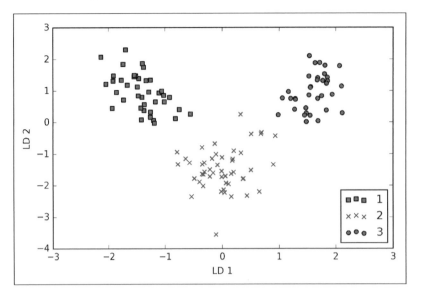

LDA via scikit-learn

The step-by-step implementation was a good exercise for understanding the inner workings of LDA and understanding the differences between LDA and PCA. Now, let's take a look at the LDA class implemented in scikit-learn:

```
>>> from sklearn.lda import LDA
>>> lda = LDA(n_components=2)
>>> X_train_lda = lda.fit_transform(X_train_std, y_train)
```

Next, let's see how the logistic regression classifier handles the lower-dimensional training dataset after the LDA transformation:

```
>>> lr = LogisticRegression()
>>> lr = lr.fit(X_train_lda, y_train)
>>> plot_decision_regions(X_train_lda, y_train, classifier=lr)
>>> plt.xlabel('LD 1')
>>> plt.ylabel('LD 2')
>>> plt.legend(loc='lower left')
>>> plt.show()
```

Looking at the resulting plot, we see that the logistic regression model misclassifies one of the samples from class 2:

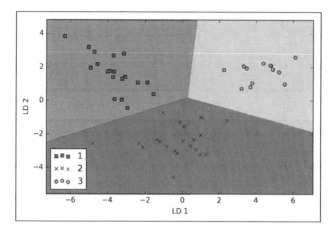

By lowering the regularization strength, we could probably shift the decision boundaries so that the logistic regression models classify all samples in the training dataset correctly. However, let's take a look at the results on the test set:

```
>>> X_test_lda = lda.transform(X_test_std)
>>> plot_decision_regions(X_test_lda, y_test, classifier=lr)
>>> plt.xlabel('LD 1')
>>> plt.ylabel('LD 2')
>>> plt.legend(loc='lower left')
>>> plt.show()
```

As we can see in the resulting plot, the logistic regression classifier is able to get a perfect accuracy score for classifying the samples in the test dataset by only using a two-dimensional feature subspace instead of the original 13 *Wine* features:

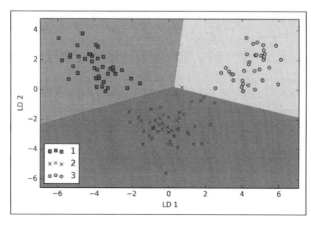

Using kernel principal component analysis for nonlinear mappings

Many machine learning algorithms make assumptions about the linear separability of the input data. You learned that the perceptron even requires perfectly linearly separable training data to converge. Other algorithms that we have covered so far assume that the lack of perfect linear separability is due to noise: Adaline, logistic regression, and the (standard) **support vector machine (SVM)** to just name a few. However, if we are dealing with nonlinear problems, which we may encounter rather frequently in real-world applications, linear transformation techniques for dimensionality reduction, such as PCA and LDA, may not be the best choice. In this section, we will take a look at a kernelized version of PCA, or *kernel PCA*, which relates to the concepts of kernel SVM that we remember from *Chapter 3, A Tour of Machine Learning Classifiers Using Scikit-learn*. Using kernel PCA, we will learn how to transform data that is not linearly separable onto a new, lower-dimensional subspace that is suitable for linear classifiers.

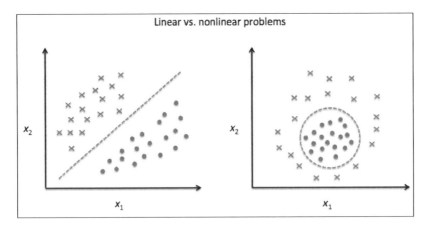

Kernel functions and the kernel trick

As we remember from our discussion about kernel SVMs in *Chapter 3, A Tour of Machine Learning Classifiers Using Scikit-learn*, we can tackle nonlinear problems by projecting them onto a new feature space of higher dimensionality where the classes become linearly separable. To transform the samples $x \in \mathbb{R}^d$ onto this higher k-dimensional subspace, we defined a nonlinear mapping function ϕ:

$$\phi : \mathbb{R}^d \to \mathbb{R}^k \ \ (k \gg d)$$

We can think of ϕ as a function that creates nonlinear combinations of the original features to map the original d-dimensional dataset onto a larger, k-dimensional feature space. For example, if we had feature vector $x \in \mathbb{R}^d$ (x is a column vector consisting of d features) with two dimensions $(d = 2)$, a potential mapping onto a 3D space could be as follows:

$$x = \left[x_1, \ x_2\right]^T$$

$$\downarrow \phi$$

$$\mathbf{z} = \left[x_1^2, \sqrt{2x_1 x_2}, x_2^2 \right]^T$$

In other words, via kernel PCA we perform a nonlinear mapping that transforms the data onto a higher-dimensional space and use standard PCA in this higher-dimensional space to project the data back onto a lower-dimensional space where the samples can be separated by a linear classifier (under the condition that the samples can be separated by density in the input space). However, one downside of this approach is that it is computationally very expensive, and this is where we use the *kernel trick*. Using the kernel trick, we can compute the similarity between two high-dimension feature vectors in the original feature space.

Before we proceed with more details about using the kernel trick to tackle this computationally expensive problem, let's look back at the *standard* PCA approach that we implemented at the beginning of this chapter. We computed the covariance between two features k and j as follows:

$$\sigma_{jk} = \frac{1}{n} \sum_{i=1}^{n} \left(x_j^{(i)} - \mu_j\right)\left(x_k^{(i)} - \mu_k\right)$$

Since the standardizing of features centers them at mean zero, for instance, $\mu_j = 0$ and $\mu_k = 0$, we can simplify this equation as follows:

$$\sigma_{jk} = \frac{1}{n} \sum_{i=1}^{n} x_j^{(i)} x_k^{(i)}$$

Note that the preceding equation refers to the covariance between two features; now, let's write the general equation to calculate the covariance *matrix* Σ:

$$\Sigma = \frac{1}{n}\sum_{i=1}^{n} x^{(i)} x^{(i)T}$$

Bernhard Scholkopf generalized this approach (B. Scholkopf, A. Smola, and K.-R. Muller. *Kernel Principal Component Analysis*. pages 583–588, 1997) so that we can replace the dot products between samples in the original feature space by the nonlinear feature combinations via ϕ:

$$\Sigma = \frac{1}{n}\sum_{i=1}^{n} \phi\left(x^{(i)}\right)\phi(x^{(i)})^{T}$$

To obtain the eigenvectors—the principal components—from this covariance matrix, we have to solve the following equation:

$$\Sigma v = \lambda v$$

$$\Rightarrow \frac{1}{n}\sum_{i=1}^{n} \phi\left(x^{(i)}\right)\phi\left(x^{(i)}\right)^{T} v = \lambda v$$

$$\Rightarrow v = \frac{1}{n\lambda}\sum_{i=1}^{n} \phi\left(x^{(i)}\right)\phi\left(x^{(i)}\right)^{T} v = \frac{1}{n}\sum_{i=1}^{n} a^{(i)}\phi\left(x^{(i)}\right)$$

Here, λ and v are the eigenvalues and eigenvectors of the covariance matrix Σ, and a can be obtained by extracting the eigenvectors of the kernel (similarity) matrix K as we will see in the following paragraphs.

The derivation of the kernel matrix is as follows:

First, let's write the covariance matrix as in matrix notation, where $\phi(X)$ is an $n \times k$ -dimensional matrix:

$$\Sigma = \frac{1}{n}\sum_{i=1}^{n} \phi\left(x^{(i)}\right)\phi\left(x^{(i)}\right)^{T} = \frac{1}{n}\phi(X)^{T}\phi(X)$$

Now, we can write the eigenvector equation as follows:

$$v = \frac{1}{n}\sum_{i=1}^{n}a^{(i)}\phi\left(x^{(i)}\right) = \lambda\phi\left(X\right)^{T}a$$

Since $\Sigma v = \lambda v$, we get:

$$\frac{1}{n}\phi\left(X\right)^{T}\phi\left(X\right)\phi\left(X\right)^{T}a = \lambda\phi\left(X\right)^{T}a$$

Multiplying it by $\phi\left(X\right)$ on both sides yields the following result:

$$\frac{1}{n}\phi\left(X\right)\phi\left(X\right)^{T}\phi\left(X\right)\phi\left(X\right)^{T}a = \lambda\phi\left(X\right)\phi\left(X\right)^{T}a$$

$$\Rightarrow \frac{1}{n}\phi\left(X\right)\phi\left(X\right)^{T}a = \lambda a$$

$$\Rightarrow \frac{1}{n}Ka = \lambda a$$

Here, K is the similarity (kernel) matrix:

$$K = \phi\left(X\right)\phi\left(X\right)^{T}$$

As we recall from the SVM section in *Chapter 3, A Tour of Machine Learning Classifiers Using Scikit-learn*, we use the kernel trick to avoid calculating the pairwise dot products of the samples x under ϕ explicitly by using a kernel function K so that we don't need to calculate the eigenvectors explicitly:

$$k\left(x^{(i)},x^{(j)}\right) = \phi\left(x^{(i)}\right)^{T}\phi\left(x^{(j)}\right)$$

In other words, what we obtain after kernel PCA are the samples already projected onto the respective components rather than constructing a transformation matrix as in the standard PCA approach. Basically, the kernel function (or simply *kernel*) can be understood as a function that calculates a dot product between two vectors — a measure of similarity.

The most commonly used kernels are as follows:

- The polynomial kernel:

$$k\left(x^{(i)}, x^{(j)}\right) = \left(x^{(i)T} x^{(j)} + \theta\right)^{p}$$

  Here, θ is the threshold and p is the power that has to be specified by the user.

- The hyperbolic tangent (sigmoid) kernel:

$$k\left(x^{(i)}, x^{(j)}\right) = \tanh\left(\eta x^{(i)T} x^{(j)} + \theta\right)$$

- The **Radial Basis Function (RBF)** or Gaussian kernel that we will use in the following examples in the next subsection:

$$k\left(x^{(i)}, x^{(j)}\right) = \exp\left(-\frac{\left\|x^{(i)} - x^{(j)}\right\|^2}{2\sigma^2}\right)$$

It is also written as follows:

$$k\left(x^{(i)}, x^{(j)}\right) = \exp\left(-\gamma \left\|x^{(i)} - x^{(j)}\right\|^2\right)$$

To summarize what we have discussed so far, we can define the following three steps to implement an RBF kernel PCA:

1. We compute the kernel (similarity) matrix k, where we need to calculate the following:

$$k\left(x^{(i)}, x^{(j)}\right) = \exp\left(-\gamma \left\|x^{(i)} - x^{(j)}\right\|^2\right)$$

We do this for each pair of samples:

$$K = \begin{bmatrix} \kappa\left(x^{(1)},x^{(1)}\right) & \kappa\left(x^{(1)},x^{(2)}\right) & \cdots & \kappa\left(x^{(1)},x^{(n)}\right) \\ \kappa\left(x^{(2)},x^{(1)}\right) & \left(x^{(2)},x^{(2)}\right) & \cdots & \kappa\left(x^{(2)},x^{(n)}\right) \\ \vdots & \vdots & \ddots & \vdots \\ \kappa\left(x^{(n)},x^{(1)}\right) & \kappa\left(x^{(n)},x^{(2)}\right) & \cdots & \kappa\left(x^{(n)},x^{(n)}\right) \end{bmatrix}$$

For example, if our dataset contains 100 training samples, the symmetric kernel matrix of the pair-wise similarities would be 100×100 dimensional.

2. We center the kernel matrix k using the following equation:

$$K' = K - 1_n K - K 1_n + 1_n K 1_n$$

Here, 1_n is an $n \times n$- dimensional matrix (the same dimensions as the kernel matrix) where all values are equal to $\frac{1}{n}$.

3. We collect the top k eigenvectors of the centered kernel matrix based on their corresponding eigenvalues, which are ranked by decreasing magnitude. In contrast to standard PCA, the eigenvectors are not the principal component axes but the samples projected onto those axes.

At this point, you may be wondering why we need to center the kernel matrix in the second step. We previously assumed that we are working with standardized data, where all features have mean zero when we formulated the covariance matrix and replaced the dot products by the nonlinear feature combinations via ϕ. Thus, the centering of the kernel matrix in the second step becomes necessary, since we do not compute the new feature space explicitly and we cannot guarantee that the new feature space is also centered at zero.

In the next section, we will put those three steps into action by implementing a kernel PCA in Python.

Implementing a kernel principal component analysis in Python

In the previous subsection, we discussed the core concepts behind kernel PCA. Now, we are going to implement an RBF kernel PCA in Python following the three steps that summarized the kernel PCA approach. Using the SciPy and NumPy helper functions, we will see that implementing a kernel PCA is actually really simple:

```python
from scipy.spatial.distance import pdist, squareform
from scipy import exp
from scipy.linalg import eigh
import numpy as np

def rbf_kernel_pca(X, gamma, n_components):
    """
    RBF kernel PCA implementation.

    Parameters
    ------------
    X: {NumPy ndarray}, shape = [n_samples, n_features]

    gamma: float
      Tuning parameter of the RBF kernel

    n_components: int
      Number of principal components to return

    Returns
    ------------
     X_pc: {NumPy ndarray}, shape = [n_samples, k_features]
       Projected dataset

    """
    # Calculate pairwise squared Euclidean distances
    # in the MxN dimensional dataset.
    sq_dists = pdist(X, 'sqeuclidean')

    # Convert pairwise distances into a square matrix.
    mat_sq_dists = squareform(sq_dists)

    # Compute the symmetric kernel matrix.
    K = exp(-gamma * mat_sq_dists)
```

```
# Center the kernel matrix.
N = K.shape[0]
one_n = np.ones((N,N)) / N
K = K - one_n.dot(K) - K.dot(one_n) + one_n.dot(K).dot(one_n)

# Obtaining eigenpairs from the centered kernel matrix
# numpy.eigh returns them in sorted order
eigvals, eigvecs = eigh(K)

# Collect the top k eigenvectors (projected samples)
X_pc = np.column_stack((eigvecs[:, -i]
                     for i in range(1, n_components + 1)))

return X_pc
```

One downside of using an RBF kernel PCA for dimensionality reduction is that we have to specify the parameter γ a priori. Finding an appropriate value for γ requires experimentation and is best done using algorithms for parameter tuning, for example, grid search, which we will discuss in more detail in *Chapter 6, Learning Best Practices for Model Evaluation and Hyperparameter Tuning*.

Example 1 – separating half-moon shapes

Now, let's apply our rbf_kernel_pca on some nonlinear example datasets. We will start by creating a two-dimensional dataset of 100 sample points representing two half-moon shapes:

```
>>> from sklearn.datasets import make_moons
>>> X, y = make_moons(n_samples=100, random_state=123)
>>> plt.scatter(X[y==0, 0], X[y==0, 1],
...             color='red', marker='^', alpha=0.5)
>>> plt.scatter(X[y==1, 0], X[y==1, 1],
...             color='blue', marker='o', alpha=0.5)
>>> plt.show()
```

For the purposes of illustration, the half-moon of triangular symbols shall represent one class and the half-moon depicted by the circular symbols represent the samples from another class:

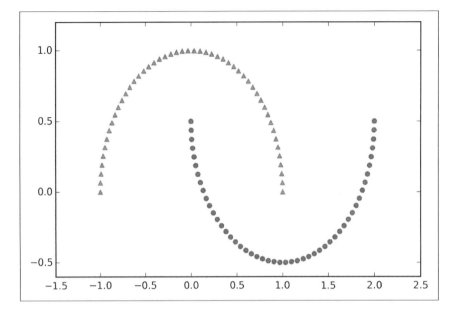

Clearly, these two half-moon shapes are not linearly separable and our goal is to *unfold* the half-moons via kernel PCA so that the dataset can serve as a suitable input for a linear classifier. But first, let's see what the dataset looks like if we project it onto the principal components via standard PCA:

```
>>> from sklearn.decomposition import PCA
>>> scikit_pca = PCA(n_components=2)
>>> X_spca = scikit_pca.fit_transform(X)
>>> fig, ax = plt.subplots(nrows=1,ncols=2, figsize=(7,3))
>>> ax[0].scatter(X_spca[y==0, 0], X_spca[y==0, 1],
...               color='red', marker='^', alpha=0.5)
>>> ax[0].scatter(X_spca[y==1, 0], X_spca[y==1, 1],
...               color='blue', marker='o', alpha=0.5)
>>> ax[1].scatter(X_spca[y==0, 0], np.zeros((50,1))+0.02,
...               color='red', marker='^', alpha=0.5)
>>> ax[1].scatter(X_spca[y==1, 0], np.zeros((50,1))-0.02,
...               color='blue', marker='o', alpha=0.5)
```

```
>>> ax[0].set_xlabel('PC1')
>>> ax[0].set_ylabel('PC2')
>>> ax[1].set_ylim([-1, 1])
>>> ax[1].set_yticks([])
>>> ax[1].set_xlabel('PC1')
>>> plt.show()
```

Clearly, we can see in the resulting figure that a linear classifier would be unable to perform well on the dataset transformed via standard PCA:

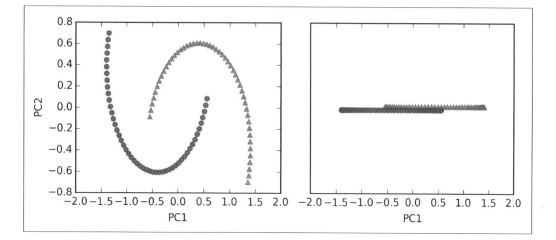

Note that when we plotted the first principal component only (right subplot), we shifted the triangular samples slightly upwards and the circular samples slightly downwards to better visualize the class overlap.

> Please remember that PCA is an unsupervised method and does not use class label information in order to maximize the variance in contrast to LDA. Here, the triangular and circular symbols were just added for visualization purposes to indicate the degree of separation.

Now, let's try out our kernel PCA function rbf_kernel_pca, which we implemented in the previous subsection:

```
>>> from matplotlib.ticker import FormatStrFormatter
>>> X_kpca = rbf_kernel_pca(X, gamma=15, n_components=2)
>>> fig, ax = plt.subplots(nrows=1,ncols=2, figsize=(7,3))
>>> ax[0].scatter(X_kpca[y==0, 0], X_kpca[y==0, 1],
...                color='red', marker='^', alpha=0.5)
>>> ax[0].scatter(X_kpca[y==1, 0], X_kpca[y==1, 1],
```

```
...                color='blue', marker='o', alpha=0.5)
>>> ax[1].scatter(X_kpca[y==0, 0], np.zeros((50,1))+0.02,
...                color='red', marker='^', alpha=0.5)
>>> ax[1].scatter(X_kpca[y==1, 0], np.zeros((50,1))-0.02,
...                color='blue', marker='o', alpha=0.5)
>>> ax[0].set_xlabel('PC1')
>>> ax[0].set_ylabel('PC2')
>>> ax[1].set_ylim([-1, 1])
>>> ax[1].set_yticks([])
>>> ax[1].set_xlabel('PC1')
>>> ax[0].xaxis.set_major_formatter(FormatStrFormatter('%0.1f'))
>>> ax[1].xaxis.set_major_formatter(FormatStrFormatter('%0.1f'))
>>> plt.show()
```

We can now see that the two classes (circles and triangles) are linearly well separated so that it becomes a suitable training dataset for linear classifiers:

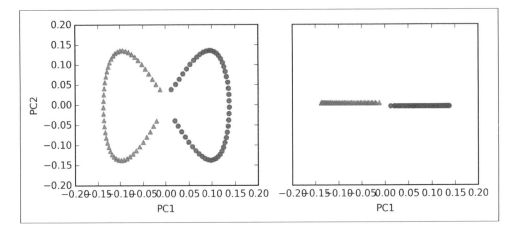

Unfortunately, there is no universal value for the tuning parameter γ that works well for different datasets. To find a γ value that is appropriate for a given problem requires experimentation. In *Chapter 6, Learning Best Practices for Model Evaluation and Hyperparameter Tuning*, we will discuss techniques that can help us to automate the task of optimizing such tuning parameters. Here, I will use values for γ that I found produce *good* results.

Example 2 – separating concentric circles

In the previous subsection, we showed you how to separate half-moon shapes via kernel PCA. Since we put so much effort into understanding the concepts of kernel PCA, let's take a look at another interesting example of a nonlinear problem: concentric circles.

The code is as follows:

```
>>> from sklearn.datasets import make_circles
>>> X, y = make_circles(n_samples=1000,
...                 random_state=123, noise=0.1, factor=0.2)
>>> plt.scatter(X[y==0, 0], X[y==0, 1],
...                 color='red', marker='^', alpha=0.5)
>>> plt.scatter(X[y==1, 0], X[y==1, 1],
...                 color='blue', marker='o', alpha=0.5)
>>> plt.show()
```

Again, we assume a two-class problem where the triangle shapes represent one class and the circle shapes represent another class, respectively:

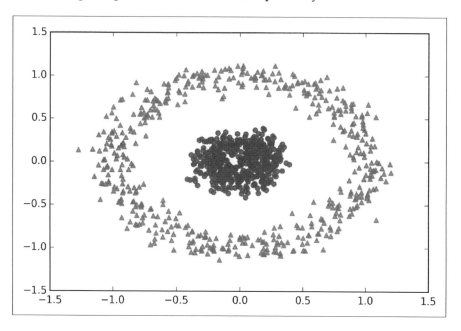

Let's start with the standard PCA approach to compare it with the results of the RBF kernel PCA:

```
>>> scikit_pca = PCA(n_components=2)
>>> X_spca = scikit_pca.fit_transform(X)
>>> fig, ax = plt.subplots(nrows=1,ncols=2, figsize=(7,3))
>>> ax[0].scatter(X_spca[y==0, 0], X_spca[y==0, 1],
...              color='red', marker='^', alpha=0.5)
>>> ax[0].scatter(X_spca[y==1, 0], X_spca[y==1, 1],
...              color='blue', marker='o', alpha=0.5)
>>> ax[1].scatter(X_spca[y==0, 0], np.zeros((500,1))+0.02,
...              color='red', marker='^', alpha=0.5)
>>> ax[1].scatter(X_spca[y==1, 0], np.zeros((500,1))-0.02,
...              color='blue', marker='o', alpha=0.5)
>>> ax[0].set_xlabel('PC1')
>>> ax[0].set_ylabel('PC2')
>>> ax[1].set_ylim([-1, 1])
>>> ax[1].set_yticks([])
>>> ax[1].set_xlabel('PC1')
>>> plt.show()
```

Again, we can see that standard PCA is not able to produce results suitable for training a linear classifier:

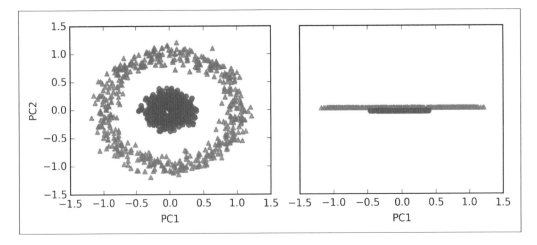

Given an appropriate value for γ, let's see if we are luckier using the RBF kernel PCA implementation:

```
>>> X_kpca = rbf_kernel_pca(X, gamma=15, n_components=2)
>>> fig, ax = plt.subplots(nrows=1,ncols=2, figsize=(7,3))
>>> ax[0].scatter(X_kpca[y==0, 0], X_kpca[y==0, 1],
...               color='red', marker='^', alpha=0.5)
>>> ax[0].scatter(X_kpca[y==1, 0], X_kpca[y==1, 1],
...               color='blue', marker='o', alpha=0.5)
>>> ax[1].scatter(X_kpca[y==0, 0], np.zeros((500,1))+0.02,
...               color='red', marker='^', alpha=0.5)
>>> ax[1].scatter(X_kpca[y==1, 0], np.zeros((500,1))-0.02,
...               color='blue', marker='o', alpha=0.5)
>>> ax[0].set_xlabel('PC1')
>>> ax[0].set_ylabel('PC2')
>>> ax[1].set_ylim([-1, 1])
>>> ax[1].set_yticks([])
>>> ax[1].set_xlabel('PC1')
>>> plt.show()
```

Again, the RBF kernel PCA projected the data onto a new subspace where the two classes become linearly separable:

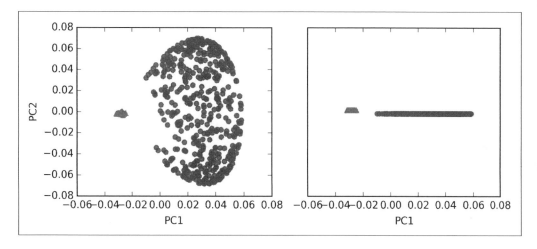

Projecting new data points

In the two previous example applications of kernel PCA, the half-moon shapes and the concentric circles, we projected a single dataset onto a new feature. In real applications, however, we may have more than one dataset that we want to transform, for example, training and test data, and typically also new samples we will collect after the model building and evaluation. In this section, you will learn how to project data points that were not part of the training dataset.

As we remember from the standard PCA approach at the beginning of this chapter, we project data by calculating the dot product between a transformation matrix and the input samples; the columns of the projection matrix are the top k eigenvectors (v) that we obtained from the covariance matrix. Now, the question is how can we transfer this concept to kernel PCA? If we think back to the idea behind kernel PCA, we remember that we obtained an eigenvector (a) of the centered kernel matrix (not the covariance matrix), which means that those are the samples that are already projected onto the principal component axis v. Thus, if we want to project a new sample x' onto this principal component axis, we'd need to compute the following:

$$\phi(x')^T v$$

Fortunately, we can use the kernel trick so that we don't have to calculate the projection $\phi(x')^T v$ explicitly. However, it is worth noting that kernel PCA, in contrast to standard PCA, is a memory-based method, which means that we have to reuse the original training set each time to project new samples. We have to calculate the pairwise RBF kernel (similarity) between each ith sample in the training dataset and the new sample x':

$$\phi(x')^T v = \sum_i a^{(i)} \phi(x')^T \phi(x^{(i)})$$

$$= \sum_i a^{(i)} k(x', x^{(i)})^T$$

Here, eigenvectors a and eigenvalues λ of the Kernel matrix K satisfy the following condition in the equation:

$$Ka = \lambda a$$

After calculating the similarity between the new samples and the samples in the training set, we have to normalize the eigenvector *a* by its eigenvalue. Thus, let's modify the `rbf_kernel_pca` function that we implemented earlier so that it also returns the eigenvalues of the kernel matrix:

```
from scipy.spatial.distance import pdist, squareform
from scipy import exp
from scipy.linalg import eigh
import numpy as np

def rbf_kernel_pca(X, gamma, n_components):
    """
    RBF kernel PCA implementation.

    Parameters
    ------------
    X: {NumPy ndarray}, shape = [n_samples, n_features]

    gamma: float
      Tuning parameter of the RBF kernel

    n_components: int
      Number of principal components to return

    Returns
    ------------
     X_pc: {NumPy ndarray}, shape = [n_samples, k_features]
        Projected dataset

     lambdas: list
        Eigenvalues

    """
    # Calculate pairwise squared Euclidean distances
    # in the MxN dimensional dataset.
    sq_dists = pdist(X, 'sqeuclidean')

    # Convert pairwise distances into a square matrix.
    mat_sq_dists = squareform(sq_dists)

    # Compute the symmetric kernel matrix.
    K = exp(-gamma * mat_sq_dists)
```

```
# Center the kernel matrix.
N = K.shape[0]
one_n = np.ones((N,N)) / N
K = K - one_n.dot(K) - K.dot(one_n) + one_n.dot(K).dot(one_n)

# Obtaining eigenpairs from the centered kernel matrix
# numpy.eigh returns them in sorted order
eigvals, eigvecs = eigh(K)

# Collect the top k eigenvectors (projected samples)
alphas = np.column_stack((eigvecs[:,-i]
                for i in range(1,n_components+1)))

# Collect the corresponding eigenvalues
lambdas = [eigvals[-i] for i in range(1,n_components+1)]

return alphas, lambdas
```

Now, let's create a new half-moon dataset and project it onto a one-dimensional subspace using the updated RBF kernel PCA implementation:

```
>>> X, y = make_moons(n_samples=100, random_state=123)
>>> alphas, lambdas =rbf_kernel_pca(X, gamma=15, n_components=1)
```

To make sure that we implement the code for projecting new samples, let's assume that the 26th point from the half-moon dataset is a new data point x', and our task is to project it onto this new subspace:

```
>>> x_new = X[25]
>>> x_new
array([ 1.8713187 ,  0.00928245])
>>> x_proj = alphas[25] # original projection
>>> x_proj
array([ 0.07877284])
>>> def project_x(x_new, X, gamma, alphas, lambdas):
...     pair_dist = np.array([np.sum(
...                 (x_new-row)**2) for row in X])
...     k = np.exp(-gamma * pair_dist)
... return k.dot(alphas / lambdas)
```

By executing the following code, we are able to reproduce the original projection. Using the project_x function, we will be able to project any new data samples as well. The code is as follows:

```
>>> x_reproj = project_x(x_new, X,
...         gamma=15, alphas=alphas, lambdas=lambdas)
>>> x_reproj
array([ 0.07877284])
```

Lastly, let's visualize the projection on the first principal component:

```
>>> plt.scatter(alphas[y==0, 0], np.zeros((50)),
...             color='red', marker='^',alpha=0.5)
>>> plt.scatter(alphas[y==1, 0], np.zeros((50)),
...             color='blue', marker='o', alpha=0.5)
>>> plt.scatter(x_proj, 0, color='black',
...             label='original projection of point X[25]',
...             marker='^', s=100)
>>> plt.scatter(x_reproj, 0, color='green',
...             label='remapped point X[25]',
...             marker='x', s=500)
>>> plt.legend(scatterpoints=1)
>>> plt.show()
```

As we can see in the following scatterplot, we mapped the sample x' onto the first principal component correctly:

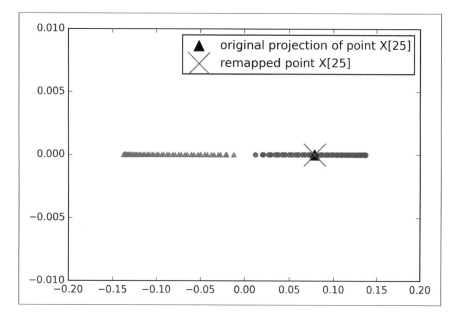

Kernel principal component analysis in scikit-learn

For our convenience, scikit-learn implements a kernel PCA class in the `sklearn.decomposition` submodule. The usage is similar to the standard PCA class, and we can specify the kernel via the `kernel` parameter:

```
>>> from sklearn.decomposition import KernelPCA
>>> X, y = make_moons(n_samples=100, random_state=123)
>>> scikit_kpca = KernelPCA(n_components=2,
...                    kernel='rbf', gamma=15)
>>> X_skernpca = scikit_kpca.fit_transform(X)
```

To see if we get results that are consistent with our own kernel PCA implementation, let's plot the transformed half-moon shape data onto the first two principal components:

```
>>> plt.scatter(X_skernpca[y==0, 0], X_skernpca[y==0, 1],
...             color='red', marker='^', alpha=0.5)
>>> plt.scatter(X_skernpca[y==1, 0], X_skernpca[y==1, 1],
...             color='blue', marker='o', alpha=0.5)
>>> plt.xlabel('PC1')
>>> plt.ylabel('PC2')
>>> plt.show()
```

As we can see, the results of the scikit-learn `KernelPCA` are consistent with our own implementation:

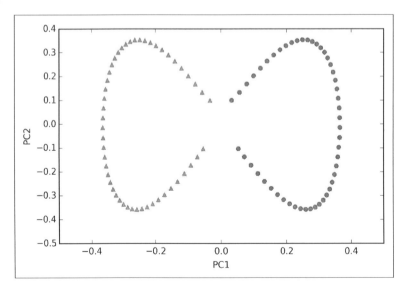

Scikit-learn also implements advanced techniques for nonlinear dimensionality reduction that are beyond the scope of this book. You can find a nice overview of the current implementations in scikit-learn complemented with illustrative examples at `http://scikit-learn.org/stable/modules/manifold.html`.

Summary

In this chapter, you learned about three different, fundamental dimensionality reduction techniques for feature extraction: standard PCA, LDA, and kernel PCA. Using PCA, we projected data onto a lower-dimensional subspace to maximize the variance along the orthogonal feature axes while ignoring the class labels. LDA, in contrast to PCA, is a technique for supervised dimensionality reduction, which means that it considers class information in the training dataset to attempt to maximize the class-separability in a linear feature space. Lastly, you learned about a kernelized version of PCA, which allows you to map nonlinear datasets onto a lower-dimensional feature space where the classes become linearly separable.

Equipped with these essential preprocessing techniques, you are now well prepared to learn about the best practices for efficiently incorporating different preprocessing techniques and evaluating the performance of different models in the next chapter.

6
Learning Best Practices for Model Evaluation and Hyperparameter Tuning

In the previous chapters, you learned about the essential machine learning algorithms for classification and how to get our data into shape before we feed it into those algorithms. Now, it's time to learn about the best practices of building good machine learning models by fine-tuning the algorithms and evaluating the model's performance! In this chapter, we will learn how to:

- Obtain unbiased estimates of a model's performance
- Diagnose the common problems of machine learning algorithms
- Fine-tune machine learning models
- Evaluate predictive models using different performance metrics

Streamlining workflows with pipelines

When we applied different preprocessing techniques in the previous chapters, such as **standardization** for feature scaling in *Chapter 4*, *Building Good Training Sets – Data Preprocessing*, or **principal component analysis** for data compression in *Chapter 5*, *Compressing Data via Dimensionality Reduction*, you learned that we have to reuse the parameters that were obtained during the fitting of the training data to scale and compress any new data, for example, the samples in the separate test dataset. In this section, you will learn about an extremely handy tool, the `Pipeline` class in scikit-learn. It allows us to fit a model including an arbitrary number of transformation steps and apply it to make predictions about new data.

Loading the Breast Cancer Wisconsin dataset

In this chapter, we will be working with the **Breast Cancer Wisconsin** dataset, which contains 569 samples of **malignant** and **benign** tumor cells. The first two columns in the dataset store the unique ID numbers of the samples and the corresponding diagnosis (*M=malignant, B=benign*), respectively. The columns 3-32 contain 30 real-value features that have been computed from digitized images of the cell nuclei, which can be used to build a model to predict whether a tumor is benign or malignant. The Breast Cancer Wisconsin dataset has been deposited on the *UCI machine learning repository* and more detailed information about this dataset can be found at https://archive.ics.uci.edu/ml/datasets/Breast+Cancer+Wisconsin+(Diagnostic).

In this section we will read in the dataset, and split it into training and test datasets in three simple steps:

1. We will start by reading in the dataset directly from the UCI website using pandas:

    ```
    >>> import pandas as pd
    >>> df = pd.read_csv('https://archive.ics.uci.edu/ml/machine-
    learning-databases/breast-cancer-wisconsin/wdbc.data',
    header=None)
    ```

2. Next, we assign the 30 features to a NumPy array X. Using LabelEncoder, we transform the class labels from their original string representation (M and B) into integers:

    ```
    >>> from sklearn.preprocessing import LabelEncoder
    >>> X = df.loc[:, 2:].values
    >>> y = df.loc[:, 1].values
    >>> le = LabelEncoder()
    >>> y = le.fit_transform(y)
    ```

    After encoding the class labels (diagnosis) in an array y, the malignant tumors are now represented as class 1, and the benign tumors are represented as class 0, respectively, which we can illustrate by calling the transform method of LabelEncoder on two dummy class labels:

    ```
    >>> le.transform(['M', 'B'])
    array([1, 0])
    ```

3. Before we construct our first model pipeline in the following subsection, let's divide the dataset into a separate training dataset (80 percent of the data) and a separate test dataset (20 percent of the data):

```
>>> from sklearn.cross_validation import train_test_split
>>> X_train, X_test, y_train, y_test = \
...     train_test_split(X, y, test_size=0.20, random_state=1)
```

Combining transformers and estimators in a pipeline

In the previous chapter, you learned that many learning algorithms require input features on the same scale for optimal performance. Thus, we need to standardize the columns in the Breast Cancer Wisconsin dataset before we can feed them to a linear classifier, such as logistic regression. Furthermore, let's assume that we want to compress our data from the initial 30 dimensions onto a lower two-dimensional subspace via **principal component analysis (PCA)**, a feature extraction technique for dimensionality reduction that we introduced in *Chapter 5, Compressing Data via Dimensionality Reduction*. Instead of going through the fitting and transformation steps for the training and test dataset separately, we can chain the StandardScaler, PCA, and LogisticRegression objects in a pipeline:

```
>>> from sklearn.preprocessing import StandardScaler
>>> from sklearn.decomposition import PCA
>>> from sklearn.linear_model import LogisticRegression
>>> from sklearn.pipeline import Pipeline
>>> pipe_lr = Pipeline([('scl', StandardScaler()),
...             ('pca', PCA(n_components=2)),
...             ('clf', LogisticRegression(random_state=1))])
>>> pipe_lr.fit(X_train, y_train)
>>> print('Test Accuracy: %.3f' % pipe_lr.score(X_test, y_test))
Test Accuracy: 0.947
```

The Pipeline object takes a list of tuples as input, where the first value in each tuple is an arbitrary identifier string that we can use to access the individual elements in the pipeline, as we will see later in this chapter, and the second element in every tuple is a scikit-learn transformer or estimator.

The intermediate steps in a pipeline constitute scikit-learn transformers, and the last step is an estimator. In the preceding code example, we built a pipeline that consisted of two intermediate steps, a StandardScaler and a PCA transformer, and a logistic regression classifier as a final estimator. When we executed the fit method on the pipeline pipe_lr, the StandardScaler performed fit and transform on the training data, and the transformed training data was then passed onto the next object in the pipeline, the PCA. Similar to the previous step, PCA also executed fit and transform on the scaled input data and passed it to the final element of the pipeline, the estimator. We should note that there is no limit to the number of intermediate steps in this pipeline. The concept of how pipelines work is summarized in the following figure:

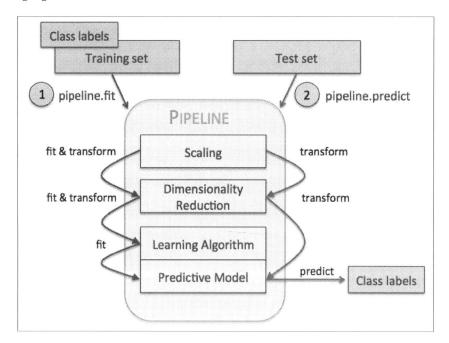

Using k-fold cross-validation to assess model performance

One of the key steps in building a machine learning model is to estimate its performance on data that the model hasn't seen before. Let's assume that we fit our model on a training dataset and use the same data to estimate how well it performs in practice. We remember from the *Tackling overfitting via regularization* section in *Chapter 3*, *A Tour of Machine Learning Classifiers Using Scikit-learn*, that a model can either suffer from underfitting (high bias) if the model is too simple, or it can overfit the training data (high variance) if the model is too complex for the underlying training data. To find an acceptable bias-variance trade-off, we need to evaluate our model carefully. In this section, you will learn about the useful cross-validation techniques **holdout cross-validation** and **k-fold cross-validation**, which can help us to obtain reliable estimates of the model's generalization error, that is, how well the model performs on unseen data.

The holdout method

A classic and popular approach for estimating the generalization performance of machine learning models is holdout cross-validation. Using the holdout method, we split our initial dataset into a separate training and test dataset—the former is used for model training, and the latter is used to estimate its performance. However, in typical machine learning applications, we are also interested in tuning and comparing different parameter settings to further improve the performance for making predictions on unseen data. This process is called **model selection**, where the term model selection refers to a given classification problem for which we want to select the *optimal* values of tuning parameters (also called **hyperparameters**). However, if we reuse the same test dataset over and over again during model selection, it will become part of our training data and thus the model will be more likely to overfit. Despite this issue, many people still use the test set for model selection, which is not a good machine learning practice.

A better way of using the holdout method for model selection is to separate the data into three parts: a training set, a validation set, and a test set. The training set is used to fit the different models, and the performance on the validation set is then used for the model selection. The advantage of having a test set that the model hasn't seen before during the training and model selection steps is that we can obtain a less biased estimate of its ability to generalize to new data. The following figure illustrates the concept of holdout cross-validation where we use a validation set to repeatedly evaluate the performance of the model after training using different parameter values. Once we are satisfied with the tuning of parameter values, we estimate the models' generalization error on the test dataset:

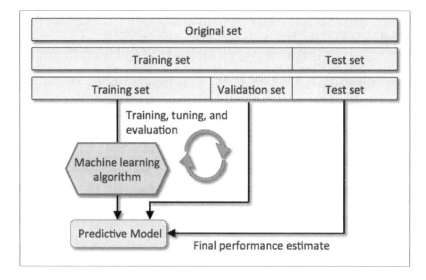

A disadvantage of the holdout method is that the performance estimate is sensitive to how we partition the training set into the training and validation subsets; the estimate will vary for different samples of the data. In the next subsection, we will take a look at a more robust technique for performance estimation, k-fold cross-validation, where we repeat the holdout method k times on k subsets of the training data.

K-fold cross-validation

In k-fold cross-validation, we randomly split the training dataset into k folds without replacement, where $k-1$ folds are used for the model training and one fold is used for testing. This procedure is repeated k times so that we obtain k models and performance estimates.

> In case you are not familiar with the terms sampling *with* and *without* replacement, let's walk through a simple thought experiment. Let's assume we are playing a lottery game where we randomly draw numbers from an urn. We start with an urn that holds five unique numbers 0, 1, 2, 3, and 4, and we draw exactly one number each turn. In the first round, the chance of drawing a particular number from the urn would be 1/5. Now, in sampling without replacement, we do not put the number back into the urn after each turn. Consequently, the probability of drawing a particular number from the set of remaining numbers in the next round depends on the previous round. For example, if we have a remaining set of numbers 0, 1, 2, and 4, the chance of drawing number 0 would become 1/4 in the next turn.
>
> However, in random sampling with replacement, we always return the drawn number to the urn so that the probabilities of drawing a particular number at each turn does not change; we can draw the same number more than once. In other words, in sampling with replacement, the samples (numbers) are independent and have a covariance zero. For example, the results from five rounds of drawing random numbers could look like this:
>
> * Random sampling without replacement: 2, 1, 3, 4, 0
> * Random sampling with replacement: 1, 3, 3, 4, 1

We then calculate the average performance of the models based on the different, independent folds to obtain a performance estimate that is less sensitive to the subpartitioning of the training data compared to the holdout method. Typically, we use k-fold cross-validation for model tuning, that is, finding the optimal hyperparameter values that yield a satisfying generalization performance. Once we have found satisfactory hyperparameter values, we can retrain the model on the complete training set and obtain a final performance estimate using the independent test set.

Since k-fold cross-validation is a resampling technique without replacement, the advantage of this approach is that each sample point will be part of a training and test dataset exactly once, which yields a lower-variance estimate of the model performance than the holdout method. The following figure summarizes the concept behind k-fold cross-validation with $k = 10$. The training data set is divided into 10 folds, and during the 10 iterations, 9 folds are used for training, and 1 fold will be used as the test set for the model evaluation. Also, the estimated performances E_i (for example, classification accuracy or error) for each fold are then used to calculate the estimated average performance E of the model:

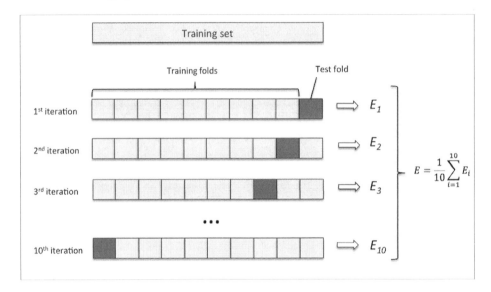

The standard value for *k* in k-fold cross-validation is 10, which is typically a reasonable choice for most applications. However, if we are working with relatively small training sets, it can be useful to increase the number of folds. If we increase the value of *k*, more training data will be used in each iteration, which results in a lower bias towards estimating the generalization performance by averaging the individual model estimates. However, large values of *k* will also increase the runtime of the cross-validation algorithm and yield estimates with higher variance since the training folds will be more similar to each other. On the other hand, if we are working with large datasets, we can choose a smaller value for *k*, for example, $k = 5$, and still obtain an accurate estimate of the average performance of the model while reducing the computational cost of refitting and evaluating the model on the different folds.

A special case of k-fold cross validation is the **leave-one-out (LOO)** cross-validation method. In LOO, we set the number of folds equal to the number of training samples ($k = n$) so that only one training sample is used for testing during each iteration. This is a recommended approach for working with very small datasets.

A slight improvement over the standard k-fold cross-validation approach is stratified k-fold cross-validation, which can yield better bias and variance estimates, especially in cases of unequal class proportions, as it has been shown in a study by R. Kohavi et al. (R. Kohavi et al. *A Study of Cross-validation and Bootstrap for Accuracy Estimation and Model Selection*. In Ijcai, volume 14, pages 1137–1145, 1995). In stratified cross-validation, the class proportions are preserved in each fold to ensure that each fold is representative of the class proportions in the training dataset, which we will illustrate by using the StratifiedKFold iterator in scikit-learn:

```
>>> import numpy as np
>>> from sklearn.cross_validation import StratifiedKFold
>>> kfold = StratifiedKFold(y=y_train,
...                         n_folds=10,
...                         random_state=1)
>>> scores = []
>>> for k, (train, test) in enumerate(kfold):
...     pipe_lr.fit(X_train[train], y_train[train])
...     score = pipe_lr.score(X_train[test], y_train[test])
...     scores.append(score)
...     print('Fold: %s, Class dist.: %s, Acc: %.3f' % (k+1,
...             np.bincount(y_train[train]), score))
Fold: 1, Class dist.: [256 153], Acc: 0.891
Fold: 2, Class dist.: [256 153], Acc: 0.978
Fold: 3, Class dist.: [256 153], Acc: 0.978
Fold: 4, Class dist.: [256 153], Acc: 0.913
Fold: 5, Class dist.: [256 153], Acc: 0.935
Fold: 6, Class dist.: [257 153], Acc: 0.978
Fold: 7, Class dist.: [257 153], Acc: 0.933
Fold: 8, Class dist.: [257 153], Acc: 0.956
Fold: 9, Class dist.: [257 153], Acc: 0.978
Fold: 10, Class dist.: [257 153], Acc: 0.956
>>> print('CV accuracy: %.3f +/- %.3f' % (
...             np.mean(scores), np.std(scores)))
CV accuracy: 0.950 +/- 0.029
```

First, we initialized the `StratifiedKfold` iterator from the `sklearn.cross_validation` module with the class labels `y_train` in the training set, and specified the number of folds via the `n_folds` parameter. When we used the `kfold` iterator to loop through the `k` folds, we used the returned indices in `train` to fit the logistic regression pipeline that we set up at the beginning of this chapter. Using the `pile_lr` pipeline, we ensured that the samples were scaled properly (for instance, standardized) in each iteration. We then used the `test` indices to calculate the accuracy score of the model, which we collected in the `scores` list to calculate the average accuracy and the standard deviation of the estimate.

Although the previous code example was useful to illustrate how k-fold cross-validation works, scikit-learn also implements a k-fold cross-validation scorer, which allows us to evaluate our model using stratified k-fold cross-validation more efficiently:

```
>>> from sklearn.cross_validation import cross_val_score
>>> scores = cross_val_score(estimator=pipe_lr,
...                          X=X_train,
...                          y=y_train,
...                          cv=10,
...                          n_jobs=1)
>>> print('CV accuracy scores: %s' % scores)
CV accuracy scores: [ 0.89130435  0.97826087  0.97826087
                      0.91304348  0.93478261  0.97777778
                      0.93333333  0.95555556  0.97777778
                      0.95555556]
>>> print('CV accuracy: %.3f +/- %.3f' % (np.mean(scores),
np.std(scores)))
CV accuracy: 0.950 +/- 0.029
```

An extremely useful feature of the `cross_val_score` approach is that we can distribute the evaluation of the different folds across multiple CPUs on our machine. If we set the `n_jobs` parameter to 1, only one CPU will be used to evaluate the performances just like in our `StratifiedKFold` example previously. However, by setting `n_jobs=2` we could distribute the 10 rounds of cross-validation to two CPUs (if available on our machine), and by setting `n_jobs=-1`, we can use all available CPUs on our machine to do the computation in parallel.

Please note that a detailed discussion of how the variance of the generalization performance is estimated in cross-validation is beyond the scope of this book, but you can find a detailed discussion in this excellent article by M. Markatou et al (M. Markatou, H. Tian, S. Biswas, and G. M. Hripcsak. *Analysis of Variance of Cross-validation Estimators of the Generalization Error. Journal of Machine Learning Research*, 6:1127–1168, 2005).

You can also read about alternative cross-validation techniques, such as the .632 Bootstrap cross-validation method (B. Efron and R. Tibshirani. *Improvements on Cross-validation: The 632+ Bootstrap Method. Journal of the American Statistical Association*, 92(438):548–560, 1997).

Debugging algorithms with learning and validation curves

In this section, we will take a look at two very simple yet powerful diagnostic tools that can help us to improve the performance of a learning algorithm: **learning curves** and **validation curves**. In the next subsections, we will discuss how we can use learning curves to diagnose if a learning algorithm has a problem with overfitting (high variance) or underfitting (high bias). Furthermore, we will take a look at validation curves that can help us address the common issues of a learning algorithm.

Diagnosing bias and variance problems with learning curves

If a model is too complex for a given training dataset—there are too many degrees of freedom or parameters in this model—the model tends to overfit the training data and does not generalize well to unseen data. Often, it can help to collect more training samples to reduce the degree of overfitting. However, in practice, it can often be very expensive or simply not feasible to collect more data. By plotting the model training and validation accuracies as functions of the training set size, we can easily detect whether the model suffers from high variance or high bias, and whether the collection of more data could help to address this problem. But before we discuss how to plot learning curves in sckit-learn, let's discuss those two common model issues by walking through the following illustration:

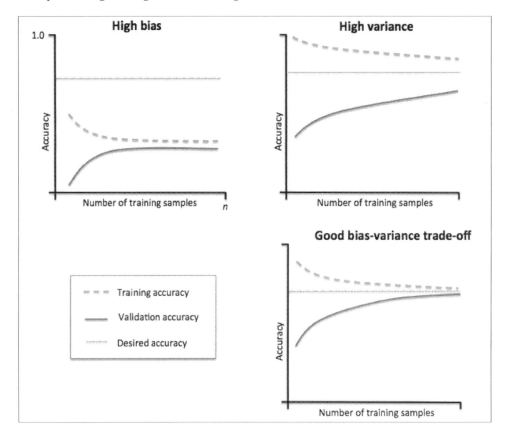

The graph in the upper-left shows a model with high bias. This model has both low training and cross-validation accuracy, which indicates that it underfits the training data. Common ways to address this issue are to increase the number of parameters of the model, for example, by collecting or constructing additional features, or by decreasing the degree of regularization, for example, in SVM or logistic regression classifiers. The graph in the upper-right shows a model that suffers from high variance, which is indicated by the large gap between the training and cross-validation accuracy. To address this problem of overfitting, we can collect more training data or reduce the complexity of the model, for example, by increasing the regularization parameter; for unregularized models, it can also help to decrease the number of features via feature selection (*Chapter 4, Building Good Training Sets – Data Preprocessing*) or feature extraction (*Chapter 5, Compressing Data via Dimensionality Reduction*). We shall note that collecting more training data decreases the chance of overfitting. However, it may not always help, for example, when the training data is extremely noisy or the model is already very close to optimal.

In the next subsection, we will see how to address those model issues using validation curves, but let's first see how we can use the learning curve function from scikit-learn to evaluate the model:

```
>>> import matplotlib.pyplot as plt
>>> from sklearn.learning_curve import learning_curve
>>> pipe_lr = Pipeline([
...             ('scl', StandardScaler()),
...             ('clf', LogisticRegression(
...                         penalty='l2', random_state=0))])
>>> train_sizes, train_scores, test_scores =\
...         learning_curve(estimator=pipe_lr,
...                        X=X_train,
...                        y=y_train,
...                        train_sizes=np.linspace(0.1, 1.0, 10),
...                        cv=10,
...                        n_jobs=1)
>>> train_mean = np.mean(train_scores, axis=1)
>>> train_std = np.std(train_scores, axis=1)
>>> test_mean = np.mean(test_scores, axis=1)
>>> test_std = np.std(test_scores, axis=1)
>>> plt.plot(train_sizes, train_mean,
...          color='blue', marker='o',
...          markersize=5,
...          label='training accuracy')
>>> plt.fill_between(train_sizes,
...                  train_mean + train_std,
...                  train_mean - train_std,
```

```
...                    alpha=0.15, color='blue')
>>> plt.plot(train_sizes, test_mean,
...          color='green', linestyle='--',
...          marker='s', markersize=5,
...          label='validation accuracy')
>>> plt.fill_between(train_sizes,
...                  test_mean + test_std,
...                  test_mean - test_std,
...                  alpha=0.15, color='green')
>>> plt.grid()
>>> plt.xlabel('Number of training samples')
>>> plt.ylabel('Accuracy')
>>> plt.legend(loc='lower right')
>>> plt.ylim([0.8, 1.0])
>>> plt.show()
```

After we have successfully executed the preceding code, we will obtain the following learning curve plot:

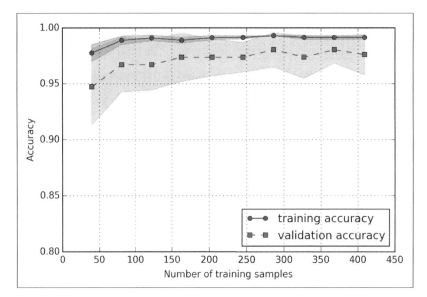

Via the `train_sizes` parameter in the `learning_curve` function, we can control the absolute or relative number of training samples that are used to generate the learning curves. Here, we set `train_sizes=np.linspace(0.1, 1.0, 10)` to use 10 evenly spaced relative intervals for the training set sizes. By default, the `learning_curve` function uses stratified k-fold cross-validation to calculate the cross-validation accuracy, and we set $k = 10$ via the `cv` parameter. Then, we simply calculate the average accuracies from the returned cross-validated training and test scores for the different sizes of the training set, which we plotted using matplotlib's `plot` function. Furthermore, we add the standard deviation of the average accuracies to the plot using the `fill_between` function to indicate the variance of the estimate.

As we can see in the preceding learning curve plot, our model performs quite well on the test dataset. However, it may be slightly overfitting the training data indicated by a relatively small, but visible, gap between the training and cross-validation accuracy curves.

Addressing overfitting and underfitting with validation curves

Validation curves are a useful tool for improving the performance of a model by addressing issues such as overfitting or underfitting. Validation curves are related to learning curves, but instead of plotting the training and test accuracies as functions of the sample size, we vary the values of the model parameters, for example, the inverse regularization parameter `C` in logistic regression. Let's go ahead and see how we create validation curves via sckit-learn:

```
>>> from sklearn.learning_curve import validation_curve
>>> param_range = [0.001, 0.01, 0.1, 1.0, 10.0, 100.0]
>>> train_scores, test_scores = validation_curve(
...                 estimator=pipe_lr,
...                 X=X_train,
...                 y=y_train,
...                 param_name='clf__C',
...                 param_range=param_range,
...                 cv=10)
>>> train_mean = np.mean(train_scores, axis=1)
>>> train_std = np.std(train_scores, axis=1)
>>> test_mean = np.mean(test_scores, axis=1)
>>> test_std = np.std(test_scores, axis=1)
```

```
>>> plt.plot(param_range, train_mean,
...          color='blue', marker='o',
...          markersize=5,
...          label='training accuracy')
>>> plt.fill_between(param_range, train_mean + train_std,
...                  train_mean - train_std, alpha=0.15,
...                  color='blue')
>>> plt.plot(param_range, test_mean,
...          color='green', linestyle='--',
...          marker='s', markersize=5,
...          label='validation accuracy')
>>> plt.fill_between(param_range,
...                  test_mean + test_std,
...                  test_mean - test_std,
...                  alpha=0.15, color='green')
>>> plt.grid()
>>> plt.xscale('log')
>>> plt.legend(loc='lower right')
>>> plt.xlabel('Parameter C')
>>> plt.ylabel('Accuracy')
>>> plt.ylim([0.8, 1.0])
>>> plt.show()
```

Using the preceding code, we obtained the validation curve plot for the parameter C:

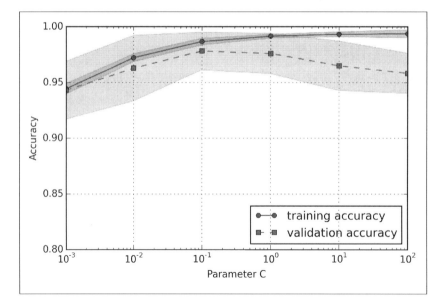

Similar to the `learning_curve` function, the `validation_curve` function uses stratified k-fold cross-validation by default to estimate the performance of the model if we are using algorithms for classification. Inside the `validation_curve` function, we specified the parameter that we wanted to evaluate. In this case, it is `C`, the inverse regularization parameter of the `LogisticRegression` classifier, which we wrote as `'clf__C'` to access the `LogisticRegression` object inside the scikit-learn pipeline for a specified value range that we set via the `param_range` parameter. Similar to the learning curve example in the previous section, we plotted the average training and cross-validation accuracies and the corresponding standard deviations.

Although the differences in the accuracy for varying values of `C` are subtle, we can see that the model slightly underfits the data when we increase the regularization strength (small values of `C`). However, for large values of `C`, it means lowering the strength of regularization, so the model tends to slightly overfit the data. In this case, the sweet spot appears to be around `C=0.1`.

Fine-tuning machine learning models via grid search

In machine learning, we have two types of parameters: those that are learned from the training data, for example, the weights in logistic regression, and the parameters of a learning algorithm that are optimized separately. The latter are the tuning parameters, also called hyperparameters, of a model, for example, the **regularization** parameter in logistic regression or the **depth** parameter of a decision tree.

In the previous section, we used validation curves to improve the performance of a model by tuning one of its hyperparameters. In this section, we will take a look at a powerful hyperparameter optimization technique called **grid search** that can further help to improve the performance of a model by finding the *optimal* combination of hyperparameter values.

Tuning hyperparameters via grid search

The approach of grid search is quite simple, it's a brute-force exhaustive search paradigm where we specify a list of values for different hyperparameters, and the computer evaluates the model performance for each combination of those to obtain the optimal set:

```
>>> from sklearn.grid_search import GridSearchCV
>>> from sklearn.svm import SVC
>>> pipe_svc = Pipeline([('scl', StandardScaler()),
...                      ('clf', SVC(random_state=1))])
>>> param_range = [0.0001, 0.001, 0.01, 0.1, 1.0, 10.0, 100.0, 1000.0]
>>> param_grid = [{'clf__C': param_range,
...                'clf__kernel': ['linear']},
...               {'clf__C': param_range,
...                'clf__gamma': param_range,
...                'clf__kernel': ['rbf']}]
>>> gs = GridSearchCV(estimator=pipe_svc,
...                   param_grid=param_grid,
...                   scoring='accuracy',
...                   cv=10,
...                   n_jobs=-1)
>>> gs = gs.fit(X_train, y_train)
>>> print(gs.best_score_)
0.978021978022
>>> print(gs.best_params_)
{'clf__C': 0.1, 'clf__kernel': 'linear'}
```

Using the preceding code, we initialized a GridSearchCV object from the sklearn.grid_search module to train and tune a **support vector machine (SVM)** pipeline. We set the param_grid parameter of GridSearchCV to a list of dictionaries to specify the parameters that we'd want to tune. For the linear SVM, we only evaluated the inverse regularization parameter C; for the RBF kernel SVM, we tuned both the C and gamma parameter. Note that the gamma parameter is specific to kernel SVMs. After we used the training data to perform the grid search, we obtained the score of the best-performing model via the best_score_ attribute and looked at its parameters, that can be accessed via the best_params_ attribute. In this particular case, the linear SVM model with 'clf__C'= 0.1' yielded the best k-fold cross-validation accuracy: 97.8 percent.

Finally, we will use the independent test dataset to estimate the performance of the best selected model, which is available via the `best_estimator_` attribute of the `GridSearchCV` object:

```
>>> clf = gs.best_estimator_
>>> clf.fit(X_train, y_train)
>>> print('Test accuracy: %.3f' % clf.score(X_test, y_test))
Test accuracy: 0.965
```

> Although grid search is a powerful approach for finding the optimal set of parameters, the evaluation of all possible parameter combinations is also computationally very expensive. An alternative approach to sampling different parameter combinations using scikit-learn is randomized search. Using the `RandomizedSearchCV` class in scikit-learn, we can draw random parameter combinations from sampling distributions with a specified budget. More details and examples for its usage can be found at `http://scikit-learn.org/stable/modules/grid_search.html#randomized-parameter-optimization`.

Algorithm selection with nested cross-validation

Using k-fold cross-validation in combination with grid search is a useful approach for fine-tuning the performance of a machine learning model by varying its hyperparameters values as we saw in the previous subsection. If we want to select among different machine learning algorithms though, another recommended approach is nested cross-validation, and in a nice study on the bias in error estimation, Varma and Simon concluded that the true error of the estimate is almost unbiased relative to the test set when nested cross-validation is used (S. Varma and R. Simon. *Bias in Error Estimation When Using Cross-validation for Model Selection.* BMC bioinformatics, 7(1):91, 2006).

In nested cross-validation, we have an outer k-fold cross-validation loop to split the data into training and test folds, and an inner loop is used to select the model using k-fold cross-validation on the training fold. After model selection, the test fold is then used to evaluate the model performance. The following figure explains the concept of nested cross-validation with five outer and two inner folds, which can be useful for large data sets where computational performance is important; this particular type of nested cross-validation is also known as **5x2 cross-validation**:

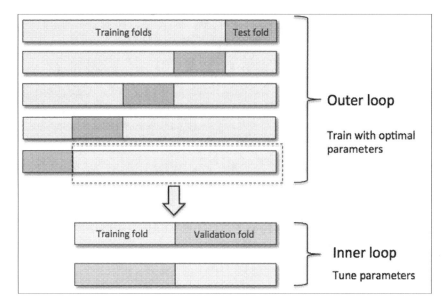

In scikit-learn, we can perform nested cross-validation as follows:

```
>>> gs = GridSearchCV(estimator=pipe_svc,
...                    param_grid=param_grid,
...                    scoring='accuracy',
...                    cv=2,
...                    n_jobs=-1)
>>> scores = cross_val_score(gs, X_train, y_train, scoring='accuracy',
cv=5)
>>> print('CV accuracy: %.3f +/- %.3f' % (
...                np.mean(scores), np.std(scores)))
CV accuracy: 0.965 +/- 0.025
```

The returned average cross-validation accuracy gives us a good estimate of what to expect if we tune the hyperparameters of a model and then use it on unseen data. For example, we can use the nested cross-validation approach to compare an SVM model to a simple decision tree classifier; for simplicity, we will only tune its depth parameter:

```
>>> from sklearn.tree import DecisionTreeClassifier
>>> gs = GridSearchCV(
...          estimator=DecisionTreeClassifier(random_state=0),
...          param_grid=[
...              {'max_depth': [1, 2, 3, 4, 5, 6, 7, None]}],
...          scoring='accuracy',
...          cv=5)
>>> scores = cross_val_score(gs,
...                          X_train,
...                          y_train,
...                          scoring='accuracy',
...                          cv=2)
>>> print('CV accuracy: %.3f +/- %.3f' % (
...                          np.mean(scores), np.std(scores)))
CV accuracy: 0.921 +/- 0.029
```

As we can see here, the nested cross-validation performance of the SVM model (97.8 percent) is notably better than the performance of the decision tree (90.8 percent). Thus, we'd expect that it might be the better choice for classifying new data that comes from the same population as this particular dataset.

Looking at different performance evaluation metrics

In the previous sections and chapters, we evaluated our models using the model accuracy, which is a useful metric to quantify the performance of a model in general. However, there are several other performance metrics that can be used to measure a model's relevance, such as **precision**, **recall**, and the **F1-score**.

Reading a confusion matrix

Before we get into the details of different scoring metrics, let's print a so-called **confusion matrix**, a matrix that lays out the performance of a learning algorithm. The confusion matrix is simply a square matrix that reports the counts of the **true positive**, **true negative**, **false positive**, and **false negative** predictions of a classifier, as shown in the following figure:

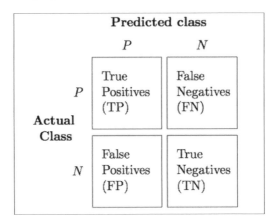

Although these metrics can be easily computed manually by comparing the true and predicted class labels, scikit-learn provides a convenient `confusion_matrix` function that we can use as follows:

```
>>> from sklearn.metrics import confusion_matrix
>>> pipe_svc.fit(X_train, y_train)
>>> y_pred = pipe_svc.predict(X_test)
>>> confmat = confusion_matrix(y_true=y_test, y_pred=y_pred)
>>> print(confmat)
[[71  1]
 [ 2 40]]
```

The array that was returned after executing the preceding code provides us with information about the different types of errors the classifier made on the test dataset that we can map onto the confusion matrix illustration in the previous figure using matplotlib's `matshow` function:

```
>>> fig, ax = plt.subplots(figsize=(2.5, 2.5))
>>> ax.matshow(confmat, cmap=plt.cm.Blues, alpha=0.3)
>>> for i in range(confmat.shape[0]):
...     for j in range(confmat.shape[1]):
...         ax.text(x=j, y=i,
...                 s=confmat[i, j],
...                 va='center', ha='center')
```

```
>>> plt.xlabel('predicted label')
>>> plt.ylabel('true label')
>>> plt.show()
```

Now, the confusion matrix plot as shown here should make the results a little bit easier to interpret:

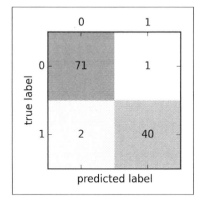

Assuming that class 1 (malignant) is the positive class in this example, our model correctly classified 71 of the samples that belong to class 0 (true negatives) and 40 samples that belong to class 1 (true positives), respectively. However, our model also incorrectly misclassified 1 sample from class 0 as class 1 (false positive), and it predicted that 2 samples are benign although it is a malignant tumor (false negatives). In the next section, we will learn how we can use this information to calculate various different error metrics.

Optimizing the precision and recall of a classification model

Both the prediction **error (ERR)** and **accuracy (ACC)** provide general information about how many samples are misclassified. The error can be understood as the sum of all false predictions divided by the number of total predictions, and the accuracy is calculated as the sum of correct predictions divided by the total number of predictions, respectively:

$$ERR = \frac{FP + FN}{FP + FN + TP + TN}$$

The prediction accuracy can then be calculated directly from the error:

$$ACC = \frac{TP + TN}{FP + FN + TP + TN} = 1 - ERR$$

The **true positive rate (TPR)** and **false positive rate (FPR)** are performance metrics that are especially useful for imbalanced class problems:

$$FPR = \frac{FP}{N} = \frac{FP}{FP + TN}$$

$$TPR = \frac{TP}{P} = \frac{TP}{FN + TP}$$

In tumor diagnosis, for example, we are more concerned about the detection of malignant tumors in order to help a patient with the appropriate treatment. However, it is also important to decrease the number of benign tumors that were incorrectly classified as malignant (false positives) to not unnecessarily concern a patient. In contrast to the FPR, the true positive rate provides useful information about the fraction of positive (or relevant) samples that were correctly identified out of the total pool of positives (**P**).

Precision (PRE) and **recall (REC)** are performance metrics that are related to those true positive and true negative rates, and in fact, recall is synonymous to the true positive rate:

$$PRE = \frac{TP}{TP + FP}$$

$$REC = TPR = \frac{TP}{P} = \frac{TP}{FN + TP}$$

In practice, often a combination of precision and recall is used, the so-called **F1-score**:

$$F1 = 2\frac{PRE \times REC}{PRE + REC}$$

These scoring metrics are all implemented in scikit-learn and can be imported from the `sklearn.metrics` module, as shown in the following snippet:

```
>>> from sklearn.metrics import precision_score
>>> from sklearn.metrics  import recall_score, f1_score
>>> print('Precision: %.3f' % precision_score(
...                 y_true=y_test, y_pred=y_pred))
Precision: 0.976
>>> print('Recall: %.3f' % recall_score(
...                 y_true=y_test, y_pred=y_pred))
Recall: 0.952
>>> print('F1: %.3f' % f1_score(
...                 y_true=y_test, y_pred=y_pred))
F1: 0.964
```

Furthermore, we can use a different scoring metric other than accuracy in `GridSearch` via the scoring parameter. A complete list of the different values that are accepted by the scoring parameter can be found at `http://scikit-learn.org/stable/modules/model_evaluation.html`.

Remember that the positive class in scikit-learn is the class that is labeled as class 1. If we want to specify a different *positive label*, we can construct our own scorer via the `make_scorer` function, which we can then directly provide as an argument to the scoring parameter in `GridSearchCV`:

```
>>> from sklearn.metrics import make_scorer, f1_score
>>> scorer = make_scorer(f1_score, pos_label=0)
>>> gs = GridSearchCV(estimator=pipe_svc,
...                   param_grid=param_grid,
...                   scoring=scorer,
...                   cv=10)
```

Plotting a receiver operating characteristic

Receiver operator characteristic (ROC) graphs are useful tools for selecting models for classification based on their performance with respect to the false positive and true positive rates, which are computed by shifting the decision threshold of the classifier. The diagonal of an ROC graph can be interpreted as random guessing, and classification models that fall below the diagonal are considered as worse than random guessing. A perfect classifier would fall into the top-left corner of the graph with a true positive rate of 1 and a false positive rate of 0. Based on the ROC curve, we can then compute the so-called **area under the curve (AUC)** to characterize the performance of a classification model.

 Similar to ROC curves, we can compute **precision-recall curves** for the different probability thresholds of a classifier. A function for plotting those precision-recall curves is also implemented in scikit-learn and is documented at `http://scikit-learn.org/stable/modules/generated/sklearn.metrics.precision_recall_curve.html`.

By executing the following code example, we will plot an ROC curve of a classifier that only uses two features from the Breast Cancer Wisconsin dataset to predict whether a tumor is benign or malignant. Although we are going to use the same logistic regression pipeline that we defined previously, we are making the classification task more challenging for the classifier so that the resulting ROC curve becomes visually more interesting. For similar reasons, we are also reducing the number of folds in the `StratifiedKFold` validator to three. The code is as follows:

```
>>> from sklearn.metrics import roc_curve, auc
>>> from scipy import interp
>>> pipe_lr = Pipeline([('scl', StandardScaler()),
...                     ('pca', PCA(n_components=2)),
...                     ('clf', LogisticRegression(penalty='l2',
...                                                random_state=0,
...                                                C=100.0))])
>>> X_train2 = X_train[:, [4, 14]]
>>> cv = StratifiedKFold(y_train,
...                      n_folds=3,
...                      random_state=1)
>>> fig = plt.figure(figsize=(7, 5))
>>> mean_tpr = 0.0
>>> mean_fpr = np.linspace(0, 1, 100)
>>> all_tpr = []

>>> for i, (train, test) in enumerate(cv):
...     probas = pipe_lr.fit(X_train2[train],
>>> y_train[train]).predict_proba(X_train2[test])
...     fpr, tpr, thresholds = roc_curve(y_train[test],
```

```
...                                probas[:, 1],
...                                pos_label=1)
...         mean_tpr += interp(mean_fpr, fpr, tpr)
...         mean_tpr[0] = 0.0
...         roc_auc = auc(fpr, tpr)
...         plt.plot(fpr,
...                  tpr,
...                  lw=1,
...                  label='ROC fold %d (area = %0.2f)'
...                         % (i+1, roc_auc))
>>> plt.plot([0, 1],
...          [0, 1],
...          linestyle='--',
...          color=(0.6, 0.6, 0.6),
...          label='random guessing')
>>> mean_tpr /= len(cv)
>>> mean_tpr[-1] = 1.0
>>> mean_auc = auc(mean_fpr, mean_tpr)
>>> plt.plot(mean_fpr, mean_tpr, 'k--',
...          label='mean ROC (area = %0.2f)' % mean_auc, lw=2)
>>> plt.plot([0, 0, 1],
...          [0, 1, 1],
...          lw=2,
...          linestyle=':',
...          color='black',
...          label='perfect performance')
>>> plt.xlim([-0.05, 1.05])
>>> plt.ylim([-0.05, 1.05])
>>> plt.xlabel('false positive rate')
>>> plt.ylabel('true positive rate')
>>> plt.title('Receiver Operator Characteristic')
>>> plt.legend(loc="lower right")
>>> plt.show()
```

In the preceding code example, we used the already familiar `StratifiedKFold` class from scikit-learn and calculated the ROC performance of the `LogisticRegression` classifier in our `pipe_lr` pipeline using the `roc_curve` function from the `sklearn.metrics` module separately for each iteration. Furthermore, we interpolated the average ROC curve from the three folds via the `interp` function that we imported from SciPy and calculated the area under the curve via the `auc` function. The resulting ROC curve indicates that there is a certain degree of variance between the different folds, and the average ROC AUC (0.75) falls between a perfect score (1.0) and random guessing (0.5):

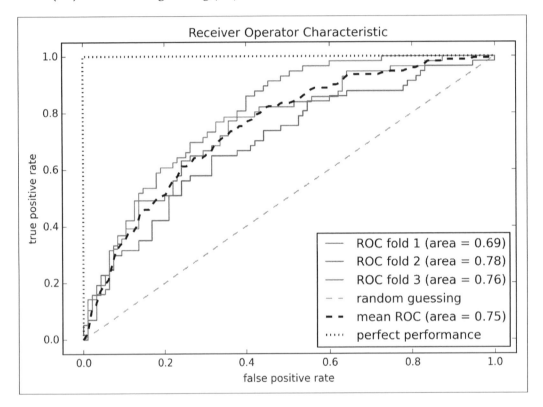

If we are just interested in the ROC AUC score, we could also directly import the `roc_auc_score` function from the `sklearn.metrics` submodule. The following code calculates the classifier's ROC AUC score on the independent test dataset after fitting it on the two-feature training set:

```
>>> pipe_lr = pipe_lr.fit(X_train2, y_train)
>>> y_pred2 = pipe_lr.predict(X_test[:, [4, 14]])
```

```
>>> from sklearn.metrics import roc_auc_score
>>> from sklearn.metrics import accuracy_score
>>> print('ROC AUC: %.3f' % roc_auc_score(
...          y_true=y_test, y_score=y_pred2))
ROC AUC: 0.662

>>> print('Accuracy: %.3f' % accuracy_score(
...          y_true=y_test, y_pred=y_pred2))
Accuracy: 0.711
```

Reporting the performance of a classifier as the ROC AUC can yield further insights in a classifier's performance with respect to imbalanced samples. However, while the accuracy score can be interpreted as a single cut-off point on a ROC curve, A. P. Bradley showed that the ROC AUC and accuracy metrics mostly agree with each other (A. P. Bradley. *The Use of the Area Under the ROC Curve in the Evaluation of Machine Learning Algorithms*. Pattern recognition, 30(7):1145–1159, 1997).

The scoring metrics for multiclass classification

The scoring metrics that we discussed in this section are specific to binary classification systems. However, scikit-learn also implements **macro** and **micro** averaging methods to extend those scoring metrics to multiclass problems via **One vs. All (OvA)** classification. The micro-average is calculated from the individual true positives, true negatives, false positives, and false negatives of the system. For example, the micro-average of the precision score in a k-class system can be calculated as follows:

$$PRE_{micro} = \frac{TP_1 + \cdots + TP_k}{TP_1 + \cdots + TP_k + FP_1 + \cdots + FP_k}$$

The macro-average is simply calculated as the average scores of the different systems:

$$PRE_{macro} = \frac{PRE_1 + \cdots + PRE_k}{k}$$

Micro-averaging is useful if we want to weight each instance or prediction equally, whereas macro-averaging weights all classes equally to evaluate the overall performance of a classifier with regard to the most frequent class labels.

If we are using binary performance metrics to evaluate multiclass classification models in scikit-learn, a normalized or weighted variant of the macro-average is used by default. The weighted macro-average is calculated by weighting the score of each class label by the number of true instances when calculating the average. The weighted macro-average is useful if we are dealing with class imbalances, that is, different numbers of instances for each label.

While the weighted macro-average is the default for multiclass problems in scikit-learn, we can specify the averaging method via the `average` parameter inside the different scoring functions that we import from the `sklearn.metrics` module, for example, the `precision_score` or `make_scorer` functions:

```
>>> pre_scorer = make_scorer(score_func=precision_score,
...                          pos_label=1,
...                          greater_is_better=True,
...                          average='micro')
```

Summary

In the beginning of this chapter, we discussed how to chain different transformation techniques and classifiers in convenient model pipelines that helped us to train and evaluate machine learning models more efficiently. We then used those pipelines to perform k-fold cross-validation, one of the essential techniques for model selection and evaluation. Using k-fold cross-validation, we plotted learning and validation curves to diagnose the common problems of learning algorithms, such as overfitting and underfitting. Using grid search, we further fine-tuned our model. We concluded this chapter by looking at a confusion matrix and various different performance metrics that can be useful to further optimize a model's performance for a specific problem task. Now, we should be well-equipped with the essential techniques to build supervised machine learning models for classification successfully.

In the next chapter, we will take a look at ensemble methods, methods that allow us to combine multiple models and classification algorithms to boost the predictive performance of a machine learning system even further.

7
Combining Different Models for Ensemble Learning

In the previous chapter, we focused on the best practices for tuning and evaluating different models for classification. In this chapter, we will build upon these techniques and explore different methods for constructing a set of classifiers that can often have a better predictive performance than any of its individual members. You will learn how to:

- Make predictions based on majority voting
- Reduce overfitting by drawing random combinations of the training set with repetition
- Build powerful models from *weak learners* that learn from their mistakes

Learning with ensembles

The goal behind **ensemble methods** is to combine different classifiers into a meta-classifier that has a better generalization performance than each individual classifier alone. For example, assuming that we collected predictions from 10 experts, ensemble methods would allow us to strategically combine these predictions by the 10 experts to come up with a prediction that is more accurate and robust than the predictions by each individual expert. As we will see later in this chapter, there are several different approaches for creating an ensemble of classifiers. In this section, we will introduce a basic perception about how ensembles work and why they are typically recognized for yielding a good generalization performance.

In this chapter, we will focus on the most popular ensemble methods that use the **majority voting** principle. Majority voting simply means that we select the class label that has been predicted by the majority of classifiers, that is, received more than 50 percent of the votes. Strictly speaking, the term **majority vote** refers to binary class settings only. However, it is easy to generalize the majority voting principle to multi-class settings, which is called **plurality voting**. Here, we select the class label that received the most votes (mode). The following diagram illustrates the concept of majority and plurality voting for an ensemble of 10 classifiers where each unique symbol (triangle, square, and circle) represents a unique class label:

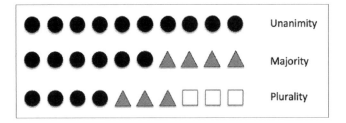

Using the training set, we start by training m different classifiers ($C_1,...,C_m$). Depending on the technique, the ensemble can be built from different classification algorithms, for example, decision trees, support vector machines, logistic regression classifiers, and so on. Alternatively, we can also use the same base classification algorithm fitting different subsets of the training set. One prominent example of this approach would be the random forest algorithm, which combines different decision tree classifiers. The following diagram illustrates the concept of a general ensemble approach using majority voting:

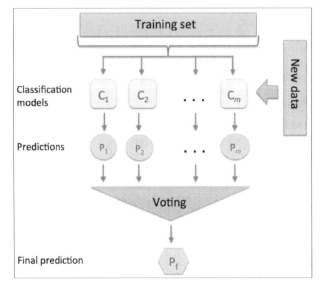

To predict a class label via a simple majority or plurality voting, we combine the predicted class labels of each individual classifier C_j and select the class label $\hat{y}$ that received the most votes:

$$\hat{y} = mode\{C_1(x), C_2(x), \ldots, C_m(x)\}$$

For example, in a binary classification task where $class1 = -1$ and $class2 = +1$, we can write the majority vote prediction as follows:

$$C(x) = sign\left[\sum_j^m C_j(x)\right] = \begin{cases} 1 & if \sum_i C_j(x) \geq 0 \\ -1 & otherwise \end{cases}$$

To illustrate why ensemble methods can work better than individual classifiers alone, let's apply the simple concepts of combinatorics. For the following example, we make the assumption that all n base classifiers for a binary classification task have an equal error rate ε. Furthermore, we assume that the classifiers are independent and the error rates are not correlated. Under those assumptions, we can simply express the error probability of an ensemble of base classifiers as a probability mass function of a binomial distribution:

$$P(y \geq k) = \sum_k^n \binom{n}{k} \varepsilon^k (1-\varepsilon)^{n-k} = \varepsilon_{ensemble}$$

Here, $\binom{n}{k}$ is the binomial coefficient n choose k. In other words, we compute the probability that the prediction of the ensemble is wrong. Now let's take a look at a more concrete example of 11 base classifiers ($n = 11$) with an error rate of 0.25 ($\varepsilon = 0.25$):

$$P(y \geq k) = \sum_{k=6}^{11} \binom{11}{k} 0.25^k (1-\varepsilon)^{11-k} = 0.034$$

As we can see, the error rate of the ensemble (0.034) is much lower than the error rate of each individual classifier (0.25) if all the assumptions are met. Note that, in this simplified illustration, a 50-50 split by an even number of classifiers n is treated as an error, whereas this is only true half of the time. To compare such an idealistic ensemble classifier to a base classifier over a range of different base error rates, let's implement the probability mass function in Python:

```
>>> from scipy.misc import comb
>>> import math
>>> def ensemble_error(n_classifier, error):
...      k_start = math.ceil(n_classifier / 2.0)
...      probs = [comb(n_classifier, k) *
...              error**k *
...              (1-error)**(n_classifier - k)
...              for k in range(k_start, n_classifier + 1)]
...      return sum(probs)
>>> ensemble_error(n_classifier=11, error=0.25)
0.034327507019042969
```

After we've implemented the `ensemble_error` function, we can compute the ensemble error rates for a range of different base errors from 0.0 to 1.0 to visualize the relationship between ensemble and base errors in a line graph:

```
>>> import numpy as np
>>> error_range = np.arange(0.0, 1.01, 0.01)
>>> ens_errors = [ensemble_error(n_classifier=11, error=error)
...               for error in error_range]
>>> import matplotlib.pyplot as plt
>>> plt.plot(error_range, ens_errors,
...          label='Ensemble error',
...          linewidth=2)
>>> plt.plot(error_range, error_range,
...          linestyle='--', label='Base error',
...          linewidth=2)
>>> plt.xlabel('Base error')
>>> plt.ylabel('Base/Ensemble error')
>>> plt.legend(loc='upper left')
>>> plt.grid()
>>> plt.show()
```

As we can see in the resulting plot, the error probability of an ensemble is always better than the error of an individual base classifier as long as the base classifiers perform better than random guessing ($\varepsilon < 0.5$). Note that the y-axis depicts the base error (dotted line) as well as the ensemble error (continuous line):

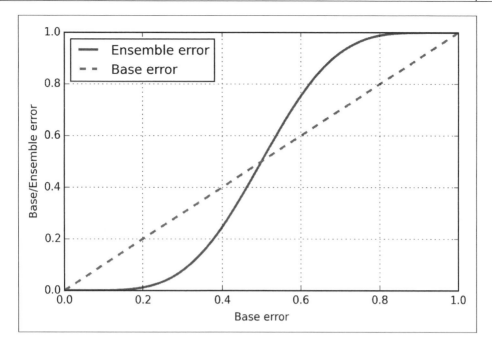

Implementing a simple majority vote classifier

After the short introduction to ensemble learning in the previous section, let's start with a warm-up exercise and implement a simple ensemble classifier for majority voting in Python. Although the following algorithm also generalizes to multi-class settings via plurality voting, we will use the term *majority voting* for simplicity as is also often done in literature.

The algorithm that we are going to implement will allow us to combine different classification algorithms associated with individual weights for confidence. Our goal is to build a stronger meta-classifier that balances out the individual classifiers' weaknesses on a particular dataset. In more precise mathematical terms, we can write the weighted majority vote as follows:

$$\hat{y} = \arg\max_i \sum_{j=1}^{m} w_j \chi_A \left(C_j \left(\boldsymbol{x} \right) = i \right)$$

Here, w_j is a weight associated with a base classifier, C_j, $\hat{y}$ is the predicted class label of the ensemble, χ_A (Greek *chi*) is the characteristic function $[C_j(x)=i \in A]$, and A is the set of unique class labels. For equal weights, we can simplify this equation and write it as follows:

$$\hat{y} = mode\{C_1(x), C_2(x), \ldots, C_m(x)\}$$

To better understand the concept of *weighting*, we will now take a look at a more concrete example. Let's assume that we have an ensemble of three base classifiers C_j ($j \in \{0,1\}$) and want to predict the class label of a given sample instance x. Two out of three base classifiers predict the class label 0, and one C_3 predicts that the sample belongs to class 1. If we weight the predictions of each base classifier equally, the majority vote will predict that the sample belongs to class 0:

$$C_1(x) \rightarrow 0, \ C_2(x) \rightarrow 0, \ C_3(x) \rightarrow 1$$

$$\hat{y} = mode\{0,0,1\} = 0$$

Now let's assign a weight of 0.6 to C_3 and weight C_1 and C_2 by a coefficient of 0.2, respectively.

$$\hat{y} = \arg\max_i \sum_{j=1}^{m} w_j \chi_A \left(C_j(x) = i \right)$$

$$= \arg\max_i \left[0.2 \times i_0 + 0.2 \times i_0 + 0.6 \times i_1 \right] = 1$$

More intuitively, since $3 \times 0.2 = 0.6$, we can say that the prediction made by C_3 has three times more weight than the predictions by C_1 or C_2, respectively. We can write this as follows:

$$\hat{y} = mode\{0,0,1,1,1\} = 1$$

To translate the concept of the weighted majority vote into Python code, we can use NumPy's convenient `argmax` and `bincount` functions:

```
>>> import numpy as np
>>> np.argmax(np.bincount([0, 0, 1],
...            weights=[0.2, 0.2, 0.6]))
1
```

As discussed in *Chapter 3, A Tour of Machine Learning Classifiers Using Scikit-learn*, certain classifiers in scikit-learn can also return the probability of a predicted class label via the `predict_proba` method. Using the predicted class probabilities instead of the class labels for majority voting can be useful if the classifiers in our ensemble are well calibrated. The modified version of the majority vote for predicting class labels from probabilities can be written as follows:

$$\hat{y} = \arg\max_i \sum_{j=1}^{m} w_j p_{ij}$$

Here, p_{ij} is the predicted probability of the *jth* classifier for class label i.

To continue with our previous example, let's assume that we have a binary classification problem with class labels $i \in \{0,1\}$ and an ensemble of three classifiers C_j ($j \in \{1,2,3\}$). Let's assume that the classifier C_j returns the following class membership probabilities for a particular sample x:

$$C_1(x) \rightarrow [0.9,0.1], \; C_2(x) \rightarrow [0.8,0.2], \; C_3(x) \rightarrow [0.4,0.6]$$

We can then calculate the individual class probabilities as follows:

$$p(i_0 \mid x) = 0.2 \times 0.9 + 0.2 \times 0.8 + 0.6 \times 0.4 = 0.58$$

$$p(i_1 \mid x) = 0.2 \times 0.1 + 0.2 \times 0.2 + 0.6 \times 0.06 = 0.42$$

$$\hat{y} = \arg\max_i \left[p(i_0 \mid x), p(i_1 \mid x) \right] = 0$$

To implement the weighted majority vote based on class probabilities, we can again make use of NumPy using numpy.average and np.argmax:

```
>>> ex = np.array([[0.9, 0.1],
...                [0.8, 0.2],
...                [0.4, 0.6]])
>>> p = np.average(ex, axis=0, weights=[0.2, 0.2, 0.6])
>>> p
array([ 0.58,  0.42])
>>> np.argmax(p)
0
```

Putting everything together, let's now implement a MajorityVoteClassifier in Python:

```
from sklearn.base import BaseEstimator
from sklearn.base import ClassifierMixin
from sklearn.preprocessing import LabelEncoder
from sklearn.externals import six
from sklearn.base import clone
from sklearn.pipeline import _name_estimators
import numpy as np
import operator


class MajorityVoteClassifier(BaseEstimator,
                             ClassifierMixin):
    """ A majority vote ensemble classifier

    Parameters
    ----------
    classifiers : array-like, shape = [n_classifiers]
      Different classifiers for the ensemble

    vote : str, {'classlabel', 'probability'}
      Default: 'classlabel'
      If 'classlabel' the prediction is based on
      the argmax of class labels. Else if
      'probability', the argmax of the sum of
      probabilities is used to predict the class label
      (recommended for calibrated classifiers).

    weights : array-like, shape = [n_classifiers]
      Optional, default: None
      If a list of `int` or `float` values are
```

provided, the classifiers are weighted by
importance; Uses uniform weights if `weights=None`.

```python
"""
def __init__(self, classifiers,
             vote='classlabel', weights=None):

    self.classifiers = classifiers
    self.named_classifiers = {key: value for
                              key, value in
                              _name_estimators(classifiers)}
    self.vote = vote
    self.weights = weights

def fit(self, X, y):
    """ Fit classifiers.

    Parameters
    ----------
    X : {array-like, sparse matrix},
        shape = [n_samples, n_features]
        Matrix of training samples.

    y : array-like, shape = [n_samples]
        Vector of target class labels.

    Returns
    -------
    self : object

    """
    # Use LabelEncoder to ensure class labels start
    # with 0, which is important for np.argmax
    # call in self.predict
    self.lablenc_ = LabelEncoder()
    self.lablenc_.fit(y)
    self.classes_ = self.lablenc_.classes_
    self.classifiers_ = []
    for clf in self.classifiers:
        fitted_clf = clone(clf).fit(X,
                          self.lablenc_.transform(y))
        self.classifiers_.append(fitted_clf)
    return self
```

I added a lot of comments to the code to better understand the individual parts. However, before we implement the remaining methods, let's take a quick break and discuss some of the code that may look confusing at first. We used the parent classes `BaseEstimator` and `ClassifierMixin` to get some base functionality *for free*, including the methods `get_params` and `set_params` to set and return the classifier's parameters as well as the `score` method to calculate the prediction accuracy, respectively. Also note that we imported `six` to make the `MajorityVoteClassifier` compatible with Python 2.7.

Next we will add the `predict` method to predict the class label via majority vote based on the class labels if we initialize a new `MajorityVoteClassifier` object with `vote='classlabel'`. Alternatively, we will be able to initialize the ensemble classifier with `vote='probability'` to predict the class label based on the class membership probabilities. Furthermore, we will also add a `predict_proba` method to return the average probabilities, which is useful to compute the **Receiver Operator Characteristic area under the curve (ROC AUC)**.

```python
def predict(self, X):
    """ Predict class labels for X.

    Parameters
    ----------
    X : {array-like, sparse matrix},
        Shape = [n_samples, n_features]
        Matrix of training samples.

    Returns
    ----------
    maj_vote : array-like, shape = [n_samples]
        Predicted class labels.

    """
    if self.vote == 'probability':
        maj_vote = np.argmax(self.predict_proba(X),
                             axis=1)
    else:  # 'classlabel' vote

        # Collect results from clf.predict calls
        predictions = np.asarray([clf.predict(X)
                                  for clf in
                                  self.classifiers_]).T

        maj_vote = np.apply_along_axis(
                       lambda x:
                       np.argmax(np.bincount(x,
```

```
                               weights=self.weights)),
                    axis=1,
                    arr=predictions)
    maj_vote = self.lablenc_.inverse_transform(maj_vote)
    return maj_vote

def predict_proba(self, X):
    """ Predict class probabilities for X.

    Parameters
    ----------
    X : {array-like, sparse matrix},
        shape = [n_samples, n_features]
        Training vectors, where n_samples is
        the number of samples and
        n_features is the number of features.

    Returns
    ----------
    avg_proba : array-like,
        shape = [n_samples, n_classes]
        Weighted average probability for
        each class per sample.

    """
    probas = np.asarray([clf.predict_proba(X)
                    for clf in self.classifiers_])
    avg_proba = np.average(probas,
                    axis=0, weights=self.weights)
    return avg_proba

def get_params(self, deep=True):
    """ Get classifier parameter names for GridSearch"""
    if not deep:
        return super(MajorityVoteClassifier,
                self).get_params(deep=False)
    else:
        out = self.named_classifiers.copy()
        for name, step in\
                six.iteritems(self.named_classifiers):
            for key, value in six.iteritems(
                    step.get_params(deep=True)):
                out['%s__%s' % (name, key)] = value
        return out
```

Also, note that we defined our own modified version of the `get_params` methods to use the `_name_estimators` function in order to access the parameters of individual classifiers in the ensemble. This may look a little bit complicated at first, but it will make perfect sense when we use grid search for hyperparameter-tuning in later sections.

> Although our `MajorityVoteClassifier` implementation is very useful for demonstration purposes, I also implemented a more sophisticated version of the majority vote classifier in scikit-learn. It will become available as `sklearn.ensemble.VotingClassifier` in the next release version (v0.17).

Combining different algorithms for classification with majority vote

Now it is about time to put the `MajorityVoteClassifier` that we implemented in the previous section into action. But first, let's prepare a dataset that we can test it on. Since we are already familiar with techniques to load datasets from CSV files, we will take a shortcut and load the **Iris** dataset from scikit-learn's dataset module. Furthermore, we will only select two features, **sepal width** and **petal length**, to make the classification task more challenging. Although our `MajorityVoteClassifier` generalizes to multiclass problems, we will only classify flower samples from the two classes, **Iris-Versicolor** and **Iris-Virginica**, to compute the **ROC AUC**. The code is as follows:

```
>>> from sklearn import datasets
>>> from sklearn.cross_validation import train_test_split
>>> from sklearn.preprocessing import StandardScaler
>>> from sklearn.preprocessing import LabelEncoder
>>> iris = datasets.load_iris()
>>> X, y = iris.data[50:, [1, 2]], iris.target[50:]
>>> le = LabelEncoder()
>>> y = le.fit_transform(y)
```

Note that scikit-learn uses the `predict_proba` method (if applicable) to compute the ROC AUC score. In *Chapter 3, A Tour of Machine Learning Classifiers Using Scikit-learn*, we saw how the class probabilities are computed in logistic regression models. In decision trees, the probabilities are calculated from a frequency vector that is created for each node at training time. The vector collects the frequency values of each class label computed from the class label distribution at that node. Then the frequencies are normalized so that they sum up to 1. Similarly, the class labels of the k-nearest neighbors are aggregated to return the normalized class label frequencies in the k-nearest neighbors algorithm. Although the normalized probabilities returned by both the decision tree and k-nearest neighbors classifier may look similar to the probabilities obtained from a logistic regression model, we have to be aware that these are actually not derived from probability mass functions.

Next we split the Iris samples into 50 percent training and 50 percent test data:

```
>>> X_train, X_test, y_train, y_test =\
...         train_test_split(X, y,
                                test_size=0.5,
                                random_state=1)
```

Using the training dataset, we now will train three different classifiers—a logistic regression classifier, a decision tree classifier, and a k-nearest neighbors classifier—and look at their individual performances via a 10-fold cross-validation on the training dataset before we combine them into an ensemble classifier:

```
>>> from sklearn.cross_validation import cross_val_score
>>> from sklearn.linear_model import LogisticRegression
>>> from sklearn.tree import DecisionTreeClassifier
>>> from sklearn.neighbors import KNeighborsClassifier
>>> from sklearn.pipeline import Pipeline
>>> import numpy as np
>>> clf1 = LogisticRegression(penalty='l2',
...                         C=0.001,
...                         random_state=0)
>>> clf2 = DecisionTreeClassifier(max_depth=1,
...                             criterion='entropy',
...                             random_state=0)
>>> clf3 = KNeighborsClassifier(n_neighbors=1,
...                             p=2,
...                             metric='minkowski')
>>> pipe1 = Pipeline([['sc', StandardScaler()],
...                     ['clf', clf1]])
```

```
>>> pipe3 = Pipeline([['sc', StandardScaler()],
...                    ['clf', clf3]])
>>> clf_labels = ['Logistic Regression', 'Decision Tree', 'KNN']
>>> print('10-fold cross validation:\n')
>>> for clf, label in zip([pipe1, clf2, pipe3], clf_labels):
...     scores = cross_val_score(estimator=clf,
>>>                              X=X_train,
>>>                              y=y_train,
>>>                              cv=10,
>>>                              scoring='roc_auc')
>>>     print("ROC AUC: %0.2f (+/- %0.2f) [%s]"
...           % (scores.mean(), scores.std(), label))
```

The output that we receive, as shown in the following snippet, shows that the predictive performances of the individual classifiers are almost equal:

```
10-fold cross validation:

ROC AUC: 0.92 (+/- 0.20) [Logistic Regression]
ROC AUC: 0.92 (+/- 0.15) [Decision Tree]
ROC AUC: 0.93 (+/- 0.10) [KNN]
```

You may be wondering why we trained the logistic regression and k-nearest neighbors classifier as part of a **pipeline**. The reason behind it is that, as discussed in *Chapter 3, A Tour of Machine Learning Classifiers Using Scikit-learn*, both the logistic regression and k-nearest neighbors algorithms (using the Euclidean distance metric) are not scale-invariant in contrast with decision trees. Although the Iris features are all measured on the same scale (cm), it is a good habit to work with standardized features.

Now let's move on to the more exciting part and combine the individual classifiers for majority rule voting in our MajorityVoteClassifier:

```
>>> mv_clf = MajorityVoteClassifier(
...              classifiers=[pipe1, clf2, pipe3])
>>> clf_labels += ['Majority Voting']
>>> all_clf = [pipe1, clf2, pipe3, mv_clf]
>>> for clf, label in zip(all_clf, clf_labels):
...     scores = cross_val_score(estimator=clf,
...                              X=X_train,
...                              y=y_train,
...                              cv=10,
...                              scoring='roc_auc')
...     print("Accuracy: %0.2f (+/- %0.2f) [%s]"
...           % (scores.mean(), scores.std(), label))
```

```
ROC AUC: 0.92 (+/- 0.20) [Logistic Regression]
ROC AUC: 0.92 (+/- 0.15) [Decision Tree]
ROC AUC: 0.93 (+/- 0.10) [KNN]
ROC AUC: 0.97 (+/- 0.10) [Majority Voting]
```

As we can see, the performance of the `MajorityVotingClassifier` has substantially improved over the individual classifiers in the 10-fold cross-validation evaluation.

Evaluating and tuning the ensemble classifier

In this section, we are going to compute the ROC curves from the test set to check if the `MajorityVoteClassifier` generalizes well to unseen data. We should remember that the test set is not to be used for model selection; its only purpose is to report an unbiased estimate of the generalization performance of a classifier system. The code is as follows:

```
>>> from sklearn.metrics import roc_curve
>>> from sklearn.metrics import auc
>>> colors = ['black', 'orange', 'blue', 'green']
>>> linestyles = [':', '--', '-.', '-']
>>> for clf, label, clr, ls \
...         in zip(all_clf, clf_labels, colors, linestyles):
...     # assuming the label of the positive class is 1
...     y_pred = clf.fit(X_train,
...                      y_train).predict_proba(X_test)[:, 1]
...     fpr, tpr, thresholds = roc_curve(y_true=y_test,
...                                      y_score=y_pred)
...     roc_auc = auc(x=fpr, y=tpr)
...     plt.plot(fpr, tpr,
...             color=clr,
...             linestyle=ls,
...             label='%s (auc = %0.2f)' % (label, roc_auc))
>>> plt.legend(loc='lower right')
>>> plt.plot([0, 1], [0, 1],
...          linestyle='--',
...          color='gray',
...          linewidth=2)
>>> plt.xlim([-0.1, 1.1])
>>> plt.ylim([-0.1, 1.1])
>>> plt.grid()
>>> plt.xlabel('False Positive Rate')
>>> plt.ylabel('True Positive Rate')
>>> plt.show()
```

As we can see in the resulting ROC, the ensemble classifier also performs well on the test set (*ROC AUC* = *0.95*), whereas the k-nearest neighbors classifier seems to be overfitting the training data (training *ROC AUC* = *0.93*, test *ROC AUC* = *0.86*):

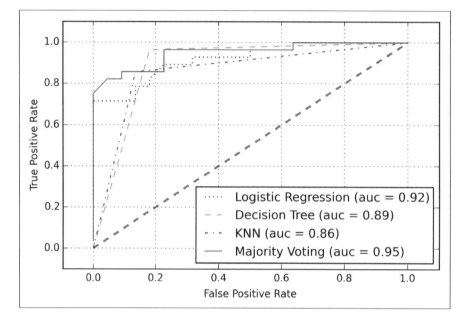

Since we only selected two features for the classification examples, it would be interesting to see what the decision region of the ensemble classifier actually looks like. Although it is not necessary to standardize the training features prior to model fitting because our logistic regression and k-nearest neighbors pipelines will automatically take care of this, we will standardize the training set so that the decision regions of the decision tree will be on the same scale for visual purposes. The code is as follows:

```
>>> sc = StandardScaler()
>>> X_train_std = sc.fit_transform(X_train)
>>> from itertools import product
>>> x_min = X_train_std[:, 0].min() - 1
>>> x_max = X_train_std[:, 0].max() + 1
>>> y_min = X_train_std[:, 1].min() - 1
>>> y_max = X_train_std[:, 1].max() + 1
```

```
>>> xx, yy = np.meshgrid(np.arange(x_min, x_max, 0.1),
...                      np.arange(y_min, y_max, 0.1))
>>> f, axarr = plt.subplots(nrows=2, ncols=2,
...                         sharex='col',
...                         sharey='row',
...                         figsize=(7, 5))
>>> for idx, clf, tt in zip(product([0, 1], [0, 1]),
...                         all_clf, clf_labels):
...     clf.fit(X_train_std, y_train)
...     Z = clf.predict(np.c_[xx.ravel(), yy.ravel()])
...     Z = Z.reshape(xx.shape)
...     axarr[idx[0], idx[1]].contourf(xx, yy, Z, alpha=0.3)
...     axarr[idx[0], idx[1]].scatter(X_train_std[y_train==0, 0],
...                                   X_train_std[y_train==0, 1],
...                                   c='blue',
...                                   marker='^',
...                                   s=50)
...     axarr[idx[0], idx[1]].scatter(X_train_std[y_train==1, 0],
...                                   X_train_std[y_train==1, 1],
...                                   c='red',
...                                   marker='o',
...                                   s=50)
...     axarr[idx[0], idx[1]].set_title(tt)
>>> plt.text(-3.5, -4.5,
...          s='Sepal width [standardized]',
...          ha='center', va='center', fontsize=12)
>>> plt.text(-10.5, 4.5,
...          s='Petal length [standardized]',
...          ha='center', va='center',
...          fontsize=12, rotation=90)
>>> plt.show()
```

Interestingly but also as expected, the decision regions of the ensemble classifier seem to be a hybrid of the decision regions from the individual classifiers. At first glance, the majority vote decision boundary looks a lot like the decision boundary of the k-nearest neighbor classifier. However, we can see that it is orthogonal to the *y* axis for *sepal width* ≥ 1, just like the decision tree stump:

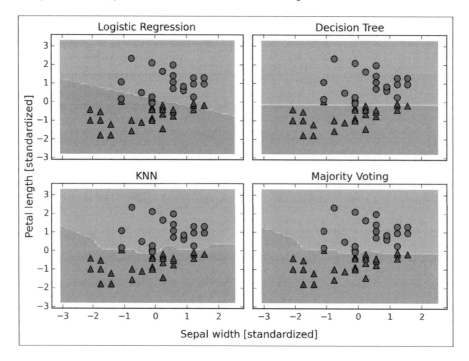

Before you learn how to tune the individual classifier parameters for ensemble classification, let's call the `get_params` method to get a basic idea of how we can access the individual parameters inside a `GridSearch` object:

```
>>> mv_clf.get_params()
{'decisiontreeclassifier': DecisionTreeClassifier(class_weight=None,
criterion='entropy', max_depth=1,
            max_features=None, max_leaf_nodes=None, min_samples_
leaf=1,
            min_samples_split=2, min_weight_fraction_leaf=0.0,
            random_state=0, splitter='best'),
 'decisiontreeclassifier__class_weight': None,
 'decisiontreeclassifier__criterion': 'entropy',
 [...]
 'decisiontreeclassifier__random_state': 0,
 'decisiontreeclassifier__splitter': 'best',
```

```
 'pipeline-1': Pipeline(steps=[('sc', StandardScaler(copy=True, with_
mean=True, with_std=True)), ('clf', LogisticRegression(C=0.001, class_
weight=None, dual=False, fit_intercept=True,
          intercept_scaling=1, max_iter=100, multi_class='ovr',
          penalty='l2', random_state=0, solver='liblinear',
tol=0.0001,
          verbose=0))]),
 'pipeline-1__clf': LogisticRegression(C=0.001, class_weight=None,
dual=False, fit_intercept=True,
          intercept_scaling=1, max_iter=100, multi_class='ovr',
          penalty='l2', random_state=0, solver='liblinear',
tol=0.0001,
          verbose=0),
 'pipeline-1__clf__C': 0.001,
 'pipeline-1__clf__class_weight': None,
 'pipeline-1__clf__dual': False,
 [...]
 'pipeline-1__sc__with_std': True,
 'pipeline-2': Pipeline(steps=[('sc', StandardScaler(copy=True, with_
mean=True, with_std=True)), ('clf', KNeighborsClassifier(algorithm='au
to', leaf_size=30, metric='minkowski',
          metric_params=None, n_neighbors=1, p=2,
weights='uniform'))]),
 'pipeline-2__clf': KNeighborsClassifier(algorithm='auto', leaf_
size=30, metric='minkowski',
          metric_params=None, n_neighbors=1, p=2,
weights='uniform'),
 'pipeline-2__clf__algorithm': 'auto',
 [...]
 'pipeline-2__sc__with_std': True}
```

Based on the values returned by the `get_params` method, we now know how to access the individual classifier's attributes. Let's now tune the inverse regularization parameter C of the logistic regression classifier and the decision tree depth via a grid search for demonstration purposes. The code is as follows:

```
>>> from sklearn.grid_search import GridSearchCV
>>> params = {'decisiontreeclassifier__max_depth': [1, 2],
...           'pipeline-1__clf__C': [0.001, 0.1, 100.0]}
>>> grid = GridSearchCV(estimator=mv_clf,
...                     param_grid=params,
...                     cv=10,
...                     scoring='roc_auc')
>>> grid.fit(X_train, y_train)
```

After the grid search has completed, we can print the different hyperparameter value combinations and the average ROC AUC scores computed via 10-fold cross-validation. The code is as follows:

```
>>> for params, mean_score, scores in grid.grid_scores_:
...     print("%0.3f+/-%0.2f %r"
...          % (mean_score, scores.std() / 2, params))
0.967+/-0.05 {'pipeline-1__clf__C': 0.001, 'decisiontreeclassifier__
max_depth': 1}
0.967+/-0.05 {'pipeline-1__clf__C': 0.1, 'decisiontreeclassifier__max_
depth': 1}
1.000+/-0.00 {'pipeline-1__clf__C': 100.0, 'decisiontreeclassifier__
max_depth': 1}
0.967+/-0.05 {'pipeline-1__clf__C': 0.001, 'decisiontreeclassifier__
max_depth': 2}
0.967+/-0.05 {'pipeline-1__clf__C': 0.1, 'decisiontreeclassifier__max_
depth': 2}
1.000+/-0.00 {'pipeline-1__clf__C': 100.0, 'decisiontreeclassifier__
max_depth': 2}

>>> print('Best parameters: %s' % grid.best_params_)
Best parameters: {'pipeline-1__clf__C': 100.0,
'decisiontreeclassifier__max_depth': 1}

>>> print('Accuracy: %.2f' % grid.best_score_)
Accuracy: 1.00
```

As we can see, we get the best cross-validation results when we choose a lower regularization strength (C = 100.0) whereas the tree depth does not seem to affect the performance at all, suggesting that a decision stump is sufficient to separate the data. To remind ourselves that it is a bad practice to use the test dataset more than once for model evaluation, we are not going to estimate the generalization performance of the tuned hyperparameters in this section. We will move on swiftly to an alternative approach for ensemble learning: **bagging**.

The majority vote approach we implemented in this section is sometimes also referred to as **stacking**. However, the stacking algorithm is more typically used in combination with a logistic regression model that predicts the final class label using the predictions of the individual classifiers in the ensemble as input, which has been described in more detail by David H. Wolpert in D. H. Wolpert. *Stacked generalization*. Neural networks, 5(2):241–259, 1992.

Bagging – building an ensemble of classifiers from bootstrap samples

Bagging is an ensemble learning technique that is closely related to the `MajorityVoteClassifier` that we implemented in the previous section, as illustrated in the following diagram:

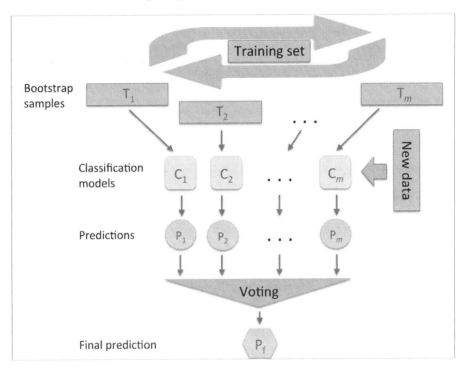

However, instead of using the same training set to fit the individual classifiers in the ensemble, we draw bootstrap samples (random samples with replacement) from the initial training set, which is why bagging is also known as **bootstrap aggregating**. To provide a more concrete example of how bootstrapping works, let's consider the example shown in the following figure. Here, we have seven different training instances (denoted as indices 1-7) that are sampled randomly with replacement in each round of bagging. Each bootstrap sample is then used to fit a classifier C_j, which is most typically an unpruned decision tree:

Sample indices	Bagging round 1	Bagging round 2	...
1	2	7	...
2	2	3	...
3	1	2	...
4	3	1	...
5	7	1	...
6	2	7	...
7	4	7	...
	C_1	C_2	C_m

Bagging is also related to the random forest classifier that we introduced in *Chapter 3, A Tour of Machine Learning Classifiers Using Scikit-learn*. In fact, random forests are a special case of bagging where we also use random feature subsets to fit the individual decision trees. Bagging was first proposed by Leo Breiman in a technical report in 1994; he also showed that bagging can improve the accuracy of unstable models and decrease the degree of overfitting. I highly recommend you read about his research in L. Breiman. *Bagging Predictors*. Machine Learning, 24(2):123–140, 1996, which is freely available online, to learn more about bagging.

To see bagging in action, let's create a more complex classification problem using the **Wine** dataset that we introduced in *Chapter 4, Building Good Training Sets – Data Preprocessing*. Here, we will only consider the Wine classes 2 and 3, and we select two features: **Alcohol** and **Hue**.

```
>>> import pandas as pd
>>> df_wine = pd.read_csv('https://archive.ics.uci.edu/ml/machine-
learning-databases/wine/wine.data', header=None)
>>> df_wine.columns = ['Class label', 'Alcohol',
...                    'Malic acid', 'Ash',
...                    'Alcalinity of ash',
...                    'Magnesium', 'Total phenols',
...                    'Flavanoids', 'Nonflavanoid phenols',
...                    'Proanthocyanins',
...                    'Color intensity', 'Hue',
...                    'OD280/OD315 of diluted wines',
...                    'Proline']
>>> df_wine = df_wine[df_wine['Class label'] != 1]
>>> y = df_wine['Class label'].values
>>> X = df_wine[['Alcohol', 'Hue']].values
```

Next we encode the class labels into binary format and split the dataset into 60 percent training and 40 percent test set, respectively:

```
>>> from sklearn.preprocessing import LabelEncoder
>>> from sklearn.cross_validation import train_test_split
>>> le = LabelEncoder()
>>> y = le.fit_transform(y)
>>> X_train, X_test, y_train, y_test =\
...         train_test_split(X, y,
...                          test_size=0.40,
...                          random_state=1)
```

A `BaggingClassifier` algorithm is already implemented in scikit-learn, which we can import from the `ensemble` submodule. Here, we will use an unpruned decision tree as the base classifier and create an ensemble of 500 decision trees fitted on different bootstrap samples of the training dataset:

```
>>> from sklearn.ensemble import BaggingClassifier
>>> tree = DecisionTreeClassifier(criterion='entropy',
...                               max_depth=None,
...                               random_state=1)
>>> bag = BaggingClassifier(base_estimator=tree,
```

```
...                        n_estimators=500,
...                        max_samples=1.0,
...                        max_features=1.0,
...                        bootstrap=True,
...                        bootstrap_features=False,
...                        n_jobs=1,
...                        random_state=1)
```

Next we will calculate the accuracy score of the prediction on the training and test dataset to compare the performance of the bagging classifier to the performance of a single unpruned decision tree:

```
>>> from sklearn.metrics import accuracy_score
>>> tree = tree.fit(X_train, y_train)
>>> y_train_pred = tree.predict(X_train)
>>> y_test_pred = tree.predict(X_test)
>>> tree_train = accuracy_score(y_train, y_train_pred)
>>> tree_test = accuracy_score(y_test, y_test_pred)
>>> print('Decision tree train/test accuracies %.3f/%.3f'
...         % (tree_train, tree_test))
Decision tree train/test accuracies 1.000/0.833
```

Based on the accuracy values that we printed by executing the preceding code snippet, the unpruned decision tree predicts all class labels of the training samples correctly; however, the substantially lower test accuracy indicates high variance (overfitting) of the model:

```
>>> bag = bag.fit(X_train, y_train)
>>> y_train_pred = bag.predict(X_train)
>>> y_test_pred = bag.predict(X_test)
>>> bag_train = accuracy_score(y_train, y_train_pred)
>>> bag_test = accuracy_score(y_test, y_test_pred)
>>> print('Bagging train/test accuracies %.3f/%.3f'
...         % (bag_train, bag_test))
Bagging train/test accuracies 1.000/0.896
```

Although the training accuracies of the decision tree and bagging classifier are similar on the training set (both 1.0), we can see that the bagging classifier has a slightly better generalization performance as estimated on the test set. Next let's compare the decision regions between the decision tree and bagging classifier:

```
>>> x_min = X_train[:, 0].min() - 1
>>> x_max = X_train[:, 0].max() + 1
>>> y_min = X_train[:, 1].min() - 1
>>> y_max = X_train[:, 1].max() + 1
>>> xx, yy = np.meshgrid(np.arange(x_min, x_max, 0.1),
...                      np.arange(y_min, y_max, 0.1))
```

```
>>> f, axarr = plt.subplots(nrows=1, ncols=2,
...                         sharex='col',
...                         sharey='row',
...                         figsize=(8, 3))
>>> for idx, clf, tt in zip([0, 1],
...                         [tree, bag],
...                         ['Decision Tree', 'Bagging']):
...     clf.fit(X_train, y_train)
...
...     Z = clf.predict(np.c_[xx.ravel(), yy.ravel()])
...     Z = Z.reshape(xx.shape)
...     axarr[idx].contourf(xx, yy, Z, alpha=0.3)
...     axarr[idx].scatter(X_train[y_train==0, 0],
...                       X_train[y_train==0, 1],
...                       c='blue', marker='^')
...     axarr[idx].scatter(X_train[y_train==1, 0],
...                       X_train[y_train==1, 1],
...                       c='red', marker='o')
...     axarr[idx].set_title(tt)
>>> axarr[0].set_ylabel(Alcohol', fontsize=12)
>>> plt.text(10.2, -1.2,
...          s=Hue',
...          ha='center', va='center', fontsize=12)
>>> plt.show()
```

As we can see in the resulting plot, the piece-wise linear decision boundary of the three-node deep decision tree looks smoother in the bagging ensemble:

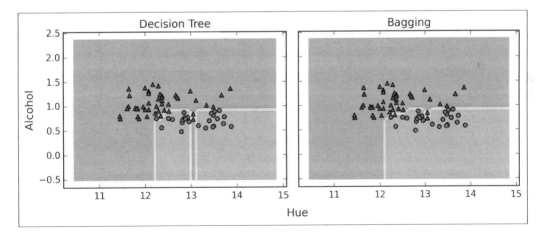

We only looked at a very simple bagging example in this section. In practice, more complex classification tasks and datasets' high dimensionality can easily lead to overfitting in single decision trees and this is where the bagging algorithm can really play out its strengths. Finally, we shall note that the bagging algorithm can be an effective approach to reduce the variance of a model. However, bagging is ineffective in reducing model bias, which is why we want to choose an ensemble of classifiers with low bias, for example, unpruned decision trees.

Leveraging weak learners via adaptive boosting

In this section about ensemble methods, we will discuss **boosting** with a special focus on its most common implementation, **AdaBoost** (short for **Adaptive Boosting**).

> The original idea behind AdaBoost was formulated by Robert Schapire in 1990 (R. E. Schapire. *The Strength of Weak Learnability*. Machine learning, 5(2):197–227, 1990). After Robert Schapire and Yoav Freund presented the AdaBoost algorithm in the Proceedings of the Thirteenth International Conference (ICML 1996), AdaBoost became one of the most widely used ensemble methods in the years that followed (Y. Freund, R. E. Schapire, et al. *Experiments with a New Boosting Algorithm*. In ICML, volume 96, pages 148–156, 1996). In 2003, Freund and Schapire received the *Goedel Prize* for their groundbreaking work, which is a prestigious prize for the most outstanding publications in the computer science field.

In boosting, the ensemble consists of very simple base classifiers, also often referred to as **weak learners**, that have only a slight performance advantage over random guessing. A typical example of a weak learner would be a decision tree stump. The key concept behind boosting is to focus on training samples that are hard to classify, that is, to let the weak learners subsequently learn from misclassified training samples to improve the performance of the ensemble. In contrast to bagging, the initial formulation of boosting, the algorithm uses random subsets of training samples drawn from the training dataset without replacement. The original boosting procedure is summarized in four key steps as follows:

1. Draw a random subset of training samples d_1 without replacement from the training set D to train a weak learner C_1.

2. Draw second random training subset d_2 without replacement from the training set and add 50 percent of the samples that were previously misclassified to train a weak learner C_2.

3. Find the training samples d_3 in the training set D on which C_1 and C_2 disagree to train a third weak learner C_3.

4. Combine the weak learners C_1, C_2, and C_3 via majority voting.

As discussed by Leo Breiman (L. Breiman. *Bias, Variance, and Arcing Classifiers*. 1996), boosting can lead to a decrease in bias as well as variance compared to bagging models. In practice, however, boosting algorithms such as AdaBoost are also known for their high variance, that is, the tendency to overfit the training data (G. Raetsch, T. Onoda, and K. R. Mueller. *An Improvement of Adaboost to Avoid Overfitting*. In Proc. of the Int. Conf. on Neural Information Processing. Citeseer, 1998).

In contrast to the original boosting procedure as described here, AdaBoost uses the complete training set to train the weak learners where the training samples are reweighted in each iteration to build a strong classifier that learns from the mistakes of the previous weak learners in the ensemble. Before we dive deeper into the specific details of the AdaBoost algorithm, let's take a look at the following figure to get a better grasp of the basic concept behind AdaBoost:

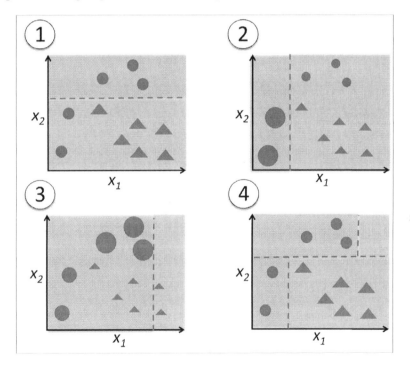

To walk through the AdaBoost illustration step by step, we start with subfigure **1**, which represents a training set for binary classification where all training samples are assigned equal weights. Based on this training set, we train a decision stump (shown as a dashed line) that tries to classify the samples of the two classes (triangles and circles) as well as possible by minimizing the cost function (or the impurity score in the special case of decision tree ensembles). For the next round (subfigure **2**), we assign a larger weight to the two previously misclassified samples (circles). Furthermore, we lower the weight of the correctly classified samples. The next decision stump will now be more focused on the training samples that have the largest weights, that is, the training samples that are supposedly hard to classify. The weak learner shown in subfigure **2** misclassifies three different samples from the circle-class, which are then assigned a larger weight as shown in subfigure **3**. Assuming that our AdaBoost ensemble only consists of three rounds of boosting, we would then combine the three weak learners trained on different reweighted training subsets by a weighted majority vote, as shown in subfigure **4**.

Now that have a better understanding behind the basic concept of AdaBoost, let's take a more detailed look at the algorithm using pseudo code. For clarity, we will denote element-wise multiplication by the cross symbol ($\times$) and the dot product between two vectors by a dot symbol ($\cdot$), respectively. The steps are as follows:

1. Set weight vector w to uniform weights where $\sum_i w_i = 1$
2. For j in m boosting rounds, do the following:
3. Train a weighted weak learner: $C_j = \text{train}(X, y, w)$.
4. Predict class labels: $\hat{y} = \text{predict}(C_j, X)$.
5. Compute weighted error rate: $\varepsilon = w \cdot (\hat{y} == y)$.
6. Compute coefficient: $\alpha_j = 0.5 \log \dfrac{1-\varepsilon}{\varepsilon}$.
7. Update weights: $w := w \times \exp(-\alpha_j \times \hat{y} \times y)$.
8. Normalize weights to sum to 1: $w := w / \sum_i w_i$.
9. Compute final prediction: $\hat{y} = \left(\sum_{j=1}^{m} (\alpha_j \times \text{predict}(C_j, X)) > 0 \right)$.

Note that the expression $(\hat{y} == y)$ in step 5 refers to a vector of 1s and 0s, where a 1 is assigned if the prediction is incorrect and 0 is assigned otherwise.

Although the AdaBoost algorithm seems to be pretty straightforward, let's walk through a more concrete example using a training set consisting of 10 training samples as illustrated in the following table:

Sample indices	x	y	Weights	$\hat{y}(x \le 3.0)$?	Correct?	Updated weights
1	1.0	1	0.1	1	Yes	0.072
2	2.0	1	0.1	1	Yes	0.072
3	3.0	1	0.1	1	Yes	0.072
4	4.0	-1	0.1	-1	Yes	0.072
5	5.0	-1	0.1	-1	Yes	0.072
6	6.0	-1	0.1	-1	Yes	0.072
7	7.0	1	0.1	-1	No	0.167
8	8.0	1	0.1	-1	No	0.167
9	9.0	1	0.1	-1	No	0.167
10	10.0	-1	0.1	-1	Yes	0.072

The first column of the table depicts the sample indices of the training samples 1 to 10. In the second column, we see the feature values of the individual samples assuming this is a one-dimensional dataset. The third column shows the true class label y_i for each training sample x_i, where $y_i \in \{1, -1\}$. The initial weights are shown in the fourth column; we initialize the weights to uniform and normalize them to sum to one. In the case of the 10 sample training set, we therefore assign the 0.1 to each weight w_i in the weight vector w. The predicted class labels $\hat{y}$ are shown in the fifth column, assuming that our splitting criterion is $x \le 3.0$. The last column of the table then shows the updated weights based on the update rules that we defined in the pseudocode.

Since the computation of the weight updates may look a little bit complicated at first, we will now follow the calculation step by step. We start by computing the weighted error rate ε as described in step 5:

$$\varepsilon = 0.1 \times 0 + 0.1 \times 0 + 0.1 \times 0 + 0.1 \times 0 + 0.1 \times 0 + 0.1 \times 0 + 0.1 \times 1 + 0.1 \times 1$$

$$+ 0.1 \times 1 + 0.1 \times 0 = \frac{3}{10} = 0.3$$

Next we compute the coefficient α_j (shown in step 6), which is later used in step 7 to update the weights as well as for the weights in majority vote prediction (step 10):

$$\alpha_j = 0.5 \log\left(\frac{1-\varepsilon}{\varepsilon}\right) \approx 0.424$$

After we have computed the coefficient α_j we can now update the weight vector using the following equation:

$$w := w \times \exp\left(-\alpha_j \times \hat{y} \times y\right)$$

Here, $\hat{y} \times y$ is an element-wise multiplication between the vectors of the predicted and true class labels, respectively. Thus, if a prediction $\hat{y}_i$ is correct, $\hat{y}_i \times y_i$ will have a positive sign so that we decrease the *ith* weight since α_j is a positive number as well:

$$0.1 \times \exp\left(-0.424 \times 1 \times 1\right) \approx 0.065$$

Similarly, we will increase the *ith* weight if $\hat{y}_i$ predicted the label incorrectly like this:

$$0.1 \times \exp\left(-0.424 \times 1 \times (-1)\right) \approx 0.153$$

Or like this:

$$0.1 \times \exp\left(-0.424 \times (-1) \times (1)\right) \approx 0.153$$

After we update each weight in the weight vector, we normalize the weights so that they sum up to 1 (step 8):

$$w := \frac{w}{\sum_i w_i}$$

Here, $\sum_i w_i = 7 \times 0.065 + 3 \times 0.153 = 0.914$.

Thus, each weight that corresponds to a correctly classified sample will be reduced from the initial value of 0.1 to $0.065 / 0.914 \approx 0.071$ for the next round of boosting. Similarly, the weights of each incorrectly classified sample will increase from 0.1 to $0.153 / 0.914 \approx 0.167$.

This was AdaBoost in a nutshell. Skipping to the more practical part, let's now train an AdaBoost ensemble classifier via scikit-learn. We will use the same Wine subset that we used in the previous section to train the bagging meta-classifier. Via the `base_estimator` attribute, we will train the `AdaBoostClassifier` on 500 decision tree stumps:

```
>>> from sklearn.ensemble import AdaBoostClassifier
>>> tree = DecisionTreeClassifier(criterion='entropy',
...                               max_depth=None,
...                               random_state=0)
>>> ada = AdaBoostClassifier(base_estimator=tree,
...                          n_estimators=500,
...                          learning_rate=0.1,
...                          random_state=0)
>>> tree = tree.fit(X_train, y_train)
>>> y_train_pred = tree.predict(X_train)
>>> y_test_pred = tree.predict(X_test)
>>> tree_train = accuracy_score(y_train, y_train_pred)
>>> tree_test = accuracy_score(y_test, y_test_pred)
>>> print('Decision tree train/test accuracies %.3f/%.3f'
...       % (tree_train, tree_test))
Decision tree train/test accuracies 0.845/0.854
```

As we can see, the decision tree stump tends to underfit the training data in contrast with the unpruned decision tree that we saw in the previous section:

```
>>> ada = ada.fit(X_train, y_train)
>>> y_train_pred = ada.predict(X_train)
>>> y_test_pred = ada.predict(X_test)
>>> ada_train = accuracy_score(y_train, y_train_pred)
>>> ada_test = accuracy_score(y_test, y_test_pred)
>>> print('AdaBoost train/test accuracies %.3f/%.3f'
...       % (ada_train, ada_test))
AdaBoost train/test accuracies 1.000/0.875
```

As we can see, the AdaBoost model predicts all class labels of the training set correctly and also shows a slightly improved test set performance compared to the decision tree stump. However, we also see that we introduced additional variance by our attempt to reduce the model bias.

Although we used another simple example for demonstration purposes, we can see that the performance of the AdaBoost classifier is slightly improved compared to the decision stump and achieved very similar accuracy scores to the bagging classifier that we trained in the previous section. However, we should note that it is considered bad practice to select a model based on the repeated usage of the test set. The estimate of the generalization performance may be too optimistic, which we discussed in more detail in *Chapter 6, Learning Best Practices for Model Evaluation and Hyperparameter Tuning.*

Finally, let's check what the decision regions look like:

```
>>> x_min = X_train[:, 0].min() - 1
>>> x_max = X_train[:, 0].max() + 1
>>> y_min = X_train[:, 1].min() - 1
>>> y_max = X_train[:, 1].max() + 1
>>> xx, yy = np.meshgrid(np.arange(x_min, x_max, 0.1),
...                      np.arange(y_min, y_max, 0.1))
>>> f, axarr = plt.subplots(1, 2,
...                         sharex='col',
...                         sharey='row',
...                         figsize=(8, 3))
>>> for idx, clf, tt in zip([0, 1],
...                         [tree, ada],
...                         ['Decision Tree', 'AdaBoost']):
...     clf.fit(X_train, y_train)
...     Z = clf.predict(np.c_[xx.ravel(), yy.ravel()])
...     Z = Z.reshape(xx.shape)
...     axarr[idx].contourf(xx, yy, Z, alpha=0.3)
...     axarr[idx].scatter(X_train[y_train==0, 0],
...                        X_train[y_train==0, 1],
...                        c='blue',
...                        marker='^')
...     axarr[idx].scatter(X_train[y_train==1, 0],
...                        X_train[y_train==1, 1],
...                        c='red',
...                        marker='o')
... axarr[idx].set_title(tt)
... axarr[0].set_ylabel('Alcohol', fontsize=12)
>>> plt.text(10.2, -1.2,
...          s=Hue',
...          ha='center',
...          va='center',
...          fontsize=12)
>>> plt.show()
```

By looking at the decision regions, we can see that the decision boundary of the AdaBoost model is substantially more complex than the decision boundary of the decision stump. In addition, we note that the AdaBoost model separates the feature space very similarly to the bagging classifier that we trained in the previous section.

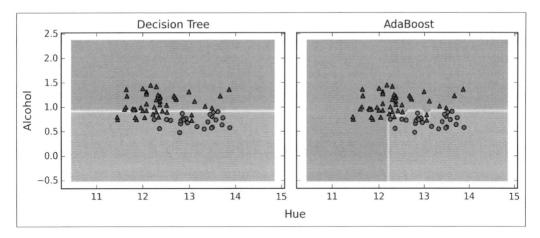

As concluding remarks about ensemble techniques, it is worth noting that ensemble learning increases the computational complexity compared to individual classifiers. In practice, we need to think carefully whether we want to pay the price of increased computational costs for an often relatively modest improvement of predictive performance.

An often-cited example of this trade-off is the famous *$1 Million Netflix Prize*, which was won using ensemble techniques. The details about the algorithm were published in A. Toescher, M. Jahrer, and R. M. Bell. *The Bigchaos Solution to the Netflix Grand Prize*. Netflix prize documentation, 2009 (which is available at `http://www.stat.osu.edu/~dmsl/GrandPrize2009_BPC_BigChaos.pdf`). Although the winning team received the $1 million prize money, Netflix never implemented their model due to its complexity, which made it unfeasible for a real-world application. To quote their exact words (`http://techblog.netflix.com/2012/04/netflix-recommendations-beyond-5-stars.html`):

> *"[...] additional accuracy gains that we measured did not seem to justify the engineering effort needed to bring them into a production environment."*

Summary

In this chapter, we looked at some of the most popular and widely used techniques for ensemble learning. Ensemble methods combine different classification models to cancel out their individual weaknesses, which often results in stable and well-performing models that are very attractive for industrial applications as well as machine learning competitions.

In the beginning of this chapter, we implemented a `MajorityVoteClassifier` in Python that allows us to combine different algorithms for classification. We then looked at bagging, a useful technique to reduce the variance of a model by drawing random bootstrap samples from the training set and combining the individually trained classifiers via majority vote. Then we discussed AdaBoost, which is an algorithm that is based on weak learners that subsequently learn from mistakes.

Throughout the previous chapters, we discussed different learning algorithms, tuning, and evaluation techniques. In the following chapter, we will look at a particular application of machine learning, sentiment analysis, which has certainly become an interesting topic in the era of the Internet and social media.

8

Applying Machine Learning to Sentiment Analysis

In this Internet and social media time and age, people's opinions, reviews, and recommendations have become a valuable resource for political science and businesses. Thanks to modern technologies, we are now able to collect and analyze such data most efficiently. In this chapter, we will delve into a subfield of **natural language processing** (**NLP**) called **sentiment analysis** and learn how to use machine learning algorithms to classify documents based on their polarity: the attitude of the writer. The topics that we will cover in the following sections include:

- Cleaning and preparing text data
- Building feature vectors from text documents
- Training a machine learning model to classify positive and negative movie reviews
- Working with large text datasets using *out-of-core* learning

Obtaining the IMDb movie review dataset

Sentiment analysis, sometimes also called **opinion mining**, is a popular sub-discipline of the broader field of NLP; it analyzes the **polarity** of documents. A popular task in sentiment analysis is the classification of documents based on the expressed opinions or emotions of the authors with regard to a particular topic.

In this chapter, we will be working with a large dataset of movie reviews from the **Internet Movie Database (IMDb)** that has been collected by Maas et al. (A. L. Maas, R. E. Daly, P. T. Pham, D. Huang, A. Y. Ng, and C. Potts. *Learning Word Vectors for Sentiment Analysis*. In the proceedings of the 49th Annual Meeting of the Association for Computational Linguistics: Human Language Technologies, pages 142–150, Portland, Oregon, USA, June 2011. Association for Computational Linguistics). The movie review dataset consists of 50,000 polar movie reviews that are labeled as either *positive* or *negative*; here, positive means that a movie was rated with more than six stars on IMDb, and negative means that a movie was rated with fewer than five stars on IMDb. In the following sections, we will learn how to extract meaningful information from a subset of these movie reviews to build a machine learning model that can predict whether a certain reviewer liked or disliked a movie.

A compressed archive of the movie review dataset (84.1 MB) can be downloaded from http://ai.stanford.edu/~amaas/data/sentiment/ as a gzip-compressed tarball archive:

- If you are working with Linux or Mac OS X, you can open a new terminal window, use cd to go into the download directory, and execute tar -zxf aclImdb_v1.tar.gz to decompress the dataset

- If you are working with Windows, you can download a free archiver such as 7-Zip (http://www.7-zip.org) to extract the files from the download archive

Having successfully extracted the dataset, we will now assemble the individual text documents from the decompressed download archive into a single CSV file. In the following code section, we will be reading the movie reviews into a pandas DataFrame object, which can take up to 10 minutes on a standard desktop computer. To visualize the progress and estimated time until completion, we will use the **PyPrind** (Python Progress Indicator, https://pypi.python.org/pypi/PyPrind/) package that I developed several years ago for such purposes. PyPrind can be installed by executing the command: pip install pyprind.

```
>>> import pyprind
>>> import pandas as pd
>>> import os
>>> pbar = pyprind.ProgBar(50000)
>>> labels = {'pos':1, 'neg':0}
>>> df = pd.DataFrame()
>>> for s in ('test', 'train'):
...     for l in ('pos', 'neg'):
...         path ='./aclImdb/%s/%s' % (s, l)
...         for file in os.listdir(path):
```

```
...                    with open(os.path.join(path, file), 'r') as infile:...
txt = infile.read()
...                        df = df.append([[txt, labels[l]]], ignore_index=True)
...                        pbar.update()
>>> df.columns = ['review', 'sentiment']
0%                        100%
[############################] | ETA[sec]: 0.000
Total time elapsed: 725.001 sec
```

Executing the preceding code, we first initialized a new progress bar object `pbar` with 50,000 iterations, which is the number of documents we were going to read in. Using the nested `for` loops, we iterated over the `train` and `test` subdirectories in the main `aclImdb` directory and read the individual text files from the `pos` and `neg` subdirectories that we eventually appended to the `DataFrame df` — together with an integer class label (1 = positive and 0 = negative).

Since the class labels in the assembled dataset are sorted, we will now shuffle `DataFrame` using the `permutation` function from the `np.random` submodule — this will be useful to split the dataset into training and test sets in later sections when we will stream the data from our local drive directly. For our own convenience, we will also store the assembled and shuffled movie review dataset as a CSV file:

```
>>> import numpy as np
>>> np.random.seed(0)
>>> df = df.reindex(np.random.permutation(df.index))
>>> df.to_csv('./movie_data.csv', index=False)
```

Since we are going to use this dataset later in this chapter, let us quickly confirm that we successfully saved the data in the right format by reading in the CSV and printing an excerpt of the first three samples:

```
>>> df = pd.read_csv('./movie_data.csv')
>>> df.head(3)
```

If you are running the code examples in IPython Notebook, you should now see the first three samples of the dataset, as shown in the following table:

	review	sentiment
0	In 1974, the teenager Martha Moxley (Maggie Gr...	1
1	OK... so... I really like Kris Kristofferson a...	0
2	***SPOILER*** Do not read this, if you think a...	0

Introducing the bag-of-words model

We remember from *Chapter 4, Building Good Training Sets – Data Preprocessing,* that we have to convert categorical data, such as text or words, into a numerical form before we can pass it on to a machine learning algorithm. In this section, we will introduce the **bag-of-words** model that allows us to represent text as numerical feature vectors. The idea behind the bag-of-words model is quite simple and can be summarized as follows:

1. We create a **vocabulary** of unique **tokens**—for example, words—from the entire set of documents.

2. We construct a feature vector from each document that contains the counts of how often each word occurs in the particular document.

Since the unique words in each document represent only a small subset of all the words in the bag-of-words vocabulary, the feature vectors will consist of mostly zeros, which is why we call them **sparse**. Do not worry if this sounds too abstract; in the following subsections, we will walk through the process of creating a simple bag-of-words model step-by-step.

Transforming words into feature vectors

To construct a bag-of-words model based on the word counts in the respective documents, we can use the CountVectorizer class implemented in scikit-learn. As we will see in the following code section, the CountVectorizer class takes an array of text data, which can be documents or just sentences, and constructs the bag-of-words model for us:

```
>>> import numpy as np
>>> from sklearn.feature_extraction.text import CountVectorizer
>>> count = CountVectorizer()
>>> docs = np.array([
...           'The sun is shining',
...           'The weather is sweet',
...           'The sun is shining and the weather is sweet'])
>>> bag = count.fit_transform(docs)
```

By calling the fit_transform method on CountVectorizer, we just constructed the vocabulary of the bag-of-words model and transformed the following three sentences into sparse feature vectors:

1. The sun is shining

2. The weather is sweet

3. The sun is shining and the weather is sweet

Now let us print the contents of the vocabulary to get a better understanding of the underlying concepts:

```
>>> print(count.vocabulary_)
{'the': 5, 'shining': 2, 'weather': 6, 'sun': 3, 'is': 1, 'sweet': 4,
'and': 0}
```

As we can see from executing the preceding command, the vocabulary is stored in a Python dictionary, which maps the unique words that are mapped to integer indices. Next let us print the feature vectors that we just created:

```
>>> print(bag.toarray())
[[0 1 1 1 0 1 0]
 [0 1 0 0 1 1 1]
 [1 2 1 1 1 2 1]]
```

Each index position in the feature vectors shown here corresponds to the integer values that are stored as dictionary items in the CountVectorizer vocabulary. For example, the first feature at index position 0 resembles the count of the word and, which only occurs in the last document, and the word is at index position 1 (the 2nd feature in the document vectors) occurs in all three sentences. Those values in the feature vectors are also called the **raw term frequencies**: *tf (t,d)* — the number of times a term *t* occurs in a document *d*.

> The sequence of items in the bag-of-words model that we just created is also called the **1-gram** or **unigram** model—each item or token in the vocabulary represents a single word. More generally, the contiguous sequences of items in NLP—words, letters, or symbols—is also called an **n-gram**. The choice of the number *n* in the n-gram model depends on the particular application; for example, a study by Kanaris et al. revealed that n-grams of size 3 and 4 yield good performances in anti-spam filtering of e-mail messages (Ioannis Kanaris, Konstantinos Kanaris, Ioannis Houvardas, and Efstathios Stamatatos. *Words vs Character N-Grams for Anti-Spam Filtering*. International Journal on Artificial Intelligence Tools, 16(06):1047–1067, 2007). To summarize the concept of the n-gram representation, the 1-gram and 2-gram representations of our first document "the sun is shining" would be constructed as follows:
>
> - **1-gram**: "the", "sun", "is", "shining"
> - **2-gram**: "the sun", "sun is", "is shining"
>
> The CountVectorizer class in scikit-learn allows us to use different n-gram models via its ngram_range parameter. While a 1-gram representation is used by default, we could switch to a 2-gram representation by initializing a new CountVectorizer instance with ngram_range=(2,2).

Assessing word relevancy via term frequency-inverse document frequency

When we are analyzing text data, we often encounter words that occur across multiple documents from both classes. Those frequently occurring words typically don't contain useful or discriminatory information. In this subsection, we will learn about a useful technique called **term frequency-inverse document frequency** (**tf-idf**) that can be used to downweight those frequently occurring words in the feature vectors. The tf-idf can be defined as the product of the **term frequency** and the **inverse document frequency**:

$$\text{tf-idf}(t,d) = tf(t,d) \times \text{idf}(t,d)$$

Here the *tf(t, d)* is the term frequency that we introduced in the previous section, and the inverse document frequency *idf(t, d)* can be calculated as:

$$\text{idf}(t,d) = log\frac{n_d}{1+\text{df}(d,t)},$$

where n_d is the total number of documents, and *df(d, t)* is the number of documents *d* that contain the term *t*. Note that adding the constant 1 to the denominator is optional and serves the purpose of assigning a non-zero value to terms that occur in all training samples; the log is used to ensure that low document frequencies are not given too much weight.

Scikit-learn implements yet another transformer, the `TfidfTransformer`, that takes the raw term frequencies from `CountVectorizer` as input and transforms them into tf-idfs:

```
>>> from sklearn.feature_extraction.text import TfidfTransformer
>>> tfidf = TfidfTransformer()
>>> np.set_printoptions(precision=2)
>>> print(tfidf.fit_transform(count.fit_transform(docs)).toarray())
[[ 0.    0.43  0.56  0.56  0.    0.43  0.  ]
 [ 0.    0.43  0.    0.    0.56  0.43  0.56]
 [ 0.4   0.48  0.31  0.31  0.31  0.48  0.31]]
```

As we saw in the previous subsection, the word is had the largest term frequency in the 3rd document, being the most frequently occurring word. However, after transforming the same feature vector into tf-idfs, we see that the word is is now associated with a relatively small tf-idf (0.31) in document 3 since it is also contained in documents 1 and 2 and thus is unlikely to contain any useful, discriminatory information.

However, if we'd manually calculated the tf-idfs of the individual terms in our feature vectors, we'd have noticed that the TfidfTransformer calculates the tf-idfs slightly differently compared to the *standard* textbook equations that we defined earlier. The equations for the idf and tf-idf that were implemented in scikit-learn are:

$$\text{idf}(t,d) = log \frac{1+n_d}{1+\text{df}(d,t)}$$

The tf-idf equation that was implemented in scikit-learn is as follows:

$$\text{tf-idf}(t,d) = \textit{tf}(t,d) \times \left(\text{idf}(t,d)+1\right)$$

While it is also more typical to normalize the raw term frequencies before calculating the tf-idfs, the TfidfTransformer normalizes the tf-idfs directly. By default (norm='l2'), scikit-learn's TfidfTransformer applies the L2-normalization, which returns a vector of length 1 by dividing an un-normalized feature vector v by its L2-norm:

$$v_{norm} = \frac{v}{\|v\|_2} = \frac{v}{\sqrt{v_1^2 + v_2^2 + \cdots + v_n^2}} = \frac{v}{\left(\sum_{i=1}^{n} v_i^2\right)^{1/2}}$$

To make sure that we understand how TfidfTransformer works, let us walk through an example and calculate the tf-idf of the word is in the 3rd document.

The word is has a term frequency of 2 (tf = 2) in document 3, and the document frequency of this term is 3 since the term is occurs in all three documents (df = 3). Thus, we can calculate the idf as follows:

$$\textit{idf}\left(\text{"is"}, d3\right) = log\frac{1+3}{1+3} = 0$$

Now in order to calculate the tf-idf, we simply need to add 1 to the inverse document frequency and multiply it by the term frequency:

$$\text{tf-idf}\left("is",\text{d3}\right) = 2 \times \left(0 + 1\right) = 2$$

If we repeated these calculations for all terms in the 3rd document, we'd obtain the following tf-idf vectors: [1.69, 2.00, 1.29, 1.29, 1.29, 2.00, and 1.29]. However, we notice that the values in this feature vector are different from the values that we obtained from the TfidfTransformer that we used previously. The final step that we are missing in this tf-idf calculation is the L2-normalization, which can be applied as follows:

$$\text{tf-idf}\left("is",\text{d3}\right) = 0.48$$

As we can see, the results now match the results returned by scikit-learn's TfidfTransformer. Since we now understand how tf-idfs are calculated, let us proceed to the next sections and apply those concepts to the movie review dataset.

Cleaning text data

In the previous subsections, we learned about the bag-of-words model, term frequencies, and tf-idfs. However, the first important step—before we build our bag-of-words model—is to clean the text data by stripping it of all unwanted characters. To illustrate why this is important, let us display the last 50 characters from the first document in the reshuffled movie review dataset:

```
>>> df.loc[0, 'review'][-50:]
'is seven.<br /><br />Title (Brazil): Not Available'
```

As we can see here, the text contains HTML markup as well as punctuation and other non-letter characters. While HTML markup does not contain much useful semantics, punctuation marks can represent useful, additional information in certain NLP contexts. However, for simplicity, we will now remove all punctuation marks but only keep **emoticon** characters such as ":)" since those are certainly useful for sentiment analysis. To accomplish this task, we will use Python's **regular expression (regex)** library, re, as shown here:

```
>>> import re
>>> def preprocessor(text):
```

```
...        text = re.sub('<[^>]*>', '', text)
...        emoticons = re.findall('(?::|;|=)(?:-)?(?:\)|\(|D|P)', text)
...        text = re.sub('[\W]+', ' ', text.lower()) + \
...                '.join(emoticons).replace('-', '')
...        return text
```

Via the first regex `<[^>]*>` in the preceding code section, we tried to remove the entire HTML markup that was contained in the movie reviews. Although many programmers generally advise against the use of regex to parse HTML, this regex should be sufficient to *clean* this particular dataset. After we removed the HTML markup, we used a slightly more complex regex to find emoticons, which we temporarily stored as `emoticons`. Next we removed all non-word characters from the text via the regex `[\W]+`, converted the text into lowercase characters, and eventually added the temporarily stored `emoticons` to the end of the processed document string. Additionally, we removed the *nose* character (-) from the emoticons for consistency.

Although regular expressions offer an efficient and convenient approach to searching for characters in a string, they also come with a steep learning curve. Unfortunately, an in-depth discussion of regular expressions is beyond the scope of this book. However, you can find a great tutorial on the Google Developers portal at `https://developers.google.com/edu/python/regular-expressions` or check out the official documentation of Python's re module at `https://docs.python.org/3.4/library/re.html`.

Although the addition of the emoticon characters to the end of the cleaned document strings may not look like the most elegant approach, the order of the words doesn't matter in our bag-of-words model if our vocabulary only consists of 1-word tokens. But before we talk more about splitting documents into individual terms, words, or tokens, let us confirm that our preprocessor works correctly:

```
>>> preprocessor(df.loc[0, 'review'][-50:])
'is seven title brazil not available'
>>> preprocessor("</a>This :) is :( a test :-)!")
'this is a test :) :( :)'
```

Lastly, since we will make use of the *cleaned* text data over and over again during the next sections, let us now apply our `preprocessor` function to all movie reviews in our `DataFrame`:

```
>>> df['review'] = df['review'].apply(preprocessor)
```

Processing documents into tokens

Having successfully prepared the movie review dataset, we now need to think about how to split the text corpora into individual elements. One way to *tokenize* documents is to split them into individual words by splitting the cleaned document at its whitespace characters:

```
>>> def tokenizer(text):
...     return text.split()
>>> tokenizer('runners like running and thus they run')
['runners', 'like', 'running', 'and', 'thus', 'they', 'run']
```

In the context of tokenization, another useful technique is **word stemming**, which is the process of transforming a word into its root form that allows us to map related words to the same stem. The original stemming algorithm was developed by Martin F. Porter in 1979 and is hence known as the **Porter stemmer** algorithm (Martin F. Porter. *An algorithm for suffix stripping*. Program: electronic library and information systems, 14(3):130–137, 1980). The Natural Language Toolkit for Python (NLTK, http://www.nltk.org) implements the Porter stemming algorithm, which we will use in the following code section. In order to install the NLTK, you can simply execute pip install nltk.

```
>>> from nltk.stem.porter import PorterStemmer
>>> porter = PorterStemmer()
>>> def tokenizer_porter(text):
...     return [porter.stem(word) for word in text.split()]
>>> tokenizer_porter('runners like running and thus they run')
['runner', 'like', 'run', 'and', 'thu', 'they', 'run']
```

 Although NLTK is not the focus of the chapter, I highly recommend you to visit the NLTK website as well as the official NLTK book, which is freely available at http://www.nltk.org/book/, if you are interested in more advanced applications in NLP.

Using PorterStemmer from the nltk package, we modified our tokenizer function to reduce words to their root form, which was illustrated by the previous simple example where the word running was stemmed to its root form run.

The Porter stemming algorithm is probably the oldest and simplest stemming algorithm. Other popular stemming algorithms include the newer **Snowball stemmer** (Porter2 or "English" stemmer) or the **Lancaster stemmer** (Paice-Husk stemmer), which is faster but also more aggressive than the Porter stemmer. Those alternative stemming algorithms are also available through the NLTK package (`http://www.nltk.org/api/nltk.stem.html`).

While stemming can create non-real words, such as thu, (from `thus`) as shown in the previous example, a technique called **lemmatization** aims to obtain the canonical (grammatically correct) forms of individual words — the so-called **lemmas**. However, lemmatization is computationally more difficult and expensive compared to stemming and, in practice, it has been observed that stemming and lemmatization have little impact on the performance of text classification (Michal Toman, Roman Tesar, and Karel Jezek. *Influence of word normalization on text classification*. Proceedings of InSciT, pages 354–358, 2006).

Before we jump into the next section where we will train a machine learning model using the bag-of-words model, let us briefly talk about another useful topic called **stop-word removal**. Stop-words are simply those words that are extremely common in all sorts of texts and likely bear no (or only little) useful information that can be used to distinguish between different classes of documents. Examples of stop-words are *is*, *and*, *has*, and the like. Removing stop-words can be useful if we are working with raw or normalized term frequencies rather than tf-idfs, which are already downweighting frequently occurring words.

In order to remove stop-words from the movie reviews, we will use the set of 127 English stop-words that is available from the NLTK library, which can be obtained by calling the `nltk.download` function:

```
>>> import nltk
>>> nltk.download('stopwords')
```

After we have downloaded the stop-words set, we can load and apply the English stop-word set as follows:

```
>>> from nltk.corpus import stopwords
>>> stop = stopwords.words('english')
>>> [w for w in tokenizer_porter('a runner likes running and runs a lot')[-10:] if w not in stop]

['runner', 'like', 'run', 'run', 'lot']
```

Training a logistic regression model for document classification

In this section, we will train a logistic regression model to classify the movie reviews into positive and negative reviews. First, we will divide the DataFrame of cleaned text documents into 25,000 documents for training and 25,000 documents for testing:

```
>>> X_train = df.loc[:25000, 'review'].values
>>> y_train = df.loc[:25000, 'sentiment'].values
>>> X_test = df.loc[25000:, 'review'].values
>>> y_test = df.loc[25000:, 'sentiment'].values
```

Next we will use a GridSearchCV object to find the optimal set of parameters for our logistic regression model using 5-fold stratified cross-validation:

```
>>> from sklearn.grid_search import GridSearchCV
>>> from sklearn.pipeline import Pipeline
>>> from sklearn.linear_model import LogisticRegression
>>> from sklearn.feature_extraction.text import TfidfVectorizer
>>> tfidf = TfidfVectorizer(strip_accents=None,
...                         lowercase=False,
...                         preprocessor=None)
>>> param_grid = [{'vect__ngram_range': [(1,1)],
...                'vect__stop_words': [stop, None],
...                'vect__tokenizer': [tokenizer,
...                                    tokenizer_porter],
...                'clf__penalty': ['l1', 'l2'],
...                'clf__C': [1.0, 10.0, 100.0]},
...               {'vect__ngram_range': [(1,1)],
...                'vect__stop_words': [stop, None],
...                'vect__tokenizer': [tokenizer,
...                                    tokenizer_porter],
...                'vect__use_idf':[False],
...                'vect__norm':[None],
...                'clf__penalty': ['l1', 'l2'],
...                'clf__C': [1.0, 10.0, 100.0]}
...               ]
>>> lr_tfidf = Pipeline([('vect', tfidf),
...                      ('clf',
...                      LogisticRegression(random_state=0))])
>>> gs_lr_tfidf = GridSearchCV(lr_tfidf, param_grid,
...                            scoring='accuracy',
...                            cv=5, verbose=1,
...                            n_jobs=-1)
>>> gs_lr_tfidf.fit(X_train, y_train)
```

When we initialized the `GridSearchCV` object and its parameter grid using the preceding code, we restricted ourselves to a limited number of parameter combinations since the number of feature vectors, as well as the large vocabulary, can make the grid search computationally quite expensive; using a standard Desktop computer, our grid search may take up to 40 minutes to complete.

In the previous code example, we replaced the `CountVectorizer` and `TfidfTransformer` from the previous subsection with the `TfidfVectorizer`, which combines the latter transformer objects. Our `param_grid` consisted of two parameter dictionaries. In the first dictionary, we used the `TfidfVectorizer` with its default settings (`use_idf=True`, `smooth_idf=True`, and `norm='l2'`) to calculate the tf-idfs; in the second dictionary, we set those parameters to `use_idf=False`, `smooth_idf=False`, and `norm=None` in order to train a model based on raw term frequencies. Furthermore, for the logistic regression classifier itself, we trained models using L2 and L1 regularization via the penalty parameter and compared different regularization strengths by defining a range of values for the inverse-regularization parameter `C`.

After the grid search has finished, we can print the best parameter set:

```
>>> print('Best parameter set: %s ' % gs_lr_tfidf.best_params_)
Best parameter set: {'clf__C': 10.0, 'vect__stop_words': None,
'clf__penalty': 'l2', 'vect__tokenizer': <function tokenizer at
0x7f6c704948c8>, 'vect__ngram_range': (1, 1)}
```

As we can see here, we obtained the best grid search results using the regular tokenizer without Porter stemming, no stop-word library, and tf-idfs in combination with a logistic regression classifier that uses L2 regularization with the regularization strength `C=10.0`.

Using the best model from this grid search, let us print the average 5-fold cross-validation accuracy score on the training set and the classification accuracy on the test dataset:

```
>>> print('CV Accuracy: %.3f'
...        % gs_lr_tfidf.best_score_)
CV Accuracy: 0.897
>>> clf = gs_lr_tfidf.best_estimator_
>>> print('Test Accuracy: %.3f'
...       % clf.score(X_test, y_test))
Test Accuracy: 0.899
```

The results reveal that our machine learning model can predict whether a movie review is positive or negative with 90 percent accuracy.

> A still very popular classifier for text classification is the Naïve Bayes classifier, which gained popularity in applications of e-mail spam filtering. Naïve Bayes classifiers are easy to implement, computationally efficient, and tend to perform particularly well on relatively small datasets compared to other algorithms. Although we don't discuss Naïve Bayes classifiers in this book, the interested reader can find my article about Naïve Text classification that I made freely available on arXiv (S. Raschka. *Naive Bayes and Text Classification I - introduction and Theory*. Computing Research Repository (CoRR), abs/1410.5329, 2014. http://arxiv.org/pdf/1410.5329v3.pdf).

Working with bigger data – online algorithms and out-of-core learning

If you executed the code examples in the previous section, you may have noticed that it could be computationally quite expensive to construct the feature vectors for the 50,000 movie review dataset during grid search. In many real-world applications it is not uncommon to work with even larger datasets that may even exceed our computer's memory. Since not everyone has access to supercomputer facilities, we will now apply a technique called out-of-core learning that allows us to work with such large datasets.

Back in *Chapter 2, Training Machine Learning Algorithms for Classification*, we introduced the concept of **stochastic gradient descent**, which is an optimization algorithm that updates the model's weights using one sample at a time. In this section, we will make use of the `partial_fit` function of the SGDClassifier in scikit-learn to stream the documents directly from our local drive and train a logistic regression model using small minibatches of documents.

First, we define a `tokenizer` function that cleans the unprocessed text data from our `movie_data.csv` file that we constructed in the beginning of this chapter and separates it into word tokens while removing stop words.

```
>>> import numpy as np
>>> import re
>>> from nltk.corpus import stopwords
>>> stop = stopwords.words('english')
>>> def tokenizer(text):
...     text = re.sub('<[^>]*>', '', text)
...     emoticons = re.findall('(?::|;|=)(?:-)?(?:\)|\(|D|P)',
...                            text.lower())
...     text = re.sub('[\W]+', ' ', text.lower()) \
```

```
...             + ' '.join(emoticons).replace('-', '')
...         tokenized = [w for w in text.split() if w not in stop]
...         return tokenized
```

Next we define a generator function, `stream_docs`, that reads in and returns one document at a time:

```
>>> def stream_docs(path):
...     with open(path, 'r', encoding='utf-8') as csv:
...         next(csv) # skip header
...         for line in csv:
...             text, label = line[:-3], int(line[-2])
...             yield text, label
```

To verify that our `stream_docs` function works correctly, let us read in the first document from the `movie_data.csv` file, which should return a tuple consisting of the review text as well as the corresponding class label:

```
>>> next(stream_docs(path='./movie_data.csv'))
('"In 1974, the teenager Martha Moxley ... ',1)
```

We will now define a function, `get_minibatch`, that will take a document stream from the `stream_docs` function and return a particular number of documents specified by the `size` parameter:

```
>>> def get_minibatch(doc_stream, size):
...     docs, y = [], []
...     try:
...         for _ in range(size):
...             text, label = next(doc_stream)
...             docs.append(text)
...             y.append(label)
...     except StopIteration:
...         return None, None
...     return docs, y
```

Unfortunately, we can't use the `CountVectorizer` for out-of-core learning since it requires holding the complete vocabulary in memory. Also, the `TfidfVectorizer` needs to keep the all feature vectors of the training dataset in memory to calculate the inverse document frequencies. However, another useful vectorizer for text processing implemented in scikit-learn is `HashingVectorizer`. `HashingVectorizer` is data-independent and makes use of the Hashing trick via the 32-bit MurmurHash3 algorithm by Austin Appleby (`https://sites.google.com/site/murmurhash/`).

```
>>> from sklearn.feature_extraction.text import HashingVectorizer
>>> from sklearn.linear_model import SGDClassifier
```

```
>>> vect = HashingVectorizer(decode_error='ignore',
...                          n_features=2**21,
...                          preprocessor=None,
...                          tokenizer=tokenizer)
>>> clf = SGDClassifier(loss='log', random_state=1, n_iter=1)
>>> doc_stream = stream_docs(path='./movie_data.csv')
```

Using the preceding code, we initialized HashingVectorizer with our tokenizer function and set the number of features to 2^{21}. Furthermore, we reinitialized a logistic regression classifier by setting the loss parameter of the SGDClassifier to log—note that, by choosing a large number of features in the HashingVectorizer, we reduce the chance to cause hash collisions but we also increase the number of coefficients in our logistic regression model.

Now comes the really interesting part. Having set up all the complementary functions, we can now start the out-of-core learning using the following code:

```
>>> import pyprind
>>> pbar = pyprind.ProgBar(45)
>>> classes = np.array([0, 1])
>>> for _ in range(45):
...     X_train, y_train = get_minibatch(doc_stream, size=1000)
...     if not X_train:
...         break
...     X_train = vect.transform(X_train)
...     clf.partial_fit(X_train, y_train, classes=classes)
...     pbar.update()
0%                              100%
[##############################] | ETA[sec]: 0.000
Total time elapsed: 50.063 sec
```

Again, we made use of the PyPrind package in order to estimate the progress of our learning algorithm. We initialized the progress bar object with 45 iterations and, in the following for loop, we iterated over 45 minibatches of documents where each minibatch consists of 1,000 documents each.

Having completed the incremental learning process, we will use the last 5,000 documents to evaluate the performance of our model:

```
>>> X_test, y_test = get_minibatch(doc_stream, size=5000)
>>> X_test = vect.transform(X_test)
>>> print('Accuracy: %.3f' % clf.score(X_test, y_test))
Accuracy: 0.868
```

As we can see, the accuracy of the model is 87 percent, slightly below the accuracy that we achieved in the previous section using the grid search for hyperparameter tuning. However, out-of-core learning is very memory-efficient and took less than a minute to complete. Finally, we can use the last 5,000 documents to update our model:

```
>>> clf = clf.partial_fit(X_test, y_test)
```

If you are planning to continue directly with *Chapter 9, Embedding a Machine Learning Model into a Web Application*, I recommend you to keep the current Python session open. In the next chapter, we will use the model that we just trained to learn how to save it to disk for later use and embed it into a web application.

> Although the bag-of-words model is still the most commonly used model for text classification, it does not consider sentence structure and grammar. A popular extension of the bag-of-words model is **Latent Dirichlet allocation**, which is a topic model that considers the latent semantics of words (D. M. Blei, A. Y. Ng, and M. I. Jordan. *Latent Dirichlet allocation*. The Journal of machine Learning research, 3:993–1022, 2003).
>
> A more modern alternative to the bag-of-words model is **word2vec**, an algorithm that Google released in 2013 (T. Mikolov, K. Chen, G. Corrado, and J. Dean. *Efficient Estimation of Word Representations in Vector Space*. arXiv preprint arXiv:1301.3781, 2013). The word2vec algorithm is an unsupervised learning algorithm based on neural networks that attempts to automatically learn the relationship between words. The idea behind word2vec is to put words that have similar meanings into similar clusters; via clever vector-spacing, the model can reproduce certain words using simple vector math, for example, *king – man + woman = queen*.
>
> The original C-implementation, with useful links to the relevant papers and alternative implementations, can be found at `https://code.google.com/p/word2vec/`.

Summary

In this chapter, we learned how to use machine learning algorithms to classify text documents based on their polarity, which is a basic task in sentiment analysis in the field of natural language processing. Not only did we learn how to encode a document as a feature vector using the bag-of-words model, but we also learned how to weight the term frequency by relevance using term frequency-inverse document frequency.

Working with text data can be computationally quite expensive due to the large feature vectors that are created during this process; in the last section, we learned how to utilize out-of-core or incremental learning to train a machine learning algorithm without loading the whole dataset into a computer's memory.

In the next chapter, we will use our document classifier and learn how to embed it into a web application.

Embedding a Machine Learning Model into a Web Application

In the previous chapters, you learned about the many different machine learning concepts and algorithms that can help us with better and more efficient decision-making. However, machine learning techniques are not limited to offline applications and analyses, and they can be the predictive engine of your web services. For example, popular and useful applications of machine learning models in web applications include spam detection in submission forms, search engines, recommendation systems for media or shopping portals, and many more.

In this chapter, you will learn how to embed a machine learning model into a web application that can not only classify but also learn from data in real-time. The topics that we will cover are as follows:

- Saving the current state of a trained machine learning model
- Using SQLite databases for data storage
- Developing a web application using the popular Flask web framework
- Deploying a machine learning application to a public web server

Serializing fitted scikit-learn estimators

Training a machine learning model can be computationally quite expensive, as we have seen in *Chapter 8, Applying Machine Learning to Sentiment Analysis*. Surely, we don't want to train our model every time we close our Python interpreter and want to make a new prediction or reload our web application? One option for **model persistence** is Python's in-built pickle module (https://docs.python.org/3.4/ library/pickle.html), which allows us to serialize and de-serialize Python object structures to compact byte code, so that we can save our classifier in its current state and reload it if we want to classify new samples without needing to learn the model from the training data all over again. Before you execute the following code, please make sure that you have trained the out-of-core logistic regression model from the last section of *Chapter 8, Applying Machine Learning to Sentiment Analysis*, and have it ready in your current Python session:

```
>>> import pickle
>>> import os
>>> dest = os.path.join('movieclassifier', 'pkl_objects')
>>> if not os.path.exists(dest):
...     os.makedirs(dest)
>>> pickle.dump(stop,
...             open(os.path.join(dest, 'stopwords.pkl'),'wb'),
...             protocol=4)
>>> pickle.dump(clf,
...             open(os.path.join(dest, 'classifier.pkl'), 'wb'),
...             protocol=4)
```

Using the preceding code, we created a movieclassifier directory where we will later store the files and data for our web application. Within this movieclassifier directory, we created a pkl_objects subdirectory to save the serialized Python objects to our local drive. Via pickle's dump method, we then serialized the trained logistic regression model as well as the stop word set from the NLTK library so that we don't have to install the NLTK vocabulary on our server. The dump method takes as its first argument the object that we want to pickle, and for the second argument we provided an open file object that the Python object will be written to. Via the wb argument inside the open function, we opened the file in binary mode for pickle, and we set protocol=4 to choose the latest and most efficient pickle protocol that has been added to Python 3.4. (If you have problems using protocol 4, please check if you are using the latest Python 3 version install. Alternatively, you may consider choosing a lower protocol number.)

> Our logistic regression model contains several NumPy arrays, such as the weight vector, and a more efficient way to serialize NumPy arrays is to use the alternative joblib library. To ensure compatibility with the server environment that we will use in later sections, we will use the standard pickle approach. If you are interested, you can find more information about joblib at `https://pypi.python.org/pypi/joblib`.

We don't need to pickle the `HashingVectorizer`, since it does not need to be fitted. Instead, we can create a new Python script file, from which we can import the vectorizer into our current Python session. Now, copy the following code and save it as `vectorizer.py` in the `movieclassifier` directory:

```
from sklearn.feature_extraction.text import HashingVectorizer
import re
import os
import pickle

cur_dir = os.path.dirname(__file__)
stop = pickle.load(open(
                os.path.join(cur_dir,
                'pkl_objects',
                'stopwords.pkl'), 'rb'))

def tokenizer(text):
    text = re.sub('<[^>]*>', '', text)
    emoticons = re.findall('(?::|;|=)(?:-)?(?:\)|\(|D|P)',
                        text.lower())
    text = re.sub('[\W]+', ' ', text.lower()) \
                + ' '.join(emoticons).replace('-', '')
    tokenized = [w for w in text.split() if w not in stop]
    return tokenized

vect = HashingVectorizer(decode_error='ignore',
                        n_features=2**21,
                        preprocessor=None,
                        tokenizer=tokenizer)
```

After we have pickled the Python objects and created the `vectorizer.py` file, it would now be a good idea to restart our Python interpreter or IPython Notebook kernel to test if we can deserialize the objects without error. However, please note that unpickling data from an untrusted source can be a potential security risk since the pickle module is not secure against malicious code. From your terminal, navigate to the `movieclassifier` directory, start a new Python session and execute the following code to verify that you can import the vectorizer and unpickle the classifier:

```
>>> import pickle
>>> import re
>>> import os
>>> from vectorizer import vect
>>> clf = pickle.load(open(
...         os.path.join('pkl_objects',
...                      'classifier.pkl'), 'rb'))
```

After we have successfully loaded the vectorizer and unpickled the classifier, we can now use these objects to pre-process document samples and make predictions about their sentiment:

```
>>> import numpy as np
>>> label = {0:'negative', 1:'positive'}
>>> example = ['I love this movie']
>>> X = vect.transform(example)
>>> print('Prediction: %s\nProbability: %.2f%%' %\
...         (label[clf.predict(X)[0]],
...          np.max(clf.predict_proba(X))*100))
Prediction: positive
Probability: 91.56%
```

Since our classifier returns the class labels as integers, we defined a simple Python dictionary to map those integers to their sentiment. We then used the `HashingVectorizer` to transform the simple example document into a word vector X. Finally, we used the `predict` method of the logistic regression classifier to predict the class label as well as the `predict_proba` method to return the corresponding probability of our prediction. Note that the `predict_proba` method call returns an array with a probability value for each unique class label. Since the class label with the largest probability corresponds to the class label that is returned by the `predict` call, we used the `np.max` function to return the probability of the predicted class.

Setting up a SQLite database for data storage

In this section, we will set up a simple **SQLite database** to collect optional feedback about the predictions from users of the web application. We can use this feedback to update our classification model. SQLite is an open source SQL database engine that doesn't require a separate server to operate, which makes it ideal for smaller projects and simple web applications. Essentially, a SQLite database can be understood as a single, self-contained database file that allows us to directly access storage files. Furthermore, SQLite doesn't require any system-specific configuration and is supported by all common operating systems. It has gained a reputation for being very reliable as it is used by popular companies, such as Google, Mozilla, Adobe, Apple, Microsoft, and many more. If you want to learn more about SQLite, I recommend you visit the official website at http://www.sqlite.org.

Fortunately, following Python's *batteries included* philosophy, there is already an API in the Python standard library, **sqlite3**, which allows us to work with SQLite databases (for more information about sqlite3, please visit https://docs.python.org/3.4/library/sqlite3.html).

By executing the following code, we will create a new SQLite database inside the `movieclassifier` directory and store two example movie reviews:

```
>>> import sqlite3
>>> import os
>>> conn = sqlite3.connect('reviews.sqlite')
>>> c = conn.cursor()
>>> c.execute('CREATE TABLE review_db'\
...           ' (review TEXT, sentiment INTEGER, date TEXT)')
>>> example1 = 'I love this movie'
>>> c.execute("INSERT INTO review_db"\
...           " (review, sentiment, date) VALUES"\
...           " (?, ?, DATETIME('now'))", (example1, 1))
>>> example2 = 'I disliked this movie'
>>> c.execute("INSERT INTO review_db"\
...           " (review, sentiment, date) VALUES"\
...           " (?, ?, DATETIME('now'))", (example2, 0))
>>> conn.commit()
>>> conn.close()
```

Following the preceding code example, we created a connection (conn) to an SQLite database file by calling sqlite3's connect method, which created the new database file reviews.sqlite in the movieclassifier directory if it didn't already exist. Please note that SQLite doesn't implement a replace function for existing tables; you need to delete the database file manually from your file browser if you want to execute the code a second time. Next, we created a cursor via the cursor method, which allows us to traverse over the database records using the powerful SQL syntax. Via the first execute call, we then created a new database table, review_db. We used this to store and access database entries. Along with review_db, we also created three columns in this database table: review, sentiment, and date. We used these to store two example movie reviews and respective class labels (sentiments). Using the SQL command DATETIME('now'), we also added date-and timestamps to our entries. In addition to the timestamps, we used the question mark symbols (?) to pass the movie review texts (example1 and example2) and the corresponding class labels (1 and 0) as positional arguments to the execute method as members of a tuple. Lastly, we called the commit method to save the changes that we made to the database and closed the connection via the close method.

To check if the entries have been stored in the database table correctly, we will now reopen the connection to the database and use the SQL SELECT command to fetch all rows in the database table that have been committed between the beginning of the year 2015 and today:

```
>>> conn = sqlite3.connect('reviews.sqlite')
>>> c = conn.cursor()
>>> c.execute("SELECT * FROM review_db WHERE date"\
...     " BETWEEN '2015-01-01 00:00:00' AND DATETIME('now')")
>>> results = c.fetchall()
>>> conn.close()
>>> print(results)
[('I love this movie', 1, '2015-06-02 16:02:12'), ('I disliked this
movie', 0, '2015-06-02 16:02:12')]
```

Alternatively, we could also use the free Firefox browser plugin **SQLite Manager** (available at https://addons.mozilla.org/en-US/firefox/addon/sqlite-manager/), which offers a nice GUI interface for working with SQLite databases as shown in the following screenshot:

rowid	review	sentiment	date
1	I love this movie	1	2015-06-02 16:02:12
2	I disliked this movie	0	2015-06-02 16:02:12

TABLE review_db Search Show All Add

reviews.sqlite

▶ Master Table (1)
▼ Tables (1)
  ▼ review_db
    review
    sentiment
    date
▶ Views (0)
▶ Indexes (0)
▶ Triggers (0)

Directory ▶ (Select Profile Database) Go

Structure | Browse & Search | Execute SQL

SQLite 3.8.5 Gecko 33.1 0.8.3.1-signed **Exclusive** Number of files in selected directory: 7

Developing a web application with Flask

After we have prepared the code to classify movie reviews in the previous subsection, let's discuss the basics of the Flask web framework to develop our web application. After Armin Ronacher's initial release of Flask in 2010, the framework has gained huge popularity over the years and examples of popular applications that make use of Flask include LinkedIn and Pinterest. Since Flask is written in Python, it provides us Python programmers with a convenient interface for embedding existing Python code such as our movie classifier.

Flask is also known as a *microframework*, which means that its core is kept lean and simple but can be easily extended with other libraries. Although the learning curve of the lightweight Flask API is not nearly as steep as those of other popular Python web frameworks, such as Django, I encourage you to take a look at the official Flask documentation at http://flask.pocoo.org/docs/0.10/ to learn more about its functionality.

If the Flask library is not already installed in your current Python environment, you can simply install it via pip from your terminal (at the time of writing, the latest stable release was Version 0.10.1):

```
pip install flask
```

Our first Flask web application

In this subsection, we will develop a very simple web application to become more familiar with the Flask API before we implement our movie classifier. First, we create a directory tree:

```
1st_flask_app_1/
    app.py
    templates/
        first_app.html
```

The app.py file will contain the main code that will be executed by the Python interpreter to run the Flask web application. The templates directory is the directory in which Flask will look for static HTML files for rendering in the web browser. Let's now take a look at the contents of app.py:

```python
from flask import Flask, render_template

app = Flask(__name__)

@app.route('/')
def index():
    return render_template('first_app.html')

if __name__ == '__main__':
    app.run()
```

In this case, we run our application as a single module, thus we initialized a new Flask instance with the argument __name__ to let Flask know that it can find the HTML template folder (templates) in the same directory where it is located. Next, we used the route decorator (@app.route('/')) to specify the URL that should trigger the execution of the index function. Here, our index function simply renders the HTML file first_app.html, which is located in the templates folder. Lastly, we used the run function to only run the application on the server when this script is directly executed by the Python interpreter, which we ensured using the if statement with __name__ == '__main__'.

Now, let's take a look at the contents of the `first_app.html` file. If you are not familiar with the HTML syntax yet, I recommend you visit `https://developer.mozilla.org/en-US/docs/Web/HTML` for useful tutorials for learning the basics of HTML.

```
<!doctype html>
<html>
  <head>
    <title>First app</title>
  </head>
  <body>
  <div>Hi, this is my first Flask web app!</div>
  </body>
</html>
```

Here, we have simply filled an empty HTML template file with a `div` element (a block level element) that contains the sentence: `Hi, this is my first Flask web app!`. Conveniently, Flask allows us to run our apps locally, which is useful for developing and testing web applications before we deploy them on a public web server. Now, let's start our web application by executing the command from the terminal inside the `1st_flask_app_1` directory:

```
python3 app.py
```

We should now see a line such as the following displayed in the terminal:

```
* Running on http://127.0.0.1:5000/
```

This line contains the address of our local server. We can now enter this address in our web browser to see the web application in action. If everything has executed correctly, we should now see a simple website with the content: **Hi, this is my first Flask web app!**.

Form validation and rendering

In this subsection, we will extend our simple Flask web application with HTML form elements to learn how to collect data from a user using the **WTForms** library (`https://wtforms.readthedocs.org/en/latest/`), which can be installed via pip:

```
pip install wtforms
```

This web app will prompt a user to type in his or her name into a text field, as shown in the following screenshot:

After the submission button (**Say Hello**) has been clicked and the form is validated, a new HTML page will be rendered to display the user's name.

The new directory structure that we need to set up for this application looks like this:

```
1st_flask_app_2/
    app.py
    static/
        style.css
    templates/
        _formhelpers.html
        first_app.html
        hello.html
```

The following are the contents of our modified app.py file:

```
from flask import Flask, render_template, request
from wtforms import Form, TextAreaField, validators
```

```
app = Flask(__name__)

class HelloForm(Form):
    sayhello = TextAreaField('',[validators.DataRequired()])

@app.route('/')
def index():
    form = HelloForm(request.form)
    return render_template('first_app.html', form=form)

@app.route('/hello', methods=['POST'])
def hello():
    form = HelloForm(request.form)
    if request.method == 'POST' and form.validate():
        name = request.form['sayhello']
        return render_template('hello.html', name=name)
    return render_template('first_app.html', form=form)

if __name__ == '__main__':
    app.run(debug=True)
```

Using wtforms, we extended the index function with a text field that we will embed in our start page using the TextAreaField class, which automatically checks whether a user has provided valid input text or not. Furthermore, we defined a new function, hello, which will render an HTML page hello.html if the form has been validated. Here, we used the POST method to transport the form data to the server in the message body. Finally, by setting the argument debug=True inside the app.run method, we further activated Flask's debugger. This is a useful feature for developing new web applications.

Now, we will implement a generic macro in the file _formhelpers.html via the **Jinja2** templating engine, which we will later import in our first_app.html file to render the text field:

```
{% macro render_field(field) %}
  <dt>{{ field.label }}
  <dd>{{ field(**kwargs)|safe }}
  {% if field.errors %}
    <ul class=errors>
    {% for error in field.errors %}
      <li>{{ error }}</li>
    {% endfor %}
    </ul>
  {% endif %}
  </dd>
  </dt>
{% endmacro %}
```

An in-depth discussion about the Jinja2 templating language is beyond the scope of this book. However, you can find a comprehensive documentation of the Jinja2 syntax at `http://jinja.pocoo.org`.

Next, we set up a simple **Cascading Style Sheets (CSS)** file, `style.css`, to demonstrate how the look and feel of HTML documents can be modified. We have to save the following CSS file, which will simply double the font size of our HTML body elements, in a subdirectory called `static`, which is the default directory where Flask looks for static files such as CSS. The code is as follows:

```css
body {
    font-size: 2em;
}
```

The following are the contents of the modified `first_app.html` file that will now render a text form where a user can enter a name:

```html
<!doctype html>
<html>
  <head>
    <title>First app</title>
    <link rel="stylesheet" href="{{ url_for('static',
    filename='style.css') }}">
  </head>
  <body>

{% from "_formhelpers.html" import render_field %}

<div>What's your name?</div>
<form method=post action="/hello">
  <dl>
    {{ render_field(form.sayhello) }}
  </dl>
  <input type=submit value='Say Hello' name='submit_btn'>
</form>
  </body>
</html>
```

In the header section of `first_app.html`, we loaded the CSS file. It should now alter the size of all text elements in the HTML body. In the HTML body section, we imported the form macro from `_formhelpers.html` and we rendered the `sayhello` form that we specified in the `app.py` file. Furthermore, we added a button to the same form element so that a user can submit the text field entry.

Lastly, we create a `hello.html` file that will be rendered via the line return `render_template('hello.html', name=name)` inside the `hello` function, which we defined in the `app.py` script to display the text that a user submitted via the text field. The code is as follows:

```
<!doctype html>
<html>
  <head>
    <title>First app</title>
    <link rel="stylesheet" href="{{ url_for('static',
      filename='style.css') }}">
  </head>
  <body>

<div>Hello {{ name }}</div>
  </body>
</html>
```

Having set up our modified Flask web application, we can run it locally by executing the following command from the app's main directory and we can view the result in our web browser at `http://127.0.0.1:5000/`:

python3 app.py

> If you are new to web development, some of those concepts may seem very complicated at first sight. In that case, I encourage you to simply set up the preceding files in a directory on your hard drive and examine them closely. You will see that the Flask web framework is actually pretty straightforward and much simpler than it might initially appear! Also, for more help, don't forget to look at the excellent Flask documentation and examples at `http://flask.pocoo.org/docs/0.10/`.

Turning the movie classifier into a web application

Now that we are somewhat familiar with the basics of Flask web development, let's advance to the next step and implement our movie classifier into a web application. In this section, we will develop a web application that will first prompt a user to enter a movie review, as shown in the following screenshot:

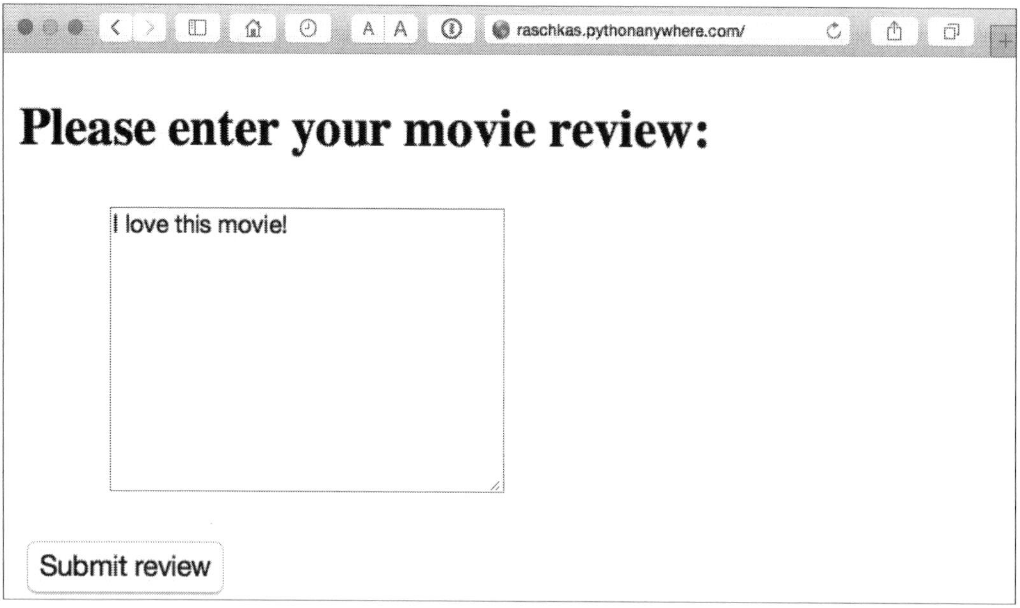

After the review has been submitted, the user will see a new page that shows the predicted class label and the probability of the prediction. Furthermore, the user will be able to provide feedback about this prediction by clicking on the **Correct** or **Incorrect** button, as shown in the following screenshot:

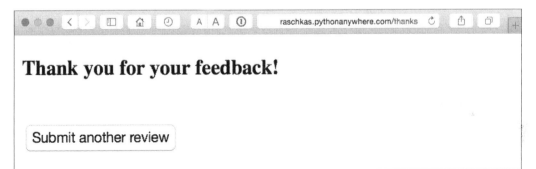

If a user clicked on either the **Correct** or **Incorrect** button, our classification model will be updated with respect to the user's feedback. Furthermore, we will also store the movie review text provided by the user as well as the suggested class label, which can be inferred from the button click, in a SQLite database for future reference. The third page that the user will see after clicking on one of the feedback buttons is a simple *thank you* screen with a **Submit another review** button that redirects the user back to the start page. This is shown in the following screenshot:

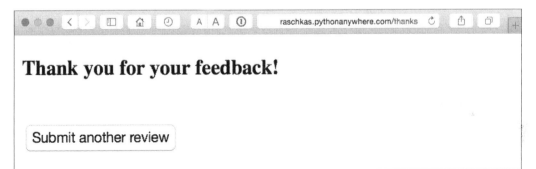

Before we take a closer look at the code implementation of this web application, I encourage you to take a look at the live demo that I uploaded at `http://raschkas.pythonanywhere.com` to get a better understanding of what we are trying to accomplish in this section.

To start with the big picture, let's take a look at the directory tree that we are going to create for this movie classification app, which is shown here:

In the previous section of this chapter, we already created the vectorizer.py file, the SQLite database reviews.sqlite, and the pkl_objects subdirectory with the pickled Python objects.

The app.py file in the main directory is the Python script that contains our Flask code, and we will use the review.sqlite database file (which we created earlier in this chapter) to store the movie reviews that are being submitted to our web app. The templates subdirectory contains the HTML templates that will be rendered by Flask and displayed in the browser, and the static subdirectory will contain a simple CSS file to adjust the look of the rendered HTML code.

Since the app.py file is rather long, we will conquer it in two steps. The first section of app.py imports the Python modules and objects that we are going to need, as well as the code to unpickle and set up our classification model:

```
from flask import Flask, render_template, request
from wtforms import Form, TextAreaField, validators
import pickle
import sqlite3
import os
import numpy as np
```

```
# import HashingVectorizer from local dir
from vectorizer import vect

app = Flask(__name__)

######## Preparing the Classifier
cur_dir = os.path.dirname(__file__)
clf = pickle.load(open(os.path.join(cur_dir,
                  'pkl_objects/classifier.pkl'), 'rb'))
db = os.path.join(cur_dir, 'reviews.sqlite')

def classify(document):
    label = {0: 'negative', 1: 'positive'}
    X = vect.transform([document])
    y = clf.predict(X)[0]
    proba = clf.predict_proba(X).max()
    return label[y], proba

def train(document, y):
    X = vect.transform([document])
    clf.partial_fit(X, [y])

def sqlite_entry(path, document, y):
    conn = sqlite3.connect(path)
    c = conn.cursor()
    c.execute("INSERT INTO review_db (review, sentiment, date)"\
    " VALUES (?, ?, DATETIME('now'))", (document, y))
    conn.commit()
    conn.close()
```

This first part of the app.py script should look very familiar to us by now. We simply imported the HashingVectorizer and unpickled the logistic regression classifier. Next, we defined a classify function to return the predicted class label as well as the corresponding probability prediction of a given text document. The train function can be used to update the classifier given that a document and a class label are provided. Using the sqlite_entry function, we can store a submitted movie review in our SQLite database along with its class label and timestamp for our personal records. Note that the clf object will be reset to its original, pickled state if we restart the web application. At the end of this chapter, you will learn how to use the data that we collect in the SQLite database to update the classifier permanently.

The concepts in the second part of the `app.py` script should also look quite familiar to us:

```python
app = Flask(__name__)
class ReviewForm(Form):
    moviereview = TextAreaField('',
                                [validators.DataRequired(),
                                validators.length(min=15)])

@app.route('/')
def index():
    form = ReviewForm(request.form)
    return render_template('reviewform.html', form=form)

@app.route('/results', methods=['POST'])
def results():
    form = ReviewForm(request.form)
    if request.method == 'POST' and form.validate():
        review = request.form['moviereview']
        y, proba = classify(review)
        return render_template('results.html',
                               content=review,
                               prediction=y,
                               probability=round(proba*100, 2))
    return render_template('reviewform.html', form=form)

@app.route('/thanks', methods=['POST'])
def feedback():
    feedback = request.form['feedback_button']
    review = request.form['review']
    prediction = request.form['prediction']

    inv_label = {'negative': 0, 'positive': 1}
    y = inv_label[prediction]
    if feedback == 'Incorrect':
        y = int(not(y))
    train(review, y)
    sqlite_entry(db, review, y)
    return render_template('thanks.html')

if __name__ == '__main__':
    app.run(debug=True)
```

We defined a `ReviewForm` class that instantiates a `TextAreaField`, which will be rendered in the `reviewform.html` template file (the landing page of our web app). This, in turn, is rendered by the `index` function. With the `validators. length(min=15)` parameter, we require the user to enter a review that contains at least 15 characters. Inside the `results` function, we fetch the contents of the submitted web form and pass it on to our classifier to predict the sentiment of the movie classifier, which will then be displayed in the rendered `results.html` template.

The `feedback` function may look a little bit complicated at first glance. It essentially fetches the predicted class label from the `results.html` template if a user clicked on the **Correct** or **Incorrect** feedback button, and transforms the predicted sentiment back into an integer class label that will be used to update the classifier via the `train` function, which we implemented in the first section of the `app.py` script. Also, a new entry to the SQLite database will be made via the `sqlite_entry` function if feedback was provided, and eventually the `thanks.html` template will be rendered to thank the user for the feedback.

Next, let's take a look at the `reviewform.html` template, which constitutes the starting page of our application:

```html
<!doctype html>
<html>
<head>
    <title>Movie Classification</title>
</head>
  <body>

<h2>Please enter your movie review:</h2>

{% from "_formhelpers.html" import render_field %}

<form method=post action="/results">
  <dl>
    {{ render_field(form.moviereview, cols='30', rows='10') }}
  </dl>
  <div>
    <input type=submit value='Submit review' name='submit_btn'>
  </div>
</form>

  </body>
</html>
```

Here, we simply imported the same _formhelpers.html template that we defined in the *Form validation and rendering* section earlier in this chapter. The render_field function of this macro is used to render a TextAreaField where a user can provide a movie review and submit it via the **Submit review** button displayed at the bottom of the page. This TextAreaField is 30 columns wide and 10 rows tall.

Our next template, results.html, looks a little bit more interesting:

```html
<!doctype html>
<html>
  <head>
    <title>Movie Classification</title>
    <link rel="stylesheet" href="{{ url_for('static',
      filename='style.css') }}">
  </head>
  <body>

<h3>Your movie review:</h3>
<div>{{ content }}</div>

<h3>Prediction:</h3>
<div>This movie review is <strong>{{ prediction }}</strong>
  (probability: {{ probability }}%).</div>

<div class='button'>
  <form action="/thanks" method="post">
    <input type=submit value='Correct' name='feedback_button'>
    <input type=submit value='Incorrect' name='feedback_button'>
    <input type=hidden value='{{ prediction }}' name='prediction'>
    <input type=hidden value='{{ content }}' name='review'>
  </form>
</div>

<div class='button'>
  <form action="/">
    <input type=submit value='Submit another review'>
  </form>
</div>

  </body>
</html>
```

First, we inserted the submitted review as well as the results of the prediction in the corresponding fields {{ content }}, {{ prediction }}, and {{ probability }}. You may notice that we used the {{ content }} and {{ prediction }} placeholder variables a second time in the form that contains the **Correct** and **Incorrect** buttons. This is a workaround to POST those values back to the server to update the classifier and store the review in case the user clicks on one of those two buttons. Furthermore, we imported a CSS file (style.css) at the beginning of the results.html file. The setup of this file is quite simple; it limits the width of the contents of this web app to 600 pixels and moves the **Incorrect** and **Correct** buttons labeled with the div id button down by 20 pixels:

```
body{
  width:600px;
}
.button{
  padding-top: 20px;
}
```

This CSS file is merely a placeholder, so please feel free to adjust it to adjust the look and feel of the web app to your liking.

The last HTML file we will implement for our web application is the thanks.html template. As the name suggests, it simply provides a nice *thank you* message to the user after providing feedback via the **Correct** or **Incorrect** button. Furthermore, we put a **Submit another review** button at the bottom of this page, which will redirect the user to the starting page. The contents of the thanks.html file are as follows:

```
<!doctype html>
<html>
  <head>
    <title>Movie Classification</title>
</head>
  <body>

<h3>Thank you for your feedback!</h3>
<div id='button'>
  <form action="/">
    <input type=submit value='Submit another review'>
  </form>
</div>

  </body>
</html>
```

Now, it would be a good idea to start the web app locally from our terminal via the following command before we advance to the next subsection and deploy it on a public web server:

```
python3 app.py
```

After we have finished testing our app, we also shouldn't forget to remove the `debug=True` argument in the `app.run()` command of our `app.py` script.

Deploying the web application to a public server

After we have tested the web application locally, we are now ready to deploy our web application onto a public web server. For this tutorial, we will be using the **PythonAnywhere** web hosting service, which specializes in the hosting of Python web applications and makes it extremely simple and hassle-free. Furthermore, PythonAnywhere offers a beginner account option that lets us run a single web application free of charge.

To create a new PythonAnywhere account, we visit the website at `https://www.pythonanywhere.com` and click on the **Pricing & signup** link that is located in the top-right corner. Next, we click on the **Create a Beginner account** button where we need to provide a username, password, and a valid e-mail address. After we have read and agreed to the terms and conditions, we should have a new account.

Unfortunately, the free beginner account doesn't allow us to access the remote server via the SSH protocol from our command-line terminal. Thus, we need to use the PythonAnywhere web interface to manage our web application. But before we can upload our local application files to the server, we need to create a new web application for our PythonAnywhere account. After we click on the **Dashboard** button in the top-right corner, we have access to the control panel shown at the top of the page. Next, we click on the **Web** tab that is now visible at the top of the page. We proceed by clicking on the **Add a new web app** button on the left, which lets us create a new Python 3.4 Flask web application that we name `movieclassifier`.

After creating a new application for our PythonAnywhere account, we head over to the **Files** tab to upload the files from our local `movieclassifier` directory using the PythonAnywhere web interface. After uploading the web application files that we created locally on our computer, we should have a `movieclassifier` directory in our PythonAnywhere account. It contains the same directories and files as our local `movieclassifier` directory has, as shown in the following screenshot:

Lastly, we head over to the **Web** tab one more time and click on the **Reload \<username\>.pythonanywhere.com** button to propagate the changes and refresh our web application. Finally, our web app should now be up and running and publicly available via the address `<username>.pythonanywhere.com`.

Unfortunately, web servers can be quite sensitive to the tiniest problems in our web app. If you are experiencing problems with running the web application on PythonAnywhere and are receiving error messages in your browser, you can check the server and error logs which can be accessed from the **Web** tab in your PythonAnywhere account to better diagnose the problem.

Updating the movie review classifier

While our predictive model is updated on-the-fly whenever a user provides feedback about the classification, the updates to the clf object will be reset if the web server crashes or restarts. If we reload the web application, the clf object will be reinitialized from the classifier.pkl pickle file. One option to apply the updates permanently would be to pickle the clf object once again after each update. However, this would become computationally very inefficient with a growing number of users and could corrupt the pickle file if users provide feedback simultaneously. An alternative solution is to update the predictive model from the feedback data that is being collected in the SQLite database. One option would be to download the SQLite database from the PythonAnywhere server, update the clf object locally on our computer, and upload the new pickle file to PythonAnywhere. To update the classifier locally on our computer, we create an update.py script file in the movieclassifier directory with the following contents:

```python
import pickle
import sqlite3
import numpy as np
import os

# import HashingVectorizer from local dir
from vectorizer import vect

def update_model(db_path, model, batch_size=10000):

    conn = sqlite3.connect(db_path)
    c = conn.cursor()
    c.execute('SELECT * from review_db')

    results = c.fetchmany(batch_size)
    while results:
        data = np.array(results)
        X = data[:, 0]
        y = data[:, 1].astype(int)

        classes = np.array([0, 1])
        X_train = vect.transform(X)
        model.partial_fit(X_train, y, classes=classes)
        results = c.fetchmany(batch_size)

    conn.close()
    return model
```

```
cur_dir = os.path.dirname(__file__)

clf = pickle.load(open(os.path.join(cur_dir,
                  'pkl_objects',
                  'classifier.pkl'), 'rb'))
db = os.path.join(cur_dir, 'reviews.sqlite')

update_model(db_path=db, model=clf, batch_size=10000)

# Uncomment the following lines if you are sure that
# you want to update your classifier.pkl file
# permanently.

# pickle.dump(clf, open(os.path.join(cur_dir,
#             'pkl_objects', 'classifier.pkl'), 'wb')
#             , protocol=4)
```

The `update_model` function will fetch entries from the SQLite database in batches of 10,000 entries at a time unless the database contains fewer entries. Alternatively, we could also fetch one entry at a time by using `fetchone` instead of `fetchmany`, which would be computationally very inefficient. Using the alternative `fetchall` method could be a problem if we are working with large datasets that exceed the computer or server's memory capacity.

Now that we have created the `update.py` script, we could also upload it to the `movieclassifier` directory on PythonAnywhere and import the `update_model` function in the main application script `app.py` to update the classifier from the SQLite database every time we restart the web application. In order to do so, we just need to add a line of code to import the `update_model` function from the `update.py` script at the top of `app.py`:

```
# import update function from local dir
from update import update_model
```

We then need to call the `update_model` function in the main application body:

```
...
if __name__ == '__main__':
    clf = update_model(db_path="db", model=clf, batch_size=10000)
...
```

Summary

In this chapter, you learned about many useful and practical topics that extend our knowledge of machine learning theory. You learned how to serialize a model after training and how to load it for later use cases. Furthermore, we created a SQLite database for efficient data storage and created a web application that lets us make our movie classifier available to the outside world.

Throughout this book, we have really discussed a lot about machine learning concepts, best practices, and supervised models for classification. In the next chapter, we will take a look at another subcategory of supervised learning, regression analysis, which lets us predict outcome variables on a continuous scale, in contrast to the categorical class labels of the classification models that we have been working with so far.

10
Predicting Continuous Target Variables with Regression Analysis

Throughout the previous chapters, you learned a lot about the main concepts behind *supervised learning* and trained many different models for classification tasks to predict group memberships or categorical variables. In this chapter, we will take a dive into another subcategory of supervised learning: *regression analysis*.

Regression models are used to predict target variables on a *continuous* scale, which makes them attractive for addressing many questions in science as well as applications in industry, such as understanding relationships between variables, evaluating trends, or making forecasts. One example would be predicting the sales of a company in future months.

In this chapter, we will discuss the main concepts of regression models and cover the following topics:

- Exploring and visualizing datasets
- Looking at different approaches to implement linear regression models
- Training regression models that are robust to outliers
- Evaluating regression models and diagnosing common problems
- Fitting regression models to nonlinear data

Introducing a simple linear regression model

The goal of simple (*univariate*) linear regression is to model the relationship between a single feature (explanatory variable x) and a continuous valued *response* (target variable y). The equation of a linear model with one explanatory variable is defined as follows:

$$y = w_0 + w_1 x$$

Here, the weight w_0 represents the y axis intercepts and w_1 is the coefficient of the explanatory variable. Our goal is to learn the weights of the linear equation to describe the relationship between the explanatory variable and the target variable, which can then be used to predict the responses of new explanatory variables that were not part of the training dataset.

Based on the linear equation that we defined previously, linear regression can be understood as finding the best-fitting straight line through the sample points, as shown in the following figure:

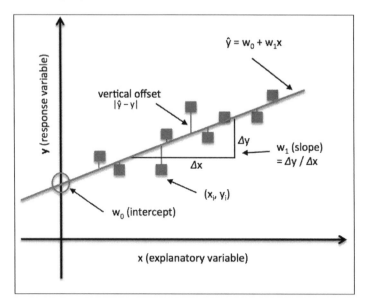

This best-fitting line is also called the **regression line**, and the vertical lines from the regression line to the sample points are the so-called **offsets** or **residuals**—the errors of our prediction.

The special case of one explanatory variable is also called **simple linear regression**, but of course we can also generalize the linear regression model to multiple explanatory variables. Hence, this process is called **multiple linear regression**:

$$y = w_0 x_0 + w_1 x_1 + \ldots + w_m x_m = \sum_{i=0}^{m} w_i x_i = w^T x$$

Here, w_0 is the y axis intercept with $x_0 = 1$.

Exploring the Housing Dataset

Before we implement our first linear regression model, we will introduce a new dataset, the **Housing Dataset**, which contains information about houses in the suburbs of Boston collected by D. Harrison and D.L. Rubinfeld in 1978. The *Housing Dataset* has been made freely available and can be downloaded from the *UCI machine learning repository* at https://archive.ics.uci.edu/ml/datasets/Housing.

The features of the 506 samples may be summarized as shown in the excerpt of the dataset description:

- **CRIM**: This is the per capita crime rate by town
- **ZN**: This is the proportion of residential land zoned for lots larger than 25,000 sq.ft.
- **INDUS**: This is the proportion of non-retail business acres per town
- **CHAS**: This is the Charles River dummy variable (this is equal to 1 if tract bounds river; 0 otherwise)
- **NOX**: This is the nitric oxides concentration (parts per 10 million)
- **RM**: This is the average number of rooms per dwelling
- **AGE**: This is the proportion of owner-occupied units built prior to 1940
- **DIS**: This is the weighted distances to five Boston employment centers
- **RAD**: This is the index of accessibility to radial highways
- **TAX**: This is the full-value property-tax rate per $10,000
- **PTRATIO**: This is the pupil-teacher ratio by town
- **B**: This is calculated as *1000(Bk - 0.63)^2*, where Bk is the proportion of people of African American descent by town
- **LSTAT**: This is the percentage lower status of the population
- **MEDV**: This is the median value of owner-occupied homes in $1000s

For the rest of this chapter, we will regard the housing prices (MEDV) as our target variable – the variable that we want to predict using one or more of the 13 explanatory variables. Before we explore this dataset further, let's fetch it from the UCI repository into a pandas `DataFrame`:

```
>>> import pandas as pd
>>> df = pd.read_csv('https://archive.ics.uci.edu/ml/machine-learning-
databases/housing/housing.data',
...                  header=None, sep='\s+')
>>> df.columns = ['CRIM', 'ZN', 'INDUS', 'CHAS',
...               'NOX', 'RM', 'AGE', 'DIS', 'RAD',
...               'TAX', 'PTRATIO', 'B', 'LSTAT', 'MEDV']
>>> df.head()
```

To confirm that the dataset was loaded successfully, we displayed the first five lines of the dataset, as shown in the following screenshot:

	CRIM	ZN	INDUS	CHAS	NOX	RM	AGE	DIS	RAD	TAX	PTRATIO	B	LSTAT	MEDV
0	0.00632	18	2.31	0	0.538	6.575	65.2	4.0900	1	296	15.3	396.90	4.98	24.0
1	0.02731	0	7.07	0	0.469	6.421	78.9	4.9671	2	242	17.8	396.90	9.14	21.6
2	0.02729	0	7.07	0	0.469	7.185	61.1	4.9671	2	242	17.8	392.83	4.03	34.7
3	0.03237	0	2.18	0	0.458	6.998	45.8	6.0622	3	222	18.7	394.63	2.94	33.4
4	0.06905	0	2.18	0	0.458	7.147	54.2	6.0622	3	222	18.7	396.90	5.33	36.2

Visualizing the important characteristics of a dataset

Exploratory Data Analysis (EDA) is an important and recommended first step prior to the training of a machine learning model. In the rest of this section, we will use some simple yet useful techniques from the graphical EDA toolbox that may help us to visually detect the presence of outliers, the distribution of the data, and the relationships between features.

First, we will create a *scatterplot matrix* that allows us to visualize the pair-wise correlations between the different features in this dataset in one place. To plot the scatterplot matrix, we will use the `pairplot` function from the `seaborn` library (http://stanford.edu/~mwaskom/software/seaborn/), which is a Python library for drawing statistical plots based on matplotlib:

```
>>> import matplotlib.pyplot as plt
>>> import seaborn as sns
>>> sns.set(style='whitegrid', context='notebook')
```

```
>>> cols = ['LSTAT', 'INDUS', 'NOX', 'RM', 'MEDV']
>>> sns.pairplot(df[cols], size=2.5)
>>> plt.show()
```

As we can see in the following figure, the scatterplot matrix provides us with a useful graphical summary of the relationships in a dataset:

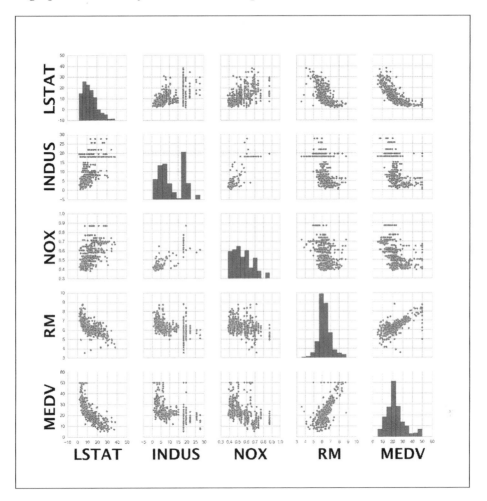

Importing the seaborn library modifies the default aesthetics of matplotlib for the current Python session. If you do not want to use seaborn's style settings, you can reset the matplotlib settings by executing the following command:

```
>>> sns.reset_orig()
```

Due to space constraints and for purposes of readability, we only plotted five columns from the dataset: **LSTAT, INDUS, NOX, RM,** and **MEDV**. However, you are encouraged to create a scatterplot matrix of the whole `DataFrame` to further explore the data.

Using this scatterplot matrix, we can now quickly eyeball how the data is distributed and whether it contains outliers. For example, we can see that there is a linear relationship between **RM** and the housing prices **MEDV** (the fifth column of the fourth row). Furthermore, we can see in the histogram (the lower right subplot in the scatter plot matrix) that the **MEDV** variable seems to be normally distributed but contains several outliers.

> Note that in contrast to common belief, training a linear regression model does not require that the explanatory or target variables are normally distributed. The normality assumption is only a requirement for certain statistical tests and hypothesis tests that are beyond the scope of this book (Montgomery, D. C., Peck, E. A., and Vining, G. G. *Introduction to linear regression analysis*. John Wiley and Sons, 2012, pp.318–319).

To quantify the linear relationship between the features, we will now create a correlation matrix. A correlation matrix is closely related to the covariance matrix that we have seen in the section about **principal component analysis (PCA)** in *Chapter 4, Building Good Training Sets – Data Preprocessing*. Intuitively, we can interpret the correlation matrix as a rescaled version of the covariance matrix. In fact, the correlation matrix is identical to a covariance matrix computed from standardized data.

The correlation matrix is a square matrix that contains the **Pearson product-moment correlation coefficients** (often abbreviated as **Pearson's r**), which measure the linear dependence between pairs of features. The correlation coefficients are bounded to the range -1 and 1. Two features have a perfect positive correlation if $r = 1$, no correlation if $r = 0$, and a perfect negative correlation if $r = -1$, respectively. As mentioned previously, Pearson's correlation coefficient can simply be calculated as the covariance between two features x and y (numerator) divided by the product of their standard deviations (denominator):

$$r = \frac{\sum_{i=1}^{n}\left[\left(x^{(i)} - \mu_x\right)\left(y^{(i)} - \mu_y\right)\right]}{\sqrt{\sum_{i=1}^{n}\left(x^{(i)} - \mu_x\right)^2}\sqrt{\sum_{i=1}^{n}\left(y^{(i)} - \mu_y\right)^2}} = \frac{\sigma_{xy}}{\sigma_x \sigma_y}$$

Here, μ denotes the sample mean of the corresponding feature, σ_{xy} is the covariance between the features x and y, and σ_x and σ_y are the features' standard deviations, respectively.

We can show that the covariance between standardized features is in fact equal to their linear correlation coefficient.

Let's first standardize the features x and y, to obtain their z-scores which we will denote as x' and y', respectively:

$$x' = \frac{x - \mu_x}{\sigma_x}, y' = \frac{y - \mu_y}{\sigma_y}$$

Remember that we calculate the (population) covariance between two features as follows:

$$\sigma_{xy} = \frac{1}{n} \sum_{i}^{n} \left(x^{(i)} - \mu_x \right)\left(y^{(i)} - \mu_y \right)$$

Since standardization centers a feature variable at mean 0, we can now calculate the covariance between the scaled features as follows:

$$\sigma'_{xy} = \frac{1}{n} \sum_{i}^{n} (x' - 0)(y' - 0)$$

Through resubstitution, we get the following result:

$$\frac{1}{n} \sum_{i}^{n} \left(\frac{x - \mu_x}{\sigma_x} \right)\left(\frac{y - \mu_y}{\sigma_y} \right)$$

$$\frac{1}{n \cdot \sigma_x \sigma_y} \sum_{i}^{n} \left(x^{(i)} - \mu_x \right)\left(y^{(i)} - \mu_y \right)$$

We can simplify it as follows:

$$\sigma'_{xy} = \frac{\sigma_{xy}}{\sigma_x \sigma_y}$$

In the following code example, we will use NumPy's `corrcoef` function on the five feature columns that we previously visualized in the scatterplot matrix, and we will use seaborn's `heatmap` function to plot the correlation matrix array as a heat map:

```
>>> import numpy as np
>>> cm = np.corrcoef(df[cols].values.T)
>>> sns.set(font_scale=1.5)
>>> hm = sns.heatmap(cm,
...                  cbar=True,
...                  annot=True,
...                  square=True,
...                  fmt='.2f',
...                  annot_kws={'size': 15},
...                  yticklabels=cols,
...                  xticklabels=cols)
>>> plt.show()
```

As we can see in the resulting figure, the correlation matrix provides us with another useful summary graphic that can help us to select features based on their respective linear correlations:

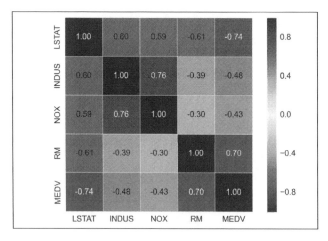

To fit a linear regression model, we are interested in those features that have a high correlation with our target variable **MEDV**. Looking at the preceding correlation matrix, we see that our target variable **MEDV** shows the largest correlation with the **LSTAT** variable (-0.74). However, as you might remember from the scatterplot matrix, there is a clear nonlinear relationship between **LSTAT** and **MEDV**. On the other hand, the correlation between **RM** and **MEDV** is also relatively high (0.70) and given the linear relationship between those two variables that we observed in the scatterplot, **RM** seems to be a good choice for an explanatory variable to introduce the concepts of a simple linear regression model in the following section.

Implementing an ordinary least squares linear regression model

At the beginning of this chapter, we discussed that linear regression can be understood as finding the best-fitting straight line through the sample points of our training data. However, we have neither defined the term *best-fitting* nor have we discussed the different techniques of fitting such a model. In the following subsections, we will fill in the missing pieces of this puzzle using the **Ordinary Least Squares (OLS)** method to estimate the parameters of the regression line that minimizes the sum of the squared vertical distances (residuals or errors) to the sample points.

Solving regression for regression parameters with gradient descent

Consider our implementation of the **ADAptive LInear NEuron (Adaline)** from *Chapter 2, Training Machine Learning Algorithms for Classification*; we remember that the artificial neuron uses a linear activation function and we defined a cost function $J(\cdot)$, which we minimized to learn the weights via optimization algorithms, such as **Gradient Descent (GD)** and **Stochastic Gradient Descent (SGD)**. This cost function in Adaline is the **Sum of Squared Errors (SSE)**. This is identical to the OLS cost function that we defined:

$$J(w) = \frac{1}{2} \sum_{i=1}^{n} \left(y^{(i)} - \hat{y}^{(i)} \right)^2$$

Here, $\hat{y}$ is the predicted value $\hat{y} = w^T x$ (note that the term $1/2$ is just used for convenience to derive the update rule of GD). Essentially, OLS linear regression can be understood as Adaline without the unit step function so that we obtain continuous target values instead of the class labels -1 and 1. To demonstrate the similarity, let's take the GD implementation of *Adaline* from *Chapter 2, Training Machine Learning Algorithms for Classification*, and remove the unit step function to implement our first linear regression model:

```
class LinearRegressionGD(object):

    def __init__(self, eta=0.001, n_iter=20):
        self.eta = eta
```

```
        self.n_iter = n_iter

    def fit(self, X, y):
        self.w_ = np.zeros(1 + X.shape[1])
        self.cost_ = []

        for i in range(self.n_iter):
            output = self.net_input(X)
            errors = (y - output)
            self.w_[1:] += self.eta * X.T.dot(errors)
            self.w_[0] += self.eta * errors.sum()
            cost = (errors**2).sum() / 2.0
            self.cost_.append(cost)
        return self

    def net_input(self, X):
        return np.dot(X, self.w_[1:]) + self.w_[0]

    def predict(self, X):
        return self.net_input(X)
```

If you need a refresher about how the weights are being updated—taking a step in the opposite direction of the gradient—please revisit the Adaline section in *Chapter 2, Training Machine Learning Algorithms for Classification*.

To see our `LinearRegressionGD` regressor in action, let's use the RM (number of rooms) variable from the Housing Data Set as the explanatory variable to train a model that can predict MEDV (the housing prices). Furthermore, we will standardize the variables for better convergence of the GD algorithm. The code is as follows:

```
>>> X = df[['RM']].values
>>> y = df['MEDV'].values
>>> from sklearn.preprocessing import StandardScaler
>>> sc_x = StandardScaler()
>>> sc_y = StandardScaler()
>>> X_std = sc_x.fit_transform(X)
>>> y_std = sc_y.fit_transform(y)
>>> lr = LinearRegressionGD()
>>> lr.fit(X_std, y_std)
```

We discussed in *Chapter 2, Training Machine Learning Algorithms for Classification,* that it is always a good idea to plot the cost as a function of the number of epochs (passes over the training dataset) when we are using optimization algorithms, such as gradient descent, to check for convergence. To cut a long story short, let's plot the cost against the number of epochs to check if the linear regression has converged:

```
>>> plt.plot(range(1, lr.n_iter+1), lr.cost_)
>>> plt.ylabel('SSE')
>>> plt.xlabel('Epoch')
>>> plt.show()
```

As we can see in the following plot, the GD algorithm converged after the fifth epoch:

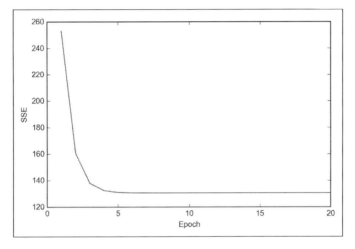

Next, let's visualize how well the linear regression line fits the training data. To do so, we will define a simple helper function that will plot a scatterplot of the training samples and add the regression line:

```
>>> def lin_regplot(X, y, model):
...     plt.scatter(X, y, c='blue')
...     plt.plot(X, model.predict(X), color='red')
...     return None
```

Now, we will use this `lin_regplot` function to plot the number of rooms against house prices:

```
>>> lin_regplot(X_std, y_std, lr)
>>> plt.xlabel('Average number of rooms [RM] (standardized)')
>>> plt.ylabel('Price in $1000\'s [MEDV] (standardized)')
>>> plt.show()
```

As we can see in the following plot, the linear regression line reflects the general trend that house prices tend to increase with the number of rooms:

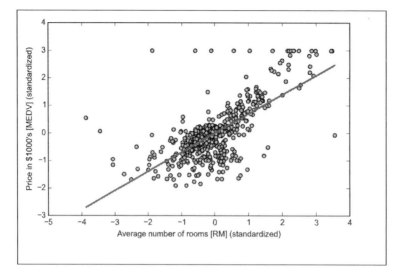

Although this observation makes intuitive sense, the data also tells us that the number of rooms does not explain the house prices very well in many cases. Later in this chapter, we will discuss how to quantify the performance of a regression model. Interestingly, we also observe a curious line $y = 3$, which suggests that the prices may have been clipped. In certain applications, it may also be important to report the predicted outcome variables on their original scale. To scale the predicted price outcome back on the **Price in $1000's** axes, we can simply apply the inverse_transform method of the StandardScaler:

```
>>> num_rooms_std = sc_x.transform([5.0])
>>> price_std = lr.predict(num_rooms_std)
>>> print("Price in $1000's: %.3f" % \
...        sc_y.inverse_transform(price_std))
Price in $1000's: 10.840
```

In the preceding code example, we used the previously trained linear regression model to predict the price of a house with five rooms. According to our model, such a house is worth $10,840.

On a side note, it is also worth mentioning that we technically don't have to update the weights of the intercept if we are working with standardized variables since the *y* axis intercept is always 0 in those cases. We can quickly confirm this by printing the weights:

```
>>> print('Slope: %.3f' % lr.w_[1])
Slope: 0.695
>>> print('Intercept: %.3f' % lr.w_[0])
Intercept: -0.000
```

Estimating the coefficient of a regression model via scikit-learn

In the previous section, we implemented a working model for regression analysis. However, in a real-world application, we may be interested in more efficient implementations, for example, scikit-learn's `LinearRegression` object that makes use of the **LIBLINEAR** library and advanced optimization algorithms that work better with unstandardized variables. This is sometimes desirable for certain applications:

```
>>> from sklearn.linear_model import LinearRegression
>>> slr = LinearRegression()
>>> slr.fit(X, y)
>>> print('Slope: %.3f' % slr.coef_[0])
Slope: 9.102
>>> print('Intercept: %.3f' % slr.intercept_)
Intercept: -34.671
```

As we can see by executing the preceding code, scikit-learn's `LinearRegression` model fitted with the unstandardized **RM** and **MEDV** variables yielded different model coefficients. Let's compare it to our own GD implementation by plotting MEDV against RM:

```
>>> lin_regplot(X, y, slr)
>>> plt.xlabel('Average number of rooms [RM]')
>>> plt.ylabel('Price in $1000\'s [MEDV]')
>>> plt.show()w
```

Now, when we plot the training data and our fitted model by executing the code above, we can see that the overall result looks identical to our GD implementation:

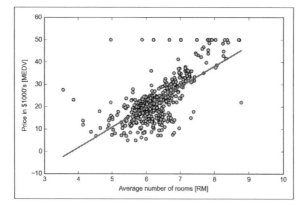

As an alternative to using machine learning libraries, there is also a closed-form solution for solving OLS involving a system of linear equations that can be found in most introductory statistics textbooks:

$$w = \left(X^T X \right)^{-1} X^T y$$

We can implement it in Python as follows:

```
# adding a column vector of "ones"
>>> Xb = np.hstack((np.ones((X.shape[0], 1)), X))
>>> w = np.zeros(X.shape[1])
>>> z = np.linalg.inv(np.dot(Xb.T, Xb))
>>> w = np.dot(z, np.dot(Xb.T, y))
>>> print('Slope: %.3f' % w[1])
Slope: 9.102
>>> print('Intercept: %.3f' % w[0])
Intercept: -34.671
```

The advantage of this method is that it is guaranteed to find the optimal solution analytically. However, if we are working with very large datasets, it can be computationally too expensive to invert the matrix in this formula (sometimes also called the **normal equation**) or the sample matrix may be singular (non-invertible), which is why we may prefer iterative methods in certain cases.

If you are interested in more information on how to obtain the normal equations, I recommend you take a look at Dr. Stephen Pollock's chapter, *The Classical Linear Regression Model* from his lectures at the University of Leicester, which are available for free at http://www.le.ac.uk/users/dsgp1/COURSES/MESOMET/ECMETXT/06mesmet.pdf.

Fitting a robust regression model using RANSAC

Linear regression models can be heavily impacted by the presence of outliers. In certain situations, a very small subset of our data can have a big effect on the estimated model coefficients. There are many statistical tests that can be used to detect outliers, which are beyond the scope of the book. However, removing outliers always requires our own judgment as a data scientist, as well as our domain knowledge.

As an alternative to throwing out outliers, we will look at a robust method of regression using the **RANdom SAmple Consensus (RANSAC)** algorithm, which fits a regression model to a subset of the data, the so-called *inliers*.

We can summarize the iterative RANSAC algorithm as follows:

1. Select a random number of samples to be inliers and fit the model.
2. Test all other data points against the fitted model and add those points that fall within a user-given tolerance to the inliers.
3. Refit the model using all inliers.
4. Estimate the error of the fitted model versus the inliers.
5. Terminate the algorithm if the performance meets a certain user-defined threshold or if a fixed number of iterations has been reached; go back to step 1 otherwise.

Let's now wrap our linear model in the RANSAC algorithm using scikit-learn's `RANSACRegressor` object:

```
>>> from sklearn.linear_model import RANSACRegressor
>>> ransac = RANSACRegressor(LinearRegression(),
...             max_trials=100,
...             min_samples=50,
...             residual_metric=lambda x: np.sum(np.abs(x), axis=1),
...             residual_threshold=5.0,
...             random_state=0)
>>> ransac.fit(X, y)
```

We set the maximum number of iterations of the RANSACRegressor to 100, and using min_samples=50, we set the minimum number of the randomly chosen samples to be at least 50. Using the residual_metric parameter, we provided a callable lambda function that simply calculates the absolute vertical distances between the fitted line and the sample points. By setting the residual_threshold parameter to 5.0, we only allowed samples to be included in the inlier set if their vertical distance to the fitted line is within 5 distance units, which works well on this particular dataset. By default, scikit-learn uses the MAD estimate to select the inlier threshold, where **MAD** stands for the **Median Absolute Deviation** of the target values y. However, the choice of an appropriate value for the inlier threshold is problem-specific, which is one disadvantage of RANSAC. Many different approaches have been developed over the recent years to select a good inlier threshold automatically. You can find a detailed discussion in R. Toldo and A. Fusiello's. *Automatic Estimation of the Inlier Threshold in Robust Multiple Structures Fitting* (in Image Analysis and Processing–ICIAP 2009, pages 123–131. Springer, 2009).

After we have fitted the RANSAC model, let's obtain the inliers and outliers from the fitted RANSAC linear regression model and plot them together with the linear fit:

```
>>> inlier_mask = ransac.inlier_mask_
>>> outlier_mask = np.logical_not(inlier_mask)
>>> line_X = np.arange(3, 10, 1)
>>> line_y_ransac = ransac.predict(line_X[:, np.newaxis])
>>> plt.scatter(X[inlier_mask], y[inlier_mask],
...             c='blue', marker='o', label='Inliers')
>>> plt.scatter(X[outlier_mask], y[outlier_mask],
...             c='lightgreen', marker='s', label='Outliers')
>>> plt.plot(line_X, line_y_ransac, color='red')
>>> plt.xlabel('Average number of rooms [RM]')
>>> plt.ylabel('Price in $1000\'s [MEDV]')
>>> plt.legend(loc='upper left')
>>> plt.show()
```

As we can see in the following scatterplot, the linear regression model was fitted on the detected set of inliers shown as circles:

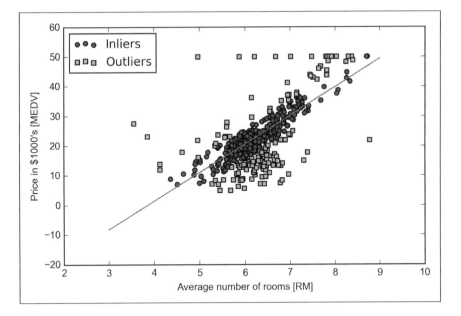

When we print the slope and intercept of the model executing the following code, we can see that the linear regression line is slightly different from the fit that we obtained in the previous section without RANSAC:

```
>>> print('Slope: %.3f' % ransac.estimator_.coef_[0])
Slope: 9.621
>>> print('Intercept: %.3f' % ransac.estimator_.intercept_)
Intercept: -37.137
```

Using RANSAC, we reduced the potential effect of the outliers in this dataset, but we don't know if this approach has a positive effect on the predictive performance for unseen data. Thus, in the next section we will discuss how to evaluate a regression model for different approaches, which is a crucial part of building systems for predictive modeling.

Evaluating the performance of linear regression models

In the previous section, we discussed how to fit a regression model on training data. However, you learned in previous chapters that it is crucial to test the model on data that it hasn't seen during training to obtain an unbiased estimate of its performance.

As we remember from *Chapter 6, Learning Best Practices for Model Evaluation and Hyperparameter Tuning,* we want to split our dataset into separate training and test datasets where we use the former to fit the model and the latter to evaluate its performance to generalize to unseen data. Instead of proceeding with the simple regression model, we will now use all variables in the dataset and train a multiple regression model:

```
>>> from sklearn.cross_validation import train_test_split
>>> X = df.iloc[:, :-1].values
>>> y = df['MEDV'].values
>>> X_train, X_test, y_train, y_test = train_test_split(
...          X, y, test_size=0.3, random_state=0)
>>> slr = LinearRegression()
>>> slr.fit(X_train, y_train)
>>> y_train_pred = slr.predict(X_train)
>>> y_test_pred = slr.predict(X_test)
```

Since our model uses multiple explanatory variables, we can't visualize the linear regression line (or hyperplane to be precise) in a two-dimensional plot, but we can plot the residuals (the differences or vertical distances between the actual and predicted values) versus the predicted values to diagnose our regression model. Those **residual plots** are a commonly used graphical analysis for diagnosing regression models to detect nonlinearity and outliers, and to check if the errors are randomly distributed.

Using the following code, we will now plot a residual plot where we simply subtract the true target variables from our predicted responses:

```
>>> plt.scatter(y_train_pred, y_train_pred - y_train,
...             c='blue', marker='o', label='Training data')
>>> plt.scatter(y_test_pred,  y_test_pred - y_test,
...             c='lightgreen', marker='s', label='Test data')
>>> plt.xlabel('Predicted values')
>>> plt.ylabel('Residuals')
>>> plt.legend(loc='upper left')
>>> plt.hlines(y=0, xmin=-10, xmax=50, lw=2, color='red')
>>> plt.xlim([-10, 50])
>>> plt.show()
```

After executing the code, we should see a residual plot with a line passing through the *x* axis origin as shown here:

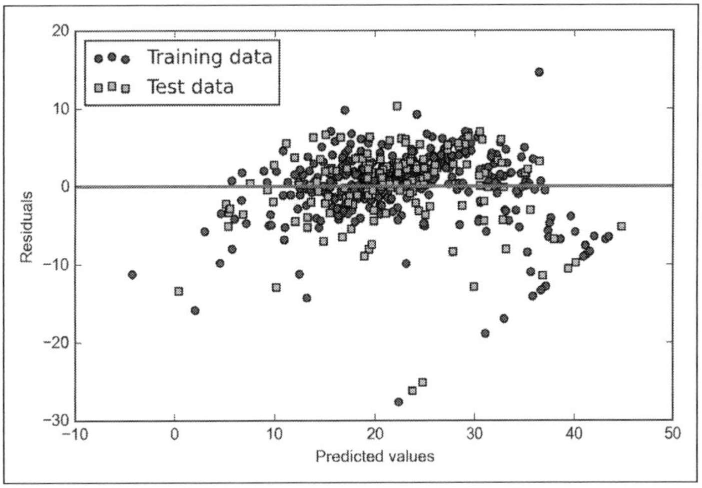

In the case of a perfect prediction, the residuals would be exactly zero, which we will probably never encounter in realistic and practical applications. However, for a good regression model, we would expect that the errors are randomly distributed and the residuals should be randomly scattered around the centerline. If we see patterns in a residual plot, it means that our model is unable to capture some explanatory information, which is leaked into the residuals as we can slightly see in our preceding residual plot. Furthermore, we can also use residual plots to detect outliers, which are represented by the points with a large deviation from the centerline.

Another useful quantitative measure of a model's performance is the so-called **Mean Squared Error (MSE)**, which is simply the average value of the SSE cost function that we minimize to fit the linear regression model. The MSE is useful to for comparing different regression models or for tuning their parameters via a grid search and cross-validation:

$$MSE = \frac{1}{n} \sum_{i=1}^{n} \left(y^{(i)} - \hat{y}^{(i)} \right)^2$$

Execute the following code:

```
>>> from sklearn.metrics import mean_squared_error
>>> print('MSE train: %.3f, test: %.3f' % (
        mean_squared_error(y_train, y_train_pred),
        mean_squared_error(y_test, y_test_pred)))
```

We will see that the MSE on the training set is 19.96, and the MSE of the test set is much larger with a value of 27.20, which is an indicator that our model is overfitting the training data.

Sometimes it may be more useful to report the coefficient of determination (R^2), which can be understood as a standardized version of the MSE, for better interpretability of the model performance. In other words, R^2 is the fraction of response variance that is captured by the model. The R^2 value is defined as follows:

$$R^2 = 1 - \frac{SSE}{SST}$$

Here, SSE is the sum of squared errors and SST is the total sum of squares $SST = \sum_{i=1}^{n}\left(y^{(i)} - \mu_y\right)^2$, or in other words, it is simply the variance of the response.

Let's quickly show that R^2 is indeed just a rescaled version of the MSE:

$$R^2 = 1 - \frac{SSE}{SST}$$

$$1 - \frac{\frac{1}{n}\sum_{i=1}^{n}\left(y^{(i)} - \hat{y}^{(i)}\right)^2}{\frac{1}{n}\sum_{i=1}^{n}\left(y^{(i)} - \mu_y\right)^2}$$

$$1 - \frac{MSE}{Var(y)}$$

For the training dataset, R^2 is bounded between 0 and 1, but it can become negative for the test set. If $R^2 = 1$, the model fits the data perfectly with a corresponding $MSE = 0$.

Evaluated on the training data, the R^2 of our model is 0.765, which doesn't sound too bad. However, the R^2 on the test dataset is only 0.673, which we can compute by executing the following code:

```
>>> from sklearn.metrics import r2_score
>>> print('R^2 train: %.3f, test: %.3f' %
```

```
...         (r2_score(y_train, y_train_pred),
...          r2_score(y_test, y_test_pred)))
```

Using regularized methods for regression

As we discussed in *Chapter 3, A Tour of Machine Learning Classifiers Using Scikit-learn*, regularization is one approach to tackle the problem of overfitting by adding additional information, and thereby shrinking the parameter values of the model to induce a penalty against complexity. The most popular approaches to regularized linear regression are the so-called **Ridge Regression, Least Absolute Shrinkage and Selection Operator (LASSO)** and **Elastic Net** method.

Ridge regression is an L2 penalized model where we simply add the squared sum of the weights to our least-squares cost function:

$$J(w)_{Ridge} = \sum_{i=1}^{n}\left(y^{(i)} - \hat{y}^{(i)}\right)^2 + \lambda \| w \|_2^2$$

Here:

$$L2: \quad \lambda \| w \|_2^2 = \lambda \sum_{j=1}^{m} w_j^2$$

By increasing the value of the hyperparameter λ, we increase the regularization strength and shrink the weights of our model. Please note that we don't regularize the intercept term w_0.

An alternative approach that can lead to sparse models is the LASSO. Depending on the regularization strength, certain weights can become zero, which makes the LASSO also useful as a supervised feature selection technique:

$$J(w)_{LASSO} = \sum_{i=1}^{n}\left(y^{(i)} - \hat{y}^{(i)}\right)^2 + \lambda \| w \|_1$$

Here:

$$L1: \lambda \| w \|_1 = \lambda \sum_{j=1}^{m} \left| w_j \right|$$

However, a limitation of the LASSO is that it selects at most n variables if $m > n$. A compromise between Ridge regression and the LASSO is the Elastic Net, which has a L1 penalty to generate sparsity and a L2 penalty to overcome some of the limitations of the LASSO, such as the number of selected variables.

$$J(w)_{ElasticNet} = \sum_{i=1}^{n} \left(y^{(i)} - \hat{y}^{(i)} \right)^2 + \lambda_1 \sum_{j=1}^{m} w_j^2 + \lambda_2 \sum_{j=1}^{m} \left| w_j \right|$$

Those regularized regression models are all available via scikit-learn, and the usage is similar to the regular regression model except that we have to specify the regularization strength via the parameter λ, for example, optimized via k-fold cross-validation.

A Ridge Regression model can be initialized as follows:

```
>>> from sklearn.linear_model import Ridge
>>> ridge = Ridge(alpha=1.0)
```

Note that the regularization strength is regulated by the parameter `alpha`, which is similar to the parameter λ. Likewise, we can initialize a LASSO regressor from the `linear_model` submodule:

```
>>> from sklearn.linear_model import Lasso
>>> lasso = Lasso(alpha=1.0)
```

Lastly, the `ElasticNet` implementation allows us to vary the L1 to L2 ratio:

```
>>> from sklearn.linear_model import ElasticNet
>>> lasso = ElasticNet(alpha=1.0, l1_ratio=0.5)
```

For example, if we set `l1_ratio` to `1.0`, the `ElasticNet` regressor would be equal to LASSO regression. For more detailed information about the different implementations of linear regression, please see the documentation at `http://scikit-learn.org/stable/modules/linear_model.html`.

Turning a linear regression model into a curve – polynomial regression

In the previous sections, we assumed a linear relationship between explanatory and response variables. One way to account for the violation of linearity assumption is to use a polynomial regression model by adding polynomial terms:

$$y = w_0 + w_1 x + w_2 x^2 x^2 + \ldots + w_d x^d$$

Here, d denotes the degree of the polynomial. Although we can use polynomial regression to model a nonlinear relationship, it is still considered a multiple linear regression model because of the linear regression coefficients w.

We will now discuss how to use the `PolynomialFeatures` transformer class from scikit-learn to add a quadratic term ($d = 2$) to a simple regression problem with one explanatory variable, and compare the polynomial to the linear fit. The steps are as follows:

1. Add a second degree polynomial term:

   ```
   from sklearn.preprocessing import PolynomialFeatures
   >>> X = np.array([258.0, 270.0, 294.0,
   ...                          320.0, 342.0, 368.0,
   ...                          396.0, 446.0, 480.0,
   ...                          586.0])[:, np.newaxis]

   >>> y = np.array([236.4, 234.4, 252.8,
   ...                          298.6, 314.2, 342.2,
   ...                          360.8, 368.0, 391.2,
   ...                          390.8])
   >>> lr = LinearRegression()
   >>> pr = LinearRegression()
   >>> quadratic = PolynomialFeatures(degree=2)
   >>> X_quad = quadratic.fit_transform(X)
   ```

2. Fit a simple linear regression model for comparison:

   ```
   >>> lr.fit(X, y)
   >>> X_fit = np.arange(250,600,10)[:, np.newaxis]
   >>> y_lin_fit = lr.predict(X_fit)
   ```

3. Fit a multiple regression model on the transformed features for polynomial regression:

   ```
   >>> pr.fit(X_quad, y)
   >>> y_quad_fit = pr.predict(quadratic.fit_transform(X_fit))
   Plot the results:
   >>> plt.scatter(X, y, label='training points')
   >>> plt.plot(X_fit, y_lin_fit,
   ...          label='linear fit', linestyle='--')
   >>> plt.plot(X_fit, y_quad_fit,
   ...          label='quadratic fit')
   >>> plt.legend(loc='upper left')
   >>> plt.show()
   ```

In the resulting plot, we can see that the polynomial fit captures the relationship between the response and explanatory variable much better than the linear fit:

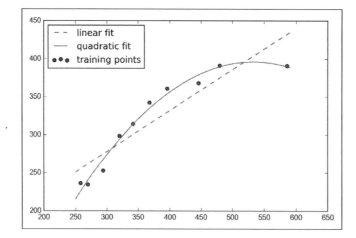

```
>>> y_lin_pred = lr.predict(X)
>>> y_quad_pred = pr.predict(X_quad)
>>> print('Training MSE linear: %.3f, quadratic: %.3f' % (
...            mean_squared_error(y, y_lin_pred),
...            mean_squared_error(y, y_quad_pred)))
Training MSE linear: 569.780, quadratic: 61.330
>>> print('Training R^2 linear: %.3f, quadratic: %.3f' % (
...            r2_score(y, y_lin_pred),
...            r2_score(y, y_quad_pred)))
Training R^2 linear: 0.832, quadratic: 0.982
```

As we can see after executing the preceding code, the MSE decreased from 570 (linear fit) to 61 (quadratic fit), and the coefficient of determination reflects a closer fit to the quadratic model ($R^2 = 0.982$) as opposed to the linear fit ($R^2 = 0.832$) in this particular toy problem.

Modeling nonlinear relationships in the Housing Dataset

After we discussed how to construct polynomial features to fit nonlinear relationships in a toy problem, let's now take a look at a more concrete example and apply those concepts to the data in the *Housing Dataset*. By executing the following code, we will model the relationship between house prices and LSTAT (percent lower status of the population) using second degree (quadratic) and third degree (cubic) polynomials and compare it to a linear fit.

The code is as follows:

```
>>> X = df[['LSTAT']].values
>>> y = df['MEDV'].values
>>> regr = LinearRegression()

# create polynomial features
>>> quadratic = PolynomialFeatures(degree=2)
>>> cubic = PolynomialFeatures(degree=3)
>>> X_quad = quadratic.fit_transform(X)
>>> X_cubic = cubic.fit_transform(X)

# linear fit
>>> X_fit = np.arange(X.min(), X.max(), 1)[:, np.newaxis]
>>> regr = regr.fit(X, y)
>>> y_lin_fit = regr.predict(X_fit)
>>> linear_r2 = r2_score(y, regr.predict(X))

# quadratic fit
>>> regr = regr.fit(X_quad, y)
>>> y_quad_fit = regr.predict(quadratic.fit_transform(X_fit))
>>> quadratic_r2 = r2_score(y, regr.predict(X_quad))

# cubic fit
>>> regr = regr.fit(X_cubic, y)
>>> y_cubic_fit = regr.predict(cubic.fit_transform(X_fit))
>>> cubic_r2 = r2_score(y, regr.predict(X_cubic))

# plot results
>>> plt.scatter(X, y,
...             label='training points',
...             color='lightgray')
>>> plt.plot(X_fit, y_lin_fit,
...          label='linear (d=1), $R^2=%.2f$'
...             % linear_r2,
...          color='blue',
...          lw=2,
...          linestyle=':')
>>> plt.plot(X_fit, y_quad_fit,
...          label='quadratic (d=2), $R^2=%.2f$'
...             % quadratic_r2,
...          color='red',
...          lw=2,
...          linestyle='-')
```

```
>>> plt.plot(X_fit, y_cubic_fit,
...            label='cubic (d=3), $R^2=%.2f$'
...              % cubic_r2,
...            color='green',
...            lw=2,
...            linestyle='--')
>>> plt.xlabel('% lower status of the population [LSTAT]')
>>> plt.ylabel('Price in $1000\'s [MEDV]')
>>> plt.legend(loc='upper right')
>>> plt.show()
```

As we can see in the resulting plot, the cubic fit captures the relationship between the house prices and **LSTAT** better than the linear and quadratic fit. However, we should be aware that adding more and more polynomial features increases the complexity of a model and therefore increases the chance of overfitting. Thus, in practice, it is always recommended that you evaluate the performance of the model on a separate test dataset to estimate the generalization performance:

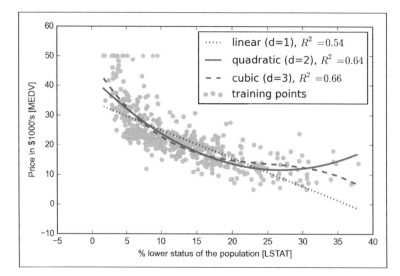

In addition, polynomial features are not always the best choice for modeling nonlinear relationships. For example, just by looking at the **MEDV-LSTAT** scatterplot, we could propose that a log transformation of the **LSTAT** feature variable and the square root of **MEDV** may project the data onto a linear feature space suitable for a linear regression fit. Let's test this hypothesis by executing the following code:

```
# transform features
>>> X_log = np.log(X)
```

```
>>> y_sqrt = np.sqrt(y)

# fit features
>>> X_fit = np.arange(X_log.min()-1,
...                   X_log.max()+1, 1)[:, np.newaxis]
>>> regr = regr.fit(X_log, y_sqrt)
>>> y_lin_fit = regr.predict(X_fit)
>>> linear_r2 = r2_score(y_sqrt, regr.predict(X_log))

# plot results
>>> plt.scatter(X_log, y_sqrt,
...             label='training points',
...             color='lightgray')
>>> plt.plot(X_fit, y_lin_fit,
...          label='linear (d=1), $R^2=%.2f$' % linear_r2,
...          color='blue',
...          lw=2)
>>> plt.xlabel('log(% lower status of the population [LSTAT])')
>>> plt.ylabel('$\sqrt{Price \; in \; \$1000\'s [MEDV]}$')
>>> plt.legend(loc='lower left')
>>> plt.show()
```

After transforming the explanatory onto the log space and taking the square root of the target variables, we were able to capture the relationship between the two variables with a linear regression line that seems to fit the data better ($R^2 = 0.69$) than any of the polynomial feature transformations previously:

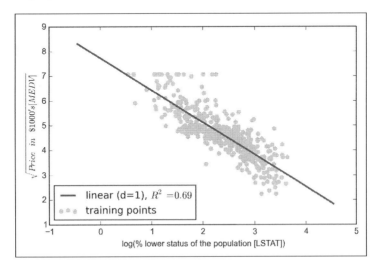

Dealing with nonlinear relationships using random forests

In this section, we are going to take a look at **random forest** regression, which is conceptually different from the previous regression models in this chapter. A random forest, which is an ensemble of multiple **decision trees**, can be understood as the sum of piecewise linear functions in contrast to the global linear and polynomial regression models that we discussed previously. In other words, via the decision tree algorithm, we are subdividing the input space into smaller regions that become more *manageable*.

Decision tree regression

An advantage of the decision tree algorithm is that it does not require any transformation of the features if we are dealing with nonlinear data. We remember from *Chapter 3, A Tour of Machine Learning Classifiers Using Scikit-learn*, that we grow a decision tree by iteratively splitting its nodes until the leaves are pure or a stopping criterion is satisfied. When we used decision trees for classification, we defined entropy as a measure of impurity to determine which feature split maximizes the **Information Gain** (**IG**), which can be defined as follows for a binary split:

$$IG\left(D_p, x_i\right) = I\left(D_p\right) - \frac{N_{left}}{N_p} I\left(D_{left}\right) - \frac{N_{right}}{N_p} I\left(D_{right}\right)$$

Here, x is the feature to perform the split, N_p is the number of samples in the parent node, I is the impurity function, D_p is the subset of training samples in the parent node, and D_{left} and D_{right} are the subsets of training samples in the left and right child node after the split. Remember that our goal is to find the feature split that maximizes the information gain, or in other words, we want to find the feature split that reduces the impurities in the child nodes. In *Chapter 3, A Tour of Machine Learning Classifiers Using Scikit-learn*, we used *entropy* as a measure of impurity, which is a useful criterion for classification. To use a decision tree for regression, we will replace entropy as the impurity measure of a node t by the MSE:

$$I\left(t\right) = MSE\left(t\right) = \frac{1}{N_t} \sum_{i \in D_t} \left(y^{(i)} - \hat{y}_t\right)^2$$

Here, N_t is the number of training samples at node t, D_t is the training subset at node t, $y^{(i)}$ is the true target value, and $\hat{y}_t$ is the predicted target value (sample mean):

$$\hat{y}_t = \frac{1}{N}\sum_{i\in D_t} y^{(i)}$$

In the context of decision tree regression, the MSE is often also referred to as within-node variance, which is why the splitting criterion is also better known as *variance reduction*. To see what the line fit of a decision tree looks like, let's use the DecisionTreeRegressor implemented in scikit-learn to model the nonlinear relationship between the **MEDV** and **LSTAT** variables:

```
>>> from sklearn.tree import DecisionTreeRegressor
>>> X = df[['LSTAT']].values
>>> y = df['MEDV'].values
>>> tree = DecisionTreeRegressor(max_depth=3)
>>> tree.fit(X, y)
>>> sort_idx = X.flatten().argsort()
    >>> lin_regplot(X[sort_idx], y[sort_idx], tree)
>>> plt.xlabel('% lower status of the population [LSTAT]')
>>> plt.ylabel('Price in $1000\'s [MEDV]')
>>> plt.show()
```

As we can see from the resulting plot, the decision tree captures the general trend in the data. However, a limitation of this model is that it does not capture the continuity and differentiability of the desired prediction. In addition, we need to be careful about choosing an appropriate value for the depth of the tree to not overfit or underfit the data; here, a depth of 3 seems to be a good choice:

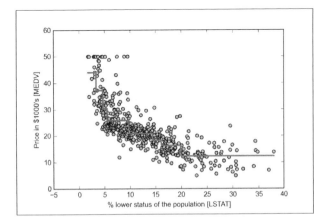

In the next section, we will take a look at a more robust way for fitting regression trees: random forests.

Random forest regression

As we discussed in *Chapter 3, A Tour of Machine Learning Classifiers Using Scikit-learn*, the random forest algorithm is an ensemble technique that combines multiple decision trees. A random forest usually has a better generalization performance than an individual decision tree due to randomness that helps to decrease the model variance. Other advantages of random forests are that they are less sensitive to outliers in the dataset and don't require much parameter tuning. The only parameter in random forests that we typically need to experiment with is the number of trees in the ensemble. The basic random forests algorithm for regression is almost identical to the random forest algorithm for classification that we discussed in *Chapter 3, A Tour of Machine Learning Classifiers Using Scikit-learn*. The only difference is that we use the MSE criterion to grow the individual decision trees, and the predicted target variable is calculated as the average prediction over all decision trees.

Now, let's use all the features in the Housing Dataset to fit a random forest regression model on 60 percent of the samples and evaluate its performance on the remaining 40 percent. The code is as follows:

```
>>> X = df.iloc[:, :-1].values
>>> y = df['MEDV'].values
>>> X_train, X_test, y_train, y_test =\
...        train_test_split(X, y,
...                         test_size=0.4,
...                         random_state=1)

>>> from sklearn.ensemble import RandomForestRegressor
>>> forest = RandomForestRegressor(
                               n_estimators=1000,
...                              criterion='mse',
...                              random_state=1,
...                              n_jobs=-1)
>>> forest.fit(X_train, y_train)
>>> y_train_pred = forest.predict(X_train)
>>> y_test_pred = forest.predict(X_test)
```

```
>>> print('MSE train: %.3f, test: %.3f' % (
...         mean_squared_error(y_train, y_train_pred),
...         mean_squared_error(y_test, y_test_pred)))
>>> print('R^2 train: %.3f, test: %.3f' % (
...         r2_score(y_train, y_train_pred),
...         r2_score(y_test, y_test_pred)))
MSE train: 1.642, test: 11.635
R^2 train: 0.960, test: 0.871
```

Unfortunately, we see that the random forest tends to overfit the training data. However, it's still able to explain the relationship between the target and explanatory variables relatively well ($R^2 = 0.871$ on the test dataset).

Lastly, let's also take a look at the residuals of the prediction:

```
>>> plt.scatter(y_train_pred,
...             y_train_pred - y_train,
...             c='black',
...             marker='o',
...             s=35,
...             alpha=0.5,
...             label='Training data')
>>> plt.scatter(y_test_pred,
...             y_test_pred - y_test,
...             c='lightgreen',
...             marker='s',
...             s=35,
...             alpha=0.7,
...             label='Test data')
>>> plt.xlabel('Predicted values')
>>> plt.ylabel('Residuals')
>>> plt.legend(loc='upper left')
>>> plt.hlines(y=0, xmin=-10, xmax=50, lw=2, color='red')
>>> plt.xlim([-10, 50])
>>> plt.show()
```

As it was already summarized by the R^2 coefficient, we can see that the model fits the training data better than the test data, as indicated by the outliers in the y axis direction. Also, the distribution of the residuals does not seem to be completely random around the zero center point, indicating that the model is not able to capture all the exploratory information. However, the residual plot indicates a large improvement over the residual plot of the linear model that we plotted earlier in this chapter:

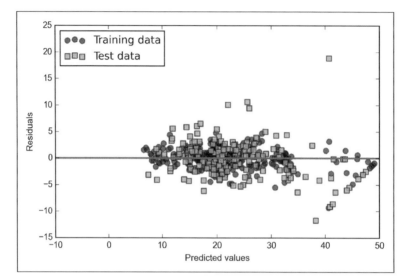

In *Chapter 3, A Tour of Machine Learning Classifiers Using Scikit-learn*, we also discussed the kernel trick that can be used in combination with **support vector machine (SVM)** for classification, which is useful if we are dealing with nonlinear problems. Although a discussion is beyond of the scope of this book, SVMs can also be used in nonlinear regression tasks. The interested reader can find more information about Support Vector Machines for regression in an excellent report by S. R. Gunn: S. R. Gunn et al. *Support Vector Machines for Classification and Regression.* (ISIS technical report, 14, 1998). An SVM regressor is also implemented in scikit-learn, and more information about its usage can be found at http://scikit-learn.org/stable/modules/generated/sklearn.svm.SVR.html#sklearn.svm.SVR.

Summary

At the beginning of this chapter, you learned about using simple linear regression analysis to model the relationship between a single explanatory variable and a continuous response variable. We then discussed a useful explanatory data analysis technique to look at patterns and anomalies in data, which is an important first step in predictive modeling tasks.

We built our first model by implementing linear regression using a gradient-based optimization approach. We then saw how to utilize scikit-learn's linear models for regression and also implement a robust regression technique (RANSAC) as an approach for dealing with outliers. To assess the predictive performance of regression models, we computed the mean sum of squared errors and the related R^2 metric. Furthermore, we also discussed a useful graphical approach to diagnose the problems of regression models: the residual plot.

After we discussed how regularization can be applied to regression models to reduce the model complexity and avoid overfitting, we also introduced several approaches to model nonlinear relationships, including polynomial feature transformation and random forest regressors.

We discussed supervised learning, classification, and regression analysis, in great detail throughout the previous chapters. In the next chapter, we are going to discuss another interesting subfield of machine learning: unsupervised learning. In the next chapter, you will learn how to use cluster analysis for finding hidden structures in data in the absence of target variables.

11
Working with Unlabeled Data – Clustering Analysis

In the previous chapters, we used supervised learning techniques to build machine learning models using data where the answer was already known—the class labels were already available in our training data. In this chapter, we will switch gears and explore cluster analysis, a category of **unsupervised learning** techniques that allows us to discover hidden structures in data where we do not know the right answer upfront. The goal of clustering is to find a natural grouping in data such that items in the same cluster are more similar to each other than those from different clusters.

Given its exploratory nature, clustering is an exciting topic and, in this chapter, you will learn about the following concepts that can help you to organize data into meaningful structures:

- Finding centers of similarity using the popular k-means algorithm
- Using a bottom-up approach to build hierarchical cluster trees
- Identifying arbitrary shapes of objects using a density-based clustering approach

Grouping objects by similarity using k-means

In this section, we will discuss one of the most popular **clustering** algorithms, **k-means**, which is widely used in academia as well as in industry. Clustering (or cluster analysis) is a technique that allows us to find groups of similar objects, objects that are more related to each other than to objects in other groups. Examples of business-oriented applications of clustering include the grouping of documents, music, and movies by different topics, or finding customers that share similar interests based on common purchase behaviors as a basis for recommendation engines.

As we will see in a moment, the k-means algorithm is extremely easy to implement but is also computationally very efficient compared to other clustering algorithms, which might explain its popularity. The k-means algorithm belongs to the category of prototype-based clustering. We will discuss two other categories of clustering, **hierarchical** and **density-based** clustering, later in this chapter. **Prototype-based** clustering means that each cluster is represented by a prototype, which can either be the **centroid** (*average*) of similar points with continuous features, or the **medoid** (the most *representative* or most frequently occurring point) in the case of categorical features. While k-means is very good at identifying clusters of spherical shape, one of the drawbacks of this clustering algorithm is that we have to specify the number of clusters k a priori. An inappropriate choice for k can result in poor clustering performance. Later in this chapter, we will discuss the **elbow** method and **silhouette plots**, which are useful techniques to evaluate the quality of a clustering to help us determine the optimal number of clusters k.

Although k-means clustering can be applied to data in higher dimensions, we will walk through the following examples using a simple two-dimensional dataset for the purpose of visualization:

```
>>> from sklearn.datasets import make_blobs
>>> X, y = make_blobs(n_samples=150,
...                    n_features=2,
...                    centers=3,
...                    cluster_std=0.5,
...                    shuffle=True,
...                    random_state=0)

>>> import matplotlib.pyplot as plt
>>> plt.scatter(X[:,0],
...             X[:,1],
...             c='white',
```

```
...                    marker='o',
...                    s=50)
>>> plt.grid()
>>> plt.show()
```

The dataset that we just created consists of 150 randomly generated points that are roughly grouped into three regions with higher density, which is visualized via a two-dimensional scatterplot:

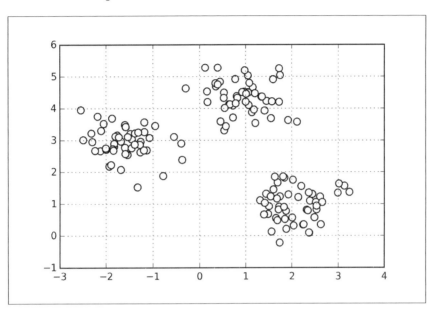

In real-world applications of clustering, we do not have any ground truth category information about those samples; otherwise, it would fall into the category of supervised learning. Thus, our goal is to group the samples based on their feature similarities, which we can be achieved using the k-means algorithm that can be summarized by the following four steps:

1. Randomly pick k centroids from the sample points as initial cluster centers.

2. Assign each sample to the nearest centroid $\mu^{(j)}$, $j \in \{1,...,k\}$.

3. Move the centroids to the center of the samples that were assigned to it.

4. Repeat steps 2 and 3 until the cluster assignments do not change or a user-defined tolerance or a maximum number of iterations is reached.

Now the next question is *how do we measure similarity between objects?* We can define similarity as the opposite of distance, and a commonly used distance for clustering samples with continuous features is the **squared Euclidean distance** between two points x and y in *m-dimensional* space:

$$d(x, y)^2 = \sum_{j=1}^{m} (x_j - y_j)^2 = \|x - y\|_2^2$$

Note that, in the preceding equation, the index j refers to the *jth* dimension (feature column) of the sample points x and y. In the rest of this section, we will use the superscripts i and j to refer to the sample index and cluster index, respectively.

Based on this Euclidean distance metric, we can describe the k-means algorithm as a simple optimization problem, an iterative approach for minimizing the **within-cluster sum of squared errors (SSE)**, which is sometimes also called **cluster inertia**:

$$SSE = \sum_{i=1}^{n} \sum_{j=1}^{k} w^{(i,j)} \left\| x^{(i)} - \mu^{(j)} \right\|_2^2$$

Here, $\mu^{(j)}$ is the representative point (centroid) for cluster j, and $w^{(i,j)} = 1$ if the sample $x^{(i)}$ is in cluster j; $w^{(i,j)} = 0$ otherwise.

Now that you have learned how the simple k-means algorithm works, let's apply it to our sample dataset using the KMeans class from scikit-learn's cluster module:

```
>>> from sklearn.cluster import KMeans
>>> km = KMeans(n_clusters=3,
...             init='random',
...             n_init=10,
...             max_iter=300,
...             tol=1e-04,
...             random_state=0)
>>> y_km = km.fit_predict(X)
```

Using the preceding code, we set the number of desired clusters to 3; specifying the number of clusters a priori is one of the limitations of k-means. We set n_init=10 to run the k-means clustering algorithms 10 times independently with different random centroids to choose the final model as the one with the lowest SSE. Via the max_iter parameter, we specify the maximum number of iterations for each single run (here, 300). Note that the k-means implementation in scikit-learn stops early if it converges before the maximum number of iterations is reached.

However, it is possible that k-means does not reach convergence for a particular run, which can be problematic (computationally expensive) if we choose relatively large values for `max_iter`. One way to deal with convergence problems is to choose larger values for `tol`, which is a parameter that controls the tolerance with regard to the changes in the within-cluster sum-squared-error to declare convergence. In the preceding code, we chose a tolerance of `1e-04` (=0.0001).

K-means++

So far, we discussed the classic k-means algorithm that uses a random seed to place the initial centroids, which can sometimes result in bad clusterings or slow convergence if the initial centroids are chosen poorly. One way to address this issue is to run the k-means algorithm multiple times on a dataset and choose the best performing model in terms of the SSE. Another strategy is to place the initial centroids far away from each other via the **k-means++** algorithm, which leads to better and more consistent results than the classic k-means (D. Arthur and S. Vassilvitskii. k-means++: *The Advantages of Careful Seeding*. In Proceedings of the eighteenth annual ACM-SIAM symposium on Discrete algorithms, pages 1027–1035. Society for Industrial and Applied Mathematics, 2007).

The initialization in k-means++ can be summarized as follows:

1. Initialize an empty set **M** to store the k centroids being selected.
2. Randomly choose the first centroid $\mu^{(j)}$ from the input samples and assign it to **M**.
3. For each sample $x^{(i)}$ that is not in **M**, find the minimum squared distance $d\left(x^{(i)},\mathbf{M}\right)^2$ to any of the centroids in **M**.
4. To randomly select the next centroid $\mu^{(p)}$, use a weighted probability distribution equal to $\dfrac{d\left(\mu^{(p)},\mathbf{M}\right)^2}{\sum_i d\left(x^{(i)},\mathbf{M}\right)^2}$.
5. Repeat steps 2 and 3 until k centroids are chosen.
6. Proceed with the classic k-means algorithm.

To use k-means++ with scikit-learn's `KMeans` object, we just need to set the `init` parameter to `k-means++` (the default setting) instead of `random`.

Another problem with k-means is that one or more clusters can be empty. Note that this problem does not exist for k-medoids or fuzzy C-means, an algorithm that we will discuss in the next subsection. However, this problem is accounted for in the current k-means implementation in scikit-learn. If a cluster is empty, the algorithm will search for the sample that is farthest away from the centroid of the empty cluster. Then it will reassign the centroid to be this farthest point.

> When we are applying k-means to real-world data using a Euclidean distance metric, we want to make sure that the features are measured on the same scale and apply z-score standardization or min-max scaling if necessary.

After we predicted the cluster labels y_km and discussed the challenges of the k-means algorithm, let's now visualize the clusters that k-means identified in the dataset together with the cluster centroids. These are stored under the centers_ attribute of the fitted KMeans object:

```
>>> plt.scatter(X[y_km==0,0],
...             X[y_km==0,1],
...             s=50,
...             c='lightgreen',
...             marker='s',
...             label='cluster 1')
>>> plt.scatter(X[y_km==1,0],
...             X[y_km==1,1],
...             s=50,
...             c='orange',
...             marker='o',
...             label='cluster 2')
>>> plt.scatter(X[y_km==2,0],
...             X[y_km==2,1],
...             s=50,
...             c='lightblue',
...             marker='v',
...             label='cluster 3')
>>> plt.scatter(km.cluster_centers_[:,0],
...             km.cluster_centers_[:,1],
...             s=250,
...             marker='*',
...             c='red',
...             label='centroids')
>>> plt.legend()
>>> plt.grid()
>>> plt.show()
```

In the following scatterplot, we can see that k-means placed the three centroids at the center of each sphere, which looks like a reasonable grouping given this dataset:

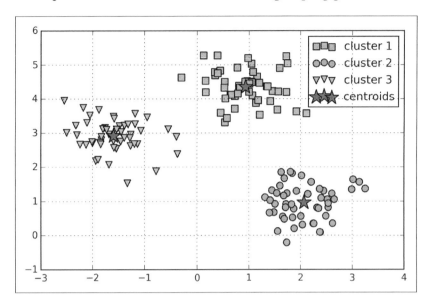

Although k-means worked well on this toy dataset, we need to note some of the main challenges of k-means. One of the drawbacks of k-means is that we have to specify the number of clusters *k* a priori, which may not always be so obvious in real-world applications, especially if we are working with a higher dimensional dataset that cannot be visualized. The other properties of k-means are that clusters do not overlap and are not hierarchical, and we also assume that there is at least one item in each cluster.

Hard versus soft clustering

Hard clustering describes a family of algorithms where each sample in a dataset is assigned to exactly one cluster, as in the k-means algorithm that we discussed in the previous subsection. In contrast, algorithms for **soft clustering** (sometimes also called **fuzzy clustering**) assign a sample to one or more clusters. A popular example of soft clustering is the **fuzzy C-means (FCM)** algorithm (also called **soft k-means** or **fuzzy k-means**). The original idea goes back to the 1970s where Joseph C. Dunn first proposed an early version of fuzzy clustering to improve k-means (J. C. Dunn. *A Fuzzy Relative of the Isodata Process and its Use in Detecting Compact Well-separated Clusters*. 1973). Almost a decade later, James C. Bedzek published his work on the improvements of the fuzzy clustering algorithm, which is now known as the FCM algorithm (J. C. Bezdek. *Pattern Recognition with Fuzzy Objective Function Algorithms*. Springer Science & Business Media, 2013).

The FCM procedure is very similar to k-means. However, we replace the hard cluster assignment by probabilities for each point belonging to each cluster. In k-means, we could express the cluster membership of a sample x by a sparse vector of binary values:

$$\begin{bmatrix} \mu^{(1)} \rightarrow 0 \\ \mu^{(2)} \rightarrow 1 \\ \mu^{(3)} \rightarrow 0 \end{bmatrix}$$

Here, the index position with value 1 indicates the cluster centroid $\mu^{(j)}$ the sample is assigned to (assuming $k = 3$, $j \in \{1, 2, 3\}$). In contrast, a membership vector in FCM could be represented as follows:

$$\begin{bmatrix} \mu^{(1)} \rightarrow 0.1 \\ \mu^{(2)} \rightarrow 0.85 \\ \mu^{(3)} \rightarrow 0.05 \end{bmatrix}$$

Here, each value falls in the range [0, 1] and represents a probability of membership to the respective cluster centroid. The sum of the memberships for a given sample is equal to 1. Similarly to the k-means algorithm, we can summarize the FCM algorithm in four key steps:

1. Specify the number of k centroids and randomly assign the cluster memberships for each point.

2. Compute the cluster centroids $\mu^{(j)}$, $j \in \{1, \ldots, k\}$.

3. Update the cluster memberships for each point.

4. Repeat steps 2 and 3 until the membership coefficients do not change or a user-defined tolerance or a maximum number of iterations is reached.

The objective function of FCM—we abbreviate it by J_m—looks very similar to the **within cluster sum-squared-error** that we minimize in k-means:

$$J_m = \sum_{i=1}^{n} \sum_{j=1}^{k} w^{m(i,j)} \left\| x^{(i)} - \mu^{(j)} \right\|_2^2 , \ m \in [1, \infty)$$

However, note that the membership indicator $w^{(i,j)}$ is not a binary value as in k-means $w^{(i,j)} \in \{0,1\}$) but a real value that denotes the cluster membership probability ($w^{(i,j)} \in [0,1]$). You also may have noticed that we added an additional exponent to $w^{(i,j)}$; the exponent m, any number greater or equal to 1 (typically $m = 2$), is the so-called **fuzziness coefficient** (or simply **fuzzifier**) that controls the degree of fuzziness. The larger the value of $\boldsymbol{m}$, the smaller the cluster membership $w^{(i,j)}$ becomes, which leads to fuzzier clusters. The cluster membership probability itself is calculated as follows:

$$w^{(i,j)} = \left[\sum_{p=1}^{k} \left(\frac{\left\| x^{(i)} - \mu^{(j)} \right\|_2}{\left\| x^{(i)} - \mu^{(p)} \right\|_2} \right)^{\frac{2}{m-1}} \right]^{-1}$$

For example, if we chose three cluster centers as in the previous k-means example, we could calculate the membership of the $x^{(i)}$ sample belonging to the $\mu^{(j)}$ cluster as:

$$w^{(i,j)} = \left[\left(\frac{\left\| x^{(i)} - \mu^{(j)} \right\|_2}{\left\| x^{(i)} - \mu^{(1)} \right\|_2} \right)^{\frac{2}{m-1}} + \left(\frac{\left\| x^{(i)} - \mu^{(j)} \right\|_2}{\left\| x^{(i)} - \mu^{(2)} \right\|_2} \right)^{\frac{2}{m-1}} + \left(\frac{\left\| x^{(i)} - \mu^{(j)} \right\|_2}{\left\| x^{(i)} - \mu^{(3)} \right\|_2} \right)^{\frac{2}{m-1}} \right]^{-1}$$

The center $\mu^{(j)}$ of a cluster itself is calculated as the mean of all samples in the cluster weighted by the membership degree of belonging to its own cluster:

$$\mu^{(j)} = \frac{\sum_{i=1}^{n} w^{m(i,j)} x^{(i)}}{\sum_{i=1}^{n} w^{m(i,j)}}$$

Just by looking at the equation to calculate the cluster memberships, it is intuitive to say that each iteration in FCM is more expensive than an iteration in k-means. However, FCM typically requires fewer iterations overall to reach convergence. Unfortunately, the FCM algorithm is currently not implemented in scikit-learn. However, it has been found in practice that both k-means and FCM produce very similar clustering outputs, as described in a study by Soumi Ghosh and Sanjay K. Dubey (S. Ghosh and S. K. Dubey. *Comparative Analysis of k-means and Fuzzy c-means Algorithms*. IJACSA, 4:35–38, 2013).

Using the elbow method to find the optimal number of clusters

One of the main challenges in unsupervised learning is that we do not know the definitive answer. We don't have the ground truth class labels in our dataset that allow us to apply the techniques that we used in *Chapter 6, Learning Best Practices for Model Evaluation and Hyperparameter Tuning,* in order to evaluate the performance of a supervised model. Thus, in order to quantify the quality of clustering, we need to use intrinsic metrics—such as the within-cluster SSE (distortion) that we discussed earlier in this chapter—to compare the performance of different k-means clusterings. Conveniently, we don't need to compute the within-cluster SSE explicitly as it is already accessible via the `inertia_` attribute after fitting a KMeans model:

```
>>> print('Distortion: %.2f' % km.inertia_)
Distortion: 72.48
```

Based on the within-cluster SSE, we can use a graphical tool, the so-called **elbow** method, to estimate the optimal number of clusters k for a given task. Intuitively, we can say that, if k increases, the distortion will decrease. This is because the samples will be closer to the centroids they are assigned to. The idea behind the elbow method is to identify the value of k where the distortion begins to increase most rapidly, which will become more clear if we plot distortion for different values of k:

```
>>> distortions = []
>>> for i in range(1, 11):
...     km = KMeans(n_clusters=i,
...                 init='k-means++',
...                 n_init=10,
...                 max_iter=300,
...                 random_state=0)
>>>     km.fit(X)
>>>     distortions.append(km.inertia_)
>>> plt.plot(range(1,11), distortions, marker='o')
>>> plt.xlabel('Number of clusters')
>>> plt.ylabel('Distortion')
>>> plt.show()
```

As we can see in the following plot, the *elbow* is located at *k* = 3, which provides evidence that *k* = 3 is indeed a good choice for this dataset:

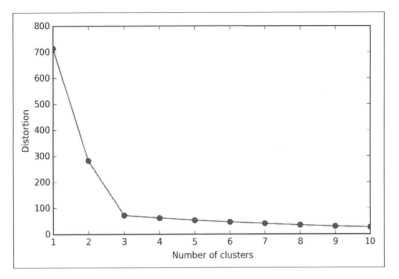

Quantifying the quality of clustering via silhouette plots

Another intrinsic metric to evaluate the quality of a clustering is **silhouette analysis**, which can also be applied to clustering algorithms other than k-means that we will discuss later in this chapter. Silhouette analysis can be used as a graphical tool to plot a measure of how tightly grouped the samples in the clusters are. To calculate the **silhouette coefficient** of a single sample in our dataset, we can apply the following three steps:

1. Calculate the cluster cohesion $a^{(i)}$ as the average distance between a sample $x^{(i)}$ and all other points in the same cluster.

2. Calculate the cluster separation $b^{(i)}$ from the next closest cluster as the average distance between the sample $x^{(i)}$ and all samples in the nearest cluster.

3. Calculate the silhouette $s^{(i)}$ as the difference between cluster cohesion and separation divided by the greater of the two, as shown here:

$$s^{(i)} = \frac{b^{(i)} - a^{(i)}}{\max\left\{b^{(i)}, a^{(i)}\right\}}$$

The silhouette coefficient is bounded in the range -1 to 1. Based on the preceding formula, we can see that the silhouette coefficient is 0 if the cluster separation and cohesion are equal ($b^{(i)} = a^{(i)}$). Furthermore, we get close to an ideal silhouette coefficient of 1 if $b^{(i)} \gg a^{(i)}$, since $b^{(i)}$ quantifies how dissimilar a sample is to other clusters, and $a^{(i)}$ tells us how similar it is to the other samples in its own cluster, respectively.

The silhouette coefficient is available as `silhouette_samples` from scikit-learn's `metric` module, and optionally the `silhouette_scores` can be imported. This calculates the average silhouette coefficient across all samples, which is equivalent to `numpy.mean(silhouette_samples(...))`. By executing the following code, we will now create a plot of the silhouette coefficients for a k-means clustering with $k = 3$:

```
>>> km = KMeans(n_clusters=3,
...             init='k-means++',
...             n_init=10,
...             max_iter=300,
...             tol=1e-04,
...             random_state=0)
>>> y_km = km.fit_predict(X)

>>> import numpy as np
>>> from matplotlib import cm
>>> from sklearn.metrics import silhouette_samples
>>> cluster_labels = np.unique(y_km)
>>> n_clusters = cluster_labels.shape[0]
>>> silhouette_vals = silhouette_samples(X,
...                                       y_km,
...                                       metric='euclidean')
>>> y_ax_lower, y_ax_upper = 0, 0
>>> yticks = []
>>> for i, c in enumerate(cluster_labels):
...     c_silhouette_vals = silhouette_vals[y_km == c]
...     c_silhouette_vals.sort()
...     y_ax_upper += len(c_silhouette_vals)
...     color = cm.jet(i / n_clusters)
...     plt.barh(range(y_ax_lower, y_ax_upper),
...             c_silhouette_vals,
...             height=1.0,
...             edgecolor='none',
...             color=color)
...     yticks.append((y_ax_lower + y_ax_upper) / 2)
...     y_ax_lower += len(c_silhouette_vals)
>>> silhouette_avg = np.mean(silhouette_vals)
>>> plt.axvline(silhouette_avg,
...             color="red",
...             linestyle="--")
>>> plt.yticks(yticks, cluster_labels + 1)
```

```
>>> plt.ylabel('Cluster')
>>> plt.xlabel('Silhouette coefficient')
>>> plt.show()
```

Through a visual inspection of the silhouette plot, we can quickly scrutinize the sizes of the different clusters and identify clusters that contain *outliers*:

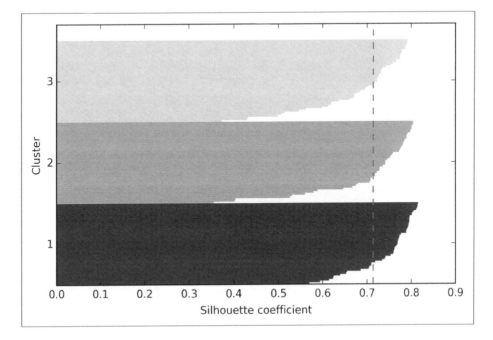

As we can see in the preceding silhouette plot, our silhouette coefficients are not even close to 0, which can be an indicator of a good clustering. Furthermore, to summarize the goodness of our clustering, we added the average silhouette coefficient to the plot (dotted line).

To see how a silhouette plot looks for a relatively *bad* clustering, let's seed the k-means algorithm with two centroids only:

```
>>> km = KMeans(n_clusters=2,
...             init='k-means++',
...             n_init=10,
...             max_iter=300,
...             tol=1e-04,
...             random_state=0)
>>> y_km = km.fit_predict(X)

>>> plt.scatter(X[y_km==0,0],
...             X[y_km==0,1],
...             s=50, c='lightgreen',
```

```
...                marker='s',
...                label='cluster 1')
>>> plt.scatter(X[y_km==1,0],
...                X[y_km==1,1],
...                s=50,
...                c='orange',
...                marker='o',
...                label='cluster 2')
>>> plt.scatter(km.cluster_centers_[:,0],
...                km.cluster_centers_[:,1],
...                s=250,
...                marker='*',
...                c='red',
...                label='centroids')
>>> plt.legend()
>>> plt.grid()
>>> plt.show()
```

As we can see in the following scatterplot, one of the centroids falls between two of the three spherical groupings of the sample points. Although the clustering does not look completely terrible, it is suboptimal.

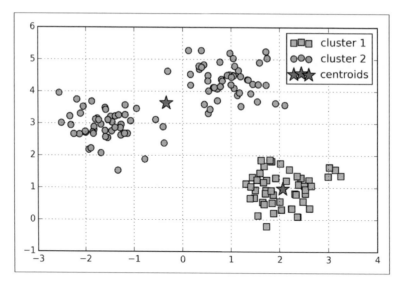

Next we create the silhouette plot to evaluate the results. Please keep in mind that we typically do not have the luxury of visualizing datasets in two-dimensional scatterplots in real-world problems, since we typically work with data in higher dimensions:

```
>>> cluster_labels = np.unique(y_km)
>>> n_clusters = cluster_labels.shape[0]
>>> silhouette_vals = silhouette_samples(X,
```

```
...                                         y_km,
...                                         metric='euclidean')
>>> y_ax_lower, y_ax_upper = 0, 0
yticks = []
>>> for i, c in enumerate(cluster_labels):
...     c_silhouette_vals = silhouette_vals[y_km == c]
...     c_silhouette_vals.sort()
...     y_ax_upper += len(c_silhouette_vals)
...     color = cm.jet(i / n_clusters)
...     plt.barh(range(y_ax_lower, y_ax_upper),
...              c_silhouette_vals,
...              height=1.0,
...              edgecolor='none',
...              color=color)
...     yticks.append((y_ax_lower + y_ax_upper) / 2)
...     y_ax_lower += len(c_silhouette_vals)
>>> silhouette_avg = np.mean(silhouette_vals)
>>> plt.axvline(silhouette_avg, color="red", linestyle="--")
>>> plt.yticks(yticks, cluster_labels + 1)
>>> plt.ylabel('Cluster')
>>> plt.xlabel('Silhouette coefficient')
>>> plt.show()
```

As we can see in the resulting plot, the silhouettes now have visibly different lengths and width, which yields further evidence for a suboptimal clustering:

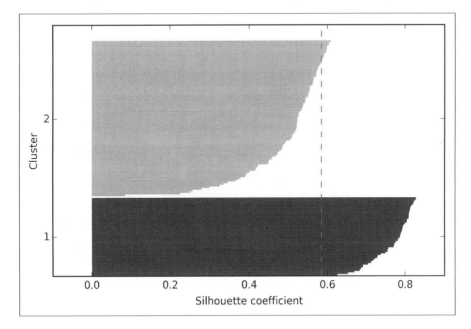

Organizing clusters as a hierarchical tree

In this section, we will take a look at an alternative approach to prototype-based clustering: **hierarchical clustering**. One advantage of hierarchical clustering algorithms is that it allows us to plot **dendrograms** (visualizations of a binary hierarchical clustering), which can help with the interpretation of the results by creating meaningful taxonomies. Another useful advantage of this hierarchical approach is that we do not need to specify the number of clusters upfront.

The two main approaches to hierarchical clustering are **agglomerative** and **divisive** hierarchical clustering. In divisive hierarchical clustering, we start with one cluster that encompasses all our samples, and we iteratively split the cluster into smaller clusters until each cluster only contains one sample. In this section, we will focus on agglomerative clustering, which takes the opposite approach. We start with each sample as an individual cluster and merge the closest pairs of clusters until only one cluster remains.

The two standard algorithms for agglomerative hierarchical clustering are **single linkage** and **complete linkage**. Using single linkage, we compute the distances between the most similar members for each pair of clusters and merge the two clusters for which the distance between the most similar members is the smallest. The complete linkage approach is similar to single linkage but, instead of comparing the most similar members in each pair of clusters, we compare the most dissimilar members to perform the merge. This is shown in the following diagram:

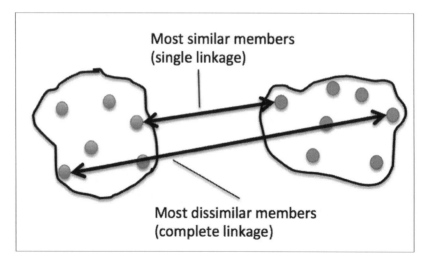

 Other commonly used algorithms for agglomerative hierarchical clustering include **average linkage** and **Ward's linkage**. In average linkage, we merge the cluster pairs based on the minimum average distances between all group members in the two clusters. In Ward's method, those two clusters that lead to the minimum increase of the total within-cluster SSE are merged.

In this section, we will focus on agglomerative clustering using the complete linkage approach. This is an iterative procedure that can be summarized by the following steps:

1. Compute the distance matrix of all samples.
2. Represent each data point as a singleton cluster.
3. Merge the two closest clusters based on the distance of the most dissimilar (distant) members.
4. Update the distance matrix.
5. Repeat steps 2 to 4 until one single cluster remains.

Now we will discuss how to compute the distance matrix (step 1). But first, let's generate some random sample data to work with. The rows represent different observations (IDs 0 to 4), and the columns are the different features (X, Y, Z) of those samples:

```
>>> import pandas as pd
>>> import numpy as np
>>> np.random.seed(123)
>>> variables = ['X', 'Y', 'Z']
>>> labels = ['ID_0','ID_1','ID_2','ID_3','ID_4']
>>> X = np.random.random_sample([5,3])*10
>>> df = pd.DataFrame(X, columns=variables, index=labels)
>>> df
```

After executing the preceding code, we should now see the following DataFrame containing the randomly generated samples:

	X	Y	Z
ID_0	6.964692	2.861393	2.268515
ID_1	5.513148	7.194690	4.231065
ID_2	9.807642	6.848297	4.809319
ID_3	3.921175	3.431780	7.290497
ID_4	4.385722	0.596779	3.980443

Performing hierarchical clustering on a distance matrix

To calculate the distance matrix as input for the hierarchical clustering algorithm, we will use the pdist function from SciPy's spatial.distance submodule:

```
>>> from scipy.spatial.distance import pdist, squareform
>>> row_dist = pd.DataFrame(squareform(
...             pdist(df, metric='euclidean')),
...             columns=labels, index=labels)
>>> row_dist
```

Using the preceding code, we calculated the Euclidean distance between each pair of sample points in our dataset based on the features X, Y, and Z. We provided the condensed distance matrix—returned by pdist—as input to the squareform function to create a symmetrical matrix of the pair-wise distances, as shown here:

	ID_0	ID_1	ID_2	ID_3	ID_4
ID_0	0.000000	4.973534	5.516653	5.899885	3.835396
ID_1	4.973534	0.000000	4.347073	5.104311	6.698233
ID_2	5.516653	4.347073	0.000000	7.244262	8.316594
ID_3	5.899885	5.104311	7.244262	0.000000	4.382864
ID_4	3.835396	6.698233	8.316594	4.382864	0.000000

Next we will apply the complete linkage agglomeration to our clusters using the `linkage` function from SciPy's `cluster.hierarchy` submodule, which returns a so-called **linkage matrix**.

However, before we call the `linkage` function, let's take a careful look at the function documentation:

```
>>> from scipy.cluster.hierarchy import linkage
>>> help(linkage)
[...]
Parameters:
  y : ndarray
    A condensed or redundant distance matrix. A condensed
    distance matrix is a flat array containing the upper
    triangular of the distance matrix. This is the form
    that pdist returns. Alternatively, a collection of m
    observation vectors in n dimensions may be passed as
    an m by n array.

  method : str, optional
    The linkage algorithm to use. See the Linkage Methods
    section below for full descriptions.

  metric : str, optional
    The distance metric to use. See the distance.pdist
    function for a list of valid distance metrics.

  Returns:
   Z : ndarray
    The hierarchical clustering encoded as a linkage matrix.
  [...]
```

Based on the function description, we conclude that we can use a condensed distance matrix (upper triangular) from the `pdist` function as an input attribute. Alternatively, we could also provide the initial data array and use the `euclidean` metric as a function argument in `linkage`. However, we should not use the squareform distance matrix that we defined earlier, since it would yield different distance values from those expected. To sum it up, the three possible scenarios are listed here:

- **Incorrect approach**: In this approach, we use the squareform distance matrix. The code is as follows:

```
>>> from scipy.cluster.hierarchy import linkage
>>> row_clusters = linkage(row_dist,
...                        method='complete',
...                        metric='euclidean')
```

- **Correct approach**: In this approach, we use the condensed distance matrix. The code is as follows:

```
>>> row_clusters = linkage(pdist(df, metric='euclidean'),
...                        method='complete')
```

- **Correct approach**: In this approach, we use the input sample matrix. The code is as follows:

```
>>> row_clusters = linkage(df.values,
...                        method='complete',
...                        metric='euclidean')
```

To take a closer look at the clustering results, we can turn them to a pandas `DataFrame` (best viewed in IPython Notebook) as follows:

```
>>> pd.DataFrame(row_clusters,
...        columns=['row label 1',
...                 'row label 2',
...                 'distance',
...                 'no. of items in clust.'],
...        index=['cluster %d' %(i+1) for i in
...                range(row_clusters.shape[0])])
```

As shown in the following table, the linkage matrix consists of several rows where each row represents one merge. The first and second columns denote the most dissimilar members in each cluster, and the third row reports the distance between those members. The last column returns the count of the members in each cluster.

	row label 1	row label 2	distance	no. of items in clust.
cluster 1	0	4	3.835396	2
cluster 2	1	2	4.347073	2
cluster 3	3	5	5.899885	3
cluster 4	6	7	8.316594	5

Now that we have computed the linkage matrix, we can visualize the results in the form of a dendrogram:

```
>>> from scipy.cluster.hierarchy import dendrogram
# make dendrogram black (part 1/2)
# from scipy.cluster.hierarchy import set_link_color_palette
# set_link_color_palette(['black'])
```

```
>>> row_dendr = dendrogram(row_clusters,
...                        labels=labels,
...                        # make dendrogram black (part 2/2)
...                        # color_threshold=np.inf
...                        )
>>> plt.tight_layout()
>>> plt.ylabel('Euclidean distance')
>>> plt.show()
```

If you are executing the preceding code or reading the e-book version of this book, you will notice that the branches in the resulting dendrogram are shown in different colors. The coloring scheme is derived from a list of matplotlib colors that are cycled for the distance thresholds in the dendrogram. For example, to display the dendrograms in black, you can uncomment the respective sections that I inserted in the preceding code.

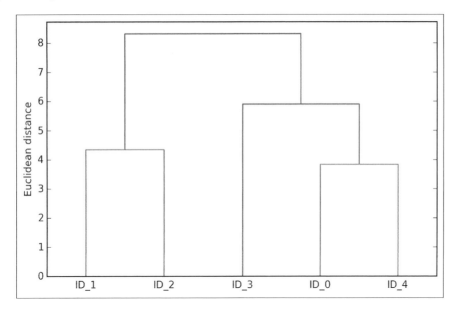

Such a dendrogram summarizes the different clusters that were formed during the agglomerative hierarchical clustering; for example, we can see that the samples **ID_0** and **ID_4**, followed by **ID_1** and **ID_2**, are the most similar ones based on the Euclidean distance metric.

Attaching dendrograms to a heat map

In practical applications, hierarchical clustering dendrograms are often used in combination with a **heat map**, which allows us to represent the individual values in the sample matrix with a color code. In this section, we will discuss how to attach a dendrogram to a heat map plot and order the rows in the heat map correspondingly.

However, attaching a dendrogram to a heat map can be a little bit tricky, so let's go through this procedure step by step:

1. We create a new `figure` object and define the *x* axis position, *y* axis position, width, and height of the dendrogram via the `add_axes` attribute. Furthermore, we rotate the dendrogram 90 degrees counter-clockwise. The code is as follows:

```
>>> fig = plt.figure(figsize=(8,8), facecolor='white')
>>> axd = fig.add_axes([0.09,0.1,0.2,0.6])
>>> row_dendr = dendrogram(row_clusters, orientation='right')
# note: for matplotlib >= v1.5.1, please use orientation='left'
```

2. Next we reorder the data in our initial `DataFrame` according to the clustering labels that can be accessed from the dendrogram object, which is essentially a Python dictionary, via the `leaves` key. The code is as follows:

```
>>> df_rowclust = df.ix[row_dendr['leaves'][::-1]]
```

3. Now we construct the heat map from the reordered `DataFrame` and position it right next to the dendrogram:

```
>>> axm = fig.add_axes([0.23,0.1,0.6,0.6])
>>> cax = axm.matshow(df_rowclust,
...                interpolation='nearest', cmap='hot_r')
```

4. Finally we will modify the aesthetics of the heat map by removing the axis ticks and hiding the axis spines. Also, we will add a color bar and assign the feature and sample names to the *x* and *y* axis tick labels, respectively. The code is as follows:

```
>>> axd.set_xticks([])
>>> axd.set_yticks([])
>>> for i in axd.spines.values():
...      i.set_visible(False)
>>> fig.colorbar(cax)
>>> axm.set_xticklabels([''] + list(df_rowclust.columns))
>>> axm.set_yticklabels([''] + list(df_rowclust.index))
>>> plt.show()
```

After following the previous steps, the heat map should be displayed with the dendrogram attached:

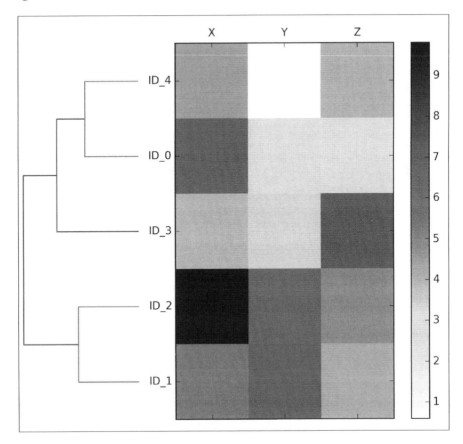

As we can see, the row order in the heat map reflects the clustering of the samples in the dendrogram. In addition to a simple dendrogram, the color-coded values of each sample and feature in the heat map provide us with a nice summary of the dataset.

Applying agglomerative clustering via scikit-learn

In this section, we saw how to perform agglomerative hierarchical clustering using SciPy. However, there is also an `AgglomerativeClustering` implementation in scikit-learn, which allows us to choose the number of clusters that we want to return. This is useful if we want to prune the hierarchical cluster tree. By setting the `n_cluster` parameter to 2, we will now cluster the samples into two groups using the same complete linkage approach based on the Euclidean distance metric as before:

```
>>> from sklearn.cluster import AgglomerativeClustering
>>> ac = AgglomerativeClustering(n_clusters=2,
...                              affinity='euclidean',
...                              linkage='complete')
>>> labels = ac.fit_predict(X)
>>> print('Cluster labels: %s' % labels)
Cluster labels: [0 1 1 0 0]
```

Looking at the predicted cluster labels, we can see that the first, fourth, and fifth sample (**ID_0, ID_3,** and **ID_4**) were assigned to one cluster (0), and the samples **ID_1** and **ID_2** were assigned to a second cluster (1), which is consistent with the results that we can observe in the dendrogram.

Locating regions of high density via DBSCAN

Although we can't cover the vast number of different clustering algorithms in this chapter, let's at least introduce one more approach to clustering: **Density-based Spatial Clustering of Applications with Noise (DBSCAN)**. The notion of density in DBSCAN is defined as the number of points within a specified radius ε.

In DBSCAN, a special label is assigned to each sample (point) using the following criteria:

- A point is considered as **core point** if at least a specified number (MinPts) of neighboring points fall within the specified radius ε
- A **border point** is a point that has fewer neighbors than MinPts within ε, but lies within the ε radius of a core point
- All other points that are neither core nor border points are considered as **noise points**

After labeling the points as core, border, or noise points, the DBSCAN algorithm can be summarized in two simple steps:

1. Form a separate cluster for each core point or a connected group of core points (core points are connected if they are no farther away than ε).

2. Assign each border point to the cluster of its corresponding core point.

To get a better understanding of what the result of DBSCAN can look like before jumping to the implementation, let's summarize what you have learned about core points, border points, and noise points in the following figure:

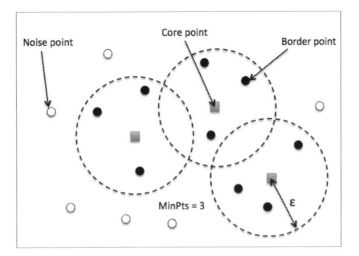

One of the main advantages of using DBSCAN is that it does not assume that the clusters have a spherical shape as in k-means. Furthermore, DBSCAN is different from k-means and hierarchical clustering in that it doesn't necessarily assign each point to a cluster but is capable of removing noise points.

For a more illustrative example, let's create a new dataset of half-moon-shaped structures to compare k-means clustering, hierarchical clustering, and DBSCAN:

```
>>> from sklearn.datasets import make_moons
>>> X, y = make_moons(n_samples=200,
...                    noise=0.05,
...                    random_state=0)
>>> plt.scatter(X[:,0], X[:,1])
>>> plt.show()
```

As we can see in the resulting plot, there are two visible, half-moon-shaped groups consisting of 100 sample points each:

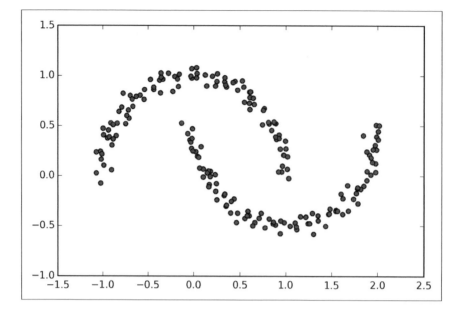

We will start by using the k-means algorithm and complete linkage clustering to see whether one of those previously discussed clustering algorithms can successfully identify the half-moon shapes as separate clusters. The code is as follows:

```
>>> f, (ax1, ax2) = plt.subplots(1, 2, figsize=(8,3))
>>> km = KMeans(n_clusters=2,
...             random_state=0)
>>> y_km = km.fit_predict(X)
>>> ax1.scatter(X[y_km==0,0],
...             X[y_km==0,1],
...             c='lightblue',
...             marker='o',
...             s=40,
...             label='cluster 1')
>>> ax1.scatter(X[y_km==1,0],
...             X[y_km==1,1],
...             c='red',
...             marker='s',
...             s=40,
...             label='cluster 2')
>>> ax1.set_title('K-means clustering')
>>> ac = AgglomerativeClustering(n_clusters=2,
```

```
...                                    affinity='euclidean',
...                                    linkage='complete')
>>> y_ac = ac.fit_predict(X)
>>> ax2.scatter(X[y_ac==0,0],
...             X[y_ac==0,1],
...             c='lightblue',
...             marker='o',
...             s=40,
...             label='cluster 1')
>>> ax2.scatter(X[y_ac==1,0],
...             X[y_ac==1,1],
...             c='red',
...             marker='s',
...             s=40,
...             label='cluster 2')
>>> ax2.set_title('Agglomerative clustering')
>>> plt.legend()
>>> plt.show()
```

Based on the visualized clustering results, we can see that the k-means algorithm is unable to separate the two clusters, and the hierarchical clustering algorithm was challenged by those complex shapes:

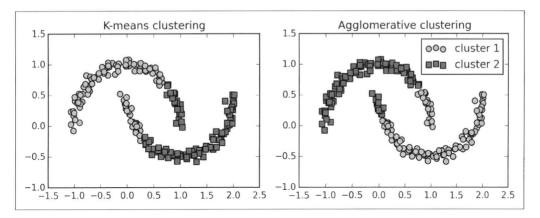

Finally, let's try the DBSCAN algorithm on this dataset to see if it can find the two half-moon-shaped clusters using a density-based approach:

```
>>> from sklearn.cluster import DBSCAN
>>> db = DBSCAN(eps=0.2,
...             min_samples=5,
...             metric='euclidean')
>>> y_db = db.fit_predict(X)
```

```
>>> plt.scatter(X[y_db==0,0],
...             X[y_db==0,1],
...             c='lightblue',
...             marker='o',
...             s=40,
...             label='cluster 1')
>>> plt.scatter(X[y_db==1,0],
...             X[y_db==1,1],
...             c='red',
...             marker='s',
...             s=40,
...             label='cluster 2')
>>> plt.legend()
>>> plt.show()
```

The DBSCAN algorithm can successfully detect the half-moon shapes, which highlights one of the strengths of DBSCAN (clustering data of arbitrary shapes)

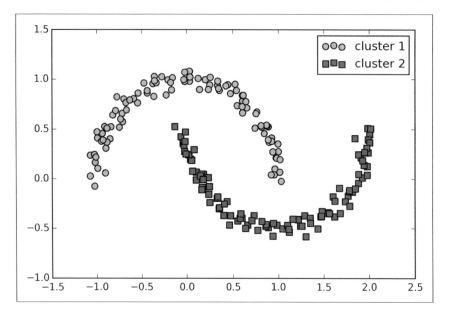

However, we should also note some of the disadvantages of DBSCAN. With an increasing number of features in our dataset—given a fixed size training set—the negative effect of the *curse of dimensionality* increases. This is especially a problem if we are using the Euclidean distance metric. However, the problem of the *curse of dimensionality* is not unique to DBSCAN; it also affects other clustering algorithms that use the Euclidean distance metric, for example, the k-means and hierarchical clustering algorithms. In addition, we have two hyperparameters in DBSCAN (MinPts and ε) that need to be optimized to yield good clustering results. Finding a good combination of MinPts and ε can be problematic if the density differences in the dataset are relatively large.

> So far, we saw three of the most fundamental categories of clustering algorithms: prototype-based clustering with k-means, agglomerative hierarchical clustering, and density-based clustering via DBSCAN. However, I also want to mention a fourth class of more advanced clustering algorithms that we have not covered in this chapter: **graph-based clustering**. Probably the most prominent members of the graph-based clustering family are **spectral clustering algorithms**. Although there are many different implementations of spectral clustering, they all have in common that they use the eigenvectors of a similarity matrix to derive the cluster relationships. Since spectral clustering is beyond the scope of this book, you can read the excellent tutorial by Ulrike von Luxburg to learn more about this topic (U. Von Luxburg. *A Tutorial on Spectral Clustering*. Statistics and computing, 17(4):395–416, 2007). It is freely available from arXiv at `http://arxiv.org/pdf/0711.0189v1.pdf`.

Note that, in practice, it is not always obvious which algorithm will perform best on a given dataset, especially if the data comes in multiple dimensions that make it hard or impossible to visualize. Furthermore, it is important to emphasize that a successful clustering does not only depend on the algorithm and its hyperparameters. Rather, the choice of an appropriate distance metric and the use of domain knowledge that can help guide the experimental setup can be even more important.

Summary

In this chapter, you learned about three different clustering algorithms that can help us with the discovery of hidden structures or information in data. We started this chapter with a prototype-based approach, k-means, which clusters samples into spherical shapes based on a specified number of cluster centroids. Since clustering is an unsupervised method, we do not enjoy the luxury of ground truth labels to evaluate the performance of a model. Thus, we looked at useful intrinsic performance metrics such as the elbow method or silhouette analysis as an attempt to quantify the quality of clustering.

We then looked at a different approach to clustering: agglomerative hierarchical clustering. Hierarchical clustering does not require specifying the number of clusters upfront, and the result can be visualized in a dendrogram representation, which can help with the interpretation of the results. The last clustering algorithm that we saw in this chapter was DBSCAN, an algorithm that groups points based on local densities and is capable of handling outliers and identifying nonglobular shapes.

After this excursion into the field of unsupervised learning, it is now about time to introduce some of the most exciting machine learning algorithms for supervised learning: multilayer artificial neural networks. After their recent resurgence, neural networks are once again the hottest topic in machine learning research. Thanks to the recently developed deep learning algorithms, neural networks are conceived as state-of-the-art for many complex tasks such as image classification and speech recognition. In *Chapter 12, Training Artificial Neural Networks for Image Recognition*, we will construct our own multilayer neural network from scratch. In *Chapter 13, Parallelizing Neural Network Training with Theano*, we will introduce powerful libraries that can help us to train complex network architectures most efficiently.

12

Training Artificial Neural Networks for Image Recognition

As you may know, **deep learning** is getting a lot of press and is without any doubt the hottest topic in the machine learning field. Deep learning can be understood as a set of algorithms that were developed to train **artificial neural networks** with many layers most efficiently. In this chapter, you will learn the basic concepts of artificial neural networks so that you will be well equipped to further explore the most exciting areas of research in the machine learning field, as well as the advanced Python-based deep learning libraries that are currently being developed.

The topics that we will cover are as follows:

- Getting a conceptual understanding of multi-layer neural networks
- Training neural networks for image classification
- Implementing the powerful backpropagation algorithm
- Debugging neural network implementations

Modeling complex functions with artificial neural networks

At the beginning of this book, we started our journey through machine learning algorithms with artificial neurons in *Chapter 2, Training Machine Learning Algorithms for Classification*. Artificial neurons represent the building blocks of the multi-layer artificial neural networks that we are going to discuss in this chapter. The basic concept behind artificial neural networks was built upon hypotheses and models of how the human brain works to solve complex problem tasks. Although artificial neural networks have gained a lot of popularity in recent years, early studies of neural networks go back to the 1940s when Warren McCulloch and Walter Pitt first described how neurons could work. However, in the decades that followed the first implementation of the **McCulloch-Pitt neuron** model, Rosenblatt's perceptron in the 1950s, many researchers and machine learning practitioners slowly began to lose interest in neural networks since no one had a good solution for training a neural network with multiple layers. Eventually, interest in neural networks was rekindled in 1986 when D.E. Rumelhart, G.E. Hinton, and R.J. Williams were involved in the (re)discovery and popularization of the **backpropagation** algorithm to train neural networks more efficiently, which we will discuss in more detail later in this chapter (Rumelhart, David E.; Hinton, Geoffrey E.; Williams, Ronald J. (1986). *Learning Representations by Back-propagating Errors*. Nature 323 (6088): 533–536).

During the previous decade, many more major breakthroughs resulted in what we now call deep learning algorithms, which can be used to create **feature detectors** from unlabeled data to pre-train deep neural networks—neural networks that are composed of many layers. Neural networks are a hot topic not only in academic research, but also in big technology companies such as Facebook, Microsoft, and Google who invest heavily in artificial neural networks and deep learning research. As of today, complex neural networks powered by deep learning algorithms are considered as state-of-the-art when it comes to complex problem solving such as image and voice recognition. Popular examples of the products in our everyday life that are powered by deep learning are Google's image search and Google Translate, an application for smartphones that can automatically recognize text in images for real-time translation into 20 languages (`http://googleresearch.blogspot.com/2015/07/how-google-translate-squeezes-deep.html`).

Many more exciting applications of deep neural networks are under active development at major tech companies, for example, Facebook's DeepFace for tagging images (Y. Taigman, M. Yang, M. Ranzato, and L. Wolf. *DeepFace: Closing the gap to human-level performance in face verification.* In Computer Vision and Pattern Recognition CVPR, 2014 IEEE Conference, pages 1701–1708) and Baidu's DeepSpeech, which is able to handle voice queries in Mandarin (A. Hannun, C. Case, J. Casper, B. Catanzaro, G. Diamos, E. Elsen, R. Prenger, S. Satheesh, S. Sengupta, A. Coates, et al. *DeepSpeech: Scaling up end-to-end speech recognition.* arXiv preprint arXiv:1412.5567, 2014). In addition, the pharmaceutical industry recently started to use deep learning techniques for drug discovery and toxicity prediction, and research has shown that these novel techniques substantially exceed the performance of traditional methods for virtual screening (T. Unterthiner, A. Mayr, G. Klambauer, and S. Hochreiter. *Toxicity prediction using deep learning.* arXiv preprint arXiv:1503.01445, 2015).

Single-layer neural network recap

This chapter is all about multi-layer neural networks, how they work, and how to train them to solve complex problems. However, before we dig deeper into a particular multi-layer neural network architecture, let's briefly reiterate some of the concepts of single-layer neural networks that we introduced in *Chapter 2, Training Machine Learning Algorithms for Classification*, namely, the **ADAptive LInear NEuron** (**Adaline**) algorithm that is shown in the following figure:

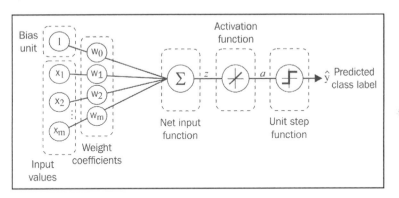

In *Chapter 2, Training Machine Learning Algorithms for Classification,* we implemented the Adaline algorithm to perform binary classification, and we used a **gradient descent** optimization algorithm to learn the weight coefficients of the model. In every **epoch** (pass over the training set), we updated the weight vector w using the following update rule:

$$w := w + \Delta w, \text{ where } \Delta w = -\eta \nabla J(w)$$

In other words, we computed the gradient based on the whole training set and updated the weights of the model by taking a step into the opposite direction of the gradient $\nabla J(w)$. In order to find the optimal weights of the model, we optimized an objective function that we defined as the **Sum of Squared Errors (SSE)** cost function $J(w)$. Furthermore, we multiplied the gradient by a factor, the **learning rate** η, which we chose carefully to balance the speed of learning against the risk of overshooting the global minimum of the cost function.

In gradient descent optimization, we updated all weights simultaneously after each epoch, and we defined the partial derivative for each weight w_j in the weight vector w as follows:

$$\frac{\partial}{\partial w_j} J(w) = \sum_i \left(y^{(i)} - a^{(i)} \right) x_j^{(i)}$$

Here $y^{(i)}$ is the target class label of a particular sample $x^{(i)}$, and $a^{(i)}$ is the **activation** of the neuron, which is a linear function in the special case of Adaline. Furthermore, we defined the *activation function* $\phi(\cdot)$ as follows:

$$\phi(z) = z = a$$

Here, the net input z is a linear combination of the weights that are connecting the input to the output layer:

$$z = \sum_j w_j x_j = w^T x$$

While we used the activation $\phi(z)$ to compute the gradient update, we implemented a **threshold function** (Heaviside function) to squash the continuous-valued output into binary class labels for prediction:

$$\hat{y} = \begin{cases} 1 & \text{if } g(z) \geq 0 \\ -1 & \text{otherwise} \end{cases}$$

Introducing the multi-layer neural network architecture

In this section, we will see how to connect multiple single neurons to a **multi-layer feedforward neural network**; this special type of network is also called a **multi-layer perceptron** (**MLP**). The following figure explains the concept of an MLP consisting of three layers: one input layer, one **hidden layer**, and one output layer. The units in the hidden layer are fully connected to the input layer, and the output layer is fully connected to the hidden layer, respectively. If such a network has more than one hidden layer, we also call it a *deep* artificial neural network.

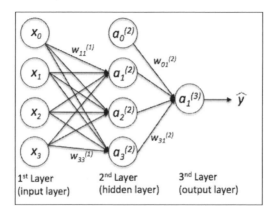

We could add an arbitrary number of hidden layers to the MLP to create deeper network architectures. Practically, we can think of the number of layers and units in a neural network as additional **hyperparameters** that we want to optimize for a given problem task using the cross-validation that we discussed in *Chapter 6, Learning Best Practices for Model Evaluation and Hyperparameter Tuning*.

However, the error gradients that we will calculate later via backpropagation would become increasingly small as more layers are added to a network. This *vanishing gradient* problem makes the model learning more challenging. Therefore, special algorithms have been developed to pretrain such deep neural network structures, which is called *deep learning*.

As shown in the preceding figure, we denote the ith activation unit in the lth layer as $a_i^{(l)}$, and the activation units $a_0^{(1)}$ and $a_0^{(2)}$ are the **bias units**, respectively, which we set equal to 1. The activation of the units in the input layer is just its input plus the bias unit:

$$a^{(1)} = \begin{bmatrix} a_0^{(1)} \\ a_1^{(1)} \\ \vdots \\ a_m^{(1)} \end{bmatrix} = \begin{bmatrix} 1 \\ x_1^{(i)} \\ \vdots \\ x_m^{(i)} \end{bmatrix}$$

Each unit in layer l is connected to all units in layer $l+1$ via a weight coefficient. For example, the connection between the kth unit in layer l to the jth unit in layer $l+1$ would be written as $w_{j,k}^{(l)}$. Please note that the superscript i in $x_m^{(i)}$ stands for the ith sample, not the ith layer. In the following paragraphs, we will often omit the superscript i for clarity.

While one unit in the output layer would suffice for a binary classification task, we saw a more general form of a neural network in the preceding figure, which allows us to perform multi-class classification via a generalization of the **One-vs-All (OvA)** technique. To better understand how this works, remember the **one-hot** representation of categorical variables that we introduced in *Chapter 4, Building Good Training Sets – Data Preprocessing*. For example, we would encode the three class labels in the familiar Iris dataset (0=Setosa, 1=Versicolor, 2=Virginica) as follows:

$$0 = \begin{bmatrix} 1 \\ 0 \\ 0 \end{bmatrix}, 1 = \begin{bmatrix} 0 \\ 1 \\ 0 \end{bmatrix}, 2 = \begin{bmatrix} 0 \\ 0 \\ 1 \end{bmatrix}$$

This one-hot vector representation allows us to tackle classification tasks with an arbitrary number of unique class labels present in the training set.

If you are new to neural network representations, the terminology around the indices (subscripts and superscripts) may look a little bit confusing at first. You may wonder why we wrote $w_{j,k}^{(l)}$ and not $w_{k,j}^{(l)}$ to refer to the weight coefficient that connects the kth unit in layer l to the jth unit in layer $l+1$. What may seem a little bit quirky at first will make much more sense in later sections when we vectorize the neural network representation. For example, we will summarize the weights that connect the input and hidden layer by a matrix $W^{(1)} \in \mathbb{R}^{h \times [m+1]}$, where h is the number of hidden units and $m+1$ is the number of input units plus bias unit. Since it is important to internalize this notation to follow the concepts later in this chapter, let's summarize what we just discussed in a descriptive illustration of a simplified 3-4-3 multi-layer perceptron:

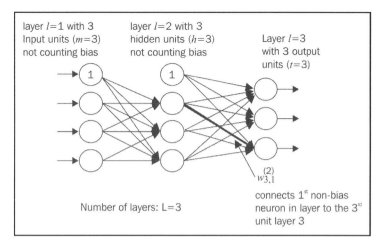

Activating a neural network via forward propagation

In this section, we will describe the process of **forward propagation** to calculate the output of an MLP model. To understand how it fits into the context of learning an MLP model, let's summarize the MLP learning procedure in three simple steps:

1. Starting at the input layer, we forward propagate the patterns of the training data through the network to generate an output.

2. Based on the network's output, we calculate the error that we want to minimize using a cost function that we will describe later.

3. We backpropagate the error, find its derivative with respect to each weight in the network, and update the model.

Finally, after repeating the steps for multiple epochs and learning the weights of the MLP, we use forward propagation to calculate the network output and apply a threshold function to obtain the predicted class labels in the one-hot representation, which we described in the previous section.

Now, let's walk through the individual steps of forward propagation to generate an output from the patterns in the training data. Since each unit in the hidden layer is connected to all units in the input layers, we first calculate the activation $a_1^{(2)}$ as follows:

$$z_1^{(2)} = a_0^{(1)} w_{1,0}^{(1)} + a_1^{(1)} w_{1,1}^{(1)} + \cdots + a_m^{(1)} w_{1,m}^{(1)}$$

$$a_1^{(2)} = \phi\left(z_1^{(2)}\right)$$

Here, $z_1^{(2)}$ is the net input and $\phi(\cdot)$ is the activation function, which has to be differentiable to learn the weights that connect the neurons using a gradient-based approach. To be able to solve complex problems such as image classification, we need nonlinear activation functions in our MLP model, for example, the **sigmoid (logistic)** activation function that we used in **logistic regression** in *Chapter 3, A Tour of Machine Learning Classifiers Using Scikit-learn*:

$$\phi(z) = \frac{1}{1 + e^{-z}}$$

As we can remember, the sigmoid function is an S-shaped curve that maps the net input z onto a logistic distribution in the range 0 to 1, which cuts the y axis at $z=0$, as shown in the following graph:

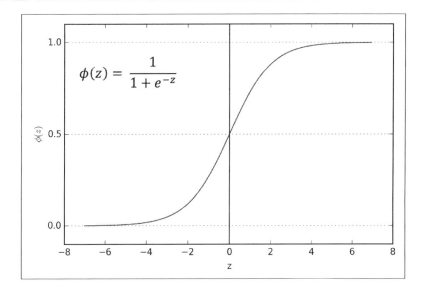

The MLP is a typical example of a *feedforward* artificial neural network. The term *feedforward* refers to the fact that each layer serves as the input to the next layer without loops, in contrast to *recurrent neural networks*, an architecture that we will discuss later in this chapter. The term multi-layer perceptron may sound a little bit confusing, since the artificial neurons in this network architecture are typically sigmoid units, not *perceptrons*. Intuitively, we can think of the neurons in the MLP as logistic regression units that return values in the continuous range between 0 and 1.

For purposes of code efficiency and readability, we will now write the activation in a more compact form using the concepts of basic linear algebra, which will allow us to **vectorize** our code implementation via NumPy rather than writing multiple nested and expensive Python `for` loops:

$$\mathbf{z}^{(2)} = \boldsymbol{W}^{(1)}\boldsymbol{a}^{(1)}$$

$$\boldsymbol{a}^{(2)} = \phi\left(\mathbf{z}^{(2)}\right)$$

[

Everywhere you read *h* on this page, you can think of *h* as *h+1* to
include the bias unit (and in order to get the dimensions right).
]

Here, $a^{(1)}$ is our $[m+1] \times 1$ dimensional feature vector of a sample $x^{(i)}$ plus bias unit.
$W^{(1)}$ is an $h \times [m+1]$ dimensional weight matrix where *h* is the number of hidden
units in our neural network. After matrix-vector multiplication, we obtain the $h \times 1$
dimensional net input vector $z^{(2)}$ to calculate the activation $a^{(2)}$ (where $a^{(2)} \in \mathbb{R}^{h \times 1}$).
Furthermore, we can generalize this computation to all n samples in the training set:

$$Z^{(2)} = W^{(1)} \left[A^{(1)} \right]^T$$

Here, $A^{(1)}$ is now an $n \times [m+1]$ matrix, and the matrix-matrix multiplication will result
in a $h \times n$ dimensional net input matrix $Z^{(2)}$. Finally, we apply the activation function
$\phi(\cdot)$ to each value in the net input matrix to get the $h \times n$ activation matrix $A^{(2)}$ for the
next layer (here, output layer):

$$A^{(2)} = \phi\left(Z^{(2)} \right)$$

Similarly, we can rewrite the activation of the output layer in the vectorized form:

$$Z^{(3)} = W^{(2)} A^{(2)}$$

Here, we multiply the $t \times h$ matrix $W^{(2)}$ (*t* is the number of output units) by the $h \times n$
dimensional matrix $A^{(2)}$ to obtain the $t \times n$ dimensional matrix $Z^{(3)}$ (the columns in this
matrix represent the outputs for each sample).

Lastly, we apply the sigmoid activation function to obtain the continuous valued
output of our network:

$$A^{(3)} = \phi\left(Z^{(3)} \right), \ A^{(3)} \in \mathbb{R}^{t \times n}$$

Classifying handwritten digits

In the previous section, we covered a lot of the theory around neural networks,
which can be a little bit overwhelming if you are new to this topic. Before we
continue with the discussion of the algorithm for learning the weights of the MLP
model, backpropagation, let's take a short break from the theory and see a neural
network in action.

Neural network theory can be quite complex, thus I want to recommend two additional resources that cover some of the concepts that we discuss in this chapter in more detail:

T. Hastie, J. Friedman, and R. Tibshirani. *The Elements of Statistical Learning*, Volume 2. Springer, 2009.

C. M. Bishop et al. *Pattern Recognition and Machine Learning*, Volume 1. Springer New York, 2006.

In this section, we will train our first multi-layer neural network to classify handwritten digits from the popular **MNIST** dataset (short for **Mixed National Institute of Standards and Technology** database) that has been constructed by Yann LeCun et al. and serves as a popular benchmark dataset for machine learning algorithms (Y. LeCun, L. Bottou, Y. Bengio, and P. Haffner. *Gradient-based Learning Applied to Document Recognition*. Proceedings of the IEEE, 86(11):2278-2324, November 1998).

Obtaining the MNIST dataset

The MNIST dataset is publicly available at `http://yann.lecun.com/exdb/mnist/` and consists of the following four parts:

- **Training set images**: `train-images-idx3-ubyte.gz` (9.9 MB, 47 MB unzipped, and 60,000 samples)

- **Training set labels**: `train-labels-idx1-ubyte.gz` (29 KB, 60 KB unzipped, and 60,000 labels)

- **Test set images**: `t10k-images-idx3-ubyte.gz` (1.6 MB, 7.8 MB, unzipped and 10,000 samples)

- **Test set labels**: `t10k-labels-idx1-ubyte.gz` (5 KB, 10 KB unzipped, and 10,000 labels)

The MNIST dataset was constructed from two datasets of the US **National Institute of Standards and Technology** (**NIST**). The training set consists of handwritten digits from 250 different people, 50 percent high school students, and 50 percent employees from the Census Bureau. Note that the test set contains handwritten digits from different people following the same split.

After downloading the files, I recommend unzipping the files using the Unix/Linux gzip tool from the command line terminal for efficiency using the following command in your local MNIST download directory:

```
gzip *ubyte.gz -d
```

Alternatively, you could use your favorite unzipping tool if you are working with a machine running on Microsoft Windows. The images are stored in byte format, and we will read them into NumPy arrays that we will use to train and test our MLP implementation:

```python
import os
import struct
import numpy as np

def load_mnist(path, kind='train'):
    """Load MNIST data from `path`"""
    labels_path = os.path.join(path,
                               '%s-labels-idx1-ubyte'
                               % kind)
    images_path = os.path.join(path,
                               '%s-images-idx3-ubyte'
                               % kind)

    with open(labels_path, 'rb') as lbpath:
        magic, n = struct.unpack('>II',
                                 lbpath.read(8))
        labels = np.fromfile(lbpath,
                             dtype=np.uint8)

    with open(images_path, 'rb') as imgpath:
        magic, num, rows, cols = struct.unpack(">IIII",
                                               imgpath.read(16))
        images = np.fromfile(imgpath,
                    dtype=np.uint8).reshape(len(labels), 784)

    return images, labels
```

The `load_mnist` function returns two arrays, the first being an $n \times m$ dimensional NumPy array (`images`), where n is the number of samples and m is the number of features. The training dataset consists of 60,000 training digits and the test set contains 10,000 samples, respectively. The images in the MNIST dataset consist of 28×28 pixels, and each pixel is represented by a gray scale intensity value. Here, we unroll the 28×28 pixels into 1D row vectors, which represent the rows in our image array (784 per row or image). The second array (`labels`) returned by the `load_mnist` function contains the corresponding target variable, the class labels (integers 0-9) of the handwritten digits.

The way we read in the image might seem a little bit strange at first:

```
magic, n = struct.unpack('>II', lbpath.read(8))
labels = np.fromfile(lbpath, dtype=np.int8)
```

To understand how these two lines of code work, let's take a look at the dataset description from the MNIST website:

[offset]	[type]	[value]	[description]
0000	32 bit integer	0x00000801(2049)	magic number (MSB first)
0004	32 bit integer	60000	number of items
0008	unsigned byte	??	label
0009	unsigned byte	??	label
....			
xxxx	unsigned byte	??	label

Using the two lines of the preceding code, we first read in the *magic number*, which is a description of the file protocol as well as the *number of items* (*n*) from the file buffer before we read the following bytes into a NumPy array using the `fromfile` method. The `fmt` parameter value `>II` that we passed as an argument to `struct.unpack` has two parts:

- `>`: This is big-endian (defines the order in which a sequence of bytes is stored); if you are unfamiliar with the terms *big-endian* and *small-endian*, you can find an excellent article about *Endianness* on Wikipedia (https://en.wikipedia.org/wiki/Endianness).
- `I`: This is an unsigned integer.

By executing the following code, we will now load the 60,000 training instances as well as the 10,000 test samples from the `mnist` directory where we unzipped the MNIST dataset:

```
>>> X_train, y_train = load_mnist('mnist', kind='train')
>>> print('Rows: %d, columns: %d'
...       % (X_train.shape[0], X_train.shape[1]))
Rows: 60000, columns: 784

>>> X_test, y_test = load_mnist('mnist', kind='t10k')
>>> print('Rows: %d, columns: %d'
...       % (X_test.shape[0], X_test.shape[1]))
Rows: 10000, columns: 784
```

To get a idea what the images in MNIST look like, let's visualize examples of the digits 0-9 after reshaping the 784-pixel vectors from our feature matrix into the original 28 × 28 image that we can plot via matplotlib's `imshow` function:

```
>>> import matplotlib.pyplot as plt
>>> fig, ax = plt.subplots(nrows=2, ncols=5, sharex=True,
sharey=True,)
>>> ax = ax.flatten()
>>> for i in range(10):
...     img = X_train[y_train == i][0].reshape(28, 28)
...     ax[i].imshow(img, cmap='Greys', interpolation='nearest')
>>> ax[0].set_xticks([])
>>> ax[0].set_yticks([])
>>> plt.tight_layout()
>>> plt.show()
```

We should now see a plot of the 2×5 subfigures showing a representative image of each unique digit:

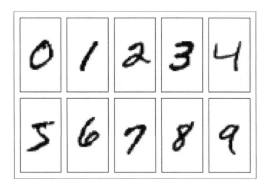

In addition, let's also plot multiple examples of the same digit to see how different those handwriting examples really are:

```
>>> fig, ax = plt.subplots(nrows=5,
...                        ncols=5,
...                        sharex=True,
...                        sharey=True,)
>>> ax = ax.flatten()
>>> for i in range(25):
...     img = X_train[y_train == 7][i].reshape(28, 28)
...     ax[i].imshow(img, cmap='Greys', interpolation='nearest')
>>> ax[0].set_xticks([])
>>> ax[0].set_yticks([])
>>> plt.tight_layout()
>>> plt.show()
```

After executing the code, we should now see the first 25 variants of the digit 7.

Optionally, we can save the MNIST image data and labels as CSV files to open them in programs that do not support their special byte format. However, we should be aware that the CSV file format will take up substantially more space on your local drive, as listed here:

- `train_img.csv`: 109.5 MB
- `train_labels.csv`: 120 KB
- `test_img.csv`: 18.3 MB
- `test_labels.csv`: 20 KB

If we decide to save those CSV files, we can execute the following code in our Python session after loading the MNIST data into NumPy arrays:

```
>>> np.savetxt('train_img.csv', X_train,
...             fmt='%i', delimiter=',')
>>> np.savetxt('train_labels.csv', y_train,
...             fmt='%i', delimiter=',')
>>> np.savetxt('test_img.csv', X_test,
...             fmt='%i', delimiter=',')
>>> np.savetxt('test_labels.csv', y_test,
...             fmt='%i', delimiter=',')
```

Once we have saved the CSV files, we can load them back into Python using NumPy's `genfromtxt` function:

```
>>> X_train = np.genfromtxt('train_img.csv',
...                          dtype=int, delimiter=',')
>>> y_train = np.genfromtxt('train_labels.csv',
...                          dtype=int, delimiter=',')
>>> X_test = np.genfromtxt('test_img.csv',
...                          dtype=int, delimiter=',')
>>> y_test = np.genfromtxt('test_labels.csv',
...                          dtype=int, delimiter=',')
```

However, it will take substantially longer to load the MNIST data from the CSV files, thus I recommend you stick to the original byte format if possible.

Implementing a multi-layer perceptron

In this subsection, we will now implement the code of an MLP with one input, one hidden, and one output layer to classify the images in the MNIST dataset. I have tried to keep the code as simple as possible. However, it may seem a little bit complicated at first, and I encourage you to download the sample code for this chapter from the Packt Publishing website, where you can find this MLP implementation annotated with comments and syntax highlighting for better readability. If you are not running the code from the accompanying IPython notebook, I recommend you copy it into a Python script file in your current working directory, for example, `neuralnet.py`, which you can then import into your current Python session via the following command:

```
from neuralnet import NeuralNetMLP
```

The code will contain parts that we have not talked about yet, such as the backpropagation algorithm, but most of the code should look familiar to you based on the Adaline implementation in *Chapter 2, Training Machine Learning Algorithms for Classification*, and the discussion of forward propagation in earlier sections. Do not worry if not all of the code makes immediate sense to you; we will follow up on certain parts later in this chapter. However, going over the code at this stage can make it easier to follow the theory later.

```
import numpy as np
from scipy.special import expit
import sys

class NeuralNetMLP(object):
    def __init__(self, n_output, n_features, n_hidden=30,
                 l1=0.0, l2=0.0, epochs=500, eta=0.001,
```

```
                alpha=0.0, decrease_const=0.0, shuffle=True,
                minibatches=1, random_state=None):
    np.random.seed(random_state)
    self.n_output = n_output
    self.n_features = n_features
    self.n_hidden = n_hidden
    self.w1, self.w2 = self._initialize_weights()
    self.l1 = l1
    self.l2 = l2
    self.epochs = epochs
    self.eta = eta
    self.alpha = alpha
    self.decrease_const = decrease_const
    self.shuffle = shuffle
    self.minibatches = minibatches

def _encode_labels(self, y, k):
    onehot = np.zeros((k, y.shape[0]))
    for idx, val in enumerate(y):
        onehot[val, idx] = 1.0
    return onehot

def _initialize_weights(self):
    w1 = np.random.uniform(-1.0, 1.0,
                size=self.n_hidden*(self.n_features + 1))
    w1 = w1.reshape(self.n_hidden, self.n_features + 1)
    w2 = np.random.uniform(-1.0, 1.0,
                size=self.n_output*(self.n_hidden + 1))
    w2 = w2.reshape(self.n_output, self.n_hidden + 1)
    return w1, w2

def _sigmoid(self, z):
    # expit is equivalent to 1.0/(1.0 + np.exp(-z))
    return expit(z)

def _sigmoid_gradient(self, z):
    sg = self._sigmoid(z)
    return sg * (1 - sg)

def _add_bias_unit(self, X, how='column'):
    if how == 'column':
        X_new = np.ones((X.shape[0], X.shape[1]+1))
        X_new[:, 1:] = X
    elif how == 'row':
```

```
        X_new = np.ones((X.shape[0]+1, X.shape[1]))
        X_new[1:, :] = X
    else:
        raise AttributeError('`how` must be `column` or `row`')
    return X_new

def _feedforward(self, X, w1, w2):
    a1 = self._add_bias_unit(X, how='column')
    z2 = w1.dot(a1.T)
    a2 = self._sigmoid(z2)
    a2 = self._add_bias_unit(a2, how='row')
    z3 = w2.dot(a2)
    a3 = self._sigmoid(z3)
    return a1, z2, a2, z3, a3

def _L2_reg(self, lambda_, w1, w2):
    return (lambda_/2.0) * (np.sum(w1[:, 1:] ** 2)\
            + np.sum(w2[:, 1:] ** 2))

def _L1_reg(self, lambda_, w1, w2):
    return (lambda_/2.0) * (np.abs(w1[:, 1:]).sum()\
            + np.abs(w2[:, 1:]).sum())

def _get_cost(self, y_enc, output, w1, w2):
    term1 = -y_enc * (np.log(output))
    term2 = (1 - y_enc) * np.log(1 - output)
    cost = np.sum(term1 - term2)
    L1_term = self._L1_reg(self.l1, w1, w2)
    L2_term = self._L2_reg(self.l2, w1, w2)
    cost = cost + L1_term + L2_term
    return cost

def _get_gradient(self, a1, a2, a3, z2, y_enc, w1, w2):
    # backpropagation
    sigma3 = a3 - y_enc
    z2 = self._add_bias_unit(z2, how='row')
    sigma2 = w2.T.dot(sigma3) * self._sigmoid_gradient(z2)
    sigma2 = sigma2[1:, :]
    grad1 = sigma2.dot(a1)
    grad2 = sigma3.dot(a2.T)

    # regularize
    grad1[:, 1:] += (w1[:, 1:] * (self.l1 + self.l2))
```

```
        grad2[:, 1:] += (w2[:, 1:] * (self.l1 + self.l2))

        return grad1, grad2

    def predict(self, X):
        a1, z2, a2, z3, a3 = self._feedforward(X, self.w1, self.w2)
        y_pred = np.argmax(z3, axis=0)
        return y_pred

    def fit(self, X, y, print_progress=False):
        self.cost_ = []
        X_data, y_data = X.copy(), y.copy()
        y_enc = self._encode_labels(y, self.n_output)

        delta_w1_prev = np.zeros(self.w1.shape)
        delta_w2_prev = np.zeros(self.w2.shape)

        for i in range(self.epochs):

            # adaptive learning rate
            self.eta /= (1 + self.decrease_const*i)

            if print_progress:
                sys.stderr.write(
                        '\rEpoch: %d/%d' % (i+1, self.epochs))
                sys.stderr.flush()

            if self.shuffle:
                idx = np.random.permutation(y_data.shape[0])
                X_data, y_enc = X_data[idx], y_enc[:,idx]

            mini = np.array_split(range(
                        y_data.shape[0]), self.minibatches)
            for idx in mini:

                # feedforward
                a1, z2, a2, z3, a3 = self._feedforward(
                                  X_data[idx], self.w1, self.w2)
                cost = self._get_cost(y_enc=y_enc[:, idx],
                                  output=a3,
                                  w1=self.w1,
                                  w2=self.w2)
                self.cost_.append(cost)
```

```
            # compute gradient via backpropagation
            grad1, grad2 = self._get_gradient(a1=a1, a2=a2,
                                              a3=a3, z2=z2,
                                              y_enc=y_enc[:, idx],
                                              w1=self.w1,
                                              w2=self.w2)

            # update weights
            delta_w1, delta_w2 = self.eta * grad1,\
                                 self.eta * grad2
            self.w1 -= (delta_w1 + (self.alpha * delta_w1_prev))
            self.w2 -= (delta_w2 + (self.alpha * delta_w2_prev))
            delta_w1_prev, delta_w2_prev = delta_w1, delta_w2

    return self
```

Now, let's initialize a new 784-50-10 MLP, a neural network with 784 input units (n_features), 50 hidden units (n_hidden), and 10 output units (n_output):

```
>>> nn = NeuralNetMLP(n_output=10,
...                   n_features=X_train.shape[1],
...                   n_hidden=50,
...                   l2=0.1,
...                   l1=0.0,
...                   epochs=1000,
...                   eta=0.001,
...                   alpha=0.001,
...                   decrease_const=0.00001,
...                   shuffle=True,
...                   minibatches=50,
...                   random_state=1)
```

As you may have noticed, by going over our preceding MLP implementation, we also implemented some additional features, which are summarized here:

- l2: The λ parameter for L2 regularization to decrease the degree of overfitting; equivalently, l1 is the λ parameter for L1 regularization.
- epochs: The number of passes over the training set.

- `eta`: The learning rate η.

- `alpha`: A parameter for momentum learning to add a factor of the previous gradient to the weight update for faster learning $\Delta w_t = \eta \nabla J(w_t) + \alpha \Delta w_{t-1}$ (where t is the current time step or epoch).

- `decrease_const`: The decrease constant d for an adaptive learning rate n that decreases over time for better convergence $\eta / 1 + t \times d$.

- `shuffle`: Shuffling the training set prior to every epoch to prevent the algorithm from getting stuck in cycles.

- `Minibatches`: Splitting of the training data into k mini-batches in each epoch. The gradient is computed for each mini-batch separately instead of the entire training data for faster learning.

Next, we train the MLP using 60,000 samples from the already shuffled MNIST training dataset. Before you execute the following code, please note that training the neural network may take 10-30 minutes on standard desktop computer hardware:

```
>>> nn.fit(X_train, y_train, print_progress=True)
Epoch: 1000/1000
```

Similar to our previous Adaline implementation, we save the cost for each epoch in a `cost_` list that we can now visualize, making sure that the optimization algorithm reached convergence. Here, we only plot every 50th step to account for the 50 mini-batches (50 mini-batches × 1000 epochs). The code is as follows:

```
>>> plt.plot(range(len(nn.cost_)), nn.cost_)
>>> plt.ylim([0, 2000])
>>> plt.ylabel('Cost')
>>> plt.xlabel('Epochs * 50')
>>> plt.tight_layout()
>>> plt.show()
```

As we see in the following plot, the graph of the cost function looks very noisy. This is due to the fact that we trained our neural network with mini-batch learning, a variant of stochastic gradient descent.

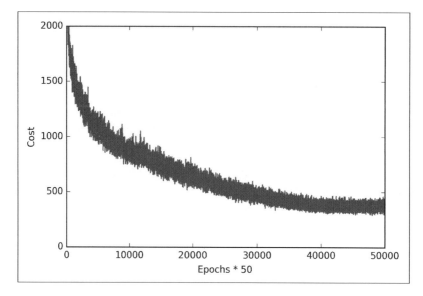

Although we can already see in the plot that the optimization algorithm converged after approximately 800 epochs (*40,000/50 = 800*), let's plot a smoother version of the cost function against the number of epochs by averaging over the mini-batch intervals. The code is as follows:

```
>>> batches = np.array_split(range(len(nn.cost_)), 1000)
>>> cost_ary = np.array(nn.cost_)
>>> cost_avgs = [np.mean(cost_ary[i]) for i in batches]

>>> plt.plot(range(len(cost_avgs)),
...          cost_avgs,
...          color='red')
>>> plt.ylim([0, 2000])
>>> plt.ylabel('Cost')
>>> plt.xlabel('Epochs')
>>> plt.tight_layout()
>>> plt.show()
```

The following plot gives us a clearer picture indicating that the training algorithm converged shortly after the 800th epoch:

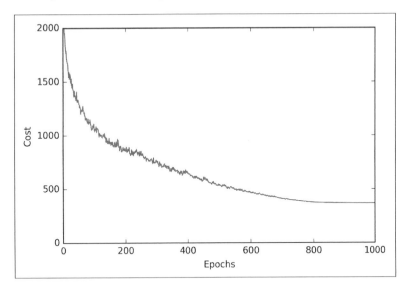

Now, let's evaluate the performance of the model by calculating the prediction accuracy:

```
>>> y_train_pred = nn.predict(X_train)
>>> acc = np.sum(y_train == y_train_pred, axis=0) / X_train.shape[0]
>>> print('Training accuracy: %.2f%%' % (acc * 100))
Training accuracy: 97.59%
```

As we can see, the model classifies most of the training digits correctly, but how does it generalize to data that it has not seen before? Let's calculate the accuracy on 10,000 images in the test dataset:

```
>>> y_test_pred = nn.predict(X_test)
>>> acc = np.sum(y_test == y_test_pred, axis=0) / X_test.shape[0]
>>> print('Test accuracy: %.2f%%' % (acc * 100))
Test accuracy: 95.62%
```

Based on the small discrepancy between training and test accuracy, we can conclude that the model only slightly overfits the training data. To further fine-tune the model, we could change the number of hidden units, values of the regularization parameters, learning rate, values of the decrease constant, or the adaptive learning using the techniques that we discussed in *Chapter 6, Learning Best Practices for Model Evaluation and Hyperparameter Tuning* (this is left as an exercise for the reader).

Now, let's take a look at some of the images that our MLP struggles with:

```
>>> miscl_img = X_test[y_test != y_test_pred][:25]
>>> correct_lab = y_test[y_test != y_test_pred][:25]
>>> miscl_lab= y_test_pred[y_test != y_test_pred][:25]

>>> fig, ax = plt.subplots(nrows=5,
...                        ncols=5,
...                        sharex=True,
...                        sharey=True,)
>>> ax = ax.flatten()
>>> for i in range(25):
...     img = miscl_img[i].reshape(28, 28)
...     ax[i].imshow(img,
...                  cmap='Greys',
...                  interpolation='nearest')
...     ax[i].set_title('%d) t: %d p: %d'
...                     % (i+1, correct_lab[i], miscl_lab[i]))
>>> ax[0].set_xticks([])
>>> ax[0].set_yticks([])
>>> plt.tight_layout()
>>> plt.show()
```

We should now see a 5×5 subplot matrix where the first number in the subtitles indicates the plot index, the second number indicates the true class label (t), and the third number stands for the predicted class label (p).

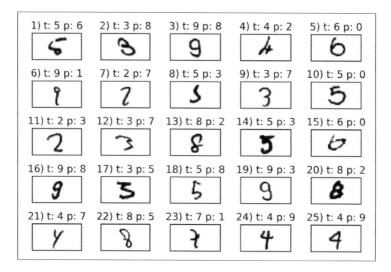

As we can see in the preceding figure, some of those images are even challenging for us humans to classify correctly. For example, we can see that the digit 9 is classified as a 3 or 8 if the lower part of the digit has a hook-like curvature (subplots 3, 16, and 17).

Training an artificial neural network

Now that we have seen a neural network in action and have gained a basic understanding of how it works by looking over the code, let's dig a little bit deeper into some of the concepts, such as the logistic cost function and the backpropagation algorithm that we implemented to learn the weights.

Computing the logistic cost function

The logistic cost function that we implemented as the _get_cost method is actually pretty simple to follow since it is the same cost function that we described in the logistic regression section in *Chapter 3, A Tour of Machine Learning Classifiers Using Scikit-learn.*

$$J(w) = -\sum_{i=1}^{n} y^{(i)} \log\left(a^{(i)}\right) + \left(1 - y^{(i)}\right) \log\left(1 - a^{(i)}\right)$$

Here, $a^{(i)}$ is the sigmoid activation of the ith unit in one of the layers which we compute in the forward propagation step:

$$a^{(i)} = \phi\left(z^{(i)}\right)$$

Now, let's add a **regularization** term, which allows us to reduce the degree of overfitting. As you will recall from earlier chapters, the L2 and L1 regularization terms are defined as follows (remember that we don't regularize the bias units):

$$L2 = \lambda \|w\|_2^2 = \lambda \sum_{j=1}^{m} w_j^2 \quad \text{and} \quad L1 = \lambda \|w\|_1^1 = \lambda \sum_{j=1}^{m} |w_j|$$

Although our MLP implementation supports both L1 and L2 regularization, we will now only focus on the L2 regularization term for simplicity. However, the same concepts apply to the L1 regularization term. By adding the L2 regularization term to our logistic cost function, we obtain the following equation:

$$J(w) = -\left[\sum_{i=1}^{n} y^{(i)} \log\left(a^{(i)}\right) + \left(1 - y^{(i)}\right) \log\left(1 - a^{(i)}\right)\right] + \frac{\lambda}{2} \|w\|_{2}^{2}$$

Since we implemented an MLP for multi-class classification, this returns an output vector of t elements, which we need to compare with the $t \times 1$ dimensional target vector in the one-hot encoding representation. For example, the activation of the third layer and the target class (here: class 2) for a particular sample may look like this:

$$a^{(3)} = \begin{bmatrix} 0.1 \\ 0.9 \\ \vdots \\ 0.3 \end{bmatrix}, \quad y = \begin{bmatrix} 0 \\ 1 \\ \vdots \\ 0 \end{bmatrix}$$

Thus, we need to generalize the logistic cost function to all activation units j in our network. So our cost function (without the regularization term) becomes:

$$J(w) = -\sum_{i=1}^{n} \sum_{j=1}^{t} y_{j}^{(i)} \log\left(a_{j}^{(i)}\right) + \left(1 - y_{j}^{(i)}\right) \log\left(1 - a_{j}^{(i)}\right)$$

Here, the superscript i is the index of a particular sample in our training set.

The following generalized regularization term may look a little bit complicated at first, but here we are just calculating the sum of all weights of a layer l (without the bias term) that we added to the first column:

$$J(w) = -\left[\sum_{i=1}^{n} \sum_{j=1}^{m} y_{j}^{(i)} \log\left(\phi\left(z_{j}^{(i)}\right)\right) + \left(1 - y_{j}^{(i)}\right) \log\left(1 - \phi\left(z_{j}^{(i)}\right)\right)\right]$$
$$+ \frac{\lambda}{2} \sum_{l=1}^{L-1} \sum_{i=1}^{u_{l}} \sum_{j=1}^{u_{l+1}} \left(w_{j,i}^{(l)}\right)^{2}$$

The following expression represents the L2-penalty term:

$$\frac{\lambda}{2}\sum_{l=1}^{L-1}\sum_{i=1}^{u_l}\sum_{j=1}^{u_{l+1}}\left(w_{j,i}^{(l)}\right)^2$$

Remember that our goal is to minimize the cost function $J(w)$. Thus, we need to calculate the partial derivative of matrix W with respect to each weight for every layer in the network:

$$\frac{\partial}{\partial w_{j,i}^{(l)}}J(W)$$

In the next section, we will talk about the backpropagation algorithm, which allows us to calculate these partial derivatives to minimize the cost function.

Note that W consists of multiple matrices. In a multi-layer perceptron with one hidden layer, we have the weight matrix $W^{(1)}$, which connects the input to the hidden layer, and $W^{(2)}$, which connects the hidden layer to the output layer. An intuitive visualization of the matrix W is provided in the following figure:

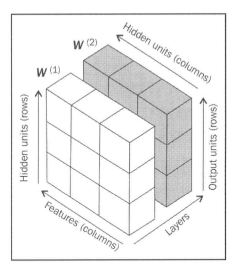

In this simplified figure, it may seem that both $W^{(1)}$ and $W^{(2)}$ have the same number of rows and columns, which is typically not the case unless we initialize an MLP with the same number of hidden units, output units, and input features.

If this may sound confusing, stay tuned for the next section where we will discuss the dimensionality of $W^{(1)}$ and $W^{(2)}$ in more detail in the context of the backpropagation algorithm.

Training neural networks via backpropagation

In this section, we will go through the math of backpropagation to understand how you can learn the weights in a neural network very efficiently. Depending on how comfortable you are with mathematical representations, the following equations may seem relatively complicated at first. Many people prefer a bottom-up approach and like to go over the equations step by step to develop an intuition for algorithms. However, if you prefer a top-down approach and want to learn about backpropagation without all the mathematical notations, I recommend you to read the next section *Developing your intuition for backpropagation* first and revisit this section later.

In the previous section, we saw how to calculate the cost as the difference between the activation of the last layer and the target class label. Now, we will see how the backpropagation algorithm works to update the weights in our MLP model, which we implemented in the _get_gradient method. As we recall from the beginning of this chapter, we first need to apply forward propagation in order to obtain the activation of the output layer, which we formulated as follows:

$$Z^{(2)} = W^{(1)} \left[A^{(1)} \right]^{T} \ \left(\text{net input of the hidden layer} \right)$$

$$A^{(2)} = \phi\left(Z^{(2)} \right) \ \left(\text{activation of the hidden layer} \right)$$

$$Z^{(3)} = W^{(2)} A^{(2)} \ \left(\text{net input of the output layer} \right)$$

$$A^{(3)} = \phi\left(Z^{(3)} \right) \ \left(\text{activation of the output layer} \right)$$

Concisely, we just forward propagate the input features through the connection in the network as shown here:

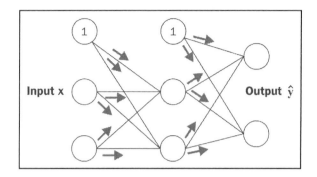

In backpropagation, we propagate the error from right to left. We start by calculating the error vector of the output layer:

$$\delta^{(3)} = a^{(3)} - y$$

Here, y is the vector of the true class labels.

Next, we calculate the error term of the hidden layer:

$$\delta^{(2)} = \left(W^{(2)}\right)^{T} \delta^{(3)} * \frac{\partial \phi\left(z^{(2)}\right)}{\partial z^{(2)}}$$

Here, $\frac{\partial \phi\left(z^{(2)}\right)}{\partial z^{(2)}}$ is simply the derivative of the sigmoid activation function, which we implemented as _sigmoid_gradient:

$$\frac{\partial \phi\left(z^{(2)}\right)}{\partial z^{(2)}} = \left(a^{(2)} * \left(1 - a^{(2)}\right)\right)$$

Note that the asterisk symbol (*) means element-wise multiplication in this context.

Although, it is not important to follow the next equations, you may be curious as to how I obtained the derivative of the activation function. I summarized the derivation step by step here:

$$\phi'(z) = \frac{\partial}{\partial z}\left(\frac{1}{1+e^{-z}}\right)$$

$$= \frac{e^{-z}}{\left(1+e^{-z}\right)^2}$$

$$= \frac{1+e^{-z}}{\left(1+e^{-z}\right)^2} - \left(\frac{1}{1+e^{-z}}\right)^2$$

$$= \frac{1}{\left(1+e^{-z}\right)} - \left(\frac{1}{1+e^{-z}}\right)^2$$

$$= \phi(z) - \left(\phi(z)\right)^2$$

$$= \phi(z)\left(1-\phi(z)\right)$$

$$= a(1-a)$$

To better understand how we compute the $\delta^{(3)}$ term, let's walk through it in more detail. In the preceding equation, we multiplied the transpose $\left(w^{(2)}\right)^T$ of the $t \times h$ dimensional matrix $W^{(2)}$; t is the number of output class labels and h is the number of hidden units. Now, $\left(w^{(2)}\right)^T$ becomes an $h \times t$ dimensional matrix with $\delta^{(3)}$, which is a $t \times 1$ dimensional vector. We then performed a pair-wise multiplication between $\left(w^{(2)}\right)^T \delta^{(3)}$ and $\left(a^{(2)} * \left(1-a^{(2)}\right)\right)$, which is also a $t \times 1$ dimensional vector. Eventually, after obtaining the δ terms, we can now write the derivation of the cost function as follows:

$$\frac{\partial}{\partial w_{i,j}^{(l)}} J(W) = a_j^{(l)} \delta_i^{(l+1)}$$

Next, we need to accumulate the partial derivative of every j th node in layer l and the ith error of the node in layer $l+1$:

$$\Delta_{i,j}^{(l)} := \Delta_{i,j}^{(l)} + a_j^{(l)} \delta_i^{(l+1)}$$

Remember that we need to compute $\Delta_{i,j}^{(l)}$ for every sample in the training set. Thus, it is easier to implement it as a vectorized version like in our preceding MLP code implementation:

$$\Delta^{(l)} = \Delta^{(l)} + \delta^{(l+1)} \left(A^{(l)} \right)^T$$

After we have accumulated the partial derivatives, we can add the regularization term as follows:

$$\Delta^{(l)} := \Delta^{(l)} + \lambda^{(l)} \ \left(\text{except for the bias term}\right)$$

Lastly, after we have computed the gradients, we can now update the weights by taking an opposite step towards the gradient:

$$W^{(l)} := W^{(l)} - \eta \Delta^{(l)}$$

To bring everything together, let's summarize backpropagation in the following figure:

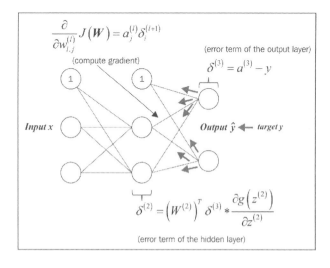

Developing your intuition for backpropagation

Although backpropagation was rediscovered and popularized almost 30 years ago, it still remains one of the most widely used algorithms to train artificial neural networks very efficiently. In this section, we'll see a more intuitive summary and the bigger picture of how this fascinating algorithm works.

In essence, backpropagation is just a very computationally efficient approach to compute the derivatives of a complex cost function. Our goal is to use those derivatives to learn the weight coefficients for parameterizing a multi-layer artificial neural network. The challenge in the parameterization of neural networks is that we are typically dealing with a very large number of weight coefficients in a high-dimensional feature space. In contrast to other cost functions that we have seen in previous chapters, the error surface of a neural network cost function is not convex or smooth. There are many bumps in this high-dimensional cost surface (local minima) that we have to overcome in order to find the global minimum of the cost function.

You may recall the concept of the chain rule from your introductory calculus classes. The chain rule is an approach to deriving a complex, nested function, for example, $f(g(x)) = y$ that is broken down into basic components:

$$\frac{\partial y}{\partial x} = \frac{\partial f}{\partial g} \frac{\partial g}{\partial x}$$

In the context of computer algebra, a set of techniques has been developed to solve such problems very efficiently, which is also known as *automatic differentiation*. If you are interested in learning more about automatic differentiation in machine learning applications, I recommend you to refer to the following resource: A. G. Baydin and B. A. Pearlmutter. *Automatic Differentiation of Algorithms for Machine Learning*. arXiv preprint arXiv:1404.7456, 2014, which is freely available on arXiv at http://arxiv.org/pdf/1404.7456.pdf.

Automatic differentiation comes with two modes, the *forward* and the *reverse* mode, respectively. Backpropagation is simply just a special case of the reverse-mode automatic differentiation. The key point is that applying the chain rule in the forward mode can be quite expensive since we would have to multiply large matrices for each layer (Jacobians) that we eventually multiply by a vector to obtain the output. The trick of the reverse mode is that we start from right to left: we multiply a matrix by a vector, which yields another vector that is multiplied by the next matrix and so on. Matrix-vector multiplication is computationally much cheaper than matrix-matrix multiplication, which is why backpropagation is one of the most popular algorithms used in neural network training.

Debugging neural networks with gradient checking

Implementations of artificial neural networks can be quite complex, and it is always a good idea to *manually* check that we have implemented backpropagation correctly. In this section, we will talk about a simple procedure called *gradient checking*, which is essentially a comparison between our analytical gradients in the network and numerical gradients. Gradient checking is not specific to feedforward neural networks but can be applied to any other neural network architecture that uses gradient-based optimization. Even if you are planning to implement more trivial algorithms using gradient-based optimization, such as linear regression, logistic regression, and support vector machines, it is generally not a bad idea to check if the gradients are computed correctly.

In the previous sections, we defined a cost function $J(W)$ where W is the matrix of the weight coefficients of an artificial network. Note that $J(W)$ is—roughly speaking—a "stacked" matrix consisting of the matrices $W^{(1)}$ and $W^{(2)}$ in a multi-layer perceptron with one hidden unit. We defined $W^{(1)}$ as the $h \times [m+1]$-dimensional matrix that connects the input layer to the hidden layer, where h is the number of hidden units and m is the number of features (input units). The matrix $W^{(2)}$ that connects the hidden layer to the output layer has the dimensions $t \times h$, where t is the number of output units. We then calculated the derivative of the cost function for a weight $w_{i,j}^{(l)}$ as follows:

$$\frac{\partial}{\partial w_{i,j}^{(l)}} J(W)$$

Remember that we are updating the weights by taking an opposite step towards the direction of the gradient. In gradient checking, we compare this analytical solution to a numerically approximated gradient:

$$\frac{\partial}{\partial w_{i,j}^{(l)}} J(W) \approx \frac{J\left(w_{i,j}^{(l)} + \varepsilon\right) - J\left(w_{i,j}^{(l)}\right)}{\varepsilon}$$

Here, ε is typically a very small number, for example 1e-5 (note that 1e-5 is just a more convenient notation for 0.00001). Intuitively, we can think of this finite difference approximation as the slope of the secant line connecting the points of the cost function for the two weights w and $w + \varepsilon$ (both are scalar values), as shown in the following figure. We are omitting the superscripts and subscripts for simplicity.

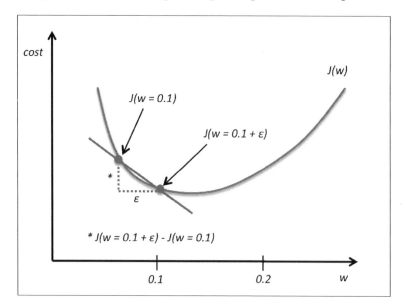

An even better approach that yields a more accurate approximation of the gradient is to compute the symmetric (or centered) difference quotient given by the two-point formula:

$$\frac{J\left(w_{i,j}^{(l)} + \varepsilon\right) - J\left(w_{i,j}^{(l)} - \varepsilon\right)}{2\varepsilon}$$

Typically, the approximated difference between the numerical gradient J'_n and analytical gradient J'_a is then calculated as the L2 vector norm. For practical reasons, we unroll the computed gradient matrices into flat vectors so that we can calculate the error (the difference between the gradient vectors) more conveniently:

$$error = \left\| J'_n - J'_a \right\|_2$$

One problem is that the error is not scale invariant (small errors are more significant if the weight vector norms are small too). Thus, it is recommended to calculate a normalized difference:

$$relative\,error = \frac{\left\| J'_n - J'_a \right\|_2}{\left\| J'_n \right\|_2 + \left\| J'_a \right\|_2}$$

Now, we want the relative error between the numerical gradient and the analytical gradient to be as small as possible. Before we implement gradient checking, we need to discuss one more detail: what is the acceptable error threshold to pass the gradient check? The relative error threshold for passing the gradient check depends on the complexity of the network architecture. As a rule of thumb, the more hidden layers we add, the larger the difference between the numerical and analytical gradient can become if backpropagation is implemented correctly. Since we have implemented a relatively simple neural network architecture in this chapter, we want to be rather strict about the threshold and define the following rules:

- Relative error <= 1e-7 means everything is okay!
- Relative error <= 1e-4 means the condition is problematic, and we should look into it.
- Relative error > 1e-4 means there is probably something wrong in our code.

Now that we have established these ground rules, let's implement gradient checking. To do so, we can simply take the `NeuralNetMLP` class that we implemented previously and add the following method to the class body:

```
def _gradient_checking(self, X, y_enc, w1,
                       w2, epsilon, grad1, grad2):
    """ Apply gradient checking (for debugging only)

    Returns
    ---------
```

```
    relative_error : float
      Relative error between the numerically
      approximated gradients and the backpropagated gradients.

    """
    num_grad1 = np.zeros(np.shape(w1))
    epsilon_ary1 = np.zeros(np.shape(w1))
    for i in range(w1.shape[0]):
        for j in range(w1.shape[1]):
            epsilon_ary1[i, j] = epsilon
            a1, z2, a2, z3, a3 = self._feedforward(
                                            X,
                                            w1 - epsilon_ary1,
                                            w2)
            cost1 = self._get_cost(y_enc,
                                    a3,
                                    w1-epsilon_ary1,
                                    w2)
            a1, z2, a2, z3, a3 = self._feedforward(
                                            X,
                                            w1 + epsilon_ary1,
                                            w2)
            cost2 = self._get_cost(y_enc,
                                    a3,
                                    w1 + epsilon_ary1,
                                    w2)
            num_grad1[i, j] = (cost2 - cost1) / (2 * epsilon)
            epsilon_ary1[i, j] = 0

    num_grad2 = np.zeros(np.shape(w2))
    epsilon_ary2 = np.zeros(np.shape(w2))
    for i in range(w2.shape[0]):
        for j in range(w2.shape[1]):
            epsilon_ary2[i, j] = epsilon
            a1, z2, a2, z3, a3 = self._feedforward(
                                            X,
                                            w1,
                                            w2 - epsilon_ary2)
            cost1 = self._get_cost(y_enc,
                                    a3,
                                    w1,
                                    w2 - epsilon_ary2)
            a1, z2, a2, z3, a3 = self._feedforward(
```

```
                                          X,
                                          w1,
                                          w2 + epsilon_ary2)
            cost2 = self._get_cost(y_enc,
                                    a3,
                                    w1,
                                    w2 + epsilon_ary2)
            num_grad2[i, j] = (cost2 - cost1) / (2 * epsilon)
            epsilon_ary2[i, j] = 0

    num_grad = np.hstack((num_grad1.flatten(),
                          num_grad2.flatten()))
    grad = np.hstack((grad1.flatten(), grad2.flatten()))
    norm1 = np.linalg.norm(num_grad - grad)
    norm2 = np.linalg.norm(num_grad)
    norm3 = np.linalg.norm(grad)
    relative_error = norm1 / (norm2 + norm3)
    return relative_error
```

The `_gradient_checking` code seems rather simple. However, my personal recommendation is to keep it as simple as possible. Our goal is to double-check the gradient computation, so we want to make sure that we do not introduce any additional mistakes in gradient checking by writing efficient but complex code. Next, we only need to make a small modification to the `fit` method. In the following code, I omitted the code at the beginning of the `fit` function for clarity, and the only lines that we need to add to the method are implemented between the comments `## start gradient checking` and `## end gradient checking`:

```
class MLPGradientCheck(object):
    [...]
    def fit(self, X, y, print_progress=False):
        [...]
                # compute gradient via backpropagation
                grad1, grad2 = self._get_gradient(
                                    a1=a1,
                                    a2=a2,
                                    a3=a3,
                                    z2=z2,
                                    y_enc=y_enc[:, idx],
                                    w1=self.w1,
                                    w2=self.w2)

                ## start gradient checking
```

```
        grad_diff = self._gradient_checking(
                        X=X[idx],
                        y_enc=y_enc[:, idx],
                        w1=self.w1,
                        w2=self.w2,
                        epsilon=1e-5,
                        grad1=grad1,
                        grad2=grad2)
        if grad_diff <= 1e-7:
            print('Ok: %s' % grad_diff)
        elif grad_diff <= 1e-4:
            print('Warning: %s' % grad_diff)
        else:
            print('PROBLEM: %s' % grad_diff)

        ## end gradient checking

        # update weights; [alpha * delta_w_prev]
        # for momentum learning
        delta_w1 = self.eta * grad1
        delta_w2 = self.eta * grad2
        self.w1 -= (delta_w1 +\
                    (self.alpha * delta_w1_prev))
        self.w2 -= (delta_w2 +\
                    (self.alpha * delta_w2_prev))
        delta_w1_prev = delta_w1
        delta_w2_prev = delta_w2

    return self
```

Assuming that we named our modified multi-layer perceptron class
MLPGradientCheck, we can now initialize a new MLP with 10 hidden layers. Also,
we disable regularization, adaptive learning, and momentum learning. In addition,
we use regular gradient descent by setting minibatches to 1. The code is as follows:

```
>>> nn_check = MLPGradientCheck(n_output=10,
                        n_features=X_train.shape[1],
                        n_hidden=10,
                        l2=0.0,
                        l1=0.0,
                        epochs=10,
                        eta=0.001,
                        alpha=0.0,
                        decrease_const=0.0,
                        minibatches=1,
                        random_state=1)
```

One downside of gradient checking is that it is computationally very, very expensive. Training a neural network with gradient checking enabled is so slow that we really only want to use it for debugging purposes. For this reason, it is not uncommon to run gradient checking only on a handful of training samples (here, we choose 5). The code is as follows:

```
>>> nn_check.fit(X_train[:5], y_train[:5], print_progress=False)
Ok: 2.56712936241e-10
Ok: 2.94603251069e-10
Ok: 2.37615620231e-10
Ok: 2.43469423226e-10
Ok: 3.37872073158e-10
Ok: 3.63466384861e-10
Ok: 2.22472120785e-10
Ok: 2.33163708438e-10
Ok: 3.44653686551e-10
Ok: 2.17161707211e-10
```

As we can see from the code output, our multi-layer perceptron passes this test with excellent results.

Convergence in neural networks

You might be wondering why we did not use regular gradient descent but mini-batch learning to train our neural network for the handwritten digit classification. You may recall our discussion on stochastic gradient descent that we used to implement online learning. In online learning, we compute the gradient based on a single training example ($k=1$) at a time to perform the weight update. Although this is a stochastic approach, it often leads to very accurate solutions with a much faster convergence than regular gradient descent. Mini-batch learning is a special form of stochastic gradient descent where we compute the gradient based on a subset k of the n training samples with $1 < k < n$. Mini-batch learning has the advantage over online learning that we can make use of our vectorized implementations to improve computational efficiency. However, we can update the weights much faster than in regular gradient descent. Intuitively, you can think of mini-batch learning as predicting the vote turnout of a presidential election from a poll by asking only a representative subset of the population rather than asking the entire population.

In addition, we added more tuning parameters such as the decrease constant and a parameter for an adaptive learning rate. The reason is that neural networks are much harder to train than simpler algorithms such as Adaline, logistic regression, or support vector machines. In multi-layer neural networks, we typically have hundreds, thousands, or even billions of weights that we need to optimize. Unfortunately, the output function has a rough surface and the optimization algorithm can easily become trapped in local minima, as shown in the following figure:

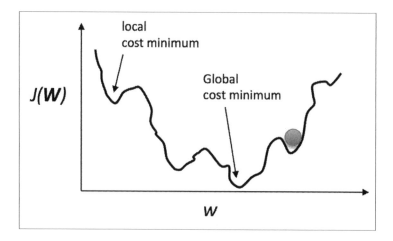

Note that this representation is extremely simplified since our neural network has many dimensions; it makes it impossible to visualize the actual cost surface for the human eye. Here, we only show the cost surface for a single weight on the x axis. However, the main message is that we do not want our algorithm to get trapped in local minima. By increasing the learning rate, we can more readily escape such local minima. On the other hand, we also increase the chance of overshooting the global optimum if the learning rate is too large. Since we initialize the weights randomly, we start with a solution to the optimization problem that is typically hopelessly wrong. A decrease constant, which we defined earlier, can help us to climb down the cost surface faster in the beginning and the adaptive learning rate allows us to better anneal to the global minimum.

Other neural network architectures

In this chapter, we discussed one of the most popular feedforward neural network representations, the multi-layer perceptron. Neural networks are currently one of the most active research topics in the machine learning field, and there are many other neural network architectures that are well beyond the scope of this book. If you are interested in learning more about neural networks and algorithms for deep learning, I recommend reading the introduction and overview; Y. Bengio. *Learning Deep Architectures for AI*. Foundations and Trends in Machine Learning, 2(1):1–127, 2009. Yoshua Bengio's book is currently freely available at `http://www.iro.umontreal.ca/~bengioy/papers/ftml_book.pdf`.

Although neural networks really are a topic for another book, let's take at least a brief look at two other popular architectures, **convolutional neural networks** and **recurrent neural networks**.

Convolutional Neural Networks

Convolutional Neural Networks (**CNNs** or **ConvNets**) gained popularity in computer vision due to their extraordinary good performance on image classification tasks. As of today, CNNs are one of the most popular neural network architectures in deep learning. The key idea behind convolutional neural networks is to build many layers of **feature detectors** to take the spatial arrangement of pixels in an input image into account. Note that there exist many different variants of CNNs. In this section, we will discuss only the general idea behind this architecture. If you are interested in learning more about CNNs, I recommend you to take a look at the publications of Yann LeCun (`http://yann.lecun.com`), who is one of the co-inventors of CNNs. In particular, I can recommend the following literature for getting started with CNNs:

- Y. LeCun, L. Bottou, Y. Bengio, and P. Haffner. *Gradient-based Learning Applied to Document Recognition*. Proceedings of the IEEE, 86(11):2278–2324, 1998.

- P. Y. Simard, D. Steinkraus, and J. C. Platt. *Best Practices for Convolutional Neural Networks Applied to Visual Document Analysis*. IEEE, 2003, p.958.

As you will recall from our multi-layer perceptron implementation, we unrolled the images into feature vectors and these inputs were fully connected to the hidden layer—spatial information was not encoded in this network architecture. In CNNs, we use **receptive fields** to connect the input layer to a feature map. These receptive fields can be understood as overlapping windows that we slide over the pixels of an input image to create a feature map. The stride lengths of the window sliding as well as the window size are additional hyperparameters of the model that we need to define *a priori*. The process of creating the **feature map** is also called **convolution**. An example of such a **convolutional layer**, the layer that connects the input pixels to each unit in the feature map, is shown in the following figure:

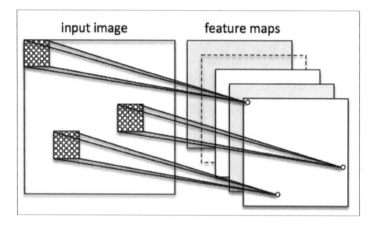

It is important to note that the feature detectors are replicates, which means that the receptive fields that map the features to the units in the next layer share the same weights. Here, the key idea is that if a feature detector is useful in one part of the image, it might be useful in another part as well. The nice side effect of this approach is that it greatly reduces the number of parameters that need to be learned. Since we allow different patches of the image to be represented in different ways, CNNs are particularly good at recognizing objects of different sizes and different positions in an image. We do not need to worry so much about rescaling and centering the images as it has been done in MNIST.

In CNNs, a convolutional layer is followed by a **pooling layer** (sometimes also called **sub-sampling**). In pooling, we summarize neighboring feature detectors to reduce the number of features for the next layer. Pooling can be understood as a simple method of feature extraction where we take the average or maximum value of a patch of neighboring features and pass it on to the next layer. To create a deep convolutional neural network, we stack multiple layers—alternating between convolutional and pooling layers—before we connect it to a multi-layer perceptron for classification. This is shown in the following figure:

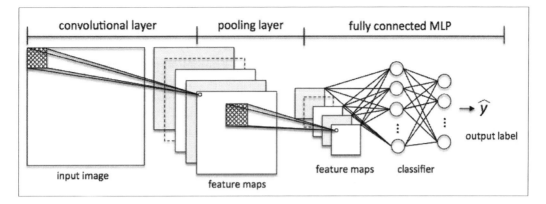

Recurrent Neural Networks

Recurrent Neural Networks (RNNs) can be thought of as feedforward neural networks with feedback loops or backpropagation through time. In RNNs, the neurons only fire for a limited amount of time before they are (temporarily) deactivated. In turn, these neurons activate other neurons that fire at a later point in time. Basically, we can think of recurrent neural networks as MLPs with an additional time variable. The time component and dynamic structure allows the network to use not only the current inputs but also the inputs that it encountered earlier.

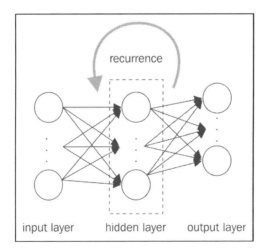

Although RNNs achieved remarkable results in speech recognition, language translation, and connected handwriting recognition, these network architectures are typically much harder to train. This is because we cannot simply backpropagate the error layer by layer; we have to consider the additional time component, which amplifies the vanishing and exploding gradient problem. In 1997, Juergen Schmidhuber and his co-workers introduced the so-called long short-term memory units to overcome this problem: **Long Short Term Memory (LSTM)** units; S. Hochreiter and J. Schmidhuber. *Long Short-term Memory*. Neural Computation, 9(8):1735–1780, 1997.

However, we should note that there are many different variants of RNNs, and a detailed discussion is beyond the scope of this book.

A few last words about neural network implementation

You might be wondering why we went through all of this theory just to implement a simple multi-layer artificial network that can classify handwritten digits instead of using an open source Python machine learning library. One reason is that at the time of writing this book, scikit-learn does not have an MLP implementation. More importantly, we (machine learning practitioners) should have at least a basic understanding of the algorithms that we are using in order to apply machine learning techniques appropriately and successfully.

Now that we know how feedforward neural networks work, we are ready to explore more sophisticated Python libraries built on top of NumPy such as Theano (http://deeplearning.net/software/theano/), which allows us to construct neural networks more efficiently. We will see this in *Chapter 13, Parallelizing Neural Network Training with Theano*. Over the last couple of years, Theano has gained a lot of popularity among machine learning researchers, who use it to construct deep neural networks because of its ability to optimize mathematical expressions for computations on multi-dimensional arrays utilizing **Graphical Processing Units (GPUs)**.

A great collection of Theano tutorials can be found at http://deeplearning.net/software/theano/tutorial/index.html#tutorial.

There are also a number of interesting libraries that are being actively developed to train neural networks in Theano, which you should keep on your radar:

- **Pylearn2** (http://deeplearning.net/software/pylearn2/)
- **Lasagne** (https://lasagne.readthedocs.org/en/latest/)
- **Keras** (http://keras.io)

Summary

In this chapter, you have learned about the most important concepts behind multi-layer artificial neural networks, which are currently the hottest topic in machine learning research. In *Chapter 2, Training Machine Learning Algorithms for Classification*, we started our journey with simple single-layer neural network structures and now we have connected multiple neurons to a powerful neural network architecture to solve complex problems such as handwritten digit recognition. We demystified the popular backpropagation algorithm, which is one of the building blocks of many neural network models that are used in deep learning. After learning about the backpropagation algorithm, we were able to update the weights of such a complex neural network. We also added useful modifications such as mini-batch learning and an adaptive learning rate that allows us to train a neural network more efficiently.

13
Parallelizing Neural Network Training with Theano

In the previous chapter, we went over a lot of mathematical concepts to understand how feedforward artificial neural networks and multilayer perceptrons in particular work. First and foremost, having a good understanding of the mathematical underpinnings of machine learning algorithms is very important, since it helps us to use those powerful algorithms most effectively and *correctly*. Throughout the previous chapters, you dedicated a lot of time to learning the best practices of machine learning, and you even practiced implementing algorithms yourself from scratch. In this chapter, you can lean back a little bit and rest on your laurels, I want you to enjoy this exciting journey through one of the most powerful libraries that is used by machine learning researchers to experiment with deep neural networks and train them very efficiently. Most of modern machine learning research utilizes computers with powerful **Graphics Processing Units (GPUs)**. If you are interested in diving into deep learning, which is currently the hottest topic in machine learning research, this chapter is definitely for you. However, do not worry if you do not have access to GPUs; in this chapter, the use of GPUs will be optional, not required.

Before we get started, let me give you a brief overview of the topics that we will cover in this chapter:

- Writing optimized machine learning code with Theano
- Choosing activation functions for artificial neural networks
- Using the Keras deep learning library for fast and easy experimentation

Building, compiling, and running expressions with Theano

In this section, we will explore the powerful Theano tool, which has been designed to train machine learning models most effectively using Python. The Theano development started back in 2008 in the **LISA** lab (short for **Laboratoire d'Informatique des Systèmes Adaptatifs** (http://lisa.iro.umontreal.ca)) lead by Yoshua Bengio.

Before we discuss what Theano really is and what it can do for us to speed up our machine learning tasks, let's discuss some of the challenges when we are running expensive calculations on our hardware. Luckily, the performance of computer processors keeps on improving constantly over the years, which allows us to train more powerful and complex learning systems to improve the predictive performance of our machine learning models. Even the cheapest desktop computer hardware that is available nowadays comes with processing units that have multiple cores. In the previous chapters, we saw that many functions in scikit-learn allow us to spread the computations over multiple processing units. However, by default, Python is limited to execution on one core, due to the **Global Interpreter Lock** (GIL). However, although we take advantage of its `multiprocessing` library to distribute computations over multiple cores, we have to consider that even advanced desktop hardware rarely comes with more than 8 or 16 such cores.

If we think back of the previous chapter where we implemented a very simple multilayer perceptron with only one hidden layer consisting of 50 units, we already had to optimize approximately 1000 weights to learn a model for a very simple image classification task. The images in MNIST are rather small (28 x 28 pixels), and we can only imagine the explosion in the number of parameters if we want to add additional hidden layers or work with images that have higher pixel densities. Such a task would quickly become unfeasible for a single processing unit. Now, the question is how can we tackle such problems more effectively? The obvious solution to this problem is to use GPUs. GPUs are real power horses. You can think of a graphics card as a small computer cluster inside your machine. Another advantage is that modern GPUs are relatively cheap compared to the state-of-the-art CPUs, as we can see in the following overview:

Specifications	Intel® Core™ i7-5960X Processor Extreme Edition	NVIDIA GeForce® GTX™ 980 Ti
Base Clock Frequency	3.0 GHz	1.0 GHz
Cores	8	2816
Memory Bandwidth	68 GB/s	336.5 GB/s
Floating-Point Calculations	354 GFLOPS	5632 GFLOPS
Cost	$1000.00	$700.00

Sources for this can be found on the following websites:

- http://www.geforce.com/hardware/desktop-gpus/geforce-gtx-980-ti/specifications
- http://ark.intel.com/products/82930/Intel-Core-i7-5960X-Processor-Extreme-Edition-20M-Cache-up-to-3_50-GHz

(date: August 20, 2015)

At 70 percent of the price of a modern CPU, we can get a GPU that has 450 times more cores, and is capable of around 15 times more floating-point calculations per second. So, what is holding us back from utilizing GPUs for our machine learning tasks? The challenge is that writing code to target GPUs is not as trivial as executing Python code in our interpreter. There are special packages such as CUDA and OpenCL that allow us to target the GPU. However, writing code in CUDA or OpenCL is probably not the most convenient environment for implementing and running machine learning algorithms. The good news is that this is what Theano was developed for!

What is Theano?

What exactly is Theano—a programming language, a compiler, or a Python library? It turns out that it fits all these descriptions. Theano has been developed to implement, compile, and evaluate mathematical expressions very efficiently with a strong focus on multidimensional arrays (tensors). It comes with an option to run code on CPU(s). However, its real power comes from utilizing GPUs to take advantage of the large memory bandwidths and great capabilities for floating point math. Using Theano, we can easily run code in parallel over shared memory as well. In 2010, the developers of Theano reported an 1.8x faster performance than NumPy when the code was run on the CPU, and if Theano targeted the GPU, it was even 11x faster than NumPy (J. Bergstra, O. Breuleux, F. Bastien, P. Lamblin, R. Pascanu, G. Desjardins, J. Turian, D. Warde-Farley, and Y. Bengio. *Theano: A CPU and GPU Math Compiler in Python*. In Proc. 9th Python in Science Conf, pages 1–7, 2010.). Now, keep in mind that this benchmark is from 2010, and Theano has improved significantly over the years, and so have the capabilities of modern graphics cards.

So, how does Theano relate to NumPy? Theano is built on top of NumPy and it has a very similar syntax, which makes the usage very convenient for people who are already familiar with the latter. To be fair, Theano is not just "NumPy on steroids" as many people would describe it, but it also shares some similarities with SymPy (http://www.sympy.org), a Python package for symbolic computations (or symbolic algebra). As we saw in previous chapters, in NumPy, we describe what our variables are, and how we want to combine them; then, the code is executed line by line. In Theano, however, we write down the problem first and the description of how we want to analyze it. Then, Theano optimizes and compiles code for us using C/C++, or CUDA/OpenCL if we want to run it on the GPU. In order to generate the optimized code for us, Theano needs to know the scope of our problem; think of it as a tree of operations (or a graph of symbolic expressions). Note that Theano is still under active development, and many new features are added and improvements are made on a regular basis. In this chapter, we will explore the basic concepts behind Theano and learn how to use it for machine learning tasks. Since Theano is a large library with many advanced features, it would be impossible to cover all of them in this book. However, I will provide useful links to the excellent online documentation (http://deeplearning.net/software/theano/) if you want to learn more about this library.

First steps with Theano

In this section, we will take our first steps with Theano. Depending on how your system is set up, you typically can just use the pip installer and install Theano from PyPI by executing the following from your command-line terminal:

```
pip install Theano
```

If you should experience problems with the installation procedure, I recommend you to read more about system and platform-specific recommendations that are provided at http://deeplearning.net/software/theano/install.html. Note that all the code in this chapter can be run on your CPU; using the GPU is entirely optional but recommended if you fully want to enjoy the benefits of Theano. If you have a graphics card that supports either CUDA or OpenCL, please refer to the up-to-date tutorial at http://deeplearning.net/software/theano/tutorial/using_gpu. html#using-gpu to set it up appropriately.

At its core, Theano is built around so-called tensors to evaluate symbolic mathematical expressions. Tensors can be understood as a generalization of scalars, vectors, matrices, and so on. More concretely, a scalar can be defined as a rank-0 tensor, a vector as a rank-1 tensor, a matrix as rank-2 tensor, and matrices stacked in a third dimension as rank-3 tensors. As a warm-up exercise, we will start with the use of simple scalars from the Theano tensor module to compute a net input z of a sample point x in a one dimensional dataset with weight w_1 and bias w_0:

$$z = x_1 \times w_1 + w_0$$

The code is as follows:

```
>>> import theano
>>> from theano import tensor as T

# initialize
>>> x1 = T.scalar()
>>> w1 = T.scalar()
>>> w0 = T.scalar()
>>> z1 = w1 * x1 + w0

# compile
>>> net_input = theano.function(inputs=[w1, x1, w0],
...                             outputs=z1)

# execute
>>> print('Net input: %.2f' % net_input(2.0, 1.0, 0.5))
Net input: 2.50
```

This was pretty straightforward, right? If we write code in Theano, we just have to follow three simple steps: define the *symbols* (`Variable` objects), compile the code, and execute it. In the initialization step, we defined three symbols, x1, w1, and w0, to compute z1. Then, we compiled a function `net_input` to compute the net input z1.

However, there is one particular detail that deserves special attention if we write Theano code: the type of our variables (`dtype`). Consider it as a blessing or burden, but in Theano we need to choose whether we want to use 64 or 32 bit integers or floats, which greatly affects the performance of the code. Let's discuss those variable types in more detail in the next section.

Configuring Theano

Nowadays, no matter whether we run Mac OS X, Linux, or Microsoft Windows, we mainly use software and applications using 64-bit memory addresses. However, if we want to accelerate the evaluation of mathematical expressions on GPUs, we still often rely on the older 32-bit memory addresses. Currently, this is the only supported computing architecture in Theano. In this section, we will see how to configure Theano appropriately. If you are interested in more details about the Theano configuration, please refer to the online documentation at http://deeplearning.net/software/theano/library/config.html.

When we are implementing machine learning algorithms, we are mostly working with floating point numbers. By default, both NumPy and Theano use the double-precision floating-point format (`float64`). However, it would be really useful to toggle back and forth `float64` (CPU), and `float32` (GPU) when we are developing Theano code for prototyping on CPU and execution on GPU. For example, to access the default settings for Theano's float variables, we can execute the following code in our Python interpreter:

```
>>> print(theano.config.floatX)
float64
```

If you have not modified any settings after the installation of Theano, the floating point default should be `float64`. However, we can simply change it to `float32` in our current Python session via the following code:

```
>>> theano.config.floatX = 'float32'
```

Note that although the current GPU utilization in Theano requires `float32` types, we can use both `float64` and `float32` on our CPUs. Thus, if you want to change the default settings globally, you can change the settings in your THEANO_FLAGS variable via the command-line (Bash) terminal:

```
export THEANO_FLAGS=floatX=float32
```

Alternatively, you can apply these settings only to a particular Python script, by running it as follows:

```
THEANO_FLAGS=floatX=float32 python your_script.py
```

So far, we discussed how to set the default floating-point types to get the best bang for the buck on our GPU using Theano. Next, let's discuss the options to toggle between CPU and GPU execution. If we execute the following code, we can check whether we are using CPU or GPU:

```
>>> print(theano.config.device)
cpu
```

My personal recommendation is to use `cpu` as default, which makes prototyping and code debugging easier. For example, you can run Theano code on your CPU by executing it as a script, as from your command-line terminal:

```
THEANO_FLAGS=device=cpu,floatX=float64 python your_script.py
```

However, once we have implemented the code and want to run it most efficiently utilizing our GPU hardware, we can then run it via the following code without making additional modifications to our original code:

```
THEANO_FLAGS=device=gpu,floatX=float32 python your_script.py
```

It may also be convenient to create a `.theanorc` file in your home directory to make these configurations permanent. For example, to always use `float32` and the GPU, you can create such a `.theanorc` file including these settings. The command is as follows:

```
echo -e "\n[global]\nfloatX=float32\ndevice=gpu\n" >> ~/.theanorc
```

If you are not operating on a MacOS X or Linux terminal, you can create a `.theanorc` file manually using your favorite text editor and add the following contents:

```
[global]
floatX=float32
device=gpu
```

Now that we know how to configure Theano appropriately with respect to our available hardware, we can discuss how to use more complex array structures in the next section.

Working with array structures

In this section, we will discuss how to use array structures in Theano using its `tensor` module. By executing the following code, we will create a simple 2 x 3 matrix, and calculate the column sums using Theano's optimized tensor expressions:

```
>>> import numpy as np

# initialize
# if you are running Theano on 64 bit mode,
# you need to use dmatrix instead of fmatrix
>>> x = T.fmatrix(name='x')
>>> x_sum = T.sum(x, axis=0)

# compile
>>> calc_sum = theano.function(inputs=[x], outputs=x_sum)

# execute (Python list)
>>> ary = [[1, 2, 3], [1, 2, 3]]
>>> print('Column sum:', calc_sum(ary))
Column sum: [ 2.   4.   6.]

# execute (NumPy array)
>>> ary = np.array([[1, 2, 3], [1, 2, 3]],
...                 dtype=theano.config.floatX)
>>> print('Column sum:', calc_sum(ary))
Column sum: [ 2.   4.   6.]
```

As we saw earlier, there are just three basic steps that we have to follow when we are using Theano: defining the variable, compiling the code, and executing it. The preceding example shows that Theano can work with both Python and NumPy types: `list` and `numpy.ndarray`.

> Note that we used the optional name argument (here, x) when we created the `fmatrix` TensorVariable, which can be helpful to debug our code or print the Theano graph. For example, if we'd print the `fmatrix` symbol x without giving it a name, the `print` function would return its TensorType:
>
> ```
> >>> print(x)
> <TensorType(float32, matrix)>
> ```
>
> However, if the TensorVariable was initialized with a name argument x as in our preceding example, it would be returned by the `print` function:
>
> ```
> >>> print(x)
> x
> ```
>
> The TensorType can be accessed via the `type` method:
>
> ```
> >>> print(x.type())
> <TensorType(float32, matrix)>
> ```

Theano also has a very smart memory management system that reuses memory
to make it fast. More concretely, Theano spreads memory space across multiple
devices, CPUs and GPUs; to track changes in the memory space, it aliases the
respective buffers. Next, we will take a look at the `shared` variable, which allows us
to spread large objects (arrays) and grants multiple functions read and write access,
so that we can also perform updates on those objects after compilation. A detailed
description of the memory handling in Theano is beyond the scope of this book.
Thus, I encourage you to follow-up on the up-to-date information about Theano and
memory management at `http://deeplearning.net/software/theano/tutorial/`
`aliasing.html`.

```
# initialize
>>> x = T.fmatrix('x')
>>> w = theano.shared(np.asarray([[0.0, 0.0, 0.0]],
                                 dtype=theano.config.floatX))
>>> z = x.dot(w.T)
>>> update = [[w, w + 1.0]]

# compile
>>> net_input = theano.function(inputs=[x],
...                             updates=update,
...                             outputs=z)

# execute
>>> data = np.array([[1, 2, 3]],
...                  dtype=theano.config.floatX)
>>> for i in range(5):
...     print('z%d:' % i, net_input(data))
z0: [[ 0.]]
z1: [[ 6.]]
z2: [[ 12.]]
z3: [[ 18.]]
z4: [[ 24.]]
```

As you can see, sharing memory via Theano is really easy: In the preceding example,
we defined an `update` variable where we declared that we want to update an array `w`
by a value `1.0` after each iteration in the `for` loop. After we defined which object we
want to update and how, we passed this information to the `update` parameter of the
`theano.function` compiler.

Another neat trick in Theano is to use the `givens` variable to insert values into the graph before compiling it. Using this approach, we can reduce the number of transfers from RAM over CPUs to GPUs to speed up learning algorithms that use shared variables. If we use the `inputs` parameter in `theano.function`, data is transferred from the CPU to the GPU multiple times, for example, if we iterate over a dataset multiple times (epochs) during gradient descent. Using `givens`, we can keep the dataset on the GPU if it fits into its memory (for example, if we are learning with mini-batches). The code is as follows:

```
# initialize
>>> data = np.array([[1, 2, 3]],
...                      dtype=theano.config.floatX)
>>> x = T.fmatrix('x')
>>> w = theano.shared(np.asarray([[0.0, 0.0, 0.0]],
...                      dtype=theano.config.floatX))
>>> z = x.dot(w.T)
>>> update = [[w, w + 1.0]]

# compile
>>> net_input = theano.function(inputs=[],
...                             updates=update,
...                             givens={x: data},
...                             outputs=z)

# execute
>>> for i in range(5):
...     print('z:', net_input())
z0: [[ 0.]]
z1: [[ 6.]]
z2: [[ 12.]]
z3: [[ 18.]]
z4: [[ 24.]]
```

Looking at the preceding code example, we also see that the `givens` attribute is a Python dictionary that maps a variable name to the actual Python object. Here, we set this name when we defined the `fmatrix`.

Wrapping things up – a linear regression example

Now that we familiarized ourselves with Theano, let's take a look at a really practical example and implement **Ordinary Least Squares** (OLS) regression. For a quick refresher on regression analysis, please refer to *Chapter 10, Predicting Continuous Target Variables with Regression Analysis*.

Let's start by creating a small one-dimensional toy dataset with ten training samples:

```
>>> X_train = np.asarray([[0.0], [1.0],
...                       [2.0], [3.0],
...                       [4.0], [5.0],
...                       [6.0], [7.0],
...                       [8.0], [9.0]],
...                       dtype=theano.config.floatX)
>>> y_train = np.asarray([1.0, 1.3,
...                       3.1, 2.0,
...                       5.0, 6.3,
...                       6.6, 7.4,
...                       8.0, 9.0],
...                       dtype=theano.config.floatX)
```

Note that we are using `theano.config.floatX` when we construct the NumPy arrays, so we can optionally toggle back and forth between CPU and GPU if we want.

Next, let's implement a training function to learn the weights of the linear regression model, using the sum of squared errors cost function. Note that w_0 is the bias unit (the *y* axis intercept at $x = 0$). The code is as follows:

```
import theano
from theano import tensor as T
import numpy as np

def train_linreg(X_train, y_train, eta, epochs):

    costs = []
    # Initialize arrays
    eta0 = T.fscalar('eta0')
    y = T.fvector(name='y')
    X = T.fmatrix(name='X')
```

```
w = theano.shared(np.zeros(
                    shape=(X_train.shape[1] + 1),
                    dtype=theano.config.floatX),
                name='w')

# calculate cost
net_input = T.dot(X, w[1:]) + w[0]
errors = y - net_input
cost = T.sum(T.pow(errors, 2))

# perform gradient update
gradient = T.grad(cost, wrt=w)
update = [(w, w - eta0 * gradient)]

# compile model
train = theano.function(inputs=[eta0],
                        outputs=cost,
                        updates=update,
                        givens={X: X_train,
                                y: y_train,})

for _ in range(epochs):
    costs.append(train(eta))

return costs, w
```

A really nice feature in Theano is the `grad` function that we used in the preceding code example. The `grad` function automatically computes the derivative of an expression *with respect to* its parameters that we passed to the function as the `wrt` argument.

After we implemented the training function, let's train our linear regression model and take a look at the values of the **Sum of Squared Errors (SSE)** cost function to check if it converged:

```
>>> import matplotlib.pyplot as plt
>>> costs, w = train_linreg(X_train, y_train, eta=0.001, epochs=10)
>>> plt.plot(range(1, len(costs)+1), costs)
>>> plt.tight_layout()
>>> plt.xlabel('Epoch')
>>> plt.ylabel('Cost')
>>> plt.show()
```

As we can see in the following plot, the learning algorithm already converged after the fifth epoch:

So far so good; by looking at the cost function, it seems that we built a working regression model from this particular dataset. Now, let's compile a new function to make predictions based on the input features:

```
def predict_linreg(X, w):
    Xt = T.matrix(name='X')
    net_input = T.dot(Xt, w[1:]) + w[0]
    predict = theano.function(inputs=[Xt],
                              givens={w: w},
                              outputs=net_input)
    return predict(X)
```

Implementing a `predict` function was pretty straightforward following the three-step procedure of Theano: define, compile, and execute. Next, let's plot the linear regression fit on the training data:

```
>>> plt.scatter(X_train,
...             y_train,
...             marker='s',
...             s=50)
>>> plt.plot(range(X_train.shape[0]),
```

```
...                 predict_linreg(X_train, w),
...                 color='gray',
...                 marker='o',
...                 markersize=4,
...                 linewidth=3)
>>> plt.xlabel('x')
>>> plt.ylabel('y')
>>> plt.show()
```

As we can see in the resulting plot, our model fits the data points appropriately:

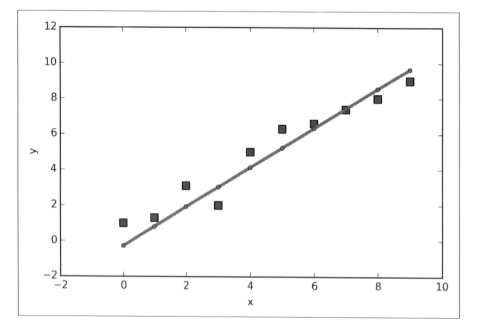

Implementing a simple regression model was a good exercise to become familiar with the Theano API. However, our ultimate goal is to play out the advantages of Theano, that is, implementing powerful artificial neural networks. We should now be equipped with all the tools we would need to implement the multilayer perceptron from *Chapter 12, Training Artificial Neural Networks for Image Recognition*, in Theano. However, this would be rather boring, right? Thus, we will take a look at one of my favorite deep learning libraries built on top of Theano to make the experimentation with neural networks as convenient as possible. However, before we introduce the Keras library, let's first discuss the different choices of activation functions in neural networks in the next section.

Choosing activation functions for feedforward neural networks

For simplicity, we have only discussed the sigmoid activation function in context of multilayer feedforward neural networks so far; we used it in the hidden layer as well as the output layer in the multilayer perceptron implementation in *Chapter 12, Training Artificial Neural Networks for Image Recognition*. Although we referred to this activation function as *sigmoid* function—as it is commonly called in literature—the more precise definition would be *logistic function* or *negative log-likelihood function*. In the following subsections, you will learn more about alternative sigmoidal functions that are useful for implementing multilayer neural networks.

Technically, we could use any function as activation function in multilayer neural networks as long as it is differentiable. We could even use linear activation functions such as in Adaline (*Chapter 2, Training Machine Learning Algorithms for Classification*). However, in practice, it would not be very useful to use linear activation functions for both hidden and output layers, since we want to introduce nonlinearity in a typical artificial neural network to be able to tackle complex problem tasks. The sum of linear functions yields a linear function after all.

The logistic activation function that we used in the previous chapter probably mimics the concept of a neuron in a brain most closely: we can think of it as probability of whether a neuron fires or not. However, logistic activation functions can be problematic if we have highly negative inputs, since the output of the sigmoid function would be close to zero in this case. If the sigmoid function returns outputs that are close to zero, the neural network would learn very slowly and it becomes more likely that it gets trapped in local minima during training. This is why people often prefer a **hyperbolic tangent** as activation function in hidden layers. Before we discuss what a hyperbolic tangent looks like, let's briefly recapitulate some of the basics of the logistic function and look at a generalization that makes it more useful for multi-class classification tasks.

Logistic function recap

As we mentioned it in the introduction to this section, the logistic function, often just called the *sigmoid function*, is in fact a special case of a sigmoid function. We recall from the section on logistic regression in *Chapter 3, A Tour of Machine Learning Classifiers Using Scikit-learn*, that we can use the logistic function to model the probability that sample x belongs to the positive class (class 1) in a binary classification task:

$$\phi_{logistic}(z) = \frac{1}{1+e^{-z}}$$

Here, the scalar variable z is defined as the net input:

$$z = w_0 x_0 + \cdots + w_m x_m = \sum_{j=0}^{m} x_j w_j = \boldsymbol{w}^T \boldsymbol{x}$$

Note that w_0 is the bias unit (y-axis intercept, $x_0 = 1$). To provide a more concrete example, let's assume a model for a two-dimensional data point x and a model with the following weight coefficients assigned to the vector w:

```
>>> X = np.array([[1, 1.4, 1.5]])
>>> w = np.array([0.0, 0.2, 0.4])

>>> def net_input(X, w):
...       z = X.dot(w)
...       return z

>>> def logistic(z):
...       return 1.0 / (1.0 + np.exp(-z))

>>> def logistic_activation(X, w):
...       z = net_input(X, w)
...       return logistic(z)

>>> print('P(y=1|x) = %.3f'
...          % logistic_activation(X, w)[0])
P(y=1|x) = 0.707
```

If we calculate the net input and use it to activate a logistic neuron with those particular feature values and weight coefficients, we get back a value of 0.707, which we can interpret as a 70.7 percent probability that this particular sample x belongs to the positive class. In *Chapter 12, Training Artificial Neural Networks for Image Recognition*, we used the one-hot encoding technique to compute the values in the output layer consisting of multiple logistic activation units. However, as we will demonstrate with the following code example, an output layer consisting of multiple logistic activation units does not produce meaningful, interpretable probability values:

```
# W : array, shape = [n_output_units, n_hidden_units+1]
#          Weight matrix for hidden layer -> output layer.
# note that first column (A[:][0] = 1) are the bias units
>>> W = np.array([[1.1, 1.2, 1.3, 0.5],
...               [0.1, 0.2, 0.4, 0.1],
...               [0.2, 0.5, 2.1, 1.9]])

# A : array, shape = [n_hidden+1, n_samples]
#          Activation of hidden layer.
# note that first element (A[0][0] = 1) is the bias unit
>>> A = np.array([[1.0],
...               [0.1],
...               [0.3],
...               [0.7]])

# Z : array, shape = [n_output_units, n_samples]
#          Net input of the output layer.
>>> Z = W.dot(A)
>>> y_probas = logistic(Z)
>>> print('Probabilities:\n', y_probas)
Probabilities:
 [[ 0.87653295]
  [ 0.57688526]
  [ 0.90114393]]
```

As we can see in the output, the probability that the particular sample belongs to the first class is almost 88 percent, the probability that the particular sample belongs to the second class is almost 58 percent, and the probability that the particular sample belongs to the third class is 90 percent, respectively. This is clearly confusing, since we all know that a percentage should intuitively be expressed as a fraction of 100. However, this is in fact not a big concern if we only use our model to predict the class labels, not the class membership probabilities.

```
>>> y_class = np.argmax(Z, axis=0)
>>> print('predicted class label: %d' % y_class[0])
predicted class label: 2
```

However, in certain contexts, it can be useful to return meaningful class probabilities for multi-class predictions. In the next section, we will take a look at a generalization of the logistic function, the **softmax** function, which can help us with this task.

Estimating probabilities in multi-class classification via the softmax function

The **softmax** function is a generalization of the logistic function that allows us to compute meaningful class-probabilities in multi-class settings (multinomial logistic regression). In softmax, the probability of a particular sample with net input z belongs to the i th class can be computed with a normalization term in the denominator that is the sum of all M linear functions:

$$P\left(y = i \mid z\right) = \phi_{softmax}\left(z\right) = \frac{e_i^z}{\sum_{m=1}^{M} e_m^z}$$

To see softmax in action, let's code it up in Python:

```
>>> def softmax(z):
...        return np.exp(z) / np.sum(np.exp(z))

>>> def softmax_activation(X, w):
...        z = net_input(X, w)
...        return softmax(z)

>>> y_probas = softmax(Z)
>>> print('Probabilities:\n', y_probas)
Probabilities:
 [[ 0.40386493]
 [ 0.07756222]
 [ 0.51857284]]
>>> y_probas.sum()
1.0
```

As we can see, the predicted class probabilities now sum up to one, as we would expect. It is also notable that the probability for the second class is close to zero, since there is a large gap between z_1 and $\max(z)$. However, note that the predicted class label is the same as in the logistic function. Intuitively, it may help to think of the softmax function as a *normalized* logistic function that is useful to obtain meaningful class-membership predictions in multi-class settings.

```
>>> y_class = np.argmax(Z, axis=0)
>>> print('predicted class label:
...        %d' % y_class[0])
predicted class label: 2
```

Broadening the output spectrum by using a hyperbolic tangent

Another sigmoid function that is often used in the hidden layers of artificial neural networks is the **hyperbolic tangent (tanh)**, which can be interpreted as a rescaled version of the logistic function.

$$\phi_{tanh}(z) = 2 \times \phi_{logistic}(2 \times z) - 1 = \frac{e^z - e^{-z}}{e^z + e^{-z}}$$

$$\phi_{logistic}(z) = \frac{1}{1 + e^{-z}}$$

The advantage of the hyperbolic tangent over the logistic function is that it has a broader output spectrum and ranges the open interval (-1, 1), which can improve the convergence of the back propagation algorithm (C. M. Bishop. *Neural networks for pattern recognition*. Oxford university press, 1995, pp. 500-501). In contrast, the logistic function returns an output signal that ranges the open interval (0, 1). For an intuitive comparison of the logistic function and the hyperbolic tangent, let's plot the two sigmoid functions:

```python
>>> import matplotlib.pyplot as plt

>>> def tanh(z):
...         e_p = np.exp(z)
...         e_m = np.exp(-z)
...         return (e_p - e_m) / (e_p + e_m)

>>> z = np.arange(-5, 5, 0.005)
>>> log_act = logistic(z)
>>> tanh_act = tanh(z)

>>> plt.ylim([-1.5, 1.5])
>>> plt.xlabel('net input $z$')
>>> plt.ylabel('activation $\phi(z)$')
>>> plt.axhline(1, color='black', linestyle='--')
>>> plt.axhline(0.5, color='black', linestyle='--')
>>> plt.axhline(0, color='black', linestyle='--')
>>> plt.axhline(-1, color='black', linestyle='--')

>>> plt.plot(z, tanh_act,
...             linewidth=2,
...             color='black',
...             label='tanh')
>>> plt.plot(z, log_act,
...             linewidth=2,
...             color='lightgreen',
...             label='logistic')

>>> plt.legend(loc='lower right')
>>> plt.tight_layout()
>>> plt.show()
```

As we can see, the shapes of the two sigmoidal curves look very similar; however, the `tanh` function has 2x larger output space than the logistic function:

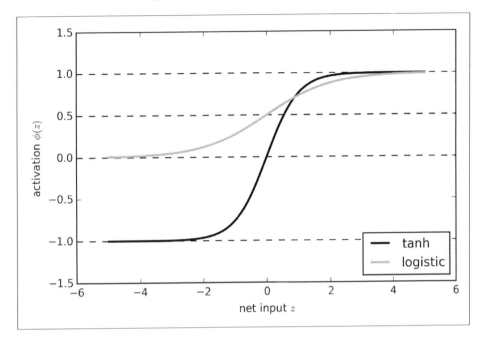

Note that we implemented the `logistic` and `tanh` functions verbosely for the purpose of illustration. In practice, we can use NumPy's `tanh` function to achieve the same results:

```
>>>   tanh_act = np.tanh(z)
```

In addition, the `logistic` function is available in SciPy's `special` module:

```
>>> from scipy.special import expit
>>> log_act = expit(z)
```

Now that we know more about the different activation functions that are commonly used in artificial neural networks, let's conclude this section with an overview of the different activation functions that we encountered in this book.

Activation function	Equation	Example	1D Graph
Unit step (Heaviside)	$\phi(z) = \begin{cases} 0, & z < 0, \\ 0.5, & z = 0, \\ 1, & z > 0, \end{cases}$	Perceptron variant	
Sign (Signum)	$\phi(z) = \begin{cases} -1, & z < 0, \\ 0, & z = 0, \\ 1, & z > 0, \end{cases}$	Perceptron variant	
Linear	$\phi(z) = z$	Adaline, linear regression	
Piece-wise linear	$\phi(z) = \begin{cases} 1, & z \geq \frac{1}{2}, \\ z + \frac{1}{2}, & -\frac{1}{2} < z < \frac{1}{2}, \\ 0, & z \leq -\frac{1}{2}, \end{cases}$	Support vector machine	
Logistic (sigmoid)	$\phi(z) = \dfrac{1}{1 + e^{-z}}$	Logistic regression, Multi-layer NN	
Hyperbolic tangent	$\phi(z) = \dfrac{e^{z} - e^{-z}}{e^{z} + e^{-z}}$	Multi-layer NN	

Training neural networks efficiently using Keras

In this section, we will take a look at Keras, one of the most recently developed libraries to facilitate neural network training. The development on Keras started in the early months of 2015; as of today, it has evolved into one of the most popular and widely used libraries that are built on top of Theano, and allows us to utilize our GPU to accelerate neural network training. One of its prominent features is that it's a very intuitive API, which allows us to implement neural networks in only a few lines of code. Once you have Theano installed, you can install Keras from PyPI by executing the following command from your terminal command line:

```
pip install Keras
```

For more information about Keras, please visit the official website at
`http://keras.io`.

To see what neural network training via Keras looks like, let's implement
a multilayer perceptron to classify the handwritten digits from the MNIST
dataset, which we introduced in the previous chapter. The MNIST dataset
can be downloaded from `http://yann.lecun.com/exdb/mnist/` in four
parts as listed here:

- `train-images-idx3-ubyte.gz`: These are training set images
  (9912422 bytes)
- `train-labels-idx1-ubyte.gz`: These are training set labels (28881 bytes)
- `t10k-images-idx3-ubyte.gz`: These are test set images (1648877 bytes)
- `t10k-labels-idx1-ubyte.gz`: These are test set labels (4542 bytes)

After downloading and unzipping the archives, we place the files into a directory
`mnist` in our current working directory, so that we can load the training as well as
the test dataset using the following function:

```
import os
import struct
import numpy as np

def load_mnist(path, kind='train'):
    """Load MNIST data from `path`"""
    labels_path = os.path.join(path,
                               '%s-labels-idx1-ubyte'
                               % kind)
    images_path = os.path.join(path,
                               '%s-images-idx3-ubyte'
                               % kind)

    with open(labels_path, 'rb') as lbpath:
        magic, n = struct.unpack('>II',
                                 lbpath.read(8))
        labels = np.fromfile(lbpath,
                             dtype=np.uint8)

    with open(images_path, 'rb') as imgpath:
        magic, num, rows, cols = struct.unpack(">IIII",
                                               imgpath.read(16))
        images = np.fromfile(imgpath,
                             dtype=np.uint8).reshape(len(labels), 784)
```

```
    return images, labels
X_train, y_train = load_mnist('mnist', kind='train')
print('Rows: %d, columns: %d' % (X_train.shape[0], X_train.shape[1]))
Rows: 60000, columns: 784
X_test, y_test = load_mnist('mnist', kind='t10k')
print('Rows: %d, columns: %d' % (X_test.shape[0], X_test.shape[1]))
Rows: 10000, columns: 784
```

On the following pages, we will walk through the code examples for using Keras step by step, which you can directly execute from your Python interpreter. However, if you are interested in training the neural network on your GPU, you can either put it into a Python script, or download the respective code from the Packt Publishing website. In order to run the Python script on your GPU, execute the following command from the directory where the mnist_keras_mlp.py file is located:

```
THEANO_FLAGS=mode=FAST_RUN,device=gpu,floatX=float32 python mnist_
keras_mlp.py
```

To continue with the preparation of the training data, let's cast the MNIST image array into 32-bit format:

```
>>> import theano
>>> theano.config.floatX = 'float32'
>>> X_train = X_train.astype(theano.config.floatX)
>>> X_test = X_test.astype(theano.config.floatX)
```

Next, we need to convert the class labels (integers 0-9) into the one-hot format. Fortunately, Keras provides a convenient tool for this:

```
>>> from keras.utils import np_utils
>>> print('First 3 labels: ', y_train[:3])
First 3 labels:  [5 0 4]
>>> y_train_ohe = np_utils.to_categorical(y_train)
>>> print('\nFirst 3 labels (one-hot):\n', y_train_ohe[:3])
First 3 labels (one-hot):
 [[ 0.  0.  0.  0.  0.  1.  0.  0.  0.  0.]
  [ 1.  0.  0.  0.  0.  0.  0.  0.  0.  0.]
  [ 0.  0.  0.  0.  1.  0.  0.  0.  0.  0.]]
```

Now, we can get to the interesting part and implement a neural network. Here, we will use the same architecture as in *Chapter 12, Training Artificial Neural Networks for Image Recognition*. However, we will replace the logistic units in the hidden layer with hyperbolic tangent activation functions, replace the logistic function in the output layer with softmax, and add an additional hidden layer. Keras makes these tasks very simple, as you can see in the following code implementation:

```
>>> from keras.models import Sequential
>>> from keras.layers.core import Dense
>>> from keras.optimizers import SGD

>>> np.random.seed(1)

>>> model = Sequential()
>>> model.add(Dense(input_dim=X_train.shape[1],
...                 output_dim=50,
...                 init='uniform',
...                 activation='tanh'))

>>> model.add(Dense(input_dim=50,
...                 output_dim=50,
...                 init='uniform',
...                 activation='tanh'))

>>> model.add(Dense(input_dim=50,
...                 output_dim=y_train_ohe.shape[1],
...                 init='uniform',
...                 activation='softmax'))

>>> sgd = SGD(lr=0.001, decay=1e-7, momentum=.9)
>>> model.compile(loss='categorical_crossentropy', optimizer=sgd)
```

First, we initialize a new model using the Sequential class to implement a feedforward neural network. Then, we can add as many layers to it as we like. However, since the first layer that we add is the input layer, we have to make sure that the input_dim attribute matches the number of features (columns) in the training set (here, 768). Also, we have to make sure that the number of output units (output_dim) and input units (input_dim) of two consecutive layers match. In the preceding example, we added two hidden layers with 50 hidden units plus 1 bias unit each. Note that bias units are initialized to 0 in fully connected networks in Keras. This is in contrast to the MLP implementation in *Chapter 12, Training Artificial Neural Networks for Image Recognition*, where we initialized the bias units to 1, which is a more common (not necessarily better) convention.

Finally, the number of units in the output layer should be equal to the number of unique class labels — the number of columns in the one-hot encoded class label array. Before we can compile our model, we also have to define an optimizer. In the preceding example, we chose a stochastic gradient descent optimization, which we are already familiar with, from previous chapters. Furthermore, we can set values for the weight decay constant and momentum learning to adjust the learning rate at each epoch as discussed in *Chapter 12, Training Artificial Neural Networks for Image Recognition*. Lastly, we set the cost (or loss) function to `categorical_crossentropy`. The (binary) cross-entropy is just the technical term for the cost function in logistic regression, and the categorical cross-entropy is its generalization for multi-class predictions via softmax. After compiling the model, we can now train it by calling the `fit` method. Here, we are using mini-batch stochastic gradient with a batch size of 300 training samples per batch. We train the MLP over 50 epochs, and we can follow the optimization of the `cost` function during training by setting `verbose=1`. The `validation_split` parameter is especially handy, since it will reserve 10 percent of the training data (here, 6,000 samples) for validation after each epoch, so that we can check if the model is overfitting during training.

```
>>> model.fit(X_train,
...           y_train_ohe,
...           nb_epoch=50,
...           batch_size=300,
...           verbose=1,
...           validation_split=0.1,
...           show_accuracy=True)
Train on 54000 samples, validate on 6000 samples
Epoch 0
54000/54000 [==============================] - 1s - loss: 2.2290 -
acc: 0.3592 - val_loss: 2.1094 - val_acc: 0.5342
Epoch 1
54000/54000 [==============================] - 1s - loss: 1.8850 -
acc: 0.5279 - val_loss: 1.6098 - val_acc: 0.5617
Epoch 2
54000/54000 [==============================] - 1s - loss: 1.3903 -
acc: 0.5884 - val_loss: 1.1666 - val_acc: 0.6707
Epoch 3
54000/54000 [==============================] - 1s - loss: 1.0592 -
acc: 0.6936 - val_loss: 0.8961 - val_acc: 0.7615
[...]
Epoch 49
54000/54000 [==============================] - 1s - loss: 0.1907 -
acc: 0.9432 - val_loss: 0.1749 - val_acc: 0.9482
```

Printing the value of the cost function is extremely useful during training, since we can quickly spot whether the cost is decreasing during training and stop the algorithm earlier if otherwise to tune the hyperparameter values.

To predict the class labels, we can then use the `predict_classes` method to return the class labels directly as integers:

```
>>> y_train_pred = model.predict_classes(X_train, verbose=0)
>>> print('First 3 predictions: ', y_train_pred[:3])
>>> First 3 predictions:  [5 0 4]
```

Finally, let's print the model accuracy on training and test sets:

```
>>> train_acc = np.sum(
...        y_train == y_train_pred, axis=0) / X_train.shape[0]
>>> print('Training accuracy: %.2f%%' % (train_acc * 100))
Training accuracy: 94.51%

>>> y_test_pred = model.predict_classes(X_test, verbose=0)
>>> test_acc = np.sum(y_test == y_test_pred,
...                   axis=0) / X_test.shape[0]
print('Test accuracy: %.2f%%' % (test_acc * 100))
Test accuracy: 94.39%
```

Note that this is just a very simple neural network without optimized tuning parameters. If you are interested in playing more with Keras, please feel free to further tweak the learning rate, momentum, weight decay, and number of hidden units.

> Although Keras is a great library for implementing and experimenting with neural networks, there are many other Theano wrapper libraries that are worth mentioning. A prominent example is Pylearn2 (http://deeplearning.net/software/pylearn2/), which has been developed in the LISA lab in Montreal. Also, Lasagne (https://github.com/Lasagne/Lasagne) may be of interest to you if you prefer a more minimalistic but extensible library, that offers more control over the underlying Theano code.

Summary

I hope you enjoyed this last chapter of an exciting tour of machine learning. Throughout this book, we covered all of the essential topics that this field has to offer, and you should now be well equipped to put those techniques into action to solve real-world problems.

We started our journey with a brief overview of the different types of learning tasks: supervised learning, reinforcement learning, and unsupervised learning. We discussed several different learning algorithms that can be used for classification, starting with simple single-layer neural networks in *Chapter 2, Training Machine Learning Algorithms for Classification*. Then, we discussed more advanced classification algorithms in *Chapter 3, A Tour of Machine Learning Classifiers Using Scikit-learn*, and you learned about the most important aspects of a machine learning pipeline in *Chapter 4, Building Good Training Sets – Data Preprocessing* and *Chapter 5, Compressing Data via Dimensionality Reduction*. Remember that even the most advanced algorithm is limited by the information in the training data that it gets to learn from. In *Chapter 6, Learning Best Practices for Model Evaluation and Hyperparameter Tuning*, you learned about the best practices to build and evaluate predictive models, which is another important aspect in machine learning applications. If one single learning algorithm does not achieve the performance we desire, it can sometimes be helpful to create an ensemble of experts to make a prediction. We discussed this in *Chapter 7, Combining Different Models for Ensemble Learning*. In *Chapter 8, Applying Machine Learning to Sentiment Analysis*, we applied machine learning to analyze the probably most interesting form of data in the modern age that is dominated by social media platforms on the Internet: text documents. However, machine learning techniques are not limited to offline data analysis, and in *Chapter 9, Embedding a Machine Learning Model into a Web Application*, we saw how to embed a machine learning model into a web application to share it with the outside world. For the most part, our focus was on algorithms for classification, probably the most popular application of machine learning. However, this is not where it ends! In *Chapter 10, Predicting Continuous Target Variables with Regression Analysis*, we explored several algorithms for regression analysis to predict continuous-valued output values. Another exciting subfield of machine learning is clustering analysis, which can help us to find hidden structures in data even if our training data does not come with the right answers to learn from. We discussed this in *Chapter 11, Working with Unlabeled Data – Clustering Analysis*.

In the last two chapters of this book, we caught a glimpse of the most beautiful and most exciting algorithms in the whole machine learning field: artificial neural networks. Although deep learning really is beyond the scope of this book, I hope I could at least kindle your interest to follow the most recent advancement in this field. If you are considering a career as a machine learning researcher, or even if you just want to keep up to date with the current advancement in this field, I can recommend you to follow the works of the leading experts in this field, such as Geoff Hinton (`http://www.cs.toronto.edu/~hinton/`), Andrew Ng (`http://www.andrewng.org`), Yann LeCun (`http://yann.lecun.com`), Juergen Schmidhuber (`http://people.idsia.ch/~juergen/`), and Yoshua Bengio (`http://www.iro.umontreal.ca/~bengioy`), just to name a few. Also, please do not hesitate to join the scikit-learn, Theano, and Keras mailing lists to participate in interesting discussions around these libraries, and machine learning in general. I am looking forward to meeting you there! You are always welcome to contact me if you have any questions about this book or need some general tips about machine learning.

I hope this journey through the different aspects of machine learning was really worthwhile, and you learned many new and useful skills to advance your career and apply them to real-world problem solving.

Index

Symbols

A

B

principal component analysis,
    scikit-learn 135-137
prototype-based clustering 312
public server
    web application, deploying to 272, 273
Pylearn2
    URL 413
PyPrind
    URL 234
Python
    about 13
    kernel principal component analysis,
        implementing in 154, 155
    packages, installing 13-15
    references 14
    using, for machine learning 13
PythonAnywhere account
    URL 272

Q

quality of clustering
    quantifying, via silhouette plots 321-324

R

Radial Basis Function (RBF)
    about 152
    implementing 152, 153
random forest regression 304-308
random forests 90
RANdom SAmple Consensus (RANSAC)
    algorithm 291
raw term frequencies 237
recall (REC) 192
receptive fields 382
Recurrent Neural
    Networks (RNNs) 383, 384
regression line 278
regular expression (regex) 240
regularization 365
regularization parameter 67, 185
regularized methods
    using, for regression 297, 298
reinforcement learning
    about 6
    interactive problems, solving with 6

residual plots 294
residuals 278
Ridge Regression 297
roadmap, for machine learning systems
    about 10
    models, evaluating 13
    predictive model, selecting 12
    predictive model, training 12
    preprocessing 11
    unseen data instances, predicting 13
robust regression model
    fitting, RANSAC used 291-293
ROC area under the curve (ROC AUC) 210

S

scatterplot matrix 280
scenarios, distance values
    correct approach 330
    incorrect approach 329
scikit-learn
    about 50
    agglomerative clustering, applying via 334
    perceptron, training via 50-55
    reference link 167
scikit-learn estimator API 102, 103
scikit-learn online documentation
    URL 55
sentiment analysis 233
sepal width 210
Sequential Backward Selection (SBS) 118
sequential feature selection
    algorithms 118-123
sigmoid function 57
sigmoid (logistic) activation function 348
silhouette analysis 321
silhouette coefficient 321
silhouette plots
    about 312
    quality of clustering,
        quantifying via 321-324
simple linear regression model 278, 279
simple majority vote classifier
    different algorithms, combining
        with majority vote 210-212
    implementing 203-210

W

Ward's linkage 327
weak learners
about 90, 224
leveraging, via adaptive boosting 224-231
web application
deploying, to public server 272, 273
developing, with Flask 257
implementation, URL 265
movie classifier, turning into 264-271
movie review classifier, updating 274, 275
Wine dataset
about 108, 221
Alcohol class 221

features 109
Hue class 221
URL 108
word2vec
about 249
URL 249
word stemming 242
workflows
streamlining, with pipelines 169
WTForms library
URL 259

Thank you for buying
Python Machine Learning

About Packt Publishing

Packt, pronounced 'packed', published its first book, *Mastering phpMyAdmin for Effective MySQL Management*, in April 2004, and subsequently continued to specialize in publishing highly focused books on specific technologies and solutions.

Our books and publications share the experiences of your fellow IT professionals in adapting and customizing today's systems, applications, and frameworks. Our solution-based books give you the knowledge and power to customize the software and technologies you're using to get the job done. Packt books are more specific and less general than the IT books you have seen in the past. Our unique business model allows us to bring you more focused information, giving you more of what you need to know, and less of what you don't.

Packt is a modern yet unique publishing company that focuses on producing quality, cutting-edge books for communities of developers, administrators, and newbies alike. For more information, please visit our website at www.packtpub.com.

About Packt Open Source

In 2010, Packt launched two new brands, Packt Open Source and Packt Enterprise, in order to continue its focus on specialization. This book is part of the Packt Open Source brand, home to books published on software built around open source licenses, and offering information to anybody from advanced developers to budding web designers. The Open Source brand also runs Packt's Open Source Royalty Scheme, by which Packt gives a royalty to each open source project about whose software a book is sold.

Writing for Packt

We welcome all inquiries from people who are interested in authoring. Book proposals should be sent to author@packtpub.com. If your book idea is still at an early stage and you would like to discuss it first before writing a formal book proposal, then please contact us; one of our commissioning editors will get in touch with you.

We're not just looking for published authors; if you have strong technical skills but no writing experience, our experienced editors can help you develop a writing career, or simply get some additional reward for your expertise.

Learning scikit-learn: Machine Learning in Python

ISBN: 978-1-78328-193-0   Paperback: 118 pages

Experience the benefits of machine learning techniques by applying them to real-world problems using Python and the open source scikit-learn library

1. Use Python and scikit-learn to create intelligent applications.

2. Apply regression techniques to predict future behaviour and learn to cluster items in groups by their similarities.

3. Make use of classification techniques to perform image recognition and document classification.

Building Machine Learning Systems with Python

ISBN: 978-1-78216-140-0   Paperback: 290 pages

Master the art of machine learning with Python and build effective machine learning systems with this intensive hands-on guide

1. Master Machine Learning using a broad set of Python libraries and start building your own Python-based ML systems.

2. Understand the best practices for modularization and code organization while putting your application to scale.

3. Covers classification, regression, feature engineering, and much more guided by practical examples.

Made in the USA
Lexington, KY
17 June 2016